PLATO AS

CRITICAL

THEORIST

PLATO AS

CRITICAL

THEORIST

JONNY THAKKAR

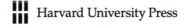 Harvard University Press

Cambridge, Massachusetts
London, England   2018

Library of Congress Cataloging-in-Publication Data

Names: Thakkar, Jonny, 1982– author.
Title: Plato as critical theorist / Jonny Thakkar.
Description: Cambridge, Massachusetts : Harvard University Press, 2018. |
    Includes bibliographical references and index.
Identifiers: LCCN 2017045234 | ISBN 9780674971769 (alk. paper)
Subjects: LCSH: Philosopher-kings. | Plato. Republic. | Political ethics. |
    Liberalism. | Political participation. | Platonists.
Classification: LCC B398.P45 T43 2018 | DDC 321/.07—dc23
LC record available at https://lccn.loc.gov/2017045234

I do not know what meaning classical studies could have for our time if they were not untimely—that is to say, acting counter to our time and thereby acting on our time and, let us hope, for the benefit of a time to come.

—*Friedrich Nietzsche, "On the Uses and Disadvantages of History for Life"*

Contents

Preface

"No BOOK CAN ever be finished," wrote Karl Popper in the preface to the second edition of *The Open Society and Its Enemies*. "While working on it we learn just enough to find it immature the moment we turn away from it." This particular book has been a long time coming. The core idea began to germinate as early as 2007 thanks to the cross-fertilization of two exceptional courses at the University of Chicago: twenty weeks on Plato's *Republic* with Jonathan Lear and twenty weeks on Marx's *Capital* with Moishe Postone.

Plato and Marx tend to be taken as the founders of opposing schools within political philosophy: "ideal theory," which seeks to change the world by changing our conception of how things might best be, and "critical theory," which seeks to change the world by changing our conception of how things actually are. My hunch was that close inspection of Plato and Marx would reveal the possibility of resolving this opposition into a higher unity. For in my view Plato's ideal theory was best understood against the background of an implicit critical theory, while Marx's critical theory was best understood against the background of an implicit ideal theory. Not only that, but it seemed to me that their respective ideals and critiques had much in common—and that by combining them we could illuminate our own world.

That a text as strange as the *Republic* could change the way we view contemporary political life is hardly obvious, but for me it had already happened: somehow the process of studying Plato had made me look at the present through his eyes. Not that I agreed with everything he seemed to be saying, of course—as a twenty-first-century Westerner, how could I? The point was rather that Plato had changed what I took to be most salient about today's world. In particular, I had begun to ask after the place of wisdom and justice in our institutions and in our everyday lives. This led me to a debate within recent political philosophy between "perfectionists" and "political liberals" over whether (or to what extent) the state can legitimately promote a particular vision of the good life. It struck me that there will always remain a difference between what the state can force citizens to do and what they ought to do of their own accord, and that this difference allows perfectionist themes to slip through the net of political liberalism so long as we frame them in terms of the demands of excellent citizenship. If this was right, I thought, it might be possible to revive Platonic political theory by thinking in terms of philosopher-citizens rather than philosopher-kings. This would then allow us to generate a powerful ideal—and, in combination with Marx, a powerful critical theory.

I was dimly aware of how long it would take to pull off a project of this size with any degree of rigor—but only dimly. The first attempt took me five years to complete; further rounds of wholesale rewriting have taken four more. The world has changed significantly in the interim: faced with the resurgence of nationalism and socialism, the neoliberal order that previously seemed all-conquering has come to seem fragile and contingent. Whether this makes the final product more or less timely is hard to say, but in any case I have come to accept, with Popper, that that is all there can ever be: a final version, not a finished one.

I would like to dedicate the final product to Jonathan Lear, without whom it would not exist. Jonathan gave me the gift of Plato at a time when my mind was set on Heidegger; he encouraged me to pursue a project that most advisers would have rejected as overly ambitious; he raised questions and objections at just the right level of resolution; and when writing and rewriting took their time, he gave me his precious support. Above all, though, he gave me a model to aspire to. One of the claims of this book is that each of our actions and works manifests a conception of the good life, however inchoately, and that since humans are set up to imitate the people and things around them, we are always generating models for others to follow. What Jonathan modeled for me was idealism about the academic life—a commitment to unearthing the possibilities for creative work latent within current scholarship as opposed to simply lamenting disciplinary limitations or submitting to them. This gave me the will to go on, and it still does.

Many other debts have accrued as this project has gestated, both to individuals and to institutions. With each passing year it becomes clearer to me just how exceptional was the intellectual environment at the University of Chicago's Committee on Social Thought, and how unlikely it is that I would have flourished as a graduate student anywhere else: blanket permission to take courses in any department across the university allowed me to rove across philosophy, social theory, and literature, both ancient and modern, until I found a project that felt like my own. Princeton University's Society of Fellows in the Liberal Arts gave me the luxury of a three-year postdoctoral position and with it the opportunity to sharpen my thinking in conversation with colleagues in the Philosophy Department and the University Center for Human Values. The Philosophy Department at the University of British Columbia then gave me shelter for one further year as I rewrote every single chapter, before the Department of Political Science at Swarthmore College appointed me to a position that allowed me to finalize the manuscript in peace.

My personal debts are so numerous that a full account would try the reader's patience, but it would be remiss of me not to single out Danielle Allen, whose pathbreaking work on Plato's politics I have tried to further; Daniel Brudney, who rekindled my interest in contemporary political philosophy; and Robert Pippin, who taught me to treat past philosophers as companions in thought. Others who have taught and supported me in various ways and to varying degrees over the course of this project include Mark Alznauer, Scott Anderson, Paul Bartha, Thomas Bartscherer, Jon Baskin, Susanna Berger, Cassandra Betts, Robert Bird, Agnes Callard, Noah Chafets,

Charles Comey, John Cooper, Dennis Feeney, Anton Ford, Gregory Freeman, Johann Frick, Raymond Geuss, Andreas Glaeser, Dimitri Gondicas, Mary Harper, Desmond Jagmohan, Hans Joas, Mark Johnston, Leon Kass, Joel Lande, Melissa Lane, Ben Laurence, Gabriel Richardson Lear, Christophe Litwin, Henrik Lorenz, M. M. McCabe, Benjamin Morison, Glenn Most, Alexander Nehamas, Alan Patten, Philip Pettit, Robert Pippin, Moishe Postone, Alexander Prescott-Couch, Tom Rogerson, Alan Ryan, Shalini Satkunanandan, Mira Siegelberg, Michael Smith, Tom Stern, Susan Stewart, Anna Stilz, Jeffrey Stout, Mark Thakkar, Joshua Trubowitz, Michael Wachtel, Rachel Wiseman, Michael Wood, and Etay Zwick. Jon Baskin, Charles Comey, Steffen Seitz, and Jenna Spitzer were kind enough to give me comments on the whole manuscript, as were three anonymous reviewers, copy editor Charles Eberline, and Brian Ostrander of Westchester Publishing Services. For their patience and trust, special thanks must be reserved for my editors at Harvard University Press, Joy Deng and Lindsay Waters; my parents, Haren and Mary Thakkar; and my wife, Camille Breton.

PLATO AS
CRITICAL
THEORIST

Introduction

§1 The Situation

1. Speaking after the collapse of the Berlin Wall in 1989, Francis Fukuyama made some infamous predictions about the future of Western democracies:

> The struggle for recognition, the willingness to risk one's life for a purely abstract goal, the worldwide ideological struggle that called forth daring, courage, imagination, and idealism, will be replaced by economic calculation, the endless solving of technical problems, environmental concerns, and the satisfaction of sophisticated consumer demands. In the post-historical period there will be neither art nor philosophy, just the perpetual caretaking of the museum of human history.[1]

These remarks have been much pilloried. Recent decades have witnessed a rise in nationalism, authoritarianism, and fundamentalism

---

1. Fukuyama, "The End of History?," 18. This article is based on "Are We Approaching the End of History?," lecture at the University of Chicago's Olin Center, February 8, 1989. (Full citations of all works cited in the notes are given in the Bibliography.)

rather than the inexorable march of liberal democracy. Liberal democracies themselves, meanwhile, remain riven by disputes over the bounds of the state, the rate and scale of immigration, the differential fates of racial and religious groups, norms concerning gender and sexuality, and many other issues besides.

2. In fairness to Fukuyama, his claim was not that political struggles would disappear after 1989, but only that they would no longer amount to anything world-historical. If we treat this as political phenomenology rather than prophecy, it seems fairly accurate. We can point to whole decades—the 1840s or the 1920s or the 1960s, for example—in which competing visions for the future abounded, so that from any given political perspective anything from heaven to hell seemed possible. By comparison with these periods, visions of fundamentally different forms of sociopolitical organization have played little role in recent politics; few have treated the present as a staging post on the way to a future way of life. Conceptions of the past have certainly energized both Left and Right, but within mainstream politics, at least, discussions of the future have remained largely technocratic, having to do with potential demographic and environmental crises rather than transformations in our basic mode of sociopolitical organization.[2]

3. If few mainstream political actors have seriously proposed transcending the current social order, as opposed to reforming or restoring it, that might be because it is more or less satisfactory. For if we have arrived at a form of life that enables us to flourish as best we can, given our essential finitude and vulnerability, there is nowhere else we should want to go. This is not to say that all would be rosy in such a society. Fukuyama thought it would inevitably lack the spiritual energy—expressed in artistic, philosophical, and ideological production—that comes from imagining future ways of life, and that this would represent a genuine loss: "I can feel in myself, and see in others around me, a powerful nostalgia for the time

---

2. There have certainly been vigorous academic debates over topics such as the future of work, a universal basic income, deliberative democracy, lottocracy, neorepublicanism, and neoauthoritarianism, but thus far they do not seem to have greatly affected mainstream political consciousness.

when history existed. Such nostalgia, in fact, will continue to fuel competition and conflict even in the post-historical world for some time to come."[3] But just as it would be irrational for scientists to wish for a return to the period when there were competing theories as to the best way to prevent smallpox, even if they might pine for the feelings of urgency that researchers must have experienced at the time, so it would be irrational to wish to transform a healthy social order.[4]

4. It is hard to believe, however, that the present social order is in fact healthy. For although nostalgia may be at work in the idioms and mannerisms of today's oppositional movements, the discontent they express goes well beyond calls for reform or restoration. From the

---

3. Fukuyama, "The End of History?," 18.

4. It is unclear how we could ever know that such a form of life had been reached. Presumably the desire for radical transformation would wane in a well-ordered society. Indeed, the absence of such desire may even be a necessary condition for a society to count as well ordered in the first place. Cf. Rawls, "The Sense of Justice," in *Theory of Justice*, 453–512. Yet this could scarcely be a sufficient condition. There may have been societies—feudal England, for instance—in which what we would now think of as egregious injustice was so entrenched, buttressed by a host of legitimating myths and traditions, that it seemed more or less natural, the kind of thing that arouses little more protest than the fact that humans cannot fly. (As a matter of historical fact, this was probably not true of feudal England, but from a philosophical perspective all that really matters is that such a society is possible.) Might we not be in a similar state? How would we know? One strategy would be to engage in a constant process of trial and error with respect to our institutions, like a sailor who gets as close as possible to the wind by pushing into it until the sail flaps. Then it would seem to follow that a situation in which radical possibilities were not being toyed with, at least to some extent, would necessarily fall short of the ideal. Another strategy, associated with Hegel, would be to demonstrate the superiority of our current views over previous ones by giving what Bernard Williams calls a "vindicatory" history, showing how the later outlook "makes sense of itself, and of the earlier outlook, and of the transition from the earlier to the later, in such terms that both parties (the holders of the earlier outlook, and the holders of the later) have reason to recognize the transition as an improvement." See Williams, *Philosophy as a Humanistic Discipline*, 189. Williams is skeptical that it is possible to give such a history concerning ethics, as opposed to science, since ethical life is hard to view as a collective learning process in which views are accepted and discarded like scientific theories. But even if a vindicatory history were possible—and it does not strike me as out of the question— this would not solve our problem, since we could be justified in taking our current institutions as the end of a process of development, rather than simply the latest stage, only if we could give an account of their perfection with respect to certain standards or values. But what reason would we have for thinking that these standards or values are not themselves to be surpassed?

religious Right to the environmentalist Left, the urban unions to the countryside conservatives, many social movements clearly draw energy from a sense that our sociopolitical order is simply not conducive to the good life. Criticisms of this kind often take as their object "neoliberalism," understood as a school of thought that places faith in free markets, private ownership, and supply-side economics.[5] But ultimately the objection is not so much to a particular set of policies as to a whole way of life. It is not easy to characterize what the objectionable features of this way of life amount to, but they might be thought to include possessive individualism, an ethos that emphasizes competition at the expense of community; economism, a mode of rationality in which political debates seem to be rendered futile by economic imperatives; and commodification, a process whereby more and more domains of life are structured by markets. This is not supposed to be an exhaustive list—the point is just that objections of this kind bespeak a longing for radical transformation.[6]

5. Recent political life has therefore been peculiar: our sociopolitical order has elicited a form of dissatisfaction, at least in many quarters, that goes well beyond specific policy concerns, yet the public sphere has not been marked by conflict between fundamentally different visions of sociopolitical organization. It might seem obvious that what is called for is a vision of a way of life that remains liberal and democratic but avoids the ills associated with neoliberalism, so that those who feel dissatisfaction with the contemporary order

---

5. Whether the term "neoliberalism" has any analytical value is disputed. Like many political concepts, it seems to have found currency as an insult rather than a self-description or a category of sober political science. For a helpful overview of the debates regarding neoliberalism and a suggested (but still loose) definition, see Thorsen and Lie, "What Is Neoliberalism?" For an analysis of neoliberalism as a form of class warfare rather than a way of life, see Harvey, *Brief History of Neoliberalism*.

6. Clearly the claims in this paragraph represent a defeasible interpretation of the present situation. I do not take that to be an objection to them, since it seems to me that for political philosophy to be genuinely political, it must begin with such an interpretation, which, like the invocation of an unspecified "we," serves as an invitation to the reader. See Charles Taylor, "Interpretation and the Sciences of Man." For recent treatments of possessive individualism, economism, and commodification, see Wendy Brown, *Undoing the Demos;* Sandel, *What Money Can't Buy;* Satz, *Why Some Things Should Not Be for Sale;* Grant, *Strings Attached;* and Skidelsky and Skidelsky, *How Much Is Enough?*

are able to face it with the energy of idealism rather than the weariness of despair. It might seem equally obvious that political philosophers who share the relevant objections ought to be at the forefront of this movement, articulating and defending a new ideal. It is easy to imagine such work being dismissed as pie in the sky by those engaged in concrete struggles over policy and power. What is harder to imagine is that political philosophers would themselves share this critique. Yet in recent years this is exactly what has happened, with various prominent philosophers charging that ideal theory is either useless or dangerous or (somehow) both.

§2 Ideal Theory and Its Critics

6. "Idealism" can be said in many ways, and it is worth distinguishing them. Sometimes it refers to the practice of trying to bring about a better world by acting as though it already existed. Sometimes it refers to the practice of holding certain values sacrosanct and therefore refusing to trade them off for the sake of putative consequences. And sometimes it refers to an attitude of viewing the actually existing in light of its highest potential. These usages are related to my own but importantly distinct from it. For the sake of clarity, let me therefore stipulate that what I mean by "idealism" is "the practice of working out and orienting oneself to ideals." Not that "ideal" has but one meaning, of course. Sometimes we speak of values such as humility or justice as ideals, especially when they appear foundational, sacrosanct, or transcendent (i.e., beyond our grasp, whether practically or cognitively). In a lower register, we also speak of theoretical abstractions or heuristics as ideals: *homo economicus*, for instance, or Max Weber's Calvinist moneymaker. These usages are not incorrect, and once again my usage is not absolutely divorced from them. But what I mean by an ideal, at least in the first instance, is an imagined best possibility—the ideal husband, for instance. In the political context, then, idealism in my sense is the practice of working out and orienting oneself toward visions of the best possible society.

7. There are three dimensions to an imagined best possibility. As a best possibility, an ideal must be good relative to some standard.

To speak of the ideal F is therefore to assume certain standards of excellence governing Fs. These standards are relative to different evaluative contexts; the ideal hammer for carpentry may be different from the ideal hammer for smithing. When what is at issue is the ideal society, we presumably mean that it is ideal with respect to some aspect of the human good. So candidate ideals will imply some vision of the human good and hence the human condition, although this vision may be thicker or thinner according to the ideal in question.[7]

8. As best possibilities, however, ideals are not only good but also possible. It follows that if something is impossible, it is not an ideal. So utopias are not ideals, and ideals are not impossible dreams. This is, I admit, stipulative. In ordinary usage we sometimes use "ideal" to connote impossibility, and we sometimes use "utopian" to describe political projects which in fact proved entirely feasible, such as the Shaker settlements in New England. And of course, there may also be no hard-and-fast criteria for distinguishing the possible and the impossible in politics. These complications notwithstanding, for the sake of conceptual clarity I want to insist that there is a genuine distinction between two kinds of states of affairs, one possible and the other impossible, one ideal and the other utopian. To the extent that a theory really is pie in the sky, then, it is not ideal at all.

9. Yet we must also distinguish between ideals and perfect cases. Ideals are not made of flesh and blood; they are models or abstractions. An abstraction is a device that helps us achieve clarity about some part of the world by bracketing certain features of reality. Maps, for example, enable us to navigate by simplifying and compressing topography. If a map were fully adequate to its subject, the two would be the same size—and then we might lose the wood for the trees. Ideals in my sense count as abstractions because they aim to sketch only the main contours of the best possible F. They abstract from some of the features that actual Fs, including perfect cases, must

---

7. Liberal ideals tend to depend on thinner visions of the human good than religious ones, for instance. It may be said that they privilege "the right" over "the good," so long as we understand that the right is in fact a part of the good, albeit a part with a special status relative to the others.

always have. So there is a sense in which ideals are always impossible to realize: no actually existing case, however perfect, could ever look quite like the ideal one. What I mean when I say that ideals (as opposed to utopias) are possible is therefore not that they can be realized as such, but rather that they model principles that are realizable.

10. This analysis allows us to accurately locate "realist" objections to ideal theory. To declare that a given ideal is not actually best—say, because it leaves no place for family life—is to claim that it is not really ideal at all. This is not a criticism of ideal theory per se, but of a particular theory that purports to be ideal. Something similar applies with respect to judgments concerning possibility. As abstractions, all ideals are unrealistic in a trivial sense. But a given ideal might also be unrealistic in the sense that the principles it models are impossible to realize. Once again, however, to call an ideal impossible or utopian is not to criticize it for being ideal theory but precisely to accuse it of not being ideal theory.

11. It is worth noting, even at the risk of digression, that the notion of possibility at work in policing the boundary between ideals and utopias may shift according to context. Outside academic philosophy the term "impossible" is used rather vaguely. Many proposals that are commonly deemed impossible, such as the abolition of private property or of the nuclear family, have in fact been carried out over the course of history; it certainly was not impossible to introduce them for a time. We should therefore distinguish between different senses of possibility. The realm of logical possibility is clearly broader, for instance, than the realm of natural possibility. It is not logically impossible for a lion to become a tiger, but it is naturally impossible. And the realm of natural possibility is in turn broader than the realm of practical possibility. The proposition that Arnold Schwarzenegger will be president of the United States goes against no laws of nature, but I see no harm in calling it impossible, practically speaking, if by impossible we mean that the possibility is so remote that its existence cannot guide our action in any meaningful way. This is a question of judgment, of course, and our judgment on such matters is likely to be clouded by the heat of conflict and the smoke of oratory. Yet it strikes me as the kind of judgment for which

political philosophy, as a branch of practical philosophy, ought to make room.

12. Some might argue that our practical aspirations ought to be utopian rather than being limited by a conception of what is possible.[8] This attack is somewhat hard to grasp from a conceptual standpoint: insofar as a state of affairs is absolutely impossible, how can it orient or guide us at all? This is not so much a matter of "ought implies can" as "intention implies capability"—we cannot coherently aim at flying to the moon unaided. In practice, however, people do seem to manage to orient themselves this way; one thinks, for example, of fakirs who starve themselves in the hope of freeing their minds from their bodies and do thereby achieve something. I am tempted to suggest that such practice still amounts to idealism rather than utopianism; the implicit claim is that our sense of possibility is somehow too narrow or unimaginative, and that we will discover what is possible only if we reach for the impossible. If this is right, then these considerations do not constitute an objection to ideal theory as such: ideal theory can be dangerous insofar as it involves an attempt to fix and thereby limit in advance our conception of what is possible—but it does not have to be.

13. A different strategy for attacking ideal theory is to deny that we ought to privilege thinking about the best over thinking about the better. In *The Idea of Justice*, for example, Amartya Sen argues that working out what would be most just is neither necessary nor sufficient for solving actual problems, such as whether a given policy would reduce injustice more than another.[9] Insofar as an ideal of justice has multiple dimensions, such as liberty and equality, it will be impossible to rank societies or policies purely by their distance from the ideal, and Sen thinks that the same problem recurs at the level of each dimension considered separately insofar as each involves

---

8. I use the phrase "practical aspirations" deliberately. There are those, like G. A. Cohen, who claim that theoretical philosophy ought not to be bound by questions of possibility (or any facts) even when it concerns practical matters, but these thinkers are not necessarily utopian in my sense. They might be, but only if they are committed to the further thesis that their reflections can guide action in the absence of considerations concerning possibility. See Cohen, *Rescuing Justice and Equality*, chap. 6.

9. See Sen, *Idea of Justice*.

complex, multifactor considerations. By itself, then, an ideal is not sufficient for guiding policy. But nor is it necessary. We can agree to ban slavery as unjust without agreeing on what a just society would look like; more abstractly, we do not need to agree that A is the best arrangement in order to agree that B is better than C. So on Sen's view, ideal theory is at best a waste of time and at worst a dangerous distraction. This does look like a genuinely universal criticism of ideal theory, but it is clear what it would take to meet the challenge: one would simply have to show how and why thinking about the best is not a waste of time.

14. A more troubling line of attack concerns the modeling involved in ideal theory. In constructing his theory of justice, for example, John Rawls makes various strategic simplifications. First, he stipulates that citizens enter society at birth and exit only by death—in other words, that there is no possibility of immigration. In the real world, of course, a perfectly just society would not forbid immigration (or at least not on Rawls's account). But assuming away immigration allows Rawls to conceive of the basic structure of society as influencing each imagined citizen to the same degree, which in turn gives everyone the same stake in justice and so allows the original-position thought experiment to get off the ground.[10] Second, he assumes that citizens will generally comply with the principles of justice.[11] This is not the case in any real-world society, but the assumption allows Rawls to assess different principles of justice on their normative merits alone rather than considering how they would be taken up by a multitude of flawed human beings with their own agendas and psychologies. Finally, he invites us to picture society as a cooperative venture aimed at the mutual advantage of its members.[12] Again, actual societies are clearly structured by conflict as much as by cooperation. But the assumption that society is a cooperative scheme among free and equal citizens is supposed to focus our attention on constructing social arrangements that everyone would have good reason to accept.

---

10. See, e.g., Rawls, *Political Liberalism*, xliii.
11. Rawls, *Theory of Justice*, 138, 245.
12. Ibid., 4.

15. Each of these three assumptions might reasonably be questioned. For one thing, a theory that brackets the possibility of immigration inevitably treats transnational questions as secondary. But if the assumption that the nation-state is the primary unit of political interest is local to a specific historical and geographic context, as it surely is, then a theory built on that assumption will be parochial. This is not in itself a particularly devastating criticism. Like good maps, good theories (whether normative or empirical) must cover over what is inessential in order to reveal what is essential. But what counts as essential will depend on our purposes, so a defense of Rawls could be made on the grounds that his abstractions were tailored to his particular purposes. As to whether those purposes were the right ones, there is surely no abstract answer. Different theories will be useful at different times and in different contexts. Any given theorist will have to make a judgment concerning the needs of the present situation and how best to contribute, given her own interests and aptitudes. To criticize Rawls's choice of project, we would have to take all of this into account and then make a speculative judgment about how he might have used his time and talents more profitably. But among the most irritating of all academic vices is surely the habit of criticizing others for pursuing a project different from one's own.

16. This live-and-let-live response faces an immediate objection, however, from those who argue that the kind of modeling that makes a theory ideal is the kind of modeling that makes a theory bad.[13] There are various ways to make this point. One involves claiming that ideal theory will never be capable of guiding action in anything more than an illusory or ideological manner since its assumptions are best characterized not as abstractions, whereby we bracket certain truths for the sake of simplicity, but rather as idealizations, whereby we assert things we know to be false.[14] A case in point

---

13. See, e.g., Geuss, *Outside Ethics*; Geuss, *Philosophy and Real Politics*; and Finlayson, *Political Is Political*.

14. For the distinction between abstractions and idealizations, see O'Neill, "Abstraction, Idealization and Ideology in Ethics," 55–69; and O'Neill, *Towards Justice and Virtue*, 40.

might be the assumption of full compliance. To assume that people will generally comply with principles of justice is not simply to abstract away from complexity; it is to build in a condition that we know is false. The resulting theory is therefore in an important sense an ideal not of a human society but rather of some fictional species in a nearby possible world. This makes it hard to see why the principles that the ideal models should have any bearing on the design of real-world societies.[15]

17. It is doubtful whether the purported distinction between abstractions and idealizations can actually hold: a road map that fails to record every twist and turn is at once bracketing truths and depicting falsehoods, so it might well be that abstractions can always be redescribed as idealizations.[16] For present purposes, however, the notion of idealization can be used in a different way, namely to refer to assumptions that are in some way favorable to the theorist's designs. A theorist is idealizing in this sense if she uses definitional fiat to reduce the distance between the object of the theory and the ideal version of that object. Theories that idealize in this sense run the risk of degenerating into empty utopian fantasies, pliant media for our wishful thinking; but they also run the risk of misleading us about the nature of our world. As Raymond Geuss argues, historically contingent power relations play a constitutive role in politics and society. Philosophical thought experiments that inquire into artificial situations whose parameters have been neatly designed

---

15. As Elizabeth Anderson puts it, "We need to tailor our principles to the motivational and cognitive capacities of human beings. Rousseau famously sought legitimate principles of government, taking people 'as they are and laws as they might be.' Rousseau's starting point, people *as they are*, is apt. A system of principles that would produce a just world if they regulated the conduct of perfectly rational and just persons will not do so when we ask human beings, with all our limitations and flaws, to follow them. Just institutions must be designed to block, work around, or cancel out our motivational and cognitive deficiencies, to harness our nonmoral motives to moral ends, to make up for each other's limitations by pooling our knowledge and wills. To craft such designs, we must analyze our motivational and cognitive biases, diagnose how they lead people to mistreat others, and how institutions may redirect them to better conduct." Anderson, *Imperative of Integration*, 3–4.

16. For a different criticism of the distinction, see Gaus, *Tyranny of the Ideal*, 36–38. Thanks to Alexander Prescott-Couch for discussions on this matter.

precisely in order to aid normative reflection will therefore tell us little about political life. But fictions can be practically efficacious, as Geuss points out: people have gone to their deaths over the divine right of kings. The real trouble is therefore not so much that ideals are useless as that they are dangerous: political action requires accurate perceptual judgment above all, and ideals can distort our perception.[17]

18. Once again we can turn to Rawls for an example. As soon as we assume that society is a cooperative venture for mutual advantage, it is hard to see how much in the way of inequality will ever be licensed; the decks are stacked against both the Randian crackpot who denies the importance of cooperation and the Oakeshottean conservative who denies that society is any kind of scheme or venture.[18] But this assumption might also stack the deck against certain subgroups in the United States, as Charles Mills complains.[19] How can African Americans view their society as a cooperative venture for mutual advantage, he asks, when most of them are descended from slaves? In Mills's view, Rawls's abstraction does not simply make his theory useless from the perspective of addressing existing injustices in American society; it also turns it into a dangerous mystification, "ideology" in the pejorative sense.[20] It is but a small step to the Nietzschean claim, made by Geuss in particular, that this kind of distortion is motivated—that theorists ascend to the realm of ideals precisely in order to flee the complexity and pain of earthly politics.[21]

---

17. Geuss seems to see the Iraq war as, among other things, an example of ideal theory (i.e., ideology) trumping perception of historically specific power structures. See *Philosophy and Real Politics*, but also see "Political Judgment in Its Historical Context," in *Politics and the Imagination*, 1–16.

18. This is not necessarily a criticism of Rawls, since he never claims to be presenting a theory that everyone can agree with; rather, he takes himself to be systematizing certain judgments implicit in the public culture of liberal democracies in the hope of reaching some surprising conclusions.

19. See Mills, "'Ideal Theory' as Ideology"; and Mills, "Rawls on Race/Race in Rawls." On the blindness caused by abstracting from racial stratification within ideal theory, see also Anderson, *Imperative of Integration*, 5–6.

20. On the different senses of ideology, see Geuss, *Idea of a Critical Theory*, chap. 1.

21. See Geuss, "Thucydides, Nietzsche, and Williams," in *Outside Ethics*, 219–233.

19. Much can be said about these accusations, and much has been said.[22] But the fundamental question is whether ideal theory *must* be vulnerable to the criticisms we have derived from Sen and Geuss. Sen assumes that for a theory to have any practical value, it must be able to help us in ordering potential policies. Geuss assumes that abstraction from history and power necessarily clouds our perception of reality. But if Geuss is wrong, Sen will be wrong too: if ideal theory can improve our perception, it also stands to improve our action.

20. Maps enable us to perceive more—not more in some absolute sense, but more of what is salient given our purposes. A map that featured contours and landmarks might make it hard for drivers to perceive the details salient to their activity, namely the highways and byways. In some situations the map that is most useful will be one that distorts reality quite dramatically. Passengers on the London Underground, for instance, orient themselves by means of a representation of London's geography that bears only a passing resemblance to satellite imagery but allows them to perceive what is most relevant for the purposes of planning a journey.

21. Might we think of Rawls's theory like this, as an abstraction that both occludes and distorts certain features of our world in order to open others to view? Rawls seems to think that specific power relations are epiphenomenal relative to what he calls the "basic structure of society," according to which the "benefits and burdens" of social cooperation, not only material resources but also rights and duties, are distributed. If he is right, then his theory helps us perceive what we otherwise would not, namely the supreme importance of a just basic structure. That is not to deny that his theory also

---

22. For just some of the debate, see Farrelly, "Justice in Ideal Theory"; Mills, "'Ideal Theory' as Ideology"; Robeyns, "Ideal Theory in Theory and Practice"; Stemplowska, "What's Ideal about Ideal Theory?"; Swift, "Value of Philosophy in Nonideal Circumstances"; Valentini, "On the Apparent Paradox of Ideal Theory"; G. A. Cohen, "Facts and Principles," *Philosophy and Public Affairs* 31, no. 3 (2003): 211–245, reprinted as chap. 6 in Cohen, *Rescuing Justice and Equality*; David Estlund, "Utopophobia: Concession and Aspiration in Democratic Theory," in Estlund, *Democratic Authority*, 258–276; Simmons, "Ideal and Nonideal Theory"; Enoch, "Ideal Theory, Utopianism, and What's the Question (in Political Theory)"; Anderson, *Imperative of Integration*, 3–7; Knight, "Imperative of Non-ideal Theory"; Rossi and Sleat, "Realism in Political Theory"; and Gaus, *Tyranny of the Ideal.*

occludes and distorts some features of our world, or that those features are vital to responsible political action—but this is only to say that there is no substitute for a balanced diet. The same might even be true with respect to history. In *Political Liberalism*, Rawls acknowledges that his theory is and can only ever be historically specific.[23] But even a theory that aimed to be timeless might conceivably enable us to perceive certain features of our world. A statement like "all societies are F," if true, might make us notice for the first time that our own society is in fact F; or if we already knew that, the statement might make it salient once more; or if we were well aware that our society was F but did not realize that the same applies to other societies, it might universalize what we previously took to be particular (thereby reversing a certain kind of Nietzschean or Foucauldian thought process).[24]

22. Now Geuss is entitled to retort that even if Rawls's theory could in principle help us perceive something that we otherwise would not, it does not in fact achieve this; or that even if it helps us perceive something, it does not help us perceive anything important; or that even if it helps us perceive something important, it occludes something more important. The most defensible of these positions is the last. In working out the implications of conceiving ourselves as free and equal citizens seeking to cooperate on terms we consider fair, Rawls produces an ideal in light of which certain aspects of the social world become more salient than they would otherwise be. But Geuss is right to observe that Rawls's theory offers few if any resources for saying anything about the rise of so-called neoliberalism since the 1970s beyond the observation that economic injustice has increased, and hence that it offers little insight into one of the most

---

23. See Rawls, introduction to *Political Liberalism*.

24. The proposition that such universalizing statements are simply never true would itself seem to depend on a universalizing claim about human life, although even of his seemingly universal proposition "If you want to think about politics, think first about power," Geuss insists that "it is merely an empirically general fact about societies we know (those that have existed in Europe during the past two thousand years or so, and some others) that in them power is going to be of interest." Geuss, *Philosophy and Real Politics*, 97.

important issues of our day. This does not imply, however, that there is no ideal theory that could enable us to grasp this situation.[25]

23. Sidney Morgenbesser famously said of pragmatism that "it's all very well in theory but it doesn't work in practice." For Geuss and company, political philosophy is and must always be an intervention into historically specific circumstances—regardless of whether it wants to be. But it may be that the best way to affect one's times is to abstract from the nooks and crannies of power and action and to think instead about social structure, and even there to abstract from the actual and to think about the ideal. It may depend on one's times. To put the point polemically: if Geuss is inclined to historicize Rawls, seeing his theoretical edifice as merely an ideological reflection of the postwar American social order, he should also consider historicizing himself.[26] For the present situation is one in

---

25. For Geuss's criticism of Rawls in this regard, see *Outside Ethics*, 38. Concerning the relationship between ideal theory and empirical insight, Elizabeth Anderson's discussion of ideal theory at the start of *The Imperative of Integration* is instructive. Although Anderson takes herself to be advocating nonideal theory, I would categorize her position as a plea for a particular kind of ideal theory that we might call Deweyan. She argues that since "ideals embody imagined solutions to identified problems in a society" (6), empirical insight is a necessary precursor to the formation of ideals: we must begin by diagnosing the "problems and complaints of our society" (6) and only then turn to the construction of ideals. It follows that we might criticize a given ideal as proceeding from an inadequate perception of the present situation and its needs: "When we alter our conceptual maps to gain a more empirically adequate understanding of our problems, we also open some and close other evaluative options. New conceptual terrain provides new perspectives from which to engage in evaluation and thereby prompts us to articulate new ideals" (5). This implies that it is possible to criticize Rawls (and Rawlsians) for failing to see the importance of neoliberalism without concluding that every ideal theory must fall into the same trap.

26. Geuss, *Philosophy and Real Politics*, 89, and *Outside Ethics*, 22. Whereas Geuss thinks that the fact that Rawls reflects his times makes him "a parochial figure" whose work does not "[deserve and repay] the most careful scrutiny," both G. A. Cohen and Patchen Markell see it as precisely the reason to engage with Rawls. For Cohen, the fact that Rawls reflects his age is part of his greatness: "John Rawls grasped his age, or, more precisely, one large reality of his age, in thought. In his work the politics of liberal (in the American sense) democracy and social (in the European sense) democracy rises to consciousness of itself." Likewise, Markell suggests that *A Theory of Justice* provides "a wonderfully rich vein of source material, one would think, for anyone who wished to launch a more radical critique of that order by identifying and sharpening its symptomatic tensions and contradictions. (I think here of Marx's attitude toward the classical political economists.)" See Cohen, *Rescuing Justice and Equality*, 11; and Markell, review of *Philosophy and Real Politics*, by Raymond Geuss, 175. I am essentially suggesting that the same strategy would be fruitful with respect

which widespread dissatisfaction with elements of our way of life that are frequently brought under the heading of "neoliberalism" is combined with a marked lack of competing visions, especially on the left. And the blanket rejection of political idealism (understood as the practice of working out and orienting oneself toward visions of the best possible society) seems to chime rather well with Margaret Thatcher's mantra that "there is no alternative."

24. It is unfair for the establishment to demand that critics supply alternatives to present arrangements, as Geuss rightly points out.[27] But for critics to make such a demand of themselves is only logical. After all, if political action requires detecting and changing power relations, as critics like Geuss tend to believe, and if ideology can be a form of power, as they also tend to believe, then it makes perfect sense for them to seek to propagate an ideology of their own. This is not a matter of producing detailed policy proposals or recipes for the cookshops of the future. It simply involves spreading a system of ideas, or a way of thinking, that serves to orient agents with respect to their sociopolitical world, enabling them to grasp it and motivating them to change it. Although this way of thinking will have to be embedded in day-to-day practices if it is to take root as a genuine way of being in the world, it might nevertheless be shaped by conscious reflection. And one method of consciously constructing a counterhegemonic ideology would surely be to work out an ideal theory that bears some relation to contemporary practices—a vision of the best possible us.[28]

---

to Geuss himself. A defense of Geuss on this point might plausibly appeal to the distinction he makes between "utopianism" (which he admires) and "moralism" (which he does not), but it seems to me that this distinction depends on construing "moralism" in such a way as to generate a straw man. See Geuss, *Reality and Its Dreams*, 42–48.

27. On the unfairness of asking critics to provide alternatives, see Geuss, *Philosophy and Real Politics*, 95–96; and Finlayson, *Political Is Political*, chap. 1.

28. On the Deweyan thought that visions of the best possible us still count as ideals, despite not being visions of the best possible society all told, see §2 of Chapter 6. It would be cheap to object that the precise bounds of the "we" implied in my "best possible us" formulation remain unclear. For one thing, the social unit in question will necessarily vary from case to case. For another, writing always involves some kind of invitation to the reader to consider herself as part of a "we," and it is always open to

25. What should such an ideal look like? It must be said, by way of truth in advertising, that this book will not offer anything approaching a complete answer to that question. My aim is just to address one part of the matter at hand. I have claimed that contemporary Western political life is marked by a peculiar combination of widespread discontent with significant elements of our way of life—such as those that I tentatively characterized under the headings of possessive individualism, economism, and commodification—and a relative absence of alternative ideals. My hunch is that our discontent and our lack of idealism are two sides of the same coin. If each of us were to work out a vision of the best possible society that we could form and to orient ourselves toward that vision in our day-to-day lives, our sociopolitical order would be transformed for the better. But current institutions often get in the way of such idealism, constraining us to play our parts in constituting a way of life with which we are dissatisfied. Whatever else a contemporary ideal should involve, then, it should involve idealism itself—idealism as a concrete, quotidian practice, supported by institutions and manifest in the day-to-day actions of citizens. Or so I shall argue.

§3 Why Plato?

26. To make this case, I turn to an unlikely source: Plato. For although recent debates over the value of ideal theory have mostly centered on the work of Rawls and his successors, the history of ideal theory is as long as the history of political philosophy—and right at the beginning of that history stands the *Republic*, which contains not only a theory of the ideal society, Kallipolis, but also, I will argue, a theory of the nature and purpose of ideal theory itself. Idealism, understood as the activity of working out and orienting ourselves toward ideals, is

---

the reader to refuse that invitation. This in turn points to a reason for rejecting Geuss's attack (in *Philosophy and Real Politics* and elsewhere) on the use of "intuitions" in mainstream Anglo-American political philosophy as inherently conservative. If philosophical reflection is inherently tied to time and place, then there is no way of completely escaping all contingent starting points.

to play one role in Kallipolis and another role in Athens. In Kallipolis, ideal theorists are to occupy the offices of state; in Athens, they are to generate a kind of critical perception among their fellow citizens. The overarching claim of the present book is that Plato's reflections can still guide us today, at least to some degree: idealism in the relevant sense ought to play a crucial role within any contemporary ideal, as a requirement of excellent citizenship; and this ideal of citizenship gives each of us a vantage point from which to critique the present situation. The first half of the book therefore consists of an interpretation of the *Republic*, metaphysics and all; the second half then argues that a Platonic approach to idealism can, if suitably revised, provide the basis for both a contemporary ideal and a contemporary critical theory.

27. It is only natural to wonder whether spending so much time arguing over how best to interpret the *Republic* is necessary for a book that aims to make a case about the present. Even if my argument is drawn from Plato, a skeptic might say, with respect to truth or falsity it must ultimately stand on its own two feet, and in that sense questions of interpretation are beside the point—they might be of interest to historians of philosophy, but from a normative point of view they cut no ice. On this view, a project that mixes textual interpretation and normative argument ought to be split into two books, each aimed at a different audience.

28. There is more than one way for philosophy to be normative, however. The most obvious way involves defending a set of propositions regarding what is right or good. We might argue, for instance, that ignorance of moral facts does not render agents blameless, or that there is no duty to obey the law, or that autonomy is an intrinsic good. Theses like these demand, or at least suit, a familiar mode of argumentation in which we aim to proceed from clear and simple premises to a clear and simple conclusion, making sure to bite off no more than we can chew. In this process the role of past philosophers can only ever be secondary. We might raid them for premises, arguments, or conclusions, or we might model our activities on theirs in some more general sense, but ultimately they can serve as nothing more than aids or crutches. A philosophical genius might be expected to have no use for them.

29. But philosophy can also aim to shape thought and action by taking as its object not so much propositions or sets of propositions as whole views or outlooks—ways of looking at the world and at ourselves, frameworks of significance that shape what we take as salient in the first place. What it means to advance a whole outlook is hard to say, admittedly, but it becomes a little clearer if we think about what constitutes the greatness of philosophers such as Plato, Hobbes, or Nietzsche. One wants to say that they produced not only arguments but also insights, and that these insights were not merely isolable perceptions, but rather somehow bound up with looking at things from a new angle. This is what gave their writings the quality of "untimeliness," to use Nietzsche's phrase—they achieved a kind of distance from their own culture that enabled them to reflect on the outlooks characteristic of it.[29]

30. There are various ways to seek such an external vantage point. Plato and Hobbes constructed ideal polities from first principles, and this allowed them to look at the actual world from the perspective of an imagined alternative. If the construction of an ideal is to count as a philosophical project, it must, of course, involve defending propositions regarding what is right or good—and in this respect, as we have seen, the history of philosophy plays a contingent role at best. But as Bernard Williams pointed out, drawing on Nietzsche, another way to generate an external vantage point is to acquire a sense of the past: "The point of any history is to achieve some distance from the present, which can help one to understand the present."[30] History provides us, we might say, with a series of static vantage points to

---

29. Compare Green, "Political Theory as Both Philosophy and History: A Defense Against Methodological Militancy," 431–432: "We must remember that the theorist, as the etymology of the word attests, is above all a seer—literally a seer of sights [theoros = thea (θέα) "a view" + horan (ὁρᾶν) "to see"]. And this root meaning of theory should be understood not in a mystical sense but in a phenomenological one: specifically as the capacity to perceive political reality more clearly, or in any case more originally and freshly, usually on the basis of certain felicitous distinctions. . . . At its best, then, political theory perceives political reality with superior clarity, so that students of political-theoretic works can come to intellectually maneuver within the political world with greater perspicacity, effectiveness, and self-awareness."

30. Williams, Sense of the Past, 258. Williams goes on to cite a remark of Nietzsche regarding classical philology in his Untimely Meditations: "I cannot imagine what [its] meaning would be in our own age, if it is not to be untimely—that is, to act against the

which we can repair in assessing our own culture. This is true of every kind of history, but the history of philosophy is especially useful in this regard, since philosophical texts come to life only when we learn to reconstruct the thought processes that underlie them. In disciplining ourselves to think alongside a given thinker, we learn to think as she would, which is to say that we learn to imitate her. And by the process of osmosis that so interested Plato, what we imitate can gradually seep into us. At a certain point we can find ourselves looking at our own world, and our own lives, through someone else's eyes (at least to some degree).[31] What the history of philosophy can yield, then, is a series of *dynamic* vantage points—ways of thinking that come alive in and through the process of interpretation, bringing into focus certain aspects of the present that would not otherwise have been salient and thereby allowing us to grasp, and perhaps alter, our own outlook. And in this process the hard work of interpretation is indispensable; one cannot simply skip to the conclusions.

31. Not all ways of thinking are equally illuminating, of course, and the suggestion that we in the twenty-first century stand to learn from Plato's political philosophy may not sound promising. After all, Plato is resolutely illiberal and antidemocratic. The *Republic* advocates censorship, eugenics, and the abolition of the family, among other things, and it repeatedly mocks democracy. Matters only get worse when one realizes that Plato's political philosophy rests on his metaphysics, which appears to be wildly out of step with the modern scientific worldview. The proposition that brings Plato's politics together with his metaphysics is the notorious claim that philosophers should rule. This is the core of the Platonic ideal, in my view, and it is also the core of the ideal that I shall propose myself. So is fair to say that I will be swimming against the current.

---

age, and by so doing to have an effect on the age, and, let us hope, to the benefit of a future age."

31. Plato's worries about *mimēsis* in theater would therefore seem to apply to the process of reconstructive interpretation. If he is right, we should devote ourselves to reconstructing the thought processes only of philosophers whose style of thinking we have reason to believe worth absorbing. There is also the danger, of course, of foisting our own views on the thinker in question, even if we have a strong incentive to avoid doing so, since that would negate the whole exercise of seeking distance from the present.

32. The notion that philosophers should rule is liable to seem absurd, given the way we usually understand philosophy and ruling; few would wish to replace Churchill with Wittgenstein or Obama with Parfit. So the first question is what Plato could have meant by philosophy and ruling such that it might have been even remotely plausible that ruling would require philosophy. The first half of this book addresses that question and draws out the implications regarding the role of political idealism in society.

33. On Plato's account, I argue, philosophy is the activity of working out the nature of particular things—their forms—by considering them as part of a teleologically structured cosmos in which every genuine entity has a particular role; the true form of each entity is that organization of its parts which best enables it to carry out its function. Ruling, meanwhile, is the activity of maintaining people's souls in optimal form, which requires maintaining the city in optimal form. This involves regulating the social division of labor with an eye to ideals of both city and soul, where ideals are models that embody our understanding of the best possible condition that a particular kind of object can have. It also demands disseminating these ideals, as well as other images and stories, in order to shape the views of citizens and therewith their souls. The symbolic dimension of ruling suggests that ideal theorists can exercise some form of rule even without political power, and hence that ideal theory has a role to play in nonideal societies as well as ideal ones. This in turn suggests a fruitful way of thinking about Plato's own activity in writing the *Republic*, namely that he intended to influence Athenian life by disseminating models and images that altered his fellow citizens' perceptions of their society. On my view, then, Plato's ideal theory was also his critical theory. This is only a rough and ready summary of an interpretation that must be argued for in depth, but for present purposes it will suffice.

34. The second half of the book is devoted to an account of how the *Republic* might bear on the present. However cogent Plato's view may have been on its own terms, the idea of rule by a metaphysically informed, soul-shaping elite will obviously be unappealing to anyone committed to liberal democracy. It would therefore seem natural for us to treat Plato's *Republic* as a historical curiosity, perhaps worth

reading for what it reveals about ancient Greek life or the premodern mind-set, perhaps worth studying to cut our philosophical and philological teeth on its argumentation and rhetoric, but definitely not worth taking seriously for our own lives in the way that, say, Rawls's *Theory of Justice* is worth taking seriously. We might follow Sir Karl Popper in thinking we ought to study Plato closely in order to know our enemy. But this is still to learn *by means of* Plato rather than to learn *from* him.

35. How, then, is it possible to learn from Plato's politics in a fuller sense? One way would be to use his arguments to attack liberal democracy. It is no accident, for instance, that a revolutionary communist such as Alain Badiou is happy to take Plato seriously.[32] But one need not go that far to find an ally in Plato. For liberal democracy is not one thing, and neither are its constituent parts, liberalism and democracy. Taking these dimensions apart, and speaking extremely generally, we might say that democrats who believe in some degree of what David Estlund calls "epistocracy," the idea that in certain domains power ought to be granted on the basis of knowledge, are likely to find themselves in closer sympathy with Plato than those who believe in "direct" democracy in all domains; and that liberals who believe in some degree of "perfectionism," the view that the state ought to promote certain forms of human flourishing, such as the capacity for autonomous decision making or the capacity to experience higher pleasures, will have more in common with Plato than "political liberals" who believe the state must try to remain neutral with respect to "extrapolitical" conceptions of the good life.[33] So while direct democrats and political liberals might take Plato seriously only as Popper did, it is conceivable that epistocratic democrats and perfectionist liberals could adapt Plato's arguments for their own purposes.[34]

---

32. See, e.g., Badiou, *Communist Hypothesis*; and Badiou, *Plato's "Republic."*

33. On epistocracy, see Estlund, *Democratic Authority*; and Brennan, *Against Democracy*. For perfectionism as against political liberalism, see Nussbaum, "Perfectionist Liberalism and Political Liberalism." One does not need to believe that either democracy or liberalism has any kind of "essence" to profit from this scalar heuristic.

34. For an account of Plato's influence on John Stuart Mill, see Giorgini, "Radical Plato." See also Lane, *Plato's Progeny*.

36. Something similar could also be true with respect to Plato's metaphysics. Assume, for the sake of this initial exposition, that what is taken to be "premodern" about Plato's metaphysics is his view that entities have objective essences, and that what is taken to be "extravagant" is his view that these essences exist independently of the objects that instantiate them. Clearly one does not have to reject either of these two views. Essentialist metaphysics, generally inspired by Aristotle, is thriving in modern philosophy, even if it remains a minority position within academia as a whole.[35] Moreover, the man who arguably founded analytic philosophy, Gottlob Frege, was an unrepentant believer in the independent existence of universals—a position that led him to be labeled a Platonist. So while some philosophers might have no reason to believe they could learn from Plato's metaphysics, still less to believe that it provides support for his politics, others might find themselves better disposed toward it from the start.[36]

37. We could therefore imagine a project that brought Plato to bear on contemporary debates concerning democracy or liberalism or metaphysics, or some combination of those three, arguing that we moderns should learn from his reflections. The goal would be to show that the baby had been thrown out with the bathwater: that accepting democracy need not and should not commit us to rejecting epistocracy in all its manifestations, that accepting liberalism need not and should not commit us to avoiding the politics of the good life, and that accepting the modern scientific method need not and should not commit us to rejecting every variant of "Platonism" in metaphysics. This might be a valuable contribution to contemporary philosophy, but it is not my project.

38. This book does not advance Plato's ideal as against liberal democracy or the modern scientific worldview. The goal is rather to show that the Platonic way of thinking allows us to construct a

---

35. See, e.g., the approach taken in Loux, *Metaphysics*. We could also make the same argument if we take the view that what is "premodern" is Plato's emphasis on teleology rather than his belief in objective essences, since Aristotelian approaches to the philosophy of nature are hardly dead either.

36. See, e.g., Berman, "Universals"; and Berman, "Platonic Theory of Truthmaking."

compelling ideal of excellent citizenship in liberal democracies and thereby to grasp our present situation anew. That does not involve pretending that Plato was secretly a liberal democrat committed to the modern scientific worldview. He was not. The claim is rather that the core of his political thought can survive the massive surgery undoubtedly required to make his ideal compatible with liberal democracy.

39. I begin by responding to Popper's famous critique of Plato, whose positive side is the requirement that political governors limit themselves to piecemeal reforms rather than aiming at large-scale social engineering, and that they be accountable to and deposable by their subjects. We can concede these points, I argue, while maintaining the Platonic position that those who govern institutions ought to engage in ideal theory in order to give themselves a criterion for stable and sound decision making. I then turn to Rawls's argument that the liberal state should remain neutral with respect to a range of conceptions of the good life, a position that might seem obviously incompatible with any kind of Platonism regarding rule. I show that Rawlsian political liberalism would still permit, and might even require, a limited form of philosophical rule at the state level. My main claim, however, is that in a liberal democracy it is often ordinary citizens who exercise rule in Plato's distinctive sense, whether through local associations or through their day-to-day activities. Each citizen ought therefore to organize their day-to-day career in light of a conception of a society organized toward the good life, an ideal "us." What we need, then, is not so much philosopher-kings as philosopher-citizens.[37]

---

37. I should stress that this strategy does not commit me to defending Rawlsian political liberalism. My proposals will be compatible with its truth but not dependent on it. This is partly a matter of intellectual hygiene: it helps to have a clear remit in a project this broad, and the approach just outlined allows me to bypass a whole array of debates that might otherwise bog me down. But it is also desirable for a theory to have the broadest possible relevance. If an electrical engineer proposes a new type of socket that will facilitate the operation of Dyson vacuum cleaners, that is one thing; if she claims that it will facilitate the operation of every electrical device on earth, that is another. There are those who believe that political philosophy need not concern itself with questions of applicability or relevance. They may be right. But it seems obvious that if a work of political philosophy does manage to be widely relevant while still being philosophically interesting, then so much the better. If the core elements in the Platonic way of thinking about society are compatible with Rawlsian political

40. I do not claim that the notion of philosophical citizenship amounts to anything like a complete ideal in the sense of a vision of a whole way of life. What I do claim is that it ought to be part of any such ideal, and that it ought to play a role in contemporary critical theory. Earlier I claimed that recent political life has been characterized by a peculiar tension, whereby widespread dissatisfaction with fundamental aspects of our socioeconomic order has coexisted with a sense that there is no alternative. There are, of course, historical reasons for that conjunction; we cannot simply dissolve it by force of will or argument. But in my view the ideal of idealistic citizenship gives us a lens through which to bring our dissatisfaction into focus and hence to locate the possibility of its dissolution. To make this case, I turn to Marx's *Capital*, showing that one of its central strands is both illuminated and bolstered by the Platonic way of thinking about economic life. More specifically, I argue that on Marx's account, ideal-typical capitalist societies institutionalize what Plato calls moneymaking, whereby workplace deliberations are not tethered to social needs. It follows that capitalist societies systematically malfunction relative to an ideal of society as a kind of team working together for the sake of the good life, guided by the Platonic virtues of justice and wisdom. Marx himself was coy about the ideals that underpinned his account of capitalism, preferring to cast the latter as a kind of immanent critique completely independent of self-standing normative considerations. I argue, by contrast, that ideals can perfectly well figure into Marxian critical theory so long as they can be seen to have roots within present practices, and that this criterion is in fact met by the ideal of philosophical citizenship. I then end with some brief suggestions as to how the ideal might guide action today, both at the level of institutional design and at the level of individual behavior.

§4 Which Plato?

41. Having outlined where I want to go with Plato, I should say something about how I propose to read him. The strategy of this

---

liberalism, they ought also to be compatible with more epistocratic and perfectionist versions of liberal democracy.

book is, as I have just said, first to interpret the *Republic* so as to yield a cogent political theory and then to argue that the core of that theory can and should serve as part of a contemporary ideal. Yet the notion of extracting any kind of "theory" from a work as complex and controversial as the *Republic* will already seem suspect to many. It therefore behooves me to articulate and defend my method of approaching Plato, however briefly.

42. One thing is clear: there is no such thing as an uncontroversial interpretation of a Platonic dialogue. Interpretation, writes Charles Taylor, is the attempt "to bring to light an underlying coherence or sense" in an object that is in some way "confused, incomplete, cloudy, seemingly contradictory—in one way or another, unclear."[38] This process is necessarily fraught since the ground for any given interpretation can only be other interpretations: we make sense of a particular part by locating it within our understanding of the whole, but how we understand the whole in turn depends on how we make sense of the parts.[39] The best we can hope for is a state of "reflective equilibrium," to use Rawls's term, wherein our judgments on the parts are no longer in tension with our judgments about the whole. If the object of interpretation is at all complex, however, it will be possible for two different interpretations to reach different equilibria, both internally consistent but each misguided from the other's perspective. And no one denies that Platonic dialogues are extraordinarily complex.[40]

43. To begin with, we might even quibble with the term "dialogues." Dialogue is speech that goes back and forth between two or more interlocutors. All of Plato's works, with the exception of the letters sometimes attributed to him, involve dialogue so understood. But the degree to which they involve dialogue varies: sometimes they go back and forth like a tennis match; sometimes one person merely

---

38. Charles Taylor, "Interpretation and the Sciences of Man," 15.
39. This is one way of describing the "hermeneutic circle" posited by Heidegger and Hans-Georg Gadamer. See ibid., 18.
40. I cannot do justice here to the immense literature on how Plato wrote and how he should be interpreted; quite apart from the explicit contributions, some of which will be referred to in what follows, every substantive interpretation implies some answer to this question. Having said that, I have profited especially from McCabe, "Plato's Ways of Writing."

lobs the ball gently over the net to allow the other to proceed as he wishes; sometimes pages pass before the ball is returned, the intervening period being occupied with a different game altogether, whether a monologue (narrative or theoretical) or a secondary dialogue (imagined or recounted); and sometimes the whole affair, with all the complexities just mentioned, is actually narrated by a single person—which makes it in the final analysis a monologue rather than a dialogue.

44. The term "dialogue" is here to stay because it evokes the signature feature of Plato's writing, namely the fact that it depicts philosophy as a form of discussion. This reminds us that philosophical positions are held always and only by people, that they are only ever debated in the context of lives, and that reflecting on what we should believe is part of the ongoing project of leading an examined life. Building this vision of human life into the structure of his work gives Plato's writing a profundity matched by little else in the history of philosophy. But it also creates a special difficulty for interpreters. For discussion is an activity that involves specific people at specific times in specific places for specific purposes. Situations can call for abstract argument, but they can call for other things too. If persuasion is the goal, for example, rhetoric may be required, whether to supplement or to replace argument; but sometimes speech of any kind must come to an end. Discussions are therefore limited in important ways. They are limited by the participants' capacities in that their course will be fundamentally shaped by the degree to which the interlocutors understand the topic, as well as the degree to which they understand not only one another but also themselves. They are limited by the participants' interests, in that for a topic to be pursued further it must always be the case that someone desires to pursue it. And they are limited by time, both in the sense that they must have an end, given the need to go on living, and in the sense that they must be occasioned and therefore have a beginning. All this means no two conversations are ever quite alike. And while one could conceivably continue a past conversation on a future occasion, threading the two together into one extended conversation, this would require a self-conscious effort on the part of the interlocutors.

45. Put together, these facts make it impossible to extract a single coherent theory from the Platonic corpus. It may be a fallacy to

assume a single coherent theory behind the writings of any thinker: most people change their minds over the course of time, and even a thinker as systematic as Aristotle seems to have been no exception.[41] But the difficulties of taking, say, the deliverances of Aristotle's theory of knowledge and plugging them into his theory of nature are paltry by comparison with the difficulties of combining thoughts from different Platonic dialogues. The questions and answers of one dialogue, not to mention the stories, come up in the context of a particular conversation between particular people, and each dialogue presents a different occasion with different topics and different interlocutors. We should therefore be wary of taking remarks made in one context and simply transposing them to another context without further reflection, as scholars are sometimes wont to do.[42] This is by no means a prohibition. It certainly can be illuminating to read dialogues in light of one another, and there are often reasonable grounds for doing so. After all, despite their differences, the *Theaetetus*, the *Sophist*, and the *Statesman* do pitch themselves as hanging together; there are clear intertextual references between some of the dialogues, such as the *Republic* and the *Timaeus*; and taken as a whole, the various dialogues do display strong family resemblances on a thematic level. Furthermore, it seems plausible to suppose that Plato was writing, at least in part, for members of his Academy and thus for an audience familiar with his corpus as it was at the time. But none of that changes the basic point, which is that we cannot simply assume coherence across the dialogues. There should be a standing presumption in favor of treating each work independently and only making arguments for reading one dialogue in light of another on a case-by-case basis, in full recognition of differing dialogical contexts.[43]

---

41. Most scholars see a development from the *Categories* to the *Metaphysics*, for example.

42. See Thakkar, review of *Blindness and Reorientation*, by C. D. C. Reeve, e1–e5.

43. Lloyd Gerson suggests that we think of Platonism as "the philosophical position arrived at by embracing the claims that contradict those claims explicitly rejected by Plato in the dialogues" (*Aristotle and Other Platonists*, 17). But such commitments would seem to delimit only the range of possible Platonic theories rather than specifying a single coherent theory. In *From Plato to Platonism*, 10, Gerson identifies the relevant commitments as "antimaterialism, antimechanism, antinominalism, antirelativism, and antiskepticism." I came to Gerson's definition of

46. Even at the level of the individual dialogue, however, it is not clear that interpretation will yield any kind of Platonic theory. One problem is that Plato never says anything in his own name.[44] This fact is liable to generate a pitched battle between those who see Plato as using certain figures (especially Socrates) as his mouthpiece and those who see him as no more identifiable with his protagonists than Shakespeare is with his.[45] Such disputes are pointless insofar as they remain abstract, since the literary character of Plato's writing itself differs dramatically from dialogue to dialogue. Some works are thick with context, characterization, and playful irony; others are relatively arid. Some have interlocutors who compete; others have interlocutors who cooperate. Some end with tentative conclusions; others end with confusion. Whether we can attribute anything to Plato himself will depend on the details of the case at hand.

47. The *Republic* is a remarkably reflexive work, one that reflects on styles of storytelling and argument while itself deploying several different forms of storytelling and argument. Book III contains an extended discussion of narration and imitation, during which Socrates suggests that a storyteller will be permitted to practice in Kallipolis, the ideal city, only insofar as he either narrates without imitating or restricts himself to imitating "the speech of a good person" (392c–398b). Yet everything that happens in the *Republic*, from the cut-and-thrust of the opening exchanges to the constructive passages and then the final myth, is being recounted by Socrates

---

Platonism via Lane, "Antianarchia," which adds antianarchism to the list of negative commitments.

44. Contra Gerson, then, there are in fact no claims explicitly rejected by Plato in the dialogues.

45. Richard Kraut, for instance, claims that "our best chance of understanding Plato is . . . to begin with the assumption that in each dialogue he uses his principal interlocutor to support or oppose certain conclusions by means of certain arguments because he, Plato, supports or opposes those conclusions for those reasons," while Leo Strauss claims that "if someone quotes a passage from the dialogues in order to prove that Plato held such and such a view, he acts about as reasonably as if he were to assert that according to Shakespeare life is a tale told by an idiot, full of sound and fury, signifying nothing." It should be noted that these statements are simplifications of Kraut's and Strauss's respective positions. Kraut's assumption is simply a starting point or working hypothesis, while Strauss is merely expressing his point in preliminary and polemical fashion. See Kraut, "Introduction to the Study of Plato," 29; and Strauss, *City and Man*, 50.

in his own voice. To take an extreme example, the myth of Er is a narrative (Er's tale) within a narrative (Socrates' report of Er's tale) within a dialogue (Socrates' discussion with Glaucon) within a narrative (Socrates' report of the day's conversation). The fact that every piece of dialogue is ultimately being narrated by Socrates means that he is frequently imitating "inferior characters," to use his own expression (396d), such as Thrasymachus in Book I and the sight lovers in Book V. And Socrates' narration is itself being imitated, one would think, by Plato. What are we to make of this situation? The answer may be simple enough. Perhaps Socrates is virtuous enough for Plato to safely imitate while nevertheless being imperfect enough to go astray regarding his own use of imitation. Or perhaps the rules that would apply to young guardians in Kallipolis do not apply to elderly private citizens in Athens. But the fact that such questions can reasonably be asked goes to show how astonishingly reflexive the *Republic* is. And this in turn might seem to speak against the thought that Plato means to convey anything so simple as a philosophical theory.[46]

48. At the same time, however, it would obviously be wrong to describe the *Republic* as essentially aporetic. Whatever else they are up to, the conversation partners frequently do pursue a philosophical agenda in a progressive manner, establishing provisional conclusions and using them as premises in further arguments. And some of those conclusions concern the primacy of philosophy—over the whole city, but also over other pursuits and especially over storytelling. So although the *Republic* is indeed a highly reticulated, interwoven literary object, it seems reasonable to suppose that the key to its coherence is its philosophical agenda.

49. The claim that the *Republic* advances a philosophical agenda is by no means equivalent to the claim that Plato uses Socrates as his mouthpiece. After all, Socrates does not make the running alone. It is certainly true that he guides the conversation according to his vision of the topic at hand. But his interlocutors also play constructive

---

46. For a sample of the many interpretations that make a special effort to do full justice to the literary character of the *Republic*, see Blondell, *Play of Character in Plato's Dialogues*; Clay, *Platonic Questions*; and Frank, *Poetic Justice*.

roles, most notably (although not only) in delineating the problem that the conversation is to address. It would therefore be better to say that Plato uses the whole conversation as his mouthpiece. But once we remember that the conversation is itself embedded in a narrative, we have to retreat to the notion that Plato uses the whole work as his mouthpiece. This is trivially true, but it brings out two important points concerning interpretive method.

50. The first concerns parts and wholes. It has sometimes been considered rigorous—and it certainly suits the requirements of journal publishing—to produce piecemeal interpretations of this or that Platonic argument as if they were intended to stand alone. Few would hold it against a scholar of the *Republic*'s metaphysics, for example, if she never wrote on its politics. But if the unit of philosophical content is the whole work, then our working assumption should be that our interpretation of one part of the text will have to answer to our interpretations of all the others. It might seem obvious that we should treat the text as a coherent object, but in what follows we will see that doing so yields surprising results.

51. The second point concerns the kind of philosophical content we should expect to uncover in our interpretations. Certainly the term "doctrine" seems inapt. We might say that a doctrine is a set of related propositions that could potentially be expressed in the form of a treatise, so that if the *Republic* does express a doctrine, we should be able to paraphrase it in treatise form. But if the locus of philosophical content is the work as a whole, and that whole includes literary elements, then it may resist such paraphrase.[47] Some will take this to imply that there is no way to extract a philosophical theory from the *Republic* without doing violence to its literary qualities. But that does not follow. For although the *Republic* may not advance a doctrine, what it does advance, it seems to me, is a *view*—not in the

---

47. There may be philosophical reasons for Plato's choosing a literary form that seems to refuse doctrine. For one thing, the substantive conclusions arrived at in the course of the *Republic*'s discussion all seem to be contingent on a hypothesis about the nature and role of goodness that Socrates admits is ungrounded (506d–507a). They therefore remain in an important sense incomplete.

sense of a single, static perspective but rather in the sense of a way of thinking about the world, a pattern of thought.[48]

52. A way of thinking necessarily goes beyond the text that expresses it. To illustrate this, imagine writing on a topic about which you have settled views. Suppose you write a few paragraphs and then mislay them. A couple of months later, having given up looking, you write a new version. But then the first document finally shows up, allowing you to compare the two drafts. If your thoughts really were settled, what you will now find yourself faced with are two different expressions of the same underlying pattern of thought—not simply the same thought, since we are talking about paragraphs and hence concatenations of thoughts, but the same pattern of thought.[49] The two texts might differ with respect to length, word choice, organization, rhetorical strategy, and other elements, but they would both make the same kind of connections, treat the same kind of features as salient, push in the same kind of direction, and the like. Now let us change the example. Suppose you write a few paragraphs and do not mislay them. You therefore have no need to create a second version. But the mere possibility of doing so demonstrates that the first version is only a contingent expression of a way of thinking that is in principle multiply realizable and can therefore be extracted from the text.[50]

53. This is not to deny that texts will always exceed the way of thinking that they express. For one thing, very few texts will be fully coherent: some may be deliberately incoherent, some may be shoddy,

---

48. On the original notion of *theōria* as a kind of viewing, see Nightingale, *Spectacles of Truth in Classical Greek Philosophy*.

49. Of course, this opens up questions about the criteria of identity for patterns of thought, but I mean to suggest a concept that serves a specific function—as a regulative ideal for interpretation—that does not call for absolute precision.

50. This might be true even if we changed the example so that what you are writing is a short story. If you end up with two texts for the reasons just described, each will be unique from an artistic perspective, but they might still both express the same underlying pattern of thought. That would be the case, for example, if what is relatively settled as you write is how you view your characters, their relationships, and their development—in short, how you are constructing the fictional world. This way of thinking may be partially unconscious—you might simply find yourself returning time and again to a given way of picturing something—but an interpreter might nevertheless have good reason to seek to excavate it from the particular formulations of your text.

and others will simply be imperfect. For another, every text will contain what Paul Ricoeur called "surplus meaning," ramifications and connotations that go beyond the author's own (conscious or unconscious) intentions.[51] The notion of a unitary way of thinking finding full expression in a text is therefore nothing more than a regulative ideal that serves a purpose in orienting interpretation. With almost every text there will come a point when the assumption of coherence gives out—the only question is when.

54. There is no a priori answer to how far the assumption of coherence can hold; the only way to find out is to propose an interpretation and defend it against alternatives. If what I have just said is correct, this will inevitably involve thinking alongside the text. In going back and forth between interpretations of the parts and interpretations of the whole, we must always project an expectation of what ought to be the case at either level. The hypothesis that the author is thinking in such and such a way at the level of the whole implies a hypothesis about what she ought to have written at the level of the parts, for instance. If the parts do not conform to one's hypothesis, then one should either alter the hypothesis or alter one's sense of how the parts might relate to the whole. In any case, the process will necessarily involve a form of reverse engineering on the part of the interpreter.

55. This brings danger. We want to interpret the text, not ourselves—but in trying to reverse engineer the underlying structure of a text, we run the risk of conflating our own judgments with those of the author. It is common, for instance, to invoke the "principle of charity" as a guide for interpretation. Roughly speaking, the idea is that if faced with two interpretations, we should pick the one that makes the text better. But a text can be good in many ways. Should our interpretations aim to maximize truth, plausibility, complexity, distinctiveness, or a bundle of such qualities? And by whose standards? Is it charitable to interpret a work of ancient philosophy so as to make it maximally rigorous by the standards of contemporary analytic philosophy? Or is that a form of violence?[52]

---

51. See Ricoeur, *Interpretation Theory*.

52. On the slipperiness of the principle of charity, see Stern, "Some Third Thing"; and Finlayson, *Political Is Political*, chap. 3.

56. Once again there is no a priori answer to such questions. It is obviously true, as Melissa Lane writes, that any responsible interpretation of a historical text needs to fall within the bounds of what the text could have meant, given the "semantics, syntactical conventions, and pragmatics of the language communities in which it was formulated and to which it was addressed."[53] We must therefore always be open to changing our interpretations in light of historical evidence regarding those communities. Beyond that, however, different projects will call for different approaches.[54] Bernard Williams distinguishes between the history of philosophy, which aims to yield a product that itself counts as philosophy, and the history of ideas, which aims to yield a product that counts as history.[55] Given that what counts as good work in philosophy and history changes over time, the methods used in the history of philosophy will depend on contemporary conceptions of philosophy, just as the methods used in the history of ideas will depend on contemporary conceptions of historiography. But this dependence can take different forms in different projects. If a historical text is of philosophical interest because it promises to yield a new position within contemporary academic debates, for instance, then it will make sense to frame our inquiry in terms of those debates. This will affect both which features of the text we take as most salient and the manner in which we present our

---

53. Lane, "Antianarchia," 2. Lane draws on R. G. Collingwood, who wrote that to understand what someone means, it is not enough to simply hear or read his statements—"You must also know what the question was . . . to which the thing he has said or written was meant as an answer." Collingwood, *Autobiography*, 31.

54. Jeffrey Green makes a powerful plea for methodological pluralism in political theory as against the monistic approaches of both analytic philosophy and the Cambridge School (especially in its early phase). Green sees Hannah Arendt and Isaiah Berlin as models of how to combine methods from both philosophy and history in the service of contemporary political thought. See Green, "Political Theory as Both Philosophy and History."

55. Williams, *Sense of the Past*, 257, referring back to the preface to Williams, *Descartes*. Williams also claims that the history of philosophy is distinguished from the history of ideas by its interest in diachronic influence, but this does not seem justified to me. In my view, questions concerning diachronic influence are better handled by the history of ideas (or intellectual history, as it should probably be called).

interpretation.[56] In the present case, by contrast, my hope is that the *Republic* will provide us with more than a set of arguments or propositions. The goal is rather to recover something like an outlook, or way of viewing the world, that will be "untimely" in the current context—a lens through which the present shows up as limited or somehow strange. With this in mind, our interpretation must aim to retain the distance between the text and ourselves while at the same time allowing it to speak to us rather than to its original audience. We must make something of the text by asking what it would make of us.[57]

57. In sum, this book attempts to bring Plato's *Republic* to bear on the present in an untimely fashion. The goal is to address a situation in which political idealism—understood as the activity of working out and orienting oneself toward visions of the best possible society— seems largely absent despite widespread dissatisfaction with at least some fundamental aspects of our form of life. My suggestion is that the *Republic* allows us to construct an ideal in light of which we can better grasp our present condition. Given this ambition, the most salient element of the *Republic* becomes its presentation of an ideal, Kallipolis, within which ideal theory itself plays a role. The first half of this book aims to understand this way of thinking without erasing its distance from our own—to get it to speak to us without removing its foreign accent. And since there is no way to hear what Plato has to say about politics without first attuning ourselves to his metaphysics, it is to that task that I now turn.

---

56. Clearly, much history of philosophy proceeds by simply assuming that a work is of interest and then applying contemporary modes of analysis to illuminate its conceptual architecture. The product of this activity is philosophy, as Williams would suggest, but in and of itself it makes no claim to being philosophy to which contemporary philosophers ought to pay attention qua philosophers—which is not to say that no case could be made for it, given the possibility of work in the vein described in the main text.

57. On the regulative ideal of interpretation as a kind of conversation with a text, see Gadamer, *Truth and Method*, especially 362–389.

1

What Is Philosophy For?

THE OVERARCHING CLAIM of this book is that political idealism, understood as the practice of working out and orienting ourselves toward visions of the best possible society, ought to play a crucial role within any liberal-democratic ideal. To make this case, I propose that we return to Plato's *Republic*, which offers a powerful way of thinking about the role of idealism in political life. At its baldest and most basic, political Platonism comes down to the proposition that if humans are to flourish, the societies into which they group must be consciously regulated by philosophers, with each citizen doing the job assigned to her. As Socrates puts it, "Until philosophers rule as kings in cities or those who are now called kings and leading men genuinely and adequately philosophize, cities will have no rest from evils" (473c–d).[1]

This claim is unlikely to command our immediate assent, to put it mildly. Karl Popper found it to be the wellspring of a long stream of poisonous thought culminating in Hitler and Stalin; Leo Strauss saw it as the most powerful reductio ad absurdum of political ide-

---

1. Line references to Plato's *Republic* will be to the Oxford Classical Texts edition of S. R. Slings, while translations will be drawn from two translations (that of C. D. C. Reeve and that of G. M. A. Grube and C. D. C. Reeve), with occasional emendations.

alism ever written.[2] Even those who dismiss such views tend not to think the idea of philosopher-rulers worth defending.[3] The fundamental contention of this book, by contrast, is that political Platonism, or at least a version of it, is actually *true*. Rulers really should engage in philosophy, and citizens really should carry out the tasks assigned to them by philosopher-rulers. To see why this might be so, we first need to understand why Plato thought it so. On what conceptions of ruling and philosophy could ruling require philosophy?

I will begin by asking about the conception of philosophy at work in the *Republic*. This will take us deep into Plato's so-called theory of forms—thorny territory, by all accounts—and correspondingly far away from anything directly political. But this is no idle detour. We can only break free of our preconceptions regarding the notion of philosophical rule if we first loosen the grip of the standard conception of forms, according to which philosophers investigate the structure of a world beyond our own.

I therefore begin by showing that the two-worlds view renders Plato's politics at best extremely implausible and at worst downright unintelligible. I offer a reading of the passages most naturally taken to support it, showing that they do not imply that philosophers cognize different objects from ordinary people, but rather that they are able to perceive a different aspect of the same objects. I then offer a hypothesis concerning the nature of this aspect of reality, namely that it concerns formal causes within a teleological picture of the cosmos. In support of this hypothesis I suggest that the sun image at the end of Book VI pictures goodness as both the formal and the final cause of forms. I then show how this reading makes room for enhanced cognition of ordinary objects before ending with the

---

2. See Popper, *Open Society and Its Enemies*, passim; and Strauss, *City and Man*, 65: "Certain it is that the *Republic* supplies the most magnificent cure ever devised for every form of political ambition." For a more fleshed-out version of the Straussian reading, see Bloom, "Interpretive Essay."

3. On Popper, see C. C. W. Taylor, "Plato's Totalitarianism," in *Plato 2*, 280–296. On Strauss, see Burnyeat, "Sphinx without a Secret." For a more sympathetic assessment, see Ferrari, "Strauss's Plato."

suggestion that we need to distinguish between substantial and structural forms.

§1 Two Worlds?

1. It is almost impossible to come to Plato's metaphysics without preconceptions. The term "Platonic" has become a feature of our ordinary language, invoked when people speak of a relationship as "Platonic" or of a particularly excellent item (such as a cat) as "the Platonic idea" of its species or kind. In the more specialized language of philosophy, meanwhile, "Platonism" has come to stand for belief in the absolute objectivity of what some would consider (in some respect or to some extent) subjective, from value to numbers. Closely associated with these usages is a picture of Platonism as positing two worlds, the "world of sense" and the "world of ideas," and a correlative picture of the Platonic philosopher as a kind of mystic who, having ascended to the mountaintop, leaves behind the sensory world and directly perceives the world of ideas.

2. A particularly cogent and concise elaboration of the two-worlds preconception is provided by Bertrand Russell in *The Problems of Philosophy*:

The "idea" *justice* is not identical with anything that is just: it is something other than particular things, which particular things partake of. Not being particular, it cannot exist in the world of sense. Moreover, it is not fleeting or changeable like the things of sense: it is eternally itself, immutable and indestructible. Thus Plato is led to a supra-sensible world, more real than the common world of sense, the unchangeable world of ideas, which alone gives to the world of sense whatever pale reflection of reality may belong to it. The truly real world, for Plato, is the world of ideas; for whatever we may attempt to say about things in the world of sense, we can only succeed in saying that they participate in such and such ideas, which, therefore, constitute all their character. Hence it is easy to pass on into a mysticism. We may hope, in a mystic illumination, to *see* the ideas as we see objects of sense; and we may imagine that the ideas exist in heaven.[4]

On this account, the sensible world—"fleeting, vague, without sharp boundaries, without any clear plan or arrangement"—is nothing more than a reflection of the eternal and unchanging, rigid, and exact world of ideas.[5] To realize this is ipso facto to form the desire to see that real world for oneself and therefore to forsake sense perception in favor of philosophy in the putatively Platonic sense.

3. The two-worlds picture has much to recommend it. Sticking just to the *Republic*, we clearly do find the notion that some entities can be cognized only by the senses, while others can be cognized only by the intellect (509a–511e); that sensible entities are in continual flux, while intelligible ones are unchanging (478e–479e); that the former are what they are in virtue of their relationship to the latter (476a; 596e–597e); and that they are inferior to them in terms of being, intelligibility, and value (478a–479e; 509a–511e; 596e–597e). Furthermore, philosophy clearly is depicted as a process of transcending everyday cognition, most famously in the image of the cave (513a–520d) but also in the requirement for years of mathematical education (521d–531c) and in the claim that only forms can truly be known (476e–480a).

4. There is an obvious problem with the two-worlds picture, however: it makes the notion of philosopher-rulers almost unintelligible. Why would anyone in their right mind offer the keys of the kingdom to a Platonic philosopher? Granted, Socrates' argument is that philosophers should rule *other things being equal*, that is, only if they "have no less experience than the others, and are not inferior to them in any other part of virtue" (484e). But why think that knowledge of forms adds anything to that experience and virtue vis-à-vis the craft of ruling? As Julia Annas writes,

The idea that study of Forms is an end in itself and is to be contrasted with the lowly status of practical concerns goes naturally

---

4. Russell, *Problems of Philosophy*, 91–92.
5. Ibid., 100.

with the view that knowledge not only begins but ends with Forms, that there is properly speaking no knowledge of particulars, only an inferior state of belief; if Forms are the only objects of knowledge, then particular people, things, and actions are not capable of being known, just because they are particulars. . . . How can the just rulers be compared to doctors and pilots when the beginning of wisdom is to turn away from mortal trash?[6]

If philosophy is knowledge of the world beyond, it would appear to offer no guidance regarding how we should act in the world around us. As such, it would appear irrelevant to ruling. But that is only the half of it. There is also the question why philosophers themselves would want to rule. "Someone engrossed in the study of impersonal Forms," Annas writes, "someone who has rejected as trash the claims of the world we experience, can hardly be keen to conduct interviews and sit on boring committees."[7]

5. It is certainly not impossible to provide an account of the relationship between knowing forms and ruling on the two-worlds view. On John Cooper's highly influential reading, for instance, Plato believes that in order to know the best course of action in a given situation, we must first know the otherworldly form of the good; since only philosophers have this knowledge, only they know how to pick the best course of action; and since their knowledge necessarily motivates them to maximize goodness in the world as a whole, they will also be motivated to maximize it in the city. It follows that philosophers should rule.[8]

6. Cooper's account is grounded in four interpretive hypotheses. The first is that Plato considers the good-itself (or the form of the good) to be an absolute standard of goodness that can serve as a kind of anchor for all partial standards, so that "the only sure criterion of goodness in any other thing is the degree to which it approximates the goodness of this perfect good."[9] This is speculative, since at no

---

6. Annas, *Introduction to Plato's "Republic,"* 262.
7. Ibid., 266.
8. Cooper, "Psychology of Justice in Plato," 22–23.
9. Ibid.

point do any of the interlocutors suggest that the way to assess something's goodness is to compare it to the good-itself. That is not an objection, however, since interpreters are perfectly entitled to speculate in order to make sense of a text so long as they are clear about what they are doing, and Cooper's hypothesis is certainly one way of making sense of Socrates' claim that we cannot know any particular good without knowing the good itself (534b–c; 505a–b). The difficulty lies in knowing what it would mean to compare something to the good-itself. Here Cooper needs two more speculative hypotheses. The first is that the good-itself is "a good thing, over and above the good things of this world," essentially pure and perfect, its goodness neither "mingled with and dependent on other features of things" nor present only "in some respect or relation or from some point of view."[10] The second is that we can "render this curious entity more concrete" if we think of it "as a perfect example of rational order, conceived in explicitly mathematical terms: a complex, ordered whole, whose orderliness is due to the mathematical relationships holding among its parts."[11] Combining the three hypotheses, each of which goes beyond the text, we arrive at the view that to assess an entity's goodness is to compare the degree of rational order that it manifests with the perfect instance of rational order that is the good-itself. If this is right, then states of affairs will be good insofar as they manifest rational order, and action will be good insofar as it promotes rational order in the world. This brings us to Cooper's fourth hypothesis, which is that for Plato to be just entails acting for the good of the cosmos rather than for one's own good. Although the best way to achieve rational order in one's own soul is to study rational order wherever it is found, if circumstances dictate that the most efficient way to promote rational order in the cosmos at large is to occupy political office, then the just person will give up her contemplation in favor of ruling.[12]

---

10. "To use Aristotelian language, one could say its essence is to be good; it is not, like every other good thing, essentially something else (a meal, a person) that, for one reason or another, happens to be good (is accidentally good)." Ibid., 22

11. Ibid., 23.

12. In Cooper's view, Plato is therefore advocating something like the consequentialism of Bernard Williams's nightmares: "No worldly thing or activity

7. Cooper's account is ingenious, but it saddles Plato with a picture that is fundamentally flawed. First, it is unclear why assessing particular entities with respect to a certain property, such as rational order, requires us to have prior cognition of a perfect instance of that property. It seems possible to judge Sweden more just than Swaziland without knowing how close either comes to perfect justice.[13] Second, we are given no account of what it would mean to recognize something as a perfect instance of rational order—absent some form of mystical perception, it looks as though we would already need to have in mind a notion of rational order as a standard against which to compare any putative perfect instance. Third, if Socrates' argument is that to be just entails acting for the good of the world rather than for one's own good—and thereby to be, as Cooper puts it, "a sort of high-minded fanatic"—then he has utterly failed to respond to the challenge that Glaucon presents in Book II, which is to show that justice is in our own interest. As Annas, who largely agrees with Cooper's interpretation, puts it: "Justice was to have been shown to be in *my* interests. But now it requires that I abstract completely from my interests. . . . We seem to be right back at the beginning."[14]

8. Faced with an interpretation that renders a text self-contradictory, we can draw two conclusions. One is that the work in question is simply flawed; the other is that the interpretation is wrong. If our goal is to learn from the work, to allow it to speak to us, then we should presume the latter until we reach the point where it becomes clearly untenable.[15] This is a useful principle for interpreting any

---

can, because of its own properties, because of what *it* is, interest the just man; anything interests him only as a means of coming nearer to the good-itself," where that itself is simply a means for promoting the impersonal good of the cosmos. Ibid., 27.

13. See Sen, *Idea of Justice.*

14. Annas, *Introduction to Plato's "Republic,"* 269. Annas also adds that on Plato's view, "justice demands that we positively stop being human" (269).

15. Annas's interpretation is particularly uncharitable. She attributes three different metaphysics to Plato, each located in a different part of the *Republic*. In Book V Plato holds that (a) one can have knowledge of both forms and particulars; (b) forms are separate from particulars; and (c) they exist only for a restricted range of terms. In Books VI and VII he maintains (b) and (c) but rejects (a): the enlightened and unenlightened "no longer occupy the same cognitive world," and "there is properly speaking no knowledge of particulars" (*Introduction to Plato's "Republic,"* 210–212, 253, 262–263). By the time of Book X he rejects (b) and (c) (227–230). Yet despite claiming

work of philosophy, but there are special reasons for thinking that it applies in the present case. The *Republic* is in all probability composed of chunks that were written separately.[16] But these chunks were put together by a mind that valued coherence above all else. For right at the center of the *Republic* lies the conjunction of goodness and unity. A good person is a unified person, a good city is a unified city—and a good book, one would think, is a unified book. What is more, the text is clearly self-reflexive in this regard: its characters make a conscious effort to keep their conversation coherent, referring back to previous sections and tying things together as best they can, as when Socrates tells Glaucon that the cave image "must be fitted together as a whole with what we said before" (517a–b). There is therefore reason to believe that Plato was aiming at coherence across the dialogue. He may have failed, of course, and given the limits of human capacities he almost certainly did fail. But it would be surprising if Plato's views on metaphysics and epistemology thoroughly undermined his political theory, given that the whole point of the *Republic*'s discussions of metaphysics and epistemology is to justify rule by philosophers.

9. It is important to remember that forms become an explicit topic of conversation in the *Republic* only after Socrates has claimed that philosophers should rule (473c–d). This proposal will sound ludicrous, Socrates acknowledges: it threatens to "drown [him] in a wave of outright ridicule and contempt" (473c). The only way to escape this wave, he suggests, is to offer accounts of philosophy and ruling that make clear why ruling well requires philosophy (474b). Roughly speaking, the idea is that ruling well requires being able to grasp forms, and that philosophy is the activity that aims at doing just that (476a–d; 484b–d). This sets a constraint on any viable interpretation: forms must be the kind of thing knowledge of which could plausibly be thought relevant to ruling. And this seems to speak against the two-worlds view from the start.

---

that there are three different metaphysics in the *Republic*, Annas is content to use only one of them in assessing the merits of Plato's politics, and it happens to be the one that renders Plato's politics most implausible.

16. See Nails, *People of Plato*, 324–326.

§2 Two Kinds of Perception

10. A one-world interpretation faces significant obstacles. There is no doubt that the *Republic* depicts philosophical inquiry as transcending everyday sensory cognition: the unchanging forms that Platonic philosophers try to grasp can be cognized only by the intellect, and they are superior in being, intelligibility, and value to the fluid items and properties cognized by means of the senses. Any interpretation will have to account for that. But the fact that these are undeniable features of Plato's view does not entail that he is positing a suprasensible realm, and therewith a contrast between "the world of sense" and "the world of ideas." There is another possibility, which is that Plato believes there to be one world with two aspects. If that is the case, then philosophical rulers might be concerned with the same concrete objects as their nonphilosophical counterparts—citizens, cities, and so on—only with the advantage of being able to see them under both their sensible and formal aspects. And a close reading of the end of Book V shows that this is a perfectly reasonable interpretation.

11. Book V's account of philosophy comes in three stages. The first characterizes the philosopher as one species of a wider genus that we might call the *philo-X* (474c–475c). The philo-X is one who loves X as such. To love X as such means to pursue it without qualification.[17] Someone who loves food as such, for example, would not pursue particular kinds of food but rather anything that counts as food. X would have a different value in the case of someone who loved (as such) food that is pleasant to her senses. Socrates claims that loves in this sense are insatiable (*aplēstos*; 475c); this might suggest that certain putative loves (such as that for food) might turn out to be parts of other loves (e.g., the love of appetitive satisfaction) that are more properly seen as insatiable. In any case, for present purposes, what is important is that the philo-X structure applies to philosophy. This

---

17. Note that the English word "love" does not necessarily imply the notion of pursuit; Socrates' concept, by contrast, is close to "insatiable desire," which does seem to entail pursuit. At 475b–c he twice speaks of appetite (*epithumia*) instead of love (*philia*).

implies that philosophy is conceived as a pursuit rather than a product—and the formal object of that pursuit, the X in question, is of course wisdom *(sophia)*.[18]

12. The second stage in Book V's account of philosophy consists of Socrates' attempt to equate wisdom *(sophia)*, the formal object of philosophy, with "learning" *(mathēma)*. This implies that the philosopher loves all learning (475b–c). Glaucon objects that there are many lovers of learning who do not seem to be philosophers, among them those who love going to the theater in order to experience novel sights and sounds *(hoi philotheamones* and *hoi philēkooi)*, as well as those who love to learn petty crafts *(hoi philotechnoi)* (475d–e). Socrates responds by specifying that what philosophers want is not just learning in this loose sense but real learning—they are "lovers of seeing the truth" *(tous tēs alētheias philotheamonas)*.[19] It is only when Glaucon asks what this means—what it is to see the truth, and in what sense those who love seeing, hearing, and making are not lovers of the truth—that Socrates responds by introducing the famous distinction between forms and sensibles:[20]

> The same argument applies . . . to just and unjust, good and bad, and all the forms: each of them is itself one thing, but because wherever they appear it is by virtue of partnership with actions and bodies, and with one another, each of them appears to be many things. (476a)[21]

---

18. The reason for speaking of the objects of desire as formal is that they might not always be coextensive with concrete particulars or objects in the ordinary sense. To use Socrates' own example, the formal object of a lover's desire, that which she is after as such, might conceivably be "snub-nosedness" rather than this particular snub-nosed person. The formal dimension of desire is what opens the possibility of viewing love as an ascent from the particular to the universal, as in Diotima's speech in the *Symposium*.

19. What philosophers love might therefore be described as "the sight of truth" *(hē theōria tēs alētheias)*.

20. The term "sensibles" is used in order to reflect the fact that the Greek does not determine whether what we are talking about are sensible types or sensible tokens—sensible qualities such as snub-nosedness or sensible particulars such as Helen. For an argument in favor of the "types" view, see Gosling, "Republic Book V," especially 116–124.

21. Amending Reeve's translation, which has "because they appear all over the place in partnership with actions and bodies." I prefer "wherever" to "everywhere" or

In the case of beauty, for instance, the distinction is between the form of beauty itself, on the one hand, and the many beautiful properties and items, on the other (476b). Socrates' claim is that to love genuine learning, as philosophers do, is to have an insatiable desire to grasp forms. The underlying thought appears to be as follows: sensible properties and items are what they are only by virtue of "participating" or "sharing" in forms; this relationship means that sensibles are only "likenesses" of forms; and genuine knowledge requires being able to discern this relationship, observing both the form and that which participates in it and not confusing the two (476c–d). Nonphilosophers fail to distinguish between forms and the sensible properties and items in which they are manifest, and this leaves them stuck in the world of appearance, in which "a likeness *[to homoion]* is not a likeness, but rather the thing that it is like" (476c). Philosophers, by contrast, are able to discern the structure of reality and therefore to grasp each thing both as what it is in itself and in its relationships to other things. A philosopher can therefore achieve knowledge (*gnōsis*), whereas the most a nonphilosopher can achieve is belief (*doxa*) (476d).

13. Putting the first and second stages together, we arrive at the thought that philosophy is an activity whose formal object is wisdom (*sophia*), where that requires knowledge in the sense of a capacity to discern the structure of reality and therefore to grasp each thing both as what it is and in its relationships, and where that in turn requires recognizing a distinction between forms and the sensibles that participate in them. The third stage sees Socrates defending this claim, and it is here that readers tend to detect the two-worlds view. The goal is to argue the lovers of seeing, hearing, and making—represented by Glaucon in a curious dialogue-within-the-dialogue—into accepting that their ways of learning, which fail to invoke forms, cannot result in stable accounts of things and their relationships to one another. It follows that the formal object of their activity is not knowledge but belief, and hence that they are not philosophers but "philodoxers."

"all over the place" for *pantachou* because it more clearly brings out the modal element of the philosophical content.

14. From an interpretive point of view this passage is extremely difficult, but if we depart from the order of presentation we can reconstruct the argument as the product of five key claims. The first is that knowledge (*epistēmē*) and belief are powers or capacities (*dunameis*) along the lines of sight and hearing (477b–c). The second is that powers are differentiated by their formal objects and the functions (*erga*) they perform with respect to those formal objects: "Those assigned to deal with the same things and do the same, I call the same; those that deal with different things and do different things, I call different" (477d).[22] Sight, for example, has the visible as its formal object, and its function is to disclose the visible, whereas hearing has the audible as its formal object, and its aim is to disclose the audible. So if knowledge and belief are different powers, they must have different formal objects and different functions. The third claim involves specifying how knowledge and belief differ in their formal objects and functions. The formal object of knowledge is "what is" (*to on*), that which "remains always the same in all respects"; and the function of knowledge is to disclose "how what is is" (*hōs esti ton on*; 477b, 478a, 479a, 479e). The formal object of belief, by contrast, is somehow not fully what it is; it suffers what scholars have termed "the compresence of opposites," being both F and not-F, whether at different times or in different respects (478e–479b).[23] The function of

---

22. This is sloppy on Socrates' part since he fails to recognize the possibility that two powers might have the same formal objects but perform different work with respect to them or perform the same work with respect to different formal objects.

23. The Greek concept of being elides four uses that one might wish to keep separate: the existential, as in "F exists"; the predicative, as in "F is blue"; the veridical, as in "F is true"; and the "is" of identity. See Lesley Brown, "Verb 'to Be' in Greek Philosophy," 212–236; and Kahn, "Greek Verb 'to Be' and the Concept of Being," 245–265. Scholars have debated which of the first three senses is operative when Socrates tells us that knowledge is "set over what is" while ignorance is "set over what is not" and opinion is set over what is and is not (477a; 478c–e). The existential reading has been promoted by Cross and Woozley, *Plato's "Republic,"* and simply assumed by Stanley Rosen, *Plato's "Republic"*; the predicative by Annas, *Introduction to Plato's "Republic,"* and Gregory Vlastos, "Degrees of Reality in Plato"; the veridical by Fine, "Knowledge and Belief in *Republic* V" and "Knowledge and Belief in *Republic* V–VII," supported to some degree by Gosling, "*Doxa* and *Dunamis* in Plato's *Republic*." Fine's interpretation has come under attack from Gonzales, "Propositions or Objects?," and Eck, "Fine's Plato." A helpful overview of the whole debate is Lee's survey article, "Interpreting Plato's *Republic*."

belief is to disclose this inherently unstable formal object.[24] The fourth claim is that the products of cognitive capacities will be just as stable as their objects, so that knowledge (which cognizes that which remains always the same in all respects) will result in stable cognition, whereas belief (which cognizes that which suffers the compresence of opposites) will result in usages *(nomima)* that are inherently unstable, like a boat tossed about on the waves (479d).[25] The fifth claim is that what remain the same in all respects are forms, while what are both F and not-F are sensibles. Putting these five claims together results in the claim that knowledge is the capacity that aims at disclosing forms and that results in stable cognition, while belief is the capacity that aims at disclosing sensibles and that results in the unstable cognition of conventional views.

15. This argument is liable to perplex English-speaking readers unused to thinking of knowledge as a capacity along the lines of sight or hearing. J. C. B. Gosling explains the difference between the Greek concept and our own by pointing to the different ways we would respond if asked what kinds of things we know.[26] Whereas English speakers would typically cite items of knowledge like the Pythagorean theorem or the location of our car, Gosling suggests that in Greek the things known, the *epistēmai*, are not propositions or theorems but whole branches of knowledge, such as medicine. Moreover, whereas in English someone might be called "knowledgeable" in virtue of knowing many facts, the Greek adjective *epistēmōn* connotes competence in performance, a little like our word "skillful"—a soccer trivia champion is "knowledgeable"; a soccer manager is *epistēmōn*.[27]

---

24. Unlike noncognizing *(agnōsia)*, belief does have a formal object (477a, 478c). I prefer the term "noncognizing" to Reeve's "ignorance" because in ordinary English usage ignorance does have a formal object even if it fails to disclose it.

25. Presumably this is what Socrates means when he says earlier that knowledge is infallible, while belief is fallible (477b, e).

26. See Gosling, *Plato*, 60.

27. Gosling grants that Plato tends to reserve *epistēmē* (as opposed to *technē*) for those skills with a strong theoretical element, usually involving an account or explanation, but he nevertheless maintains that the connotations of ordinary usage—according to which building is more naturally said to be an *epistēmē* than is archaeology—still persist in Plato's usage.

16. Even when we have the right concept in view, however, confusion remains. For why think that knowledge and belief are different capacities with different formal objects? It seems more natural to consider them as the same capacity exercised with respect to the same formal objects, only with different degrees of success. Plato does seem to hold something of this scalar conception: knowledge and belief are clearly placed in a hierarchy in which the former discloses more of reality than the latter. But the idea seems to be that this is true in virtue of their having different formal objects. It is as if sight were simply a better way of grasping the world than hearing. This may be true; certainly sight seems a better way of grasping the world, all things considered, than smell. But clearly there are some aspects of the world that are disclosed to smell but not to sight. Is the same true of belief as against knowledge? The logic of Socrates' argument suggests the answer is yes. Knowledge discloses that which is what it is always and in every respect; belief discloses that which is, at different times and in different respects, both F and not-F. Full perception of the world therefore requires both knowledge and belief. If this is right, then the problem with nonphilosophers is not that they are interested in seeing and hearing and making, but that they are not also interested in forms. To put it in the terms used in what I called the first stage, although they are lovers of certain kinds of learning, they cannot be called lovers of learning as such: "If someone is choosy about what he learns, we won't say he is a lover of learning or a philosopher" (475b–c).[28]

---

28. Gosling also emphasizes the fact that the sight lovers are presented as lovers of (some kind of) learning. See "Republic Book V," 121: "[The sight lovers] are people with a love of learning, but with no taste for dialectical discussion; their learning is culled, for instance, from attendance at festivals in the case of *philêkooi;* but they do not attend merely to fill in time, like the Saturday cinema queues; they would be more likely to be found at the Cannes Festival, studying the art: they are *hoi tôn technudriôn philosophoi.* When Socrates describes them at 476A10 he calls them *philotechnoi kai praktikoi:* they think in terms of skill, art, technique, of finding out how things are done; but they find out, for instance, about *to kalon* just by going to theatres and festivals: these are the things they are enthusiastic about, and so they become authorities in criticism, people who could set up to teach the principles of composition and so forth. They observe in practice the features that make a play a success, and they observe that there is a great variety of such features which account for the successes of different plays and in various ways produce a good effect."

17. If this reading is correct then the two-worlds interpretation is fatally flawed. Wisdom does not demand that we turn away from this world. Rather, it demands that we perceive this world in all its aspects. It is true that the capacity for knowledge has forms as its formal object, and that sensibles can only be the formal object of belief. But formal objects are not necessarily real particulars. Just as the very same concrete object—a human, say—can be both seen and heard, so it can also be disclosed by both knowledge and belief. Some of its properties are available only to sensory perception, while others are available only to intellectual perception. But just as there is no need to posit the existence of a "visual world" as against the "auditory world," so there is no need to posit the "world of ideas" as against "the world of sense."[29]

18. We can now zoom back out. Socrates' argument against the lovers of seeing, hearing, and making is part of his account of why philosophers should rule. Socrates claims that philosophers are able to perceive an aspect of the world that remains unavailable to nonphilosophers, namely the formal aspect, and this tallies with his Book VII description of the philosopher who returns to the political realm as able to "see infinitely better than the people [in the cave] and know *[gignōskō]* precisely what each image is, and also what it is an image of" (520c). This suggests that his epistemological opponents are also his political opponents, and hence that rival accounts of learning are also rival accounts of what would qualify someone to rule.[30]

19. The fact that the sight lovers are rivals for rule might be obscured by the fact that Plato adds a psychological layer to his depiction of those opponents, caricaturing them as trapped in a stupor born of frenzied curiosity: "Just as if their ears were under contract

---

29. For very specific purposes we might wish to imagine a world limited to one particular aspect, as when P. F. Strawson imagines a being with only auditory experience in order to test an argument regarding the relationship between objective experience and spatiotemporal bodies. See Strawson, *Individuals*, 59–86.

30. This is not to deny that Plato's account of knowledge will ultimately exceed its political context. The point is rather that it must first prove itself in that context, and that this requirement should guide our interpretation. See also Gosling, "Republic Book V," 120: "[It is important] to remember that [the sight lovers] are possible candidates that someone might put forward as people who would know what they were about, as those whom Socrates might mean as possible rulers."

to listen to every chorus, they run around to all the Dionysian festivals, whether in cities or in villages, and never miss one," while being the kind of people who "would never willingly attend a serious discussion or spend their time that way" (475d).[31] Against the background of the rest of the *Republic*, we can say that curiosity, the craving for novelty, is diagnosed as the appetitive metabolism of knowledge and hence as bound up with the democratic way of life.[32] Yet Socrates does not launch into a psychological or political critique of his opponents, or at least not until Book VIII. Instead he gives an argument against them. This is peculiar, since if Plato's psychological diagnosis is correct, argument may be an ineffective means of persuasion in such cases. We might conclude that the intended audience of this passage are those whose souls are sufficiently well ordered for them to be able to respond adequately to argument—that is, philosophers.[33] The dialectician must be able to "grasp an account of the being of each thing (534b–c)—including, presumably, the nature of knowledge and the nature of ruling and the relationship between the

---

31. We might say that the philosophical critique of curiosity, so prominent in Augustine, Thoreau, and Heidegger, begins with Plato. Augustine follows Plato in connecting curiosity—"the appetite for knowing"—with the faculty of sight in particular; see *Confessions* X.xxxv. Thoreau says that "to a philosopher all *news*, as it is called, is gossip, and they who edit and read it are old women over their tea"; see *Walden*, chap. 2, quote on p. 64. Heidegger draws a similar moral: "Curiosity . . . does not make present the present-at-hand in order to tarry alongside it and *understand* it; it seeks to see *only* in order to see and to have seen." See *Being and Time*, 397/346–347. He thinks that curiosity has three essential characteristics: the refusal to tarry amid one's surroundings, distraction by new possibilities, and as a result being both everywhere and nowhere. See *Being and Time*, 214–217/170–173.

32. Cf. 561b–e. Stanley Rosen points out that the whole context of the *Republic* is the festival of Bendis, which is being celebrated for the first time, and another novelty, the torch race on horseback. See Rosen, *Plato's "Republic,"* 13.

33. My interpretive strategy here allows me to sidestep a debate between those like J. C. B. Gosling and Gail Fine, who interpret 476d–e and 478e–479b as laying down a "principle of noncontroversiality" and hence sound argument, and Allan Silverman, who argues that the passage should be taken as showing that the sight lovers are too psychologically flawed to benefit from such sound argument: "The language is that of rhetorical persuasion, not logical deduction. Nowhere are there indications that certain premises are precluded because they beg questions or because they would not meet with acceptance on the part of the philodoxers. They are sick, after all, and their deliverances may not be regarded as right headed to begin with." My account allows me to come down on the side of Gosling and Fine without losing hold of Silverman's insight. See Fine, "Knowledge and Belief in *Republic* V," 68, and "Knowledge and Belief in *Republic* V–VII," 87; Gosling, "Republic Book V," 120–124; and Silverman, *Dialectic of Essence*, 67.

two—and to defend it against rivals. The debate that Socrates stages at the end of Book V therefore represents a model of the dialectical discussion that philosopher-rulers might themselves undertake in justifying the social order of Kallipolis. As we will see in Chapters 2 and 3, this recursive strategy, whereby Socrates models a pattern of reasoning for future rulers, comes up time and again in the *Republic*.

20. That said, the overall picture remains obscure. What does it really mean to perceive particulars in light of forms? And why should that be thought important for ruling? The underlying problem is that the Book V passage tells us very little about what forms actually are. To fill in the picture we must look elsewhere in the *Republic*—to the remarks on *sophia* in Book IV; to the celebrated images of the sun, the line, and the cave in Books VI and VII; to the account of dialectic in Book VII; to the discussion of forms in Book X; and to the many scattered passages that ask what makes something what it is as opposed to some other thing. All these passages must be read closely as part of this inquiry, but in the interests of efficiency, I will begin by laying down an interpretive hypothesis.

§3 The Hypothesis

21. In Book II of his *Physics*, Aristotle famously distinguishes four types of *aition* (explanatory factor) that can be adduced in order to explain why something is the way it is or changes the way it does: material, formal, efficient, and final. The material cause is "that out of which a thing comes to be and which persists . . . e.g. the bronze of the statue." The formal cause is the organization of that material into a shape or structure, "the form or archetype," reference to which specifies the object's essence; a simple example might be the shape of the statue. The efficient cause is "the primary source of the change or rest"; here an example would be the sculptor exercising her art. And the final cause is "that for the sake of which a thing is done," some good or apparent good, such as the glorification of an athlete (194b24–195a26).[34] These are the only causes

---

34. Aristotle, *Physics*, 315–447. For a helpful overview, see Shields, *Aristotle*, chap. 2. For a general account of the ancient notion of causality, see Michael Frede, "Original Notion of Cause."

there are, and any adequate explanation of change or rest will need to cite all four (although in some cases the last three turn out to be the same).[35]

22. In cataloging the four causes, Aristotle was building on what was already implicit in his teacher's work.[36] Focusing just on the *Republic*, toward the end of Book I we are told that horses, eyes, ears, daggers, carving knives, pruning knives, and souls all have functions (*erga*), characteristic activities that only they can perform or that they can perform best (352d–354a). The notion of virtue or excellence (*aretē*) falls out naturally from this teleological conception, since "each thing to which a particular function is assigned also [has] a virtue," namely that in virtue of which it can be said to perform its function well (353b–c). In Book X Socrates expands on this picture, telling us that "the excellence, beauty, and correctness of each manufactured item, living creature, and action [are] related to nothing but the use [*chreia*] for which each is made or naturally adapted"

---

35. See Aristotle, *Physics* 198a–b.

36. A careful reader of Plato will find there are many places in his work that contain thoughts often taken to be distinctively Aristotelian. To take just a few examples from the *Republic* (the *Statesman* provides yet more): in Book I we learn that humans love best what they have produced themselves (330c; cf. *Nicomachean Ethics* IX.7); in Books III and IV that virtue is inculcated through patterns of action (395c–397b; 443–444a; cf. *Nicomachean Ethics* II); in Book IV that there is one form for virtue and an unlimited number for vice (445c; cf. *Nicomachean Ethics* II.6); in Books IV and VII that learning involves creating second potentialities (424a; 518b–519b; cf. *Nicomachean Ethics* II); in Book VI that there is a set of intellectual virtues specifiable independently of the ethical virtues (485a–487a; cf. *Nicomachean Ethics* VI); and in Book IX that the natural ground for slavery is the slave's inability to rule himself (590c–d; cf. *Politics* I). In the chapters that follow I will consider further points of comparison, from the idea that the city comes into existence for the sake of mere life but goes on to exist for the sake of the good life to the idea that the essence of a city is its constitution and finally the idea that political craftsmen aim at creating virtuous souls. In most of these cases Aristotle states the relevant idea with a degree of clarity and systematicity that can help us modern readers better understand what Plato is saying, even if we must always to be alive to the important differences between the two authors. Compare Heidegger's suggestion in his lecture course *Plato's "Sophist,"* 8, that we approach Plato through Aristotle: "Previously it was usual to interpret the Platonic philosophy by proceeding from Socrates and the Presocratics to Plato. We wish to strike out in the opposite direction, from Aristotle back to Plato. This way is not unprecedented. It follows the old principle of hermeneutics, namely that interpretation should proceed from the clear into the obscure. . . . That implies no value judgment on Plato. What Aristotle said is what Plato placed at his disposal, only it is said more radically and developed more systematically. Aristotle should thus prepare us for Plato, point us in the direction of [his] characteristic questioning."

(601d).[37] In fact, the teleological picture extends not only to manufactured items, living creatures, and actions but also beyond. In Book
I, for instance, the soul is said to have a function, namely leading a
life (353d), while in Book II the city is said to have a function, namely
satisfying those of our needs that we cannot satisfy by ourselves
(369b).[38] The notion of excellence as that in virtue of which something can perform its function in turn suggests something like Aristotle's four causes. A knife can perform its function, allowing people
to cut, only if it has the right kind of material and the right form: it
should not bend much, for instance, and it must be sharp at one end
but not at the other. There ought to be a place for efficient causality
as well, since the correct material will be correctly enformed only if
it has been shaped by a craftsman who possesses the art of knife-
making, "look[ing] towards the appropriate form [idea]" (596b) while
shaping wood and metal.[39]

23. In that last quotation we came across the word idea, "form" in
the grand sense of "Plato's theory of forms." Given the teleological
context—the craftsman shaping material for a given end by looking
toward the form—it would seem reasonable to conclude that in this
example "form" means nothing more than "best possible formal
cause," the optimal principle for organizing material toward a given
end. The work of the craftsman is to give form to her object, and to
do that optimally she will need to consider, or keep in mind, the best
possible form it can have (perhaps as manifest in a paradigm or ideal
case). Much more needs to be said about why forms in the sense of

---

37. An adaptation of the Grube and Reeve translation.

38. Arguably souls count as "living creatures" and cities as "artefacts" in the
extended sense of those terms, but the words used in this passage (zōia and skeuē)
certainly connote the narrow sense.

39. Although the efficient cause will be relevant in explanations of change, it will
not be necessary to invoke it with respect to ontology. This, I think, is why Plato does
not seem particularly interested in efficient causality, a fact that in turn allows
Aristotle to claim that he lacked the concept altogether. It seems to me that god and
the craftsman in Book X, as well as the demiurge in the Timaeus, are clear instances of
efficient causes within a four-cause schema, but I see no need to argue for that position
here. For more on this question, see Fine, "Forms as Causes."

I should note that I will be using the word "craftsman" in a gender-neutral sense,
such that women can be craftsmen no less than men; this seems to be the best way of
avoiding the ugliness of "craftsperson" and "craftspersons."

best possible formal causes cannot be cognized by the senses, why they should be conceived as unchanging, and how they could make sensibles what they are. But for now the point is that if we had only Books I and X to draw from, we would likely conclude that the *Republic*'s concept of "form" ought to be understood as part of a theory of material, formal, and final causes—as part, that is, of a teleological theory of being.

24. It is possible that these proto-Aristotelian passages represent the exception rather than the rule—after all, there is evidence to suggest that Books I and X were constructed separately from the rest of the *Republic*.[40] To my mind, however, this objection is unpromising. For one thing, a teleological framework is clearly assumed in Book V, where powers (*dunameis*) are said to be naturally differentiated by their characteristic activities (477b–478b);[41] in Book VI, where Socrates declares that in the absence of philosopher-kings "no city, constitution, or individual man will ever become perfect [*teleos*]" (499b); and in many other places, as we shall see. But in any case, the fact that Plato saw fit to include Books I and X in his final version of the *Republic* ought to count for something. Gosling makes this point with characteristically dry wit:

> Especially with regard to Book I, if we suppose that Plato picked it off his shelf as a good first course for the *Republic*, we have further to suppose that he did not read it through. For as it stands it ends with a clear line on how to determine what excellence is, which is then ignored. It is at least as easy to suppose that it was chosen just because it clearly pointed how to interpret the later discussion of the soul.[42]

---

40. For a historical account of the construction of the *Republic*, see Nails, *People of Plato*.

41. Pace Gosling, who writes that "in the main body of the work [i.e., Books II–IX] there is no reference to *ergon*." Admittedly the key word at 477d is *apergasdomai* (to accomplish) rather than *ergon*, but the latter is clearly the former's root. See Gosling, *Plato*, 35.

42. Gosling, *Plato*, 35–36.

The fact that Plato chose to include Books I and X is prima facie evidence that he thought their doctrines cohered with those of the middle books.[43] So the real question, as Gosling points out, is whether Books II–IX are illuminated by reading them in light of Books I and X. If the answer is yes—as I will try to show it is—then we will have to conclude with Gosling that "even if Plato does not put out a bulletin to tell us that he is now doing what we ought to have been able to expect him to be doing, he is nevertheless doing it. Perhaps he expected his reader to notice."[44]

§4 Goodness as the Final Cause of Forms

25. The sun image at the end of Book VI would seem to confirm the teleological hypothesis (507b–509c). There is much to be said about the analogy—how to interpret it, how its various parts fit together—but what is clear is that, as with all analogies, the strategy depends on an assumed isomorphism between two domains.[45] Socrates uses the visible, which is familiar to us, to illuminate the invisible, which is not. The overarching proposal is that goodness (to agathon) bears the same relation to intellection (noēsis) and intel-

---

43. In my view, a close reading of Book I either yields or supports many of the *Republic*'s major theses, and in Chapter 4 I hope to show that the myth of Er, far from being an afterthought, encapsulates Plato's political doctrine rather neatly. Danielle Allen also makes an argument to this effect, although on different grounds. For her, what unifies the *Republic* from start to finish is Plato's attempt to counter the power of poets: "Book 10 does not, in short, change the subject but serves as the crowning conclusion of an argument about the ethical and political functions of abstraction. Its goal is to transfer authority from poets to 'constitution-painters.'" Allen, *Why Plato Wrote*, 36. One might also consider Myles Burnyeat's suggestions regarding the way the figure of the couch, so prominent in Book X, ramifies throughout the *Republic*. See Burnyeat, "Culture and Society in Plato's *Republic*," 215–255, as well as Chapter 3 of the present work.

44. Gosling, *Plato*, 37.

45. There is also a causal relation between the two domains, since the sun itself is caused by goodness, but I see no reason to assume that the isomorphism is a result of the causal relation, since the good begets many things that do not share its structure. In this respect it might be different from the city-soul analogy, which Jonathan Lear has argued is a product of the causal relationships between city and soul. See Lear, "Inside and Outside the *Republic*"; and the book-length counterargument by Ferrari, *City and Soul in Plato's "Republic."*

ligible things (*noumena*) as the sun does to sight and visible things.[46] This suggests that philosophical knowledge will be figured once again as one kind of perception alongside others.

26. Visible things are said to be cognized through the power of sight, but only in the presence of a third element that "marries" them, namely light; light actualizes the potential of the seer to see and the visible to be seen. The source of light is the sun, and when the eye's powers are actualized, it can see the cause of its own actualization. Indeed, the eye can be said to be the most "sunlike" (*hēlioeidēs*) of sensory organs insofar as it receives its power from the sun "like an influx from an overflowing treasury" (508b)—that is, while its functions do not map onto the sun's, it is the organ most closely bound up with the sun.[47] The function of the sun is not only to allow things to be seen but also to allow them to exist: it "provides for their genesis, growth and nourishment," although it is not itself equivalent to genesis (509b).[48] Taken together, these features are supposed to make the sun both the analogue and the offspring of goodness.

27. The process of understanding, meanwhile, is also said to have three necessary moments. There are intelligible things, things with the capacity to be understood; then there are intelligences, things with the capacity to understand; and finally there is goodness, which yokes the first two together, actualizing their potential to understand and be understood.[49] When its powers are fully actualized, intellection can see that goodness is the cause of that actualization, and that it (intellection) receives its power from overflowing goodness and is

---

46. I translate *to agathon* as "goodness" because "the good" sounds like an object rather than a property.

47. Plato may also be presuming his theory of perception, as outlined in the *Theaetetus* (154a–156e) and the *Timaeus* (45b), according to which the eye is not merely a passive organ but actively projects something (fire) in order to facilitate perception. Contemporary historians of science would term this an "extramission" theory.

48. I depart from Grube and Reeve in preferring "genesis" to "coming to be" here.

49. Fine notes that Plato does not equate *noumena* with forms here, but rather sticks to a formal term: just as one dies a death, so one intellects an intelligible object. This becomes relevant in the context of the question whether Plato believes knowledge of sensibles is possible, but I do not have space to consider Fine's argument to that effect in detail—see Fine, "Knowledge and Belief in *Republic* V–VII," 85–116. Against Fine, however, it must be noted that at 507b Socrates has clearly aligned the intelligible realm with forms.

therefore the most goodlike *(agathoeidēs)* faculty of all. Finally, it turns out that goodness not only allows intelligible things to be intellected but also actually causes their existence and essence *(ousia)* although it "is not essence, but superior to it in rank and power" (507c–509b).[50]

28. The analogy can be hard to keep track of, but the conclusion seems to be that goodness causes the existence and essence of forms, as well as their intelligibility, while existing on a higher ontological plane to them. The difficulty comes in understanding what this means. To do that, we need to answer the following questions: How is goodness supposed to actualize the potential of intelligence to understand and forms to be understood? In what way does goodness cause the existence and essence of forms? And in what sense is goodness superior to essence?

29. The first question can be restated more straightforwardly: how does goodness allow forms to be understood? Here it helps to connect the sun image with the notions of *epistēmē* and *sophia*. In the last section I drew on Gosling's claim that *epistēmē* concerns whole branches of knowledge rather than discrete items, and that to have it is to be skilled in performance. Gosling goes on to argue that the defining characteristic of someone who is *epistēmōn* is the ability to distinguish between good and bad instances of a kind: "An *epistēmē* is a theory-supported practical capacity employing centrally some notion or notions of good and bad states of affairs."[51] This tallies with Book IV's account of *sophia* as "the knowledge *[epistēmē]* of what is advantageous—both for each part and for the whole" (442c), and of the city as wise *(sophos)* in virtue of *epistēmē* that "does not deliberate about some particular thing in the city, but about the city as a whole, and about how its internal relations and its relations with other cities

---

50. Against Grube and Reeve, I prefer to translate *ousia* as "essence" rather than "being"; the word is clearly ambiguous among a number of different meanings, but I believe my disambiguation renders Plato's point clearer than others.

51. Gosling, *Plato*, 60; see also 115. Compare the following passage from Plato's *Statesman:* "Every sort of expert knowledge *[epistēmē]* everywhere throws away the bad so far as it can, and takes what is suitable and good, bringing all of this—both like and unlike—together into one, and so producing some single kind of thing with a single capacity" (308c; translation by Christopher Rowe).

will be the best possible" (428b–d).[52] Since *epistēmē* also involves being "able to grasp an account of the being *[ousia]* of each thing" (534b–c), it seems reasonable to conclude that to know something's being, or essence, is to know the ways in which a thing of its kind can be good or bad. If we assume that the being of things is given by their form, then to know something's form is to know the ways in which it can be good or bad. And to know that, we have to work out what the thing in question is aiming at.[53]

30. One way of understanding the claim that goodness allows objects to be known is therefore this: to know the form of an object is to know what it is best for it to be; to know this requires knowing its final cause, or good; hence the fact that there are final causes is what allows objects to be known; and the fact of final causality just is the fact of goodness.

31. We can unpack that last statement by thinking about the relationship between forms and final causes. To work out how it is best for a given object to be, we need to consider the role it plays as part of a wider functional context made up of various other objects. This means that forms hang together in a crucial respect: to work out the form of any one object, we also need to work out the forms of other objects in the same functional context. Nor does the holistic reasoning stop there, for the functional context itself will be a part of a wider whole, such that *its* optimal condition can be assessed only in the light of the optimal form of its neighbors. This chain will finish only when we arrive at the ultimate functional context, namely the cosmos, which is the systematic interconnected whole of forms and final causes. But if the cosmos is the ultimate functional context, and things are good in virtue of their relationship to final causes, as Book X suggests (601d), then in a certain sense the cosmos *just is* goodness. Goodness is nothing more than the systematic interconnectedness of goods. This explains why goodness is "beyond essence": the essence

---

52. See also 506a, where Socrates says that just and fine things need a guardian who knows why they are good.

53. My account obviously runs counter to that of Annas, who claims that "right at the start of the discussion Plato parts company with someone who believes that for something to be good is always for it to be good *for X,* or *from Y's point of view,* or *a good Z*" (Annas, *Introduction to Plato's "Republic,"* 245).

of every particular good is its role in the system of goods; although it is constituted by roles, the system itself has no role.[54]

32. We can make this more concrete by thinking about the relationship between different *epistēmai*. Gosling proposes that the very existence of an *epistēmē* of F entails the assumption that it is good for good Fs to exist; if this assumption turns out to be false, the relevant theory-supported practical capacity will be revealed as a pseudo-*epistēmē*.[55] There will be no *epistēmē* for making muscles as big as they can possibly be, for example, unless we can show that bodybuilding is healthy for the whole body. In other words, every candidate *epistēmē* necessarily stands in need of vindication, and to vindicate it will be to show that its success would be good for the whole of which its object is a part. But if every local *epistēmē* stands in need of a more global *epistēmē* to certify it, we are left with a chain that ends only once we reach the ultimate whole, the cosmos itself.

> In the end one would reach the stage where the whole universe was exhibited as an interconnected whole, the requirements of interconnection determining what constitutes the excellence of the parts. The fact that the system is of this particular interconnected sort is what makes it possible to speak correctly of Xs as good and bad, and thus makes *epistēmai* possible.[56]

If this is right, then *epistēmai* are radically interconnected, so that each *epistēmē* concerns not only its own subject matter but also, in its own way, the nature of the cosmos. "The *epistēmai* . . . can now be looked upon as parts of the *epistēmē* of the whole, just as the *epistēmē*

---

54. See Gosling, *Plato*, 67–68. Whether the fact that the system itself has no role makes it illegitimate to speak of goodness as itself being good is unclear to me. Perhaps we should say that insofar as goodness itself is good, it is not good in the way in which everything else is good. But then perhaps we should say that the question whether the system as a whole is good is "dialectical" in Kant's pejorative sense: it takes us beyond the bounds of sense. Whereof we cannot speak, thereof we should be silent. That being said, or unsaid, in §7 I will argue that Plato thinks we can ascribe justice and beauty to the system.

55. Another conclusion that might appear to fall out from this line of thought is that only things that have *telē* (objectives) can be known.

56. Gosling, *Plato*, 64.

of muscles is a part of the *epistēmē* of the body."[57] And if the cosmos is, as I have suggested, equivalent to goodness, then to disclose one small corner of the cosmos in light of its functional role just is to disclose goodness.

33. On the picture I have been developing, there is a sense in which the mystical picture of Plato has it right: we cannot grasp goodness directly. But this is not to say that we cannot grasp it at all, just that to grasp it is always to grasp something else, namely particular chains of formal and final causes. At the same time, however, we will be able to grasp those chains only if we grasp them as part of the overarching functional context of goodness itself. As Socrates says on a couple of occasions, unless we grasp goodness itself, we will never grasp individual goods, since things are good only in virtue of their relationship to goodness (505a–b; 534c). What we are faced with is therefore a two-way process of reasoning, from parts to whole and whole to parts.[58] In the absence of a complete picture of the cosmos, the proposition that goodness is the final cause of forms can be only a hunch or an intuition (cf. 506a). But once we have worked all the way up from parts to whole, we will be able to work back down from the whole to the parts. As Socrates says regarding the line analogy, dialectical discussion treats forms as

> genuine hypotheses (that is, stepping stones and links in a chain), in order to arrive at what is unhypothetical and the first principle of everything. Having grasped this principle, it reverses itself and, keeping hold of what follows from it, comes down to a conclusion, making no use of anything visible at all, but only of forms themselves, moving on through forms to forms, and ending in forms. (511b–c)

34. I will develop this picture in §6, but first let us pause to note that we are now in a position to provide initial answers to the three

---

57. See ibid. The following remark is also instructive: "A person with knowledge of the good would not thereby be good at medicine, strategy and the rest, but he would know that these were or were not pseudo-*epistēmai*."

58. On the importance of reasoning about parts and wholes in Plato's later work, see Harte, *Plato on Parts and Wholes*.

questions with which we began: How does goodness actualize the potential of intelligence to understand and intelligible objects to be understood? In what way does goodness cause the existence and essence of intelligible things? And in what sense is goodness superior to essence? The answer to the first question is that goodness is the final cause of knowledge itself—goodness is "what every soul pursues," and this generates a stable and enduring desire for knowledge as opposed to mere belief (505d–e).[59] The answer to the second question is that goodness causes the existence and essence of intelligible things by serving as their final cause. And the answer to the third question is that as nothing more than the harmonic structure of interlocking goods, goodness has no essential role and can therefore be said to be "beyond essence."

§5 Goodness as the Formal Cause of Forms

35. Although the sun analogy can plausibly be read as suggesting that goodness is the final cause of forms, this is not the end of the story, for it can also be read as suggesting that goodness is the *formal* cause of the existence and essence of forms, as Gerasimos Santas argues. These readings are not mutually exclusive, however; understood correctly, they complement and strengthen one another.

36. Santas bases his interpretation on a helpful distinction between the "ideal" and "proper" attributes of forms. The ideal attributes are those that forms have just qua forms; the proper attributes are those they have qua the particular forms they are. Forms have two sets of ideal attributes, Santas argues: (1) they do not change, they always exist, and they exist separately; and (2) they do not suffer the "compresence of opposites," and their properties are nonrelational. Since forms have these ideal attributes only in virtue of

---

59. The idea that goodness is the final cause of knowledge may be trivially true in the sense that in Plato's account goodness is the final cause of all human activity—whatever else we aim at, we are always aiming at goodness (505d–e). But it does suggest that when scholars such as Annas charge Plato with failing to distinguish between theoretical and practical reason, they ought to consider the possibility that theoretical reason is always already a type of practical reason. (See Annas, *Introduction to Plato's "Republic,"* 265–266.) In any case, one should not stress the nondistinction too strongly: Plato implicitly distinguishes between intellectual and ethical virtue in Book VI.

participating in goodness, we can say that "the ideal attributes of all the Forms other than the Form of the Good are proper attributes of the Form of the Good."[60] So on Santas's view, what makes a form count as a form is its possession of the properties that characterize goodness. Goodness is therefore the formal cause of forms.

37. The trouble with this view is that it remains unclear what (1) and (2) have to do with goodness.[61] Why should we think that the essence of goodness consists in never changing, always existing, existing separately from particular things, and being always what it is? What makes these attributes good? Santas speculates that Plato is generalizing from the realms of crafts and ethics, where reliability and durability are always good. Yet it is surely impossible to specify what it is to be a good hammer without considering what hammers are for, that is, without considering final causality. Only when we consider what hammers are for can we work out what an excellent hammer would be, since an excellent hammer is one that performs its characteristic activity well. But the way in which a hammer performs its characteristic activity will obviously depend on its proper attributes (like the length of its handle) just as much as its ideal ones (like being durable). So although Santas claims that "the more a thing of a given kind resembles the *ideal* attributes of the Form of that kind, the better it performs the function proper to things of that kind," it is also true that something will perform its function better to the degree that it manifests the proper attributes of its form, that is, those distinctive of the kind of thing that it is.[62] Finally, how do we know that good hammering is itself good, if not by reference to the teleological context of purposes and aspirations within which it finds a

---

60. Santas, "Form of the Good in Plato's *Republic*," 255. Santas thinks that these two sets of properties are what make forms cognitively reliable and hence suitable for grounding knowledge, but this does not answer the question regarding goodness.

61. David Sedley points out that by parity of reasoning the forms of unity and eternality should also be the cause of the knowability of forms. See Sedley, "Philosophy, the Forms, and the Art of Ruling," 268. A further problem is that Santas believes that forms are ideal exemplars, such that each form is the best possible object of its kind. The principle of charity would suggest that this self-predicational reading, according to which the best shield is immaterial and therefore in some obvious sense not a shield at all, ought to be avoided if possible. Admittedly there are other dialogues that do seem to manifest that view, but I do not view that fact as decisive for an interpretation of the *Republic*.

62. Santas, "Form of the Good in Plato's *Republic*," 266.

place? An activity cannot be good solely in virtue of its reliability and durability.

38. These objections can be defused by bringing in the conclusions of the last section. Once we see that goodness is the overarching functional context that serves as the final cause of particular forms, in other words, we can see why its proper attributes are the ideal attributes of forms, and hence why it is the formal cause of forms.

39. On a teleological picture, ordinary objects are structured by a combination of material, formal, and final causes. A helm, for example, is a piece of equipment with which one steers a boat. Several different arrangements of several different kinds of material might serve the relevant end. Boats may be steered by means of an object composed of a rudder plus a tiller or by means of one composed of a rudder plus a steering wheel, and these items may be made from wood, plastic, or metal. The final cause, then, is realizable in multiple forms or arrangements. But it is also true that any given form or arrangement will be realizable in multiple kinds of material and in various different particulars.[63] On this picture, every ordinary object has a form in the sense of a formal cause: a principle that organizes parts into a whole. But some forms are better than others, given the functional context. The true form of a given object, its *eidos* or *idea* in the grand sense, will therefore be the principle that best organizes its parts into a whole, given the functional context.[64]

---

63. Not any material will do for a given form. When Aristotle introduces the concept of a formal cause in *Physics* II.1–3, he does so as part of an account of change that (he thinks) requires all four causes. The four causes are therefore interrelated from the very start, and in particular the material and formal causes are unthinkable without each other. We might try to define something's nature in terms of its material, that out of which it was made, but this does not specify it as the kind of thing it actually is; to get to this, we need to make reference to its form: the shape, order, or arrangement of its material. So closely are the terms related, in fact, that it turns out that "material is a relative term" because "to each form there corresponds a special matter" (II.2); this is especially clear in the case of crafts, where the material has to be produced with a certain form in order to be able to be perform its role as material for a future form: only certain kinds of wood will be suitable for shaping helms.

64. This notion of true form is deeply bound up with that of virtue. As Socrates suggests in the *Gorgias*, something is excellent if it performs the characteristic activity of its kind of thing well, and it does this in virtue of its form: "But surely the virtue of each thing, whether of an implement or of a body, or again of a soul or any live creature, does not arrive most properly by accident, but by an order or rightness or art that is apportioned to each. . . . The virtue of each thing is a matter of regular and

40. Interpreting true forms as best possible formal causes allows us to understand why Socrates insists (during the argument against the sight lovers, for example) that forms are nonsensible. A shape or arrangement is typically sensible, to be sure, and so formal causes in the initial sense can often be cognized through our senses. But to work out something's *true* form, we will need to know what it is for, and although on a small scale this does not seem to require philosophy—everyone knows what knives are for, and the user of an instrument is an expert on what it is for (600e–602b)—Plato wants to suggest that the micro and the macro cannot be kept so readily apart. Suppose that a pruning knife is for pruning vines, which is for viticulture, which is for alcohol production, which is for alcohol consumption. Here we can return to Gosling's argument regarding the possibility of pseudo-*epistēmai*. If it is bad for humans to consume alcohol, then knowledge of what makes a good pruning knife will turn out to be a pseudo-*epistēmē*. To find out whether this is the case requires dialectic: we must go back and forth between the function of the part and the function of the whole, modifying each in light of the other.[65] True knowledge, which entails understanding, therefore requires both experience of sensible particulars *and* abstract dialectical reasoning regarding functional contexts that are not disclosed to the senses.

41. This account enables us to make a second pass at the three questions that arose out of the sun image. How does goodness actualize the potential of intelligence to understand and intelligible objects (i.e., forms) to be known? In what way does goodness cause the existence and essence of forms? And in what sense is goodness superior to essence? We have seen that all three questions are answerable if we interpret goodness as the final cause of forms, but we can also provide answers by interpreting goodness as the formal cause of forms.

---

orderly arrangement. . . . Hence it is a certain order proper to each existent thing that by its advent in each makes it good" (506d–e; translation by W. R. M. Lamb).

65. See Penner, "Forms in the *Republic*." As H. W. B. Joseph points out, the final cause for Plato is not temporal. It is not that the goodness of what follows is itself the ground for bringing into being the preceding means, as in G. A. Cohen's famous analysis of functional explanation. Rather, the goodness of the whole is to explain the goodness of the parts. See Joseph, *Knowledge and the Good in Plato's "Republic,"* chap. 3; and Cohen, *Karl Marx's Theory of History*, chap. 9.

42. It is essential to each true form that it be good. Every material object will have some arrangement or other, but its true form—which it may or may not manifest—will be that arrangement that allows it to be a good object of its kind, assuming that the kind is itself good. Goodness is therefore, as Gail Fine puts it, "part of the essence of every knowable object."[66] It is an ideal attribute of forms, shared by each form regardless of its proper attributes. It is, in other words, the form of forms—their formal cause. But if goodness is the formal cause of forms, it cannot be a form just like the rest. To use Fine's analogy, just as the form of a house is not some further element added to the material, so the form of goodness is nothing more than a certain constitution of forms.[67] Goodness is therefore not an entity in its own right, subject to formal and final causes beyond itself, but only the harmonic ordering of the intelligible realm. It is, as Socrates says, beyond essence.[68]

§6 Cognizing Ordinary Objects

43. In §1 we saw that a two-worlds interpretation in which philosophical knowledge concerns the "world of ideas" as opposed to the "world of sense" would threaten to render Plato's politics incoherent. Philosophers are supposed to rule in virtue of the fact that

---

66. Fine, "Knowledge and Belief in *Republic* V–VII," 97–98.

67. Although Fine does not say so, it might seem reasonable to conclude that forms are the material cause of the structure of which goodness is the formal and final cause. It may seem strange to think of forms as the material for anything, but in Book II of the *Physics* Aristotle considers premises as the material of a syllogism.

68. Compare Terence Irwin's statement: "We insist on pursuing other things only insofar as they are good and beneficial (505d5–10), but this does not mean that we pursue them for the sake of some good that is independent of them. . . . The good, then, may be understood not as something independent of the virtues and other specific goods, but as the appropriate combination and arrangement of them. This is why Plato believes the good is not a 'being' in its own right, but beyond being; while the good is superior to the different specific goods that constitute it, it cannot be understood, defined, or achieved without reference to them." Irwin, *Plato's Ethics*, 272–273. See also Gadamer, *The Idea of the Good in Platonic-Aristotelian Philosophy*, 27–28: "That Plato uses only the word *idea*, and never *eidos*, for the *agathon*, surely has something to do with [its] transcendence . . . in *idea*, taken as a 'view of something,' the viewing or looking is more pronounced than in *eidos*, taken as 'how something looks.' Consequently *idea tou agathou* (idea of the good) implies not so much the 'view of the good' as a 'looking to the good.'"

they study the forms, especially the form of the good. But "if they learn about something that is never to be found in experience," asks Annas, "how can their knowledge of it be the *practical* wisdom they are to have?"[69] In §2 we saw a way out of this quandary. A passage from Book V often taken to support the two-worlds reading in fact suggests only that philosophers perceive an aspect of this world to which nonphilosophers are blind, and that perception of this aspect is necessary for stable cognition. We are now in a position to understand what this might mean.

44. In Plato's view, there are standards of success inherent in each kind of thing, and "the excellence, beauty and correctness of each manufactured item, living creature, and action [are] related to nothing but the use for which each is made or naturally adapted" (601d). To work out which standards pertain to a given particular, we need to study its sensible qualities but also to go beyond them, trying to work out its true form by considering it in light of a series of ever-wider functional contexts that terminates in the interlocking structure of formal and final causes that is goodness itself. This would be an investigation not into some separate object that transcends the concrete particular before us, but into that object itself. The fact that F is the true form of Fs helps us see something about this particular F, namely that toward which it either is or ought to be striving. If we fail to perceive this aspect of the object, we will fail to perceive it in light of its potential and hence its full being.[70]

---

69. Annas, *Introduction to Plato's "Republic,"* 244.

70. In this connection we might consider Socrates' arguments against materialist explanation in the *Phaedo* (96a–100b), which seem both to assert the importance of final causality to adequate explanation ("If then one wished to know the cause of each thing, why it comes to be or perishes or exists, one had to find what was the best way for it to be, or to be acted upon, or to act" [97c–d]) and to assert that forms are causes ("I am going to try to show you the kind of cause with which I have concerned myself. I turn back to those oft-mentioned things and proceed from them. I assume the existence of a Beautiful, itself by itself, of a Good and a Great and all the rest" [100b]). We might also consider Aristotle's discussion of the nature of a bed in the *Physics* (II.1). When Aristotle talks of "the form of the bed" in a perfectly Platonic formulation—*to eidos tēs klinēs* (193a45)—it is hard not to hear echoes of Book X of the *Republic*. Aristotle might have intended these echoes to signify his solution to Plato's problematic theory, but given the reading proposed in this chapter, it looks like the two views are actually consonant with each other. Antiphon claims that bedness, the true essence of bed, must consist in material rather than form. If you plant a wooden bed in the

45. To illustrate the kind of reasoning at issue in going between a concrete particular and its true form, consider the account of the soul presented in Books IV and VIII. Socrates begins with observations from ordinary experience, and his account remains answerable to such experience. The story of Leontius, for example, allows him to draw our attention to the actual form of a particular soul (439e–440a). Leontius was on his way back to Athens from the Piraeus when he noticed the corpses of recently executed criminals outside the city walls. At one and the same time he felt a desire to behold these corpses and a desire to avert his eyes from them. He struggled for a time, putting his hand over his eyes, before finally the stronger desire won out and he opened his eyes wide, rushed toward the corpses, and shouted, "Look for yourselves, you evil wretches; take your fill of the beautiful sight." The moral of this story, Socrates tells us, is that the human soul is a complex entity composed of at least two distinct drives, and that psychological discomfort emerges when these drives are at war with one another. Two further examples along the same lines lead Socrates to conclude that the soul is a tripartite entity composed of three distinct drives, which he calls reason, spirit, and appetite. Socrates then argues that the true form of the soul—its optimal condition, given its material or parts—would be a harmonious arrangement in which spirit and appetite follow reason's lead. Souls whose form is deficient with respect to this standard will experience psychic conflict and attendant unhappiness.[71]

46. This account goes back and forth between experiential observation and reasoning in terms of forms. It will be successful only if

---

ground, or otherwise leave it unattended for years, it may well sprout a tree. This shows, Antiphon claims, that its form or arrangement is merely accidental to the material essence that persists through change. But Aristotle's view is that a bed that loses its form and becomes a tree no longer counts as a bed. In the absence of form, the wood is merely potentially a bed. What makes something an actual bed is its form and function—they give it its principle of unity and criterion of identity. Antiphon's error, we might say, was to presume that any sound explanation of bed-being would have to draw only on sensible data, since, as we have already seen, form (unlike shape) is in some sense suprasensible, being tied to function. In a certain sense, then, form will only ever be obscured by our focusing exclusively on particular concrete beds.

71. This is not to say that the just person is necessarily happy on the rack. In my view, Socrates aims to show that justice is necessary for happiness, not that it is sufficient. But there is much scholarly debate over this question, and a fuller account is not possible here.

it elucidates the phenomenon at hand, namely a certain form of psychic discomfort, and this demands both that the phenomenology be accurate and that the account be answerable to it.[72] But the account also relies on Plato's metaphysics, since the crucial move is the claim that "the same thing cannot do or undergo opposite things . . . in the same respect, in relation to the same thing, at the same time" (439e–440a; 436b–437c), and this principle, which commentators tend to call the "principle of opposites," is part and parcel of Plato's teleological ontology. It is a criterion of what makes things the same or different and therefore a criterion of essence or being; and it operates by assessing drives in terms of their natural directions or aims, which can be cashed out in terms of formal objects (along the lines that we saw in §2). The formal object of thirst, for instance, is said to be drink, so that if we experience both thirst and a drive to avoid drink at the same time, this must be because of the activation of a capacity with a different formal object (437d–439b). These natural directions or aims show up in ordinary experience, which is why Leontius experiences himself as torn. But what they reveal is the form of the different drives that make up the soul. In working out how those different drives could best come together into a coherent entity, we have to bear in mind the function of the soul. Socrates suggests that the function of the soul is to lead a life ("taking care of things, ruling, deliberating, and all other such things" [353d]), so that excellence of soul, its good form, will be that which enables someone to live well or happily (353b–354a). This functional picture, outlined in Book I, then gets spelled out further in Book IV's account of justice as the excellent order of the soul (443c–444a) and the corresponding account of injustice as the ruination of the "natural constitution of the very thing by which we live" (445a–b).

47. What we see in Plato's psychology, then, is an attempt to go back and forth between different aspects of concrete particulars: their actual form and their true form. Certainly this is not supposed to be the final, authoritative account. Socrates emphasizes that "we will never ever grasp this matter precisely by methods of the sort we

---

72. Of course, Socrates' larger goal is to generate an account of justice that will enable him to answer the challenge posed by Glaucon at the start of Book II.

are now using in our discussions," and he alludes to a "longer and more time-consuming road that does lead there" (435c–d). A little later, in Books VI and VII, he makes clear that this longer road would involve anchoring accounts of particular forms in a stable account of goodness (504b–505a; 511b–d; 534b–c). But we have reason to believe that the dialectical inquiry involved in reaching an authoritative account will be of a piece with the dialectical inquiry modeled by Socrates. For as we have seen, goodness is best understood as nothing more than the organization of particular forms into a harmonic structure or cosmos. To know goodness is therefore not to mystically apprehend some enigmatic entity—"the ultimate object of pursuit [which] yet lies outside the world," as Cooper would have it[73]—but rather to engage in a dialectical back-and-forth between our understanding of particular forms and our understanding of the whole which they constitute.[74] The longer road therefore involves holistic inquiry on two different levels: (1) a back-and-forth between our experience of concrete particulars and our functional reasoning regarding their true forms and (2) a back-and-forth between our account of particular forms and our understanding of the whole cosmos of forms.[75] A precise account requires both levels, even if only the second rises to the level of *epistēmē*.[76] In the final analysis, then, knowledge of goodness is inseparable from inquiry into particular things. "The greatest test of who is naturally dialectical," Socrates

---

73. Cooper, "Psychology of Justice in Plato," 27.

74. See Gosling, *Plato*, 117: "In short, knowledge of the Form of the Good is not an intuition of an unsubstantiated first premiss. It is rather an account of a system in terms of interrelated functions which is substantiated by its ability to 'make sense' of the universe."

75. The image of the divided line might suggest that the first of these levels amounts to "thought" (*dianoia*) only (510d–511c). But the defining characteristic of thought, as opposed to understanding (*epistēmē*), is that it fails to ground inquiry in a genuine first principle. Given that a two-level process of holistic inquiry would not fail in this way, the implications of the line image are unclear.

76. Whitney Schwab helpfully suggests that philosophical judgments regarding concrete particulars may rise to the level of *gnōsis* even if they do not amount to *epistēmē*. "Socrates uses '*gnōsis*' as a general term of cognitive praise, which he is willing to apply to distinct kinds of cognition." Uncontroversial examples include *epistēmē* (476c) and *dianoia* (527b), but a reasonable case can also be made for philosophically informed *doxa* regarding sensibles given that sensibles are said to be between the *agnōston* and the *gnōston* (477a). See Schwab, "Understanding *Epistēmē* in Plato's *Republic*," 80.

tells us in Book VII, is whether someone can take "the subjects they learned in no particular order as children [and] bring [them] together to form a unified vision of their kinship both with one another and with the nature of that which is" (537b–c). As Plato repeatedly suggests, the true philosopher really does love all knowledge.

§7 Two Classes of Forms

48. Plato's holism clearly bears on his political theory. But before we turn our attention to that theory, we must consider an important objection. My account so far has focused on the forms of artefacts and living things as opposed to the forms of justice and beauty or those of the equal and the unequal, the big and the small, the hard and the soft, the thick and the thin. How do all these forms relate to one another? Can the teleological picture really explain all of them? This question is not merely scholastic: it concerns the very unity of the *Republic*.

49. On the view I have been sketching, there are forms for all functional unities, including natural items such as eyes, artefacts such as cities, and activities such as cobbling.[77] Some would deny this. Annas, for instance, declares that although Book X seems to imply a form of the cobbler, "the obvious absurdity of this makes one think that Plato has not seen this implication."[78]

50. Those who deny the existence of forms for natural items, artefacts, and activities tend to appeal to a passage in Book VII where Socrates distinguishes between predicates in terms of their ability to turn our minds toward forms.[79] For example, a finger is a finger

77. On Plato's picture of the cosmos, forms and final causes are fundamentally ahistorical. It does not interest him that there may have been a time before there were any couches on the earth, as it might interest us. Humans need to sleep and to sit, and for this purpose they will need couches and beds. God has provided humans their place in the universe and the true, unchanging forms that will go with their final causes, although humans have to discover these by understanding things philosophically. See Dorothea Frede, "Plato on What the Body's Eye Tells the Mind's Eye," 205–206.

78. Annas, *Introduction to Plato's "Republic,"* 229–230. The passage in question is 598b–c.

79. See Nehamas, "Plato on the Imperfection of the Sensible World," 177; and Annas, *Introduction to Plato's "Republic,"* 223, 229–230.

whether it is "seen to be in the middle or at either end . . . dark or pale, thick or thin," and so "the soul of most people is not compelled to ask the understanding *[noēsis]* what a finger is, since sight does not at any point suggest to it that a finger is at the same time the opposite of a finger" (523d). In contrast, whether a given thing or property counts as hard or soft depends on the context and so cannot be determined simply by sense-perception *(aisthēsis)*, leaving the soul "inevitably puzzled as to what this sense-perception means by hardness" (524a).[80] To find a way out of this puzzle, the soul begins a dialectical investigation which determines that while hardness and softness are always mixed in sensible particulars, in and of themselves they are unitary and distinct (476a). To draw this distinction between appearance and reality is to recognize the existence of forms and thereby to set out on the road to stable cognition.

51. This passage is hardly conclusive. The claim that certain predicates encourage thinking about forms is a claim about educational psychology, not ontology; in and of itself, it entails nothing regarding the range of forms.[81] In any case, Socrates' claim is only that the soul of most people *(tôn pollôn hē psuchē)* is not compelled to ask what a finger is. Given Socrates' feelings about *hoi polloi*, it is not unreasonable to wonder whether the philosophical soul is expected to ask after the nature of fingers. On the account I have been outlining, the answer would seem to be yes. For a philosopher who understands the nature of goodness as an interlocking structure of forms and final causes will understand that we do require a wider context to predicate fingerhood of something. A finger is a paradigmatic instance of the kind of thing whose being is organic and hence dependent on the body of which it is a part, as Aristotle recognizes when he says that a finger severed from a body is a finger in name only

---

80. I am using the Reeve translation.

81. As Paul Shorey remarks in his note to 524c in the Loeb edition: "Plato merely means that this is the psychological origin of our attempt to form abstract and general ideas." Annas acknowledges that the question of what forms there are may be independent of the question of what forms the human mind is capable of coming to recognize. But although she terms this a "possible view," she quickly dismisses it as "too sophisticated to be ascribed to Plato merely because the argument is for a limited range of Forms whereas some interpreters want Plato to be arguing for more." See Annas, *Introduction to Plato's "Republic,"* 223.

("homonymously").[82] It may turn out that every predicate is incomplete in the sense that we cannot apply it without reference to a wider context. After all, we have already seen that Plato's views on goodness commit him to a kind of holism. As Gail Fine puts it, "Full knowledge of anything requires knowing its place in the system of which it is a part, or which it instantiates; we do not know things in the best way if we know them only in isolation from one another."[83] But in any case, even if some predicates do end up being complete or context independent—depending on our view of nature, "man" may be one—the argument from educational psychology will still not compel us to rule out the possibility of forms for such cases.[84]

52. Socrates says at the start of Book X that "we customarily hypothesize a single form in connection with each of the many things to which we apply the same name" (596a; see also 507b). This does not necessarily mean that Plato intends forms to be something like his "theory of universals," as Bertrand Russell thought, but it is hard to avoid the implication that we should at least presume that there will be a form for every name.[85] If language is doing its job at all—although, as we will see in Chapter 3, it will not do its job well in a

82. Aristotle, *Metaphysics* 1035b23–25. Cf. *Metaphysics* 1036b30–32; *On the Soul* 412b17–22; *Meteorology* 389b20–390a16; *Politics* 1253a20–25; *Parts of Animals* 640b30–641a6; and *Generation of Animals* 734b25–27. The *Politics* passage states the point particularly clearly: "All things derive their essential character from their function and their capacity; and it follows that if they are no longer fit to discharge their function, we ought not to say that they are still the same things, but only that, by an ambiguity, they still have the same names." For more on homonymy, see the first chapter of Aristotle, *Categories*, as well as Irwin, "Homonymy in Aristotle."

83. Fine, *Plato on Knowledge and Forms*, 99.

84. Schwab argues that "the predicate 'human being' may fail to apply to a concrete perceptible in circumstances in which it fails to manifest rationality." He worries that if "human being" is not circumstance-variant, there will be no need for Socrates to rule out *epistēmē* of perceptible human beings. Schwab, "Understanding *Epistēmē* in Plato's *Republic*," 71.

85. Annas, *Introduction to Plato's "Republic,"* 229, objects that if there is a form for every general term, then grasping the fact that there are forms no longer looks like a difficult matter that separates philosophers from nonphilosophers, but rather a simple recognition of an ordinary fact. This seems false to me. Clearly Socrates takes the thesis for granted, assuming that Glaucon will assent to it, but that does not imply that it is usual procedure for anyone outside Plato's or Socrates' circle. Annas's argument here might be applied to any metaphysical claim that applies to ordinary objects: if there is a substratum in every object that survives change, surely grasping that fact is only a simple recognition of an ordinary fact?

bad city—then it should reflect genuine unities, however loosely. Some apparent unities may turn out not to be genuine unities, and given Plato's emphasis on goodness as the formal and final cause of forms we might say that pseudounities will be those without any function. Redness, for example, might count as a linguistic universal in Russell's sense but not as a form, because there is nothing that all red things are aiming at. Forms are principles of unity—principles that determine what counts as the same and what counts as different— understood in relationship to functions.

53. If there is to be a form of the cobbler, cobbling must be understood as a functional unity that aims at something genuinely good (shoes), such that the relevant aim (shoemaking) organizes the relevant material (someone's decisions). The first aspect seems obvious enough: shoes protect the feet and enable people to move freely and easily. The second aspect seems to sit rather well with what we find in Book IV, where Socrates tells us that each of the citizens "is to be directed to what he is naturally suited for, so that, doing the one work that is his own, he will become not many but one" (423d). First we must assess the material to see what it is suited for; this will involve judging someone's natural tendencies and capabilities. Then we must get the citizen to pursue that aim in such a way that it organizes her whole life into a functional unity, which is not to say that her activities are homogeneous but rather that they are "constituted" in the sense that they are held together by an organizing principle.

54. Once we learn to recognize this pattern of reasoning, we can see it throughout the *Republic*. Consider Socrates' account of the true philosopher, for instance, as originally distinguished by her natural tendencies, basic focus, and characteristic excellences and then later directed toward her task via the city's educational system (501c–504a; 535a–540c). What Socrates is doing in these passages is working out the true nature, or form, of a philosopher, just as in other passages he works out the true nature, or form, of the city or of the soul.[86]

---

86. Myles Burnyeat argues convincingly that although Kallipolis is a *paradeigma* (model or ideal), it is not a form; but he then slides from the claim that the ideal city is not a form to the claim that there is no form of the city. This does not follow, nor can

55. When Plato engages in the procedure I have been describing, working out what something is in light of its final cause, he tends to use the word *phusis* (nature) or its cognates rather than *eidos* or *idea* (form). This usage is by no means universal, as Book X shows, and anyway I have been making the case that the form of a given object just is its nature understood a certain way, so that Plato's metaphysics is also his physics.[87] But we might still wonder whether this account can apply to all forms. After all, there are two classes of forms that do not seem to be functional unities: comparative ones such as "the equal" or "the big," "the heavy," or "the hard" (see 523e–524c) and evaluative ones such as beauty and justice. How can these be accounted for on the teleological interpretation?

56. Let us start with comparative terms like equality and heaviness. All these terms concern relative magnitude, and in that sense they are mathematical. If we wanted to place forms like these at the center of Plato's ontology without relying on his educational psychology, we might point instead to his evident fascination with mathematics. According to Aristoxenus, his teacher Aristotle used to recount the story of a lecture that Plato once gave on the topic of goodness:

Each came expecting to learn something about the things which are generally considered good for men, such as wealth, good health, physical strength, and altogether a kind of wonderful happiness. But when the mathematical demonstrations came, including numbers, geometrical figures and astronomy, and finally

---

the powerful consideration that Burnyeat adduces in its favor, namely, that "the well-known sentence at *Republic* 596a, which is so often invoked as evidence of a Form for every plurality of things we call by the same name, can equally well be construed . . . as positing just one Form for every plurality of things we call by the same name as the Form," be said to make his case definitively, much as it opens up the space for him to do so. See Burnyeat, "Utopia and Fantasy," 298.

87. As Schwab points out, Socrates certainly suggests that *epistēmē*, whose formal object is forms, requires grasping natures, whether the nature of the forms (476b) or the nature of each thing itself (490b). Dialectic, meanwhile, requires articulating or defining (the word is *diorisasthai*) an account of goodness, which seems to involve learning its nature, for when Socrates sets out to articulate or define an account of the philosopher, he then redescribes that task as learning the nature of the philosopher (485a). See Schwab, "Understanding *Epistēmē* in Plato's *Republic*," 55–61.

the statement, good is one, it all seemed to them, I imagine, utterly unexpected and strange. (*Elementa Harmonica*, II.30–31)[88]

Plato probably did hold mystical Pythagorean views about the cen-
trality of mathematics to the cosmos. He clearly believed, for example,
that every genuine branch of knowledge will involve mathematics
in some way; the opposition of one and many is reiterated throughout
the *Republic*, with the one always being good and the many always
being bad. One scholar has even claimed that his dialogues are
mathematically ordered so as to express a hidden Pythagorean doctrine.[89] More generally, as Gosling notes, "the whole trend is to assimilate value concepts to mathematical ones of measure and
proportion."[90] Given all this evidence, why not think that mathematics rather than teleology is the key to understanding Plato's conception of goodness? And if that is so, doesn't my account of forms
as natural unities in a teleological structure simply collapse?[91]

57. It turns out that the basic mathematical concepts (such as unity
and quantity) that undergird comparative forms are in fact explicable
teleologically, the crucial concept in this regard being that of proportion or harmony. Gosling highlights Plato's distinction—implicit
in the *Republic* but explicit by the time of the *Statesman*—between
"lower mathematics," composed of disciplines like arithmetic and geometry that deal with relative magnitude for the sake of practical
pursuits, and "higher mathematics," composed of disciplines like
music and astronomy that deal with the question of appropriate proportion for the sake of the study of soul, nature, and cosmos.[92] The
reason the lower kind leads upward to the higher is that dealing with
relative magnitudes involves carving the world up into units. This
necessarily raises the question of what counts as a unit, and hence
the question of which principles of unity are appropriate. It is per-

---

88. Cited in Gaiser, "Plato's Enigmatic Lecture 'On the Good,'" 5.
89. Kennedy, "Plato's Forms, Pythagorean Mathematics, and Stichometry." On the
Pythagoreans, see Aristotle, *Metaphysics A*, 985b–987a.
90. Gosling, *Plato*, 103; cf. Burnyeat, "Plato on Why Mathematics Is Good for the
Soul," 6: "The content of mathematics [is] a constitutive part of ethical
understanding."
91. Burnyeat, for instance, argues in "Plato on Why Mathematics Is Good for the
Soul," 74–81, that for Plato, goodness just is unity.
92. See *Statesman*, 283d–284c. Cf. Mitchell Miller, "Beginning the 'Longer Way.'"

fectly possible to have a set whose members are Fido, Bertrand Russell's third joke, and the square root of two, Gosling points out, but "although one can say how many members the set has . . . there is no defining property of the set in terms of which to give what is being counted and determine the 'units' of the set."[93] In other words, in the absence of a principle of unity for the set, there can be no principle of units. So the question of what counts as a unit becomes the question of how things should be grouped and hence which things should be counted as the same and which as different. And as this example shows (although Gosling does not draw the moral), there is no way to answer this question without referring to a context of purposes or final causes. When I pick up my pen, I could be picking up one object or two, depending on what the counting is for. I might want to know whether I have enough pens to be able to lend one to my friend while keeping one for myself, or I might be playing a game where the goal is to produce from one's pockets as many separable objects as possible. A trivial example, granted, but the idea holds: the question of sameness and difference can be answered only by considering the (nonsensible) functional context of interlocking parts and wholes.[94]

58. This principle lay behind my claim that redness is a linguistic universal but not a form. It is also the root of Socrates' distinction between dialectic and disputation. In Book VII disputation (*antilogia*) is characterized as mere debate, debate for debate's sake, refutation for the fun of it rather than a way of getting at the truth (539b–c); it is therefore associated with sophistry as against true philosophy (499a). In Book V, however, we see that we can fall into disputation unwittingly if we fail to understand what true refutation involves. Superficial refutation, which Socrates calls *eristic*, looks for contradiction "on the purely verbal level"; dialectical refutation, by

---

93. Gosling, *Plato*, 113; see Plato, *Parmenides*, 129c–130a. Gosling also proposes an alternative explanation of the way in which arithmetic and geometry are supposed to lead upward, namely, that they are necessary parts of astronomy and music, which themselves are necessarily connected to goodness. The limitation of mathematicians relative to philosophers would then be that the former do not connect their work to goodness by relating it to music and astronomy.

94. Of course, that teleological context is supposed to be objective, whereas my example involves the subjective and arbitrary assignment of function.

contrast, requires us to "examine what has been said by dividing it up into kinds" (454a). The word translated as "kinds" in that last quotation is in fact *eidē*—forms. So the distinction between eristical and dialectical refutation revolves around the attempt to work out forms. And Socrates spells out that distinction in terms of the importance of developing principles of sameness and difference that are pertinent given the purpose of a particular inquiry. Whether or not men and women can properly be said to have the same nature, for instance, depends on what we are asking the question for. With respect to procreation, they are different; with respect to the structure of their souls, they are the same (454a–457b). As far as the division of labor is concerned, it is the second kind of sameness and difference that matters: "We meant, for example, that a male and a female whose souls are suited for medicine have the same nature" (454d).[95] The boldness of Socrates' position regarding the sexes ought not to distract us from the underlying metaphysical claim, which is that principles of sameness and difference—and therefore principles of unity and identity—will vary in accordance with purposive context. That is not to say, of course, that all purposes are equally justified: the appropriateness of a given division of reality will depend on its contribution to the harmony and order of the cosmos.

59. This is where mathematical reasoning comes in for Plato. If we recall that goodness is nothing more—but also nothing less—than the interlocking structure of formal and final causes that organizes the cosmos, then we can see that this structure must necessarily be proportional and harmonious. Each part must fit well into the whole of which it is a part. And Plato's hypothesis, it seems, is that mathematics will provide the appropriate language for expressing truths

---

95. Socrates' position is not that men and women will on average be equally good at a given task, but rather that they both share in the three ways of life. Given this, they should be treated equally with respect to the question of profession. "Women share by nature in every way of life just as men do, but in all of them women are weaker than men" (455d–e). Strauss assumes that the equality of men and women is obviously contrary to nature, and hence that Socrates must be understood as joking here, but aside from any other reproaches we might level at him, it is far from clear that he even understands Socrates' point. See Strauss, *City and Man*, 127: "The just city is against nature because the equality of the sexes and absolute communism are against nature."

about harmony and proportion. So mathematics is the language of goodness.[96]

60. Something similar will be true of what I called the "evaluative" forms, beauty and justice. When all is said and done, beauty and justice both have to do with harmony and proportion. This is obvious in the case of beauty—think of the Parthenon—but it is equally true of justice. Justice is, as Aristotle says, a matter of proportional equality, of giving equal shares to people of equal merit.[97] Socrates puts the point by saying that "everyone must practice one of the occupations in the city for which he is naturally best suited" and, more generally, that "justice is doing one's own work and not meddling with what isn't one's own" (433a).[98] But to know one's station and keep to it just is to act in proportion to one's merit and thereby to ensure the harmony of the whole. And if we accept the general formulation that justice obtains when each part of a constituted whole does its own work, then we might extend the concept from its usual application to cities and souls all the way to the basic structure of the universe. The universe would then be just insofar as its parts all perform their own characteristic activities; for a part to do its own work is for it to fit harmoniously into the whole of which it is a part, complementing the other parts appropriately. But this suggests

---

96. As Gosling puts it, it is not that "the simple fact of a relationship's being mathematically expressible is sufficient to show it to be desirable [but rather that] the precise expression of notions of proper ordering will require mathematical techniques." Gosling, *Plato*, 104. Compare Sedley, "Philosophy, Forms, and the Art of Ruling," 270n21, who also argues that unity is subordinate to proportionality in explanatory terms, and that since goodness is ideal proportionality, it is expressible in mathematical terms. Compare also Fine: "Plato [does not] praise mathematics for the reasons one might expect. To be sure, he emphasizes its value in getting us to turn from 'becoming to truth and being' (525c), that is, in getting us to acknowledge forms. But he adds in the same breath, as though it is of equal importance, that mathematics is also of value in the practical matter of waging war (525b–c; cf. 522e, 526d). Nor does he praise mathematics for using necessary truths or for conferring some special sort of certainty. On the contrary, he believes that even if mathematical truths are necessary, they cannot be fully known until they, like all other truths, are suitably related to the form of the good." Fine, "Knowledge and Belief in *Republic* V–VII," 107.

97. Aristotle, *Nicomachean Ethics* V.3.

98. Cf. Plato's description of democracy as "assigning a sort of equality to equals and unequals alike" (Reeve translation, 558c).

that a just universe is equivalent to a beautiful universe, and that both are equivalent to a good universe—a cosmos.[99]

61. What all of this implies is that there are two classes of forms, related but distinguishable. On the one hand, there are what one might call the *substantial* forms, such as the form of the city or the form of the cobbler, which have to do with the true nature of concrete particulars. On the other hand, there are what one might call the *structural* forms, such as the relative magnitudes, justice, and beauty, which have to do with proportion and harmony and are therefore attributes of goodness. Both are bound up with a teleological conception of the universe, but each in a different way. Substantial forms concern the nature of ordinary things: to grasp them is to perceive a nonsensible aspect of the world around us, namely the fact that ordinary things are in one respect striving toward perfection and in another respect falling away from it. Structural forms concern the nature of substantial forms: to grasp them is to see that something will count as a true nature only if it is also proportional, since goodness is a matter of harmonic order, both internal and external, and goodness is both the formal and final cause of substantial forms. A city, for example, has an actual form, given by the way its parts are arranged into a whole. But it also has a true form, given by the way those parts ought to be arranged in light of the role that cities play in the wider functional context of the cosmos. And the form in this elevated sense will manifest a perfect proportion or harmony between parts and wholes, both internal and external, so that it exemplifies structural forms such as beauty and justice. Something similar will then be true of the soul and all other functional unities, whether natural or artificial. This is nothing more than an interpretive hypothesis, but it seems to illuminate the *Republic* considerably.

I BEGAN THIS chapter by warning that if we misinterpret Plato's metaphysics, we will necessarily misinterpret his politics (§1). The

---

99. It is worth registering a caveat regarding my suggestion that the universe itself might be considered just: 371e–372a might be taken to suggest that justice is a concept that applies only to some wholes, specifically those that tend toward "feverishness." Even if this is true, however, it would not affect the conclusion that justice is a structural form wherever it does apply. In Chapter 3 I will consider the relationship between beauty and goodness more fully.

two-worlds account is initially compelling, but picturing philosophers with their heads in the clouds renders the notion of philosopher-rulers all but incomprehensible. I have argued that another interpretation is possible, according to which to know forms is to see an aspect of this world that would otherwise be occluded (§2), namely its teleological structure (§3). I have proposed that goodness is the formal and final cause of forms (§4 and §5), showing how this bears on the cognition of ordinary objects (§6). Finally, I have suggested that there are two classes of forms, structural and substantial (§7). This interpretation credits Plato with a one-world metaphysics, according to which to know forms is to be able to perceive an aspect of concrete particulars that would otherwise be occluded: to understand a particular is to know its material, formal, and final causes, which is why those who refuse to leave the realm of experiential, nondialectical cognition—the sight lovers—will not even be able to understand particulars. This is important precisely because sight lovers are to be understood as rival candidates for the job of political craftsmen (§1); Plato insists that a craftsman must understand the three causes of her object.

This interpretation allows us to recognize the integrity of the *Republic* as one work from start to finish, retaining the clear implications of Books I and X while explaining Books V–VII in their light. Plato thinks philosophers are qualified to rule in virtue of their knowledge of forms, and we can now see that this does not commit him to the non sequitur that otherworldly knowledge is a necessary condition for worldly *phronēsis*.[100] When the true captain looks at the stars in Book VI's magnificent analogy of the ship of state, the other sailors deride him as a "stargazer" because they assume his knowledge to be otherworldly and so irrelevant to practical pursuits (488a–489c). But while the stars may be of the heavens, knowing them is the precondition for getting one's bearings here on earth. Likewise, the forms may be immaterial, but to know them is to be able to get one's

---

100. Cf. Annas: rulers require knowledge that is applicable to particular cases in order to "guide the person to make good particular choices," yet "if Forms are the only objects of knowledge, then particular people, things and actions are not capable of being known, just because they are particulars" (*Introduction to Plato's "Republic,"* 261–262).

bearings among the particular things here on earth—to find one's way in the cave, as it were.

Indeed, the cave image illustrates the fact that in Plato's view, just asking the right questions can have a transformative effect on one's bearings. To see this, we need to return briefly to the sun image. Goodness may be the formal and final cause of knowledge, as we have seen, but might we not also view goodness as the efficient cause of knowledge? When it rises, the sun actualizes the potential of the power of sight to see visible things by providing light. If we are in a dark room with our eyes open, the act of turning on the light is the efficient cause of sight. The parallel with goodness would fit with a common turn of phrase in English: only in light of goodness will intelligible things be understood. To open our eyes to this light is simply to ask what it would be for an F to be a good F, and whether it is good that Fs exist. To ask these questions is to view the world under the aspect of goodness, and this is like turning on a light switch in the realm of knowledge. For only if we ask after goodness will we be able to consider what the true form for Fs might be, given that function dictates form. And only if we can say what something's true form is can we be said to be *epistēmōn* with respect to it, given that—per Gosling—*epistēmē* is the capacity to discriminate between good and bad instances. As Terence Irwin suggests, then, what is necessary for grasping the existence of forms is not so much knowledge of goodness as an appeal to it.[101] Those who make no such appeals have their eyes closed—they are blind, perhaps, or dreaming.

Plato goes out of his way to make clear that knowledge of goodness is only an aspiration for Socrates (and, we can infer, himself), but that does not stop him from affirming the structural role it must play in knowledge and virtue (504d–505a). This, it seems to me, is Plato's mature understanding of Socratic ignorance. The difference between Socrates and his fellow Athenians was not only that Socrates knew that he did not know, but also that he knew what he did not

---

101. Irwin, *Plato's Ethics*, 271. In other words, you do not need to have fully grasped the form of goodness, but you do need familiarity with and competence in teleological understandings of the world, which implies knowledge that there is a form of goodness.

know: the whole interlocking structure that is goodness.[102] The cave image illustrates this. Its central suggestion is that understanding is not a matter of collecting more information—as the sight lovers would have it—but rather of having the correct orientation, being turned toward the light, and that acquiring this orientation requires one first to recognize one's current cognitive condition as insufficient. In a world where most people can see, the blind know they are blind; in a world where no one can see the role that goodness plays in the cosmos, the first challenge is to recognize that one has had one's eyes closed. The cave draws on the first kind of case to make clear the second.

Our wonder at Plato's artistic achievement should not distract us from what he is trying to tell us, which is that to turn toward the light, to be reoriented and converted, is to begin to ask questions about particular things in light of goodness. In the final analysis, then, what distinguishes the philosopher from the sight lover is that she asks the right kind of question and therefore approaches inquiry in a different way.[103] This path will in time bring her stable cognition of forms and particulars, to be sure: as Socrates puts it, "Because you've seen the truth about fine, just, and good things, you'll know each image for what it is and also that of which it is the image" (520c). But what makes someone a philosopher is not her body of knowledge but rather her orientation toward goodness. To put it another way, the formal object of philosophy may be *sophia*, "the knowledge of what is advantageous—both for each part and for the whole" (442c), but we should never forget that philosophy is essentially a pursuit rather than an achievement. This is crucial for our understanding of philosophical rule, and it will also be crucial, to anticipate a little, for our understanding of philosophical citizenship.

---

102. See 505d for Socrates' divination, which he thinks we all share.
103. This difference in orientation tends to be grounded in a difference in psychology, on Plato's view, but that does not defeat the point.

2

Why Philosophers Should Rule

PHILOSOPHY AND POLITICS seem to call for utterly different talents and temperaments. The one is theoretical, rewarding patience and precision; the other practical, rewarding chutzpah and charisma. Not that philosophy is irrelevant to politics, of course. "The ideas of economists and political philosophers, both when they are right and when they are wrong, are more powerful than is commonly understood," wrote John Maynard Keynes. "Indeed the world is ruled by little else. . . . Madmen in authority, who hear voices in the air, are distilling their frenzy from some academic scribbler of a few years back."[1] A chasm might seem to separate this sense of ruling the world from the sense implied in Plato's notion of philosopher-rulers occupying the commanding heights of the city. But things are not so simple. For Plato certainly is concerned with the power of ideas in society: that is why the *Republic* spends so much time cataloging the baleful effects of Homeric poetry, tragic drama, and Attic comedy and suggesting appropriate counter-measures—far more time, in fact, than is devoted to thinking about day-to-day governance. Just as we must avoid foisting our own prejudices regarding

---

1. Keynes, *General Theory of Employment, Interest and Money*, chap. 24.

the nature of philosophy onto Plato, then, so we must not presume that we already understand what he means by ruling.

Each of the next three chapters will take up a different dimension of ruling. The present chapter focuses on why ruling requires philosophy. Philosophy, we have seen, is a pursuit whose formal object is *sophia*, which Socrates characterizes as "the knowledge of what is advantageous—both for each part and for the whole" (442c). This pursuit requires investigating concrete particulars, such as the city or the soul, in light of the nonsensible structure of formal and final causes that is goodness. In order to see how this activity bears on ruling, we must first rid ourselves of our preconceptions. "Ruler" is a term of art for Plato, designed to pick out those who look after their subjects' souls rather than those who simply hold office (§1). Chapter 3 explores what that activity entails; the present chapter restricts itself to the question of why philosophers should be charged with it. The answer has three components: first, philosophers are uniquely capable of guarding themselves and thereby sticking to their task without further supervision (§2); second, holistic inquiry into form and function makes philosophers uniquely capable of guarding the city as an entity that in turn shapes souls beneficially (§3 and §4); third, philosophers need to rule in order to ensure their own full development (§5). Having established this, I will turn in Chapters 3 and 4 to the means by which philosophers shape souls and the extent to which this is possible even in nonideal societies.

§1 Ruling as Guarding

1. Put simply, the argument in favor of philosopher-rulers is as follows:

1. There is a kind of knowledge that a ruler must possess to rule well.
2. Such knowledge is available only to philosophers.
3. Therefore only philosophers can rule well.

In Chapter 1 we arrived at a new conception of what Plato means by philosophy: roughly speaking, a pursuit aimed at knowledge of how each kind of particular would best be organized. The outstanding question for us therefore concerns (1). What must ruling be such that ruling well requires knowledge of how each kind of particular is best organized? Does it involve administration, conducting interviews, and sitting on "boring committees," as Annas thinks, or directing "every detail" of citizens' day-to-day lives, as C. C. W. Taylor suggests?[2] Or is it something else entirely?

2. It might be helpful to get our pretheoretical understanding of ruling out in the open so we can be alive to its potential to distort our interpretation. It is, of course, hard to flesh out a pretheoretical understanding; often it will become visible only in the course of interpreting an interlocutor with different background assumptions.[3] Be that as it may, I would hazard that we tend to think of ruling as something like having control over the machinery of state, where the state is understood as a set of interlocking institutions that are more or less permanent, staffed by civil servants, and equipped with certain legally enforceable rights over citizens.

3. Plato certainly recognizes that ruling (archē) involves control. A textual analysis of the Republic suggests that for Plato rulers, good and bad, do have power over their subjects. They are variously described as authorities (kurioi), leaders (hēgemones), or chiefs (dynastai) who are able to prevail over others (kratein). They are said to make laws (tithesthai tous nomous), to serve as judges (dikastai), to give orders (prostassein), and to organize the collective (dioikein, oikein, diatassein, epitassein, apodidosthai). It seems natural to assume, then, that Plato also thinks of rule as requiring control over the machinery of state.

4. It is important to remember, however, that the ancient Greek polis is by no means equivalent to the modern state. A polis is certainly a political unit and therefore in that sense a state. But a polis is not equivalent to a state in the sense of a permanent administrative body that might conceivably develop its own interests (raison d'état, rent seeking, and so on) and therefore potentially act against

---

2. See Annas, Introduction to Plato's "Republic," 266; and C. C. W. Taylor, "Plato's Totalitarianism," in Plato 2, 295.

3. See Gadamer, Truth and Method, pts. 2 and 3.

the population. Insofar as the polis has interests, they are necessarily the interests of the citizens—there may be a conflict between the polis and certain of its members, but this is a conflict between individuals (or a class of individuals) and the collective, not between the collective and the state. The Greeks worried about tyranny, but they did not worry about tyranny by bureaucrats.[4] We should therefore translate "polis" as "society" rather than "state."[5]

5. But perhaps the original thought simply needs reformulating. Any political society will distribute positions of authority, whether or not these have anything to do with the state, so the claim would just be that for Plato, ruling always involves what he calls "holding the offices" *(echontos tas archas).*[6] This is where things begin to get interesting, however, for it turns out that Plato does not consider officeholding essential to ruling—offices are simply one way for a ruler to achieve her ends. To understand why this is, we need to look closely at the concept of a true ruler, or guardian.

6. With no little genius, Plato first places the notion of a true ruler in the mouth of Thrasymachus, who claims during his Book I skirmish with Socrates that a ruler in the precise sense *(tōi akribestatōi logōi)* is one who carries out his function without errors (340d–341b). The fact that Socrates does not challenge this claim suggests that in groping around for a way to strike back against his interlocutor, Thrasymachus has put his finger on a structure that Plato considers to be part of the architecture of reality. As we saw in Chapter 1, Plato's ontology dictates that the true F will be the good F, and that to find out what counts as a good F, we will have to inquire about its function within a wider whole. What allows Thrasymachus to speak of the "precise" sense rather than a "new" or "better" sense is that ordinary language already embodies something of the Platonic picture.

---

4. Rome obviously had something more like a modern state, albeit one with an extremely low number of civil servants by modern standards. For a long consideration of these questions, see Mann, *Sources of Social Power,* vol. 1, *History of Power from the Beginning to AD 1760;* for a shorter argument, see Mann, "Autonomous Power of the State."

5. The translation of *polis* as "city" is also misleading, since in most *poleis* the majority of land was rural. I will sometimes defer to convention in using this translation, but readers should understand "society" as opposed to "urban center."

6. On the importance of offices in Greek political thought, see Lane, "How to Emancipate History from the Past."

When someone speaks of a true judge, for instance, as opposed to a judge in the ordinary sense, we understand the distinction they have in mind: a given person can be appointed as a judge according to an established set of procedures carried through with no misfires—board certification, election by the appropriate body, official oaths, and all the rest—without actually doing what judges are supposed to do.[7] A true judge will therefore be one who does what judges are supposed to do.[8] But to determine what the role truly demands, we have to leave behind actuality and hence anything that could come under the auspices of social science, and instead enter the realm of philosophy. For if it makes sense to speak of a ruler in the precise sense, then among all the people who are or have ever been called rulers, there may never have been a single one who was truly a ruler.[9] To think about what a true ruler is, we have to ask what a ruler is supposed to do. And that demands that we think in terms of functional contexts and hence in terms of goodness. That is what Thrasymachus is unable to do. Having brought the dimension of the precise sense into view, he tries to address it with an observation that has its home in the domain of social science, claiming on the grounds of experience that the function of the true ruler is to seek and order what is advantageous for himself. Socrates, on the other hand, recognizes that functions can be specified only within wider functional wholes, and hence that if the ruler has a function, it must be a useful role within the whole that is society. His preliminary account of this role is that it involves seeking and ordering what is advantageous for one's subjects (342e; 345d–e; 347d). Hence a true ruler is one who seeks and orders without error—in other words, finds and delivers—what is advantageous for her subjects.

7. The relationship of ruler to ruled in such cases is said to be like that of a helmsman to her sailors, a shepherd to her sheep, a doctor to her patients, and a trainer to her athletes—which is to say that a

---

7. On what makes someone a judge in this ordinary sense, see John Searle's theory of institutional facts in *The Construction of Social Reality*, chaps. 1–5.

8. There might be grounds for debate on whether true judges must necessarily be judges in the institutional sense; this will become relevant when we consider rulers.

9. See Jonathan Lear, *Case for Irony*, 5–7, 22–25, for the Kierkegaardian view that such reasoning constitutes the essence of Socratic irony.

ruler's task is to take care of her subjects (who are described at 345e as *therapeuomenoi*, things taken care of). There is therefore no question of exploitation where true rule is concerned: so long as the ruler really is capable of benefiting the ruled, she is doing them a favor, since "anyone with any sense would prefer to be benefited by another than to go to the trouble of benefiting him" (347d). This implies that a true ruler must be manifestly excellent relative to her subjects; even if the relationship is one of friendship rather than domination (547c), she ought to be in a position to look down on them as inferior (*kataphronein*, 556c–d).

8. This does not yet adequately differentiate ruling as a craft. "Each craft," says Socrates, "provides us with a particular benefit different from the others" (346a). Helmsmen, shepherds, doctors, and trainers also take care of their subjects, over whom they too are superior in some respect. What then is the distinctive benefit conferred by rulers on the ruled? The clue is in the language Socrates uses to describe those who rule well. He tells us that in a well-governed city the ruled will think of their rulers neither as "masters" (*despotai*) nor even as "rulers" (*archontes*) but rather as "preservers" (*sōtēres*; 463a). And as everybody knows, those true rulers are also called *guardians* (*phulakes*).

9. The word "guardian" is liable to slip by as if it were simply Platonese for "ruler." But there is a substantive claim packed into the idea that rulers are guardians, namely that the benefit conferred by ruling is in the first instance preventive or prophylactic: a ruler preserves her subjects in the face of their tendency to corruption or dissolution. This makes sense against the background of Plato's ontology, wherein (a) for something to truly exist is for it to be in its best possible condition; (b) goodness is prior to badness, such that badness is always a falling away from goodness; and (c) "everything that comes-to-be must decay" (546a). Given this ontology, what looks like a purely negative task—preservation—is in fact often positive, since to preserve something in its full being can involve restoring it to its best condition. The obvious comparison would be medicine, whose goal is to preserve the body's health, whether by preventing disease or by counteracting it. The notion of guardianship therefore seems to place the ruler alongside the shepherd and the doctor as a steward of nature rather than a creator of artefacts.

10. What then distinguishes the doctor from the ruler, given that both aim to preserve human subjects? If the doctor is the steward of the body, the ruler, it seems, must be the steward of the soul. There is plenty of evidence for this proposition. Some is direct, as when we hear that the ruler is a "craftsman of temperance, justice, and the whole of citizenly virtue" (500d–501c), or that "there is [nothing] better for a city than that the best possible men and women should come to exist in it" (456e), or that a judge "rules a soul with a soul" (409a).[10] The rest depends on a reading of the whole dialogue.

11. When the guardians are first introduced, in Book II, it is because the city in words has become luxurious, unhealthy, feverish. In the grip of *pleonexia*, desiring more and more, surrendering itself to the "endless acquisition of money" and the endless pursuit of unnecessary pleasures, conflict with neighboring cities becomes inevitable, especially to the degree that those cities are in the same condition. The city therefore needs an army to protect its interests, and for that army to be as strong as possible it needs to be composed of professionals, whom Socrates calls guardians (372e–374d). It is natural to infer that these guardians will tackle not only that which threatens the city from the outside but also that which impels the city to butt up against that threat from the inside, namely *pleonexia*. After all, if the first city had no need for soldiers or rulers, it was because it was, as Glaucon puts it, a "city for pigs" (372d)—that is, a city for creatures whose desires will naturally tend to be more or less in tune with their environment. The human psyche is not like that. Our desires are bound up with our imagination, which means that they are potentially boundless.[11] To get them in tune with the world

---

10. Changing "popular" to "citizenly" in the translation of *dēmotikēs aretēs* (500d). For further evidence that Plato conceives of the true ruler as a steward of the soul, see *Gorgias*, 464b–c.

11. As Myles Burnyeat points out, we should not be misled by our own culture's stereotype of pigs as greedy. "For the ancient Greeks, the pig was an emblem rather of ignorance." See "Culture and Society in Plato's *Republic*," 231. Translated to humans, the ignorance in question would be bliss. "They'll enjoy sex with one another but bear no more children than their resources allow, lest they fall into either poverty or war" (372b–c). For a rewarding treatment of humanity's "expulsion from the garden," see Korsgaard, *Self-Constitution*, chap. 6.

requires considerable work. And that is why statecraft requires soul-craft and vice versa.

12. To put it another way: the city comes into being, as Socrates puts it, "because none of us is individually self-sufficient, but each has many needs he cannot satisfy" (369b). The most obvious of these needs are those required for staying alive—food, shelter, clothes, medicine—and then come other goods, like relishes. But as the transition to the second city suggests, and the rest of the *Republic* argues at length, the most important need with respect to which we depend on the city is psychic health.[12] For although the city first comes into existence for the sake of mere life, it ultimately exists for the sake of the good life as we conceive it—and in any given city there will be some who conceive of the good life in ways that threaten the city's existence.[13] "The source of the greatest evils for cities and the individuals in them" is therefore citizens who have "overstepped the limits of their necessary desires" (373d–e). *Pleonexia* must be guarded against not only in order to preserve the city from the ravages of internal and external strife but also to preserve the souls of the citizenry in the best possible condition. These two ambitions are related. The final goal of the ruler is to maintain the souls of her subjects in good condition, but this can be achieved only indirectly, through maintaining a sociocultural environment that is maximally conducive to human flourishing—and that in turn requires maintaining the city in its best possible condition.

13. To sum up, then, the true ruler is figured as a kind of soul-doctor whose remedies involve fostering a healthy psychic environment. Since this environment is at least partly dependent on political decisions, rulers will naturally want to exercise political power. We can already see, however, that there is no a priori reason to deny the possibility of rulers operating without holding office, since not

---

12. On the relationship between polis formation and soul formation, see Jonathan Lear, "Inside and Outside the *Republic*."

13. The use of Aristotelian language to describe the transition comes from Myles Burnyeat, who also points out that Plato signals the transition to a society marked by conceptions of the good life by a series of choices over the uses of couches and tables, which are associated with symposia and hence with cultural reproduction through poetry. See Burnyeat, "Culture and Society in Plato's *Republic*," 232–236.

all soul shaping must be achieved through political institutions. When Socrates says in Book IX that parents rule their children, he does not mean to invoke a new sense of rule—the goal of parental rule, he insists, is exactly the same as the goal of law, namely to shape its subjects' souls in such a way that they are ruled by reason (590c–591a).[14] We will explore the possibilities of ruling without holding office in Chapter 4, but for now let us focus on political rule in the most obvious sense. The immediate question concerns the relationship between guarding the city and engaging in philosophical inquiry. Why does Socrates claim, echoing Thrasymachus's invocation of the "precise sense," that "those who are to be made our guardians in the most exact [akribestatos] sense of the term must be philosophers" (503b)?

§2 Guarding Oneself

14. "Until philosophers rule as kings in cities or those who are now called kings and leading men genuinely and adequately philosophize . . . cities will have no rest from evils," declares Socrates in Book V (473c–d). We can now see that this refers back to the passage on *pleonexia* from Book II in which "the source of the greatest evils for cities and the individuals within them" is said to be those who have "overstepped the limits of their necessary desires" (373d–e). Guarding the city involves guarding it against *pleonexia*. But why does that require philosophy?

15. The answer emerges if we attend to Book III, where the fully fledged guardians (*phulakes panteleis*) are separated from the auxiliaries (*epikouroi*), whose function is to "support the convictions [dogmata]" of their fully fledged counterparts (414b; cf. 428d). What makes the one group truer guardians than the other is said to be their ability to guard the city against threats that come from within as well as without:

---

14. Compare also 501a, where Socrates imagines a philosophical ruler agreeing to "take either a private individual or a city in hand."

> Then wouldn't it really be most correct to call these people complete guardians—the ones who guard against external enemies and internal friends, so that the former will lack the power, and the latter the desire, to do any evil *[kakourgein]*; but to call the young people to whom we were referring as guardians just now *auxiliaries* and supporters of the guardians' convictions? (414a–b)

Complete guardians, then, are those with the capacity to guard against "internal friends" developing the desire to harm the city. Soon it becomes clear that these dangerous friends are not those who might be tempted to rebel, as one might expect, but rather the rulers themselves, who risk becoming "hostile masters" (*despotai echthroi*) of the other citizens instead of their allies (*summachoi*). The key, as before, is *pleonexia*. True guardians must be able to guard themselves against the expansion of desire; to maintain their subjects' souls in good condition, then, they must first maintain their own (417a–b).

16. Institutions can go some way toward promoting this.[15] Since the primary vector of *pleonexia* is money, we need arrangements that prevent guardians from acquiring private property and thereby turning themselves into "household managers and farmers" (417a).[16] But institutions are not self-standing. They in turn require guarding; rules need to be enforced and defended. This threatens an infinite regress: guardians need to be guarded by institutions that need to be guarded by guardians who need to be guarded by institutions, and so on. The only way out is to find a self-guarding guardian.[17] And it is precisely this capacity for self-guarding that first distinguishes the complete guardian from the auxiliary.[18] So the question now becomes

---

15. For more on this, see Thakkar, "Moneymakers and Craftsmen."

16. See Finley, *Ancient Economy*, 35–39, for a sense of how exceptional Plato's view of wealth was within the ancient world.

17. The notion of self-guarding is first introduced by Adeimantus in his Book II challenge to Socrates: "If all of you had . . . tried to persuade us from our earliest youth, we would not now be guarding against one another's injustice, but each would be his best guardian, afraid that by doing injustice he would be living on intimate terms with the worst thing possible" (367a).

18. It is worth noting that when Socrates introduces the communistic prohibitions, he describes their function as being to "guard against our auxiliaries . . . becoming

what it would mean to guard oneself, and what that has to do with philosophy.

17. There seem to be two ways in which philosophy can help a guardian guard herself: as a form of desire and as a form of cognition. Genuine rule requires rulers to benefit their subjects rather than to exploit them. The best way to ensure this, Socrates suggests, is to appoint as rulers only those who have no desire for the kind of goods to be gained from exploitation—those whose wealth consists in leading a good and rational life (521a–b). Philosophy fits the bill, since those who organize their lives around the desire for wisdom will have little use for material wealth. But this explanation cannot be sufficient, since those who devote their lives to astronomy or geometry will be in much the same situation.[19] What distinguishes philosophy from astronomy and geometry is obviously the mode of cognition that it represents, so presumably this must also feed into the capacity for self-guarding.

18. That this is so becomes clear if we consider the series of tests that Socrates proposes as a way of finding those who will always maintain the conviction (dogma) that whatever is best for the city is also best for them (412d). Since no one voluntarily gives up a belief they take to be true, Socrates posits, the threat must consist in their being involuntarily deprived of it. He divides this threat into three kinds: theft, sorcery, and force.[20] These labels sound silly—Socrates jokes that he is "making himself as clear as a tragic poet" (413b)—but

---

savage masters rather than gentle allies" (416b). Shortly afterward, Glaucon questions whether the arrangements are fair to the auxiliaries (419a–420a). It seems reasonable to infer that the auxiliaries are their primary target. This is not to say that they will not also apply to complete guardians—they definitely do, as we see in Book V (464d)—but this should be understood as a fail-safe against epistemological misfire, since it is always possible that an incomplete guardian will slip through the net. Logically speaking, the fact remains that the system for restricting pleonexia will work only if the chain terminates in a self-guarding guardian.

19. At 521b Socrates does claim that there is no other life "that looks down on [kataphronein] political offices besides that of true philosophy," but unlike Glaucon, I see no reason to accept this assertion without further argument.

20. Using the Reeve translation, but changing "compulsion" to "force" since the verb is biasdō, and "compulsion" might suggest the passage where philosophers are "compelled" to return to the cave (with the verb being anagkasdō or prosanagkasdō—see 520a, 521b), a compulsion that involves reason rather than violence.

it is worth paying attention to the categories they denote. Force is the simplest: it refers to cases where a guardian loses her conviction because she is unable to withstand physical suffering. To test for this susceptibility, we must subject candidate guardians to labors, pains, and contests, and to develop their resistance we need physical education. Sorcery refers to cases where the guardian gives up her conviction because she is "charmed by pleasure or terrified by fear." The test for this would be to see whether candidate guardians remain graceful, rhythmical, and harmonious when confronted with fear and pleasure, and to develop their resistance we need musical education. Theft refers to cases where a guardian loses her conviction either because of time (forgetfulness) or because of argument (persuasion). To test for this propensity, we would need to put our cadets in situations where they would be most likely to forget their conviction or be deceived out of it (413b–e). At this stage of the dialogue Socrates does not take up the question of how Kallipolis might generate individuals capable of resisting forgetfulness or persuasion. But the answer seems clear enough. Just as we could guard against force through physical education and against sorcery through musical education, so it would seem that we could guard against theft through education in dialectic—or, to call it by its other name, philosophy (534b–e).

19. For the only way to reliably guard against forgetting a true belief or being persuaded against it would be to understand why that belief should be thought true, and hence to be able to reconstruct the argument in favor of it. This is why in Book X Socrates tells Glaucon to use the argument against poetry as a form of spiritual exercise to preserve his psychic constitution: "Whenever we listen to [such poetry], we'll repeat the argument [*logos*] we have just now put forward like an incantation so as to preserve ourselves from slipping back into that childish passion" (608a).[21] It is also why Socrates

---

21. Stephen Halliwell points out that the *Phaedo* speaks of the need for a myth to be "repeated as incantation" (114d) and therefore interprets the notion of an incantation "as a nonepistemic, partly self-persuasive device, used by Orphics, among others, for dealing with recurrent fears or problems," citing Euripides, *Cyclops* 464, as an example of such an incantation. I see no reason to dispute that this is what "to incant" (*epaidein*) usually connotes, but in the passage just quoted, what is being repeated as incantation

says in Book VIII that "reason *[logos]* . . . mixed with music and poetry . . . alone dwells within the person who possesses it as the lifelong preserver *[sōtēr]* of his virtue" (549b), and that "knowledge, fine ways of living, and true arguments . . . are the best watchmen *[phrouroi]* and guardians *[phulakes]* of the thoughts of those men whom the gods love" (560b). The use of the terms "preserver," "watchmen," and "guardians" is by no means accidental: it clearly picks up Book III's discussion of internal guardians.

20. To tie everything together: the ultimate aim of ruling is soul-craft, but soulcraft requires statecraft; the only guardian who can truly guard the city is one who can guard herself; to guard oneself requires knowing that one's conviction concerning the relationship between the individual and collective good is not simply dogma but actually true; and this requires dialectic, or philosophy. So the complete guardian must be a philosopher.

21. The nature of the good life is, of course, the question that drives the *Republic* as a whole.[22] The following interpretive hypothesis therefore suggests itself: that Plato intends the *Republic* itself to model the kind of inquiry that a true guardian might engage in on a regular basis by way of securing herself as a guardian, justifying from scratch the belief that both psychic and political justice are beneficial for more than their simulator-accessible consequences.[23] If Plato's argument is on the right track, the guardian's process of reconstruction will mirror the text's. Convictions regarding justice will be reconstructed on the basis of an analogy between city and soul and a consideration of their mutual dependence, for example. This hypothesis certainly goes against the reading of true understanding

---

is an argument, a *logos*, and it is hard to regard argument as nonepistemic. It seems rather that Plato has in mind a form of rational spiritual exercise, as at the start of Book IX when Socrates suggests that the healthy and temperate person will go to sleep every night only after he "rouses his rational part and feasts it on fine arguments and speculations" so that it can "get on with its investigations, to yearn after and perceive something, it knows not what, whether it is past, present, or future" (571d–572a). See Halliwell, "Life-and-Death Journey of the Soul," 470–471.

22. One might protest that the nature of justice is the driving question, but at 347e and 352d in Book I Socrates clearly subordinates this question to the question of "how to live."

23. The notion of simulator-accessible consequences is taken from Reeve, "Glaucon's Thrasymachean Challenge," in *Blindness and Reorientation*, 61.

as a form of direct perception, but if the argument of Chapter 1 holds, true understanding is perception won only through the process of dialectical investigation of the mutual determination of parts and wholes within a cosmos whose first principle is goodness, and in my view that process is what the *Republic* is trying to model. To be sure, Plato would expect the philosopher-rulers' accounts to be significantly clearer and more accurate than his own, since they will have grown up in a better city, with correspondingly better education, and will therefore be able to take the "longer road" in thinking about the virtues (504b)—the road that requires us to use goodness as a first principle from which to grasp the form of each thing without depending on images (511b–c). But to the best of Plato's knowledge, at least, the basic lineaments of this investigation will already have been sketched by Socrates and his interlocutors.

§3 Guarding the City

22. We have seen that if guardians are to be trusted to act on behalf of the city, they must be able to reconstruct their convictions regarding the rationality of such action, and I have suggested that to the best of Plato's knowledge, this reconstruction will follow the lines of the *Republic* itself. I will now argue that the contribution of philosophy goes beyond enabling rulers to stick to their task—it also enables them to do that task well. But it does so in much the same way as before.

23. In Book VI Socrates qualifies the ruler of Kallipolis as a "craftsman of temperance, justice, and the whole of citizenly virtue" (*dēmotikē aretē*) who would "mix and blend the various pursuits [*epitēdeumata*] in the city until they produced . . . characters for human beings that the gods would love as much as possible" (500d; 501b–c). What it means to "mix and blend pursuits," I want to suggest, is to regulate the division of labor in the city—a task that goes well beyond maintaining the tripartite class division. In Books IV and V we hear of each citizen's being assigned to the pursuit that naturally suits her (423d; 453e–457c); Socrates gives the examples of medicine, music, carpentry, and shoemaking, and the suggestion is of an allotment of every single craft and pursuit relevant to the

organization *(kataskeuē)* or management *(dioikēsis)* of the city (455a; 454c–d; 455d).[24]

24. One might wonder what regulating the division of labor has to do with soulcraft. The answer is partly that in Plato's view habits of action structure the soul profoundly. Just as healthy actions engender health and unhealthy ones disease, for instance, so just actions engender justice and unjust ones injustice; more generally, "fine pursuits *[epitēdeumata]* lead to the possession of virtue, shameful ones to vice" (444b–e). These statements are crucial to Socrates' response to Glaucon's "why-be-just" challenge, but they might also be thought crucial to the political theory that he constructs along the way. Just as the desires of Book IX's tyrant are inflamed not only by his "bad associates" *(kakē homilia)* but also by his "habits" or "ways" *(tropoi)*, deepening his psychic disintegration, so in Kallipolis patterns of action will shape the patterns of soul, only in the opposite direction: each person "will become not many but one" as a result of "doing the one work that is his own" on a daily basis (574c–575a; 423d). To assign people to certain jobs is therefore to shape their souls in important ways. But it is also true, as Marx realized, that in transforming nature through our productive activities, we constitute a world that shapes us in turn.[25] In assigning people to different tasks, guardians therefore need to ensure not only that citizens carry out tasks appropriate to their nature, but also that their combined efforts coalesce into the production of a sociocultural environment maximally conducive to human flourishing. This is why Socrates tells us in Book II that we will have to supervise not only all the poets in the city but also "all the other craftsmen":

> [Mustn't] we look for craftsmen who are naturally capable of pursuing what is fine and graceful in their work, so that our young people will live in a healthy place and be benefited on all

---

24. I therefore reject Alan Ryan's assertion that "Plato scarcely discusses work in *Republic*." See Ryan, *On Politics*, 1:33. On carpentry, see Penner, "Forms in the *Republic*," 242–246.

25. See Marx, *Economic and Philosophical Manuscripts of 1844*, in Tucker, ed., *The Marx-Engels Reader*, 85: "*just as* society itself produces *man as man*, so is society produced by him" (cf. 89–93).

sides as the influence exerted by those fine works affects their eyes and ears like a healthy breeze from wholesome regions, and imperceptibly guides them from earliest childhood into being similar to, friendly toward, and concordant with the beauty of reason? (401c–d)

In Kallipolis, then, the rulers will pay attention to what is produced just as much as who is producing it—for both affect citizens' souls, and the true ruler is a steward of those souls.

25. I will expand on this point in Chapter 3, but for now the question is why overseeing the division of labor would amount to guarding the city. We have seen how it might amount to guarding souls, but Plato does not reduce the city to its citizens. What, then, does overseeing the division of labor have to do with preserving the city in the face of its tendency to corruption or dissolution? Plato cares deeply about calling things by their right names. We are repeatedly told that we should call things by the same name only if they are like each other in the relevant respect, and even (as we will see in Chapter 3) that such correct usage would be a feature of the ideal city. If Socrates gives the same name to the military defense of the city and to the mixing and blending of pursuits in the city, it must be because he thinks they are in essence the same task. The defense of the city must somehow find its full realization in the regulation of the city's division of labor.

26. In this connection it is worth thinking once again about the concept of guarding. In English the notion involves not only maintaining something in existence or good condition but also watching over it. Textually speaking, that seems to be true of Plato's usage as well. For all that he cares about calling things by their right names, he is also concerned to make his dialogue conversational, and he therefore sometimes rotates between a set of roughly similar terms to denote the same underlying phenomenon. The semantic field around the verb "to guard" (*phulakein*) in the *Republic* includes variants of verbs such as *phrourein, episkopein, epistatein,* and *skeptomai,* all of which have to do with supervision in the literal sense—watching over, watching out for, overseeing, and looking into. Meanwhile, the potential failure of a guardian is figured not only through concepts of

corruption and dissolution but also through words that connote missing something—the image of things slipping by without our noticing recurs time and again throughout the *Republic*, sometimes in connection with the interlocutors but just as often in connection with the rulers.[26] Recognizing this allows us to formulate a new question concerning guardianship: in preserving the city, what exactly are the guardians watching over, and what exactly are they watching out for?

27. The answer is that the guardians must supervise, oversee, and look out for the city in the face of threats to its existence. But what are these threats? What I want to suggest is that alongside the obvious threats, like famine or invasion, there are others that would escape the notice of nonphilosophers. Auxiliaries, selected for the spirited nature that makes them love what they consider to be their own (375b–376a), would most likely take their task to be defending their population and territory. But philosophers, I argue, would sometimes instruct them otherwise.

28. In Book II of his *Politics*, Aristotle asks after the essence of the city: "What exactly is the principle on which we ought to pronounce a city to be the same city as it was before, or not the same but a different city?"[27] This is a question concerning social ontology, but that does not make it academic. Suppose a tyrant makes a treaty on behalf of his city but is subsequently deposed—can the next rulers claim that it was a different city that signed the treaty? The answer, Aristotle points out, will depend on the criteria of identity for a city over time. In the background is one of the basic questions of metaphysics: how is change possible? Let X be a particular entity. If X changes into Y, X has gone out of existence. For us to say that X is changed but still remains, say, as X^1, there needs to be some X-ness that persists through the change, and this will be what makes the thing an X in the first place, its essence or being or *ousia*.[28] The essence of X is its principle of identity, that which makes it the thing it is and not some

---

26. See, e.g., 401c–d, 413b, 421e, 424b–d, 432d–e, 449c, 457e, 486a, 536a, 539b. Note also the connection between something's escaping our notice (the verb being *lanthanō*) and our forgetting it (the verb being *epilanthanomai*).

27. Aristotle, *Politics* 1276a17; cf. 1274b32.

28. It is, of course, possible to deny the antecedent, that is, to assert that we cannot make sense of change in the relevant sense. It is also possible to hold that any essence

other thing. This identity can be qualitative: here the question would be what makes a city a city rather than some other kind of association or a mere heap of people. It can also be numerical: here the question would be what makes a city the particular city that it is, as opposed to some different city. And since a principle of identity is also a principle of differentiation, it must also be a principle of unity: here the question would be what makes the city one thing and not multiple things. This last question is Aristotle's focus when he asks, "Suppose a set of men inhabit the same place, in what circumstances are we to consider their city to be a single city?"[29] The answer, he claims, is neither population (since some can die and others can be born without the city losing its unity) nor territory (since the entire Peloponnese could be walled around and still not be one state) but rather the constitution.

> For inasmuch as a city is a kind of partnership [koinonia], and is in fact a partnership of citizens in a government, when the form [eidos] of the government has been altered and is different it would appear to follow that the city is no longer the same city, just as we say that a chorus which on one occasion acts a comedy and on another a tragedy is a different chorus although it is often composed of the same persons, and similarly with any other common whole [koinonia] or composite structure [sunthesis] we say it is different if the form [eidos] of its structure [sunthesis] is different—for instance a musical tune consisting of the same notes we call a different tune if at one time it is played in the Dorian mode and at another in the Phrygian. Therefore if this is the case, it is clear that we must speak of a city as being the same city chiefly with regard to its constitution [politeia]; and it is possible for it to be called by the same or by a different designation both when its inhabitants are the same and when they are entirely different persons.[30]

---

is "merely" a feature of our concepts, as when Wittgenstein asserts that "essence is expressed in grammar" in *Philosophical Investigations*, §371.

29. Aristotle, *Politics* 1276a34.

30. Ibid., 1276b1–13; translation amended to render *polis* as "city" rather than "state."

So on Aristotle's view, that which remains the same when the city persists is the constitution: the city becomes a different city if and only if the constitution changes. The constitution is therefore the essence of the city. This is counterintuitive. Certainly it does not reflect our ordinary language, according to which it was *Athens* that became a democracy and then an oligarchy and then went back to being a democracy again.[31] Aristotle's reason for going against common sense is given in the passage just quoted. The idea is that the constitution serves as the principle of unity for the city in a very concrete way: by assigning roles and responsibilities, it binds together (or synthesizes, to stay close to the Greek) what would otherwise be a mere heap of people or associations into a common project or *koinonia*. To put it another way, the constitution actually constitutes the city—without it, there would be no city. To change the constitution is therefore to constitute a different city.

29. My suggestion is that Plato shares Aristotle's view of what makes a city a city, at least at this level of generality. To begin with, note that the Greek title of the work we have come to know as the *Republic* is in fact *Politeia*, the same word Aristotle uses for "constitution." Plato's *Republic* should therefore really be known as Plato's *Constitution*. Moreover, in Book IV Socrates himself raises the proto-Aristotelian question of what makes a city one city as opposed to two cities or a mere heap. Like Aristotle, Socrates suggests that a city's metaphysical identity depends on the degree to which it is bound together as one. If there are financial or geographical cleavages, for instance, or if the city's territory is too large, the city will not be one city at all (422e–423c). The project of outlining Kallipolis, as undertaken by Socrates and his interlocutors, is essentially the project of outlining its constitution—not in the modern sense of a written constitution that exhaustively determines political offices, rights, and duties, but in the sense of the general principles according to which social and political roles are to be distributed.[32] Given that the aim

---

31. See Kripke's account of proper names as "rigid designators" that designate the same object in every possible world, *Naming and Necessity*, 48–49.

32. Although there are important differences, it might help to think of this ur-constitution by analogy with what John Rawls calls "the basic structure of society," which precedes any formal constitution and which he describes as "the way in which

of the constitution is to synthesize a genuine whole out of various parts, there is a constitutive standard by which a constitution can be judged: "The greatest good for the organization *[kataskeuē]* of the city—the one at which the legislator should aim in making the laws" is whatever "binds it together and makes it one" (462a–b). Although Socrates goes on to discuss this binding together in terms of the "sharing of pleasures and pains" (462b ff.), the "organization *[kataskeuē]* of the city" was described a few pages earlier in terms of the allotment of crafts and pursuits within the city (455a). This suggests that affective unity is merely a supplement to the underlying scheme of roles and functions that should already bind the city together harmoniously. Under the right kind of constitution, citizens share a common purpose just by carrying out their roles in the division of labor.

30. If this interpretation is correct, to guard the city properly is to supervise and preserve its structure, where that implies supervising and preserving its division of labor (social and political as well as economic). This leads to counterintuitive conclusions: a leader who protects her population at the expense of the constitution—by cutting a deal that turns her city into a client state, say, or by promising the wealthy political favors in return for military hardware—cannot be said to be guarding her city. And in certain circumstances the best way to preserve a city might be to abandon its existing territory, as Herodotus reports the Phocaeans doing.[33]

31. In the case of Kallipolis, preserving the constitution will require special effort. No constitution is self-actualizing; a constitution has actuality only to the degree that its principles are actually observed, and this requires that they be applied to particular cases. This involves not only initial interpretation but also, as the tide of time brings wave after wave of events, continual reinterpretation. We do not preserve the constitution by allowing a particular actualization of its principles to ossify regardless of circumstances; we distort it. Yet injudicious reinterpretations will also create distortion. And since

---

the major social institutions distribute fundamental rights and duties and determine the division of advantages from social cooperation." Rawls, *Theory of Justice*, 7. See also Lane, "Founding as Legislating."

33. Herodotus, *Histories* 1.164–168; see also Strabo, *Geography* 6.1.1.

to change the constitution is to constitute a different city, to distort the constitution may even cause the city to go out of existence (whether or not anyone recognizes that fact). We may therefore say that if the city is to be perpetuated, its constitution must be continually and appropriately reactualized, and that this is the task of those who guard it. But whereas in an oligarchy it might not be very difficult to make sure that the constitution is adequately actualized in any given circumstance—the rulers might just need to keep an eye on things like inflation to make sure that the bar for holding office is not set too low—in Kallipolis the rulers will have to ensure not only that every citizen is performing her allotted role, but also that the allotment is itself correct, both in the sense that everyone has been assigned to the job for which they are best suited and in the sense that the scheme of labor is tailored to genuine social needs, including the need for a healthy psychic environment.

32. Guardians will therefore need practical wisdom (*phronēsis*) in Aristotle's sense, including the capacity to read the situation correctly; this is presumably why they must have no less experience than other candidate rulers, going off to war at an early age and so on (466e–467e, 484e, 537a). But Socrates suggests that the reason why guardians need to accurately discern particulars is so that they can give orders that either conform with the laws given by the lawgivers or imitate them in cases where discretion is required (458c; cf. 412a–b). The invocation of imitation provides an important clue regarding the nature of rule. For the core critique of poetic imitators in Book X is that they imitate without knowing "in what way [the imitated] thing is good or bad" (602b). If the ruler's imitation of the lawgiver is to escape this criticism, we can conclude, it must be conducted in light of an understanding of why some laws are good and others bad.

§4 Ruling as Refounding

33. How might a guardian come to understand the goodness of what the lawgivers have established? My hypothesis is that she would have to master the thought processes that animated the lawgivers, and that this would once again involve engaging in the same activity as Socrates and his interlocutors, namely ideal theory. Immediate

support comes from Book VI, where Socrates says that "there must always be some people in the city who have a rational account *[logos]* of the constitution, the same one that guided you, the lawgiver, when you made the laws" (497c–d). Further support comes from thinking through what that rational account amounted to and how it might bear on guarding the city.

34. The first thing Socrates says to get the founding started is this: "Well, then, a city comes to exist, I believe, because none of us is individually self-sufficient *[autarchēs]*, but each has many needs he cannot satisfy. Or do you think that a city is founded on some other principle?" (369b). This statement inaugurates the positive project of the *Republic*, its turn away from *aporia* to the construction of an ideal, and it does so in terms of final causality. The city exists in order to remedy our lack of self-sufficiency. This is its *archē*, its principle or source.

35. With this principle in place, we can now stand back and watch the city develop before our eyes: out of mutual need, "many people gather in a single place to live together as partners *[koinōnoi]* and helpers *[boēthoi]*" (369c)—and what they form is a *sunoikia*, literally a composite household. The city will develop up to the point where it allows basic human needs to be satisfied; that is its *telos* (objective) and hence its standard of completion. In designing the city we therefore need to work out what those needs are and what would satisfy them. In order to reproduce ourselves we need food, shelter, clothes, shoes, and medical care, and in order to provide these each must "contribute his own work for the common use of all" rather than keeping himself to himself (369e–370a). As soon as labor is considered collective in this way, it becomes natural to institute a division of tasks; given the importance of being able to devote one's full attention to a craft so as to be able to carry out each action at exactly the right moment (the *kairos*), as well as the fact that "each of us differs somewhat in nature from the others, one being suited to one task, another to another," it makes sense to specialize (370a–b). To meet our basic needs, we therefore need a farmer, a builder, a weaver, a cobbler, and a doctor. But the premise behind the division of labor is a principle of efficiency—"more plentiful and better-quality goods are more easily produced"—and this principle soon leads to a further expansion of the city, since production will obviously be more

efficient if each core worker can rely on tools and raw materials produced and harvested by others (370c–e). This necessitates the introduction of carpenters, metalworkers, cowherds, and shepherds, as well as the prerequisites for trade: merchants, retailers, marketplaces, and surplus production. Last, just as retailers are those "whose bodies are weakest and who aren't fit to do any other work," so there will be wage laborers "whose minds alone wouldn't qualify them for membership in our society but whose bodies are strong enough for labour [*ponos*]" (371c–371e).[34] With this, says Socrates, the city is complete *(teleios)*—it has reached its *telos*, its objective.

36. So Socrates' method for founding a city in thought is as follows: he begins by specifying its *archē*, or basic principle, as a particular end or final cause; he then works out which tasks must be fulfilled in order to achieve that end; on that basis he articulates the city into discrete parts, each with its own function; and then he repeats the process to see whether the circle needs to expand at any point. The first expansion takes place when he realizes that craftsmen should be provided with tools and raw materials for the sake of efficiency. The second comes when Glaucon pushes him on the *archē* itself, that is, on the kinds of needs that are at issue when we speak of a city coming into existence to satisfy needs that we cannot satisfy by ourselves. If citizens have psychic needs as well as material needs, they will also need guardians (§1). It would seem, then, that to found a city in thought requires thinking in terms of form and function with respect to both city and soul—and this kind of thinking, as we saw in Chapter 1, is precisely the distinguishing feature of philosophers.

37. My hypothesis is that guarding a city requires the same thought process as founding one. The guiding thought for guardians will be that the city comes into existence to satisfy the needs of individuals, and that in order for it to achieve its goal, those individuals need to work for it. Citizens must therefore share a common project—the welfare of the city—articulated into different roles, such as farming or medicine, which they will have to perform according to their abil-

---

34. So described, wage labor sounds a lot like slavery, which is mentioned a few times in the *Republic*; on the relationship between the two, see Finley, *Ancient Economy*, especially 63–84.

ities. Ruling is the craft of regulating this common project so that form is tailored to function: the parts of the city must coalesce into a coherent whole whose activity ensures that each citizen leads the best life possible; and this in turn requires ensuring that the parts of the soul cohere to the extent that nature will allow.[35] Socrates' engineering of an ideal city in which the parts are organized for the benefit of the whole and the whole is organized for the benefit of the parts therefore serves as a model for those regulating a real city. Just as he proposes that a society needs first food, shelter, clothes, shoes, and medical care, then tools, raw materials, and trading facilities, and finally guardianship, so guardians will decide what needs to be produced on the basis of an assessment of the nature of the good life and the needs of the present situation. Their inquiries might take the form of imagining a world without a certain item and then asking whether its introduction would serve a genuine need. As we will see in Chapter 3, they might instruct carpenters on the basis of an inquiry into whether a flourishing culture requires couches, and if so, what kind of couches they ought to be, given that different kinds of couches conduce to different kinds of activity (from poetry to philosophy).[36] If this is right, then ruling a city and founding a city involve one and the same thought process. Ruling, we might say, is a matter of continual refounding. And that means that rulers need to engage in ideal theory.

38. To make this clearer with an analogy, we might say that Plato seems to conceive of the city as something like a team. There are many kinds of team, from obvious cases like soccer clubs to less obvious ones like academic seminars. Let us take the intuitive example of soccer. Suppose each player wants glory. The only way for a player to get glory is to benefit the team, and the team's good is scoring more goals than the opposition. There are different tasks for each player, but every action of every player (insofar as she is doing her

---

35. On the notion that the soul has a function, see 353d–e; the question of the form of the soul is taken up in Book IV. For discussion, see §6 of Chapter 1.

36. See Burnyeat, "Culture and Society in Plato's *Republic*," 245–246. My view implies that the ultimate "user" in Book X's picture of crafts, the one who "gives instructions about good and bad [products]," is the philosopher-king acting on behalf of the city (601c–602a). Again, this will be discussed in Chapter 3.

job) aims at the team's good. The "natural" constitution for such a team—where constitution means, as before, the principle according to which roles are allocated—will involve assigning players to the positions in which they are most capable of benefiting the team at a given moment.[37] Each role carries with it constitutive standards of success and hence of potential excellence. An excellent goalkeeper, for instance, catches or stops the ball reliably, distributes the ball accurately, and marshals the defense commandingly. To be excellent at her task, she needs to stick to it: she must not wander far from her goal under delusions of outfield genius, for instance. What it is for a team to be a real team, as opposed to a mere heap of individuals chasing a ball, is for each player to stick to her task; if she sticks to her task, she will be playing with the team in mind regardless of her actual mental processes.[38] If eleven players in the same colors do that, they will be a team, no matter how little talent they have.[39]

39. Note that two distinct kinds of excellence have suggested themselves here: one specific to a particular position (e.g., the excellence of a goalkeeper) and one that applies to every player, namely sticking to one's task and thereby playing for the team. The latter is what Plato might call the virtue of justice: the generic excellence of any part in a constituted whole.[40] The word "virtue" is not being used in

---

37. We can imagine other constitutions, such as a gerontocratic one whereby the oldest player gets to pick her position first and so on down the chain, or an oligarchic one whereby the winner of an auction gets to pick first. In the natural constitution, as Aryeh Kosman puts it, there is "a quite general principle of a proper agreement between being and acting, or more precisely, between dispositional and active being: between the way things *are* and what it is that they are busy at work *being*." See Kosman, "Justice and Virtue," 129.

38. The claim is not that sticking to a goal has no effect on one's mental processes, or that it is somehow independent of them, but rather that to assess whether someone is playing with the team in mind requires reference only to those beliefs and desires that refer to the performance of her own task.

39. They would also count as a team even if their roles were for some reason directed at the "wrong" end, such as aesthetic pleasure as opposed to winning. This comes out in Book I's discussion of the necessity of justice even among a band of robbers or thieves with a common unjust purpose (351c).

40. This interpretation of justice might seem to be contradicted by Socrates' remark that justice "isn't concerned with someone's doing his own externally, but with what is inside him, with what is truly himself and his own" (443c–d). Certainly justice is in the first instance the property of wholes rather than their parts, such that it applies to cities and souls rather than to citizens and parts of the soul. But I believe we

a moralizing sense: the point is not to assess quality of will for the sake of dishing out praise and blame. Rather, both specific and generic virtues bring about the good of the team by enabling its members to do their work.[41] But they cannot do this unless the roles are well distributed. If the roles are organized so that teammates who stick to their task only end up getting in each other's way, or if they cohere around the wrong goal—maximizing ball possession, say, rather than goal-scoring opportunities—then neither generic nor particular excellences will bring about the good of the whole (or, therefore, that of the parts).

40. In order to prevent such deformation, teams need conscious regulation. This makes them different from natural entities such as horses. A horse may need a veterinarian from time to time, but (barring special circumstances) the veterinarian's job is to restore it to its natural homeostasis; when that is done, the horse can manage by itself. Teams, by contrast, do not naturally tend to fall into a happy equilibrium, all other things being equal. They typically require constant supervision. A soccer team, for instance, needs a manager, someone who looks after its organization on a continual basis. And whereas the articulation of a horse into its organs, each with its own characteristic activity, is given by nature, the articulation of a team into specific roles is always to some extent the product of design. The work of a soccer manager therefore involves more than stewardship. To maintain her team in good condition, she must engage in team building. So although a team is composed of living creatures, it can only ever be an artefact. Management is necessarily productive *poiēsis*.[42]

---

can also speak of justice in the political sense, by analogy with the "political courage" mentioned at 430c, insofar as we are referring to the individual aspect of "everyone's doing his own work" in the city (433a–b; 433e–434c). A just citizen is someone who does his own work in the city; a just person is someone whose soul is well ordered. For an account of the relationship between psychological justice and being a just citizen, see Kosman, "Justice and Virtue," 125.

41. As Socrates puts it in Book I, it is *by means of* their virtue that things perform their functions well (353c); at 351d–e justice is said to *cause* friendship.

42. One might object that there is another possibility, that of spontaneous order or equilibrium. But Plato's point seems to be that human societies do not naturally slip into happy equilibrium. For more on this, see the discussion of democracy in Chapter 4.

41. The manager's excellence consists in her capacity to think about the team as a whole. We can unpack this in terms of what we might call the micro- and macroformation of the team: there is both a specific assignment of tasks—for example, whether the wingers are to play as wide forwards or as midfielders, whether they are to press the opposition fullbacks, and suchlike—and a general division of labor among ordinary players, team leaders, and the manager. The first task of a manager is to ensure that this macroformation is adhered to, since the microformation will have no actuality if individuals ignore their instructions. The manager will therefore typically ask the captain and maybe one or two senior players to watch over the others. Once the macroformation is secure, the microformation needs to be adapted so that roles are appropriately assigned, given both personnel and circumstances. Some purported tasks will not count as genuine tasks at all, since their successful execution would in no way bring about the good of the team; although it is perfectly possible for a player to spend the game off in the corner doing star jumps, that would be ruled out as a task. Other tasks would best be carried out by certain individuals, or pairs of individuals, rather than others. And the entire microformation might need to change according to the situation. Why play with four defenders if the opposition is using only one attacker? Why have a goalkeeper if the team is down 1–0 with one minute to go? The manager's role is to address such questions. But the only way to know whether a given task needs to be revised or preserved is to know why it exists in the first place. Teams have goalkeepers to reduce the chances of the opposition scoring, and the point of that is to win the game. In certain circumstances the underlying objective will be best served by not having a goalkeeper at all. We can therefore characterize the specific excellence of a soccer manager as consisting in an ability to discern the particulars of a given situation combined with an ability to judge how a team's structure (or form) might best bring about its goal (or function). The first ability seems to correlate with practical wisdom (*phronēsis*) in Aristotle's sense, the second with what Plato calls wisdom (*sophia*)—for as Socrates tells us, *sophia* is a virtue properly attributed to those with an understanding (*epistēmē*) that

enables them to judge what is good for their object as a whole, in terms of its internal and external relations (428b–e).

42. In the passage about wisdom, Socrates is of course speaking of cities rather than teams. But it is not hard to see the parallel between cities and teams, at least on Plato's account of cities. On the macro level a city is said to have three elements, each with its particular virtue.[43] There is also one virtue that applies to each element, the master virtue that enables the city to be one city as opposed to a mere heap of individuals or two cities (the rich and the poor)—namely justice in the political sense.[44] This macroconstitution then manifests itself in the city's microconstitution, its specific division of labor, which can and should be altered according to circumstances. On reflection it may become clear that the task of a poet or a doctor has been misunderstood, or that times have changed, or that change is only apparent and the existing understanding needs defending. The way to decide is to combine accurate perception of the particulars of a situation with reflection on why we have poets or doctors at all, that is, what they are for. And this will call for someone with both *phronēsis* and *sophia*.[45]

---

43. As with justice, there is certainly a complication here in that Socrates declares temperance to be a property of the whole rather than of any given part (431e–432b). But this is because it consists in an "agreement between the naturally worse and the naturally better as to which of the two is to rule," and if we assume that each part has the propensity to want to rule, then clearly the burden is chiefly on the subordinate part to accept its place. I therefore argue that although temperance is a virtue that applies to all parts of the city, as well as to the city as a whole, it is nonetheless the distinctive virtue of the lower part.

44. See notes 40 and 43.

45. The claim that Plato has anything to say about shifting circumstances in the *Republic*—as opposed to the *Statesman*—might be thought controversial. But the term used in the *Statesman*'s treatment of this topic, *kairos* (the opportune moment), in fact comes up twice in the *Republic*, and both moments are crucial. The first we have already seen: Book II's argument for the division of labor, an argument that will ultimately be used to justify the existence of philosopher-kings, depends on the notion that craft work demands craftsmen capable of hitting the mark temporally and not missing the right moment (370b). The second is equally telling. It comes in Book VIII, where we are told that the decline of Kallipolis is inevitable. The surface details have to do with geometry and breeding cycles, but I take them to be metaphorical; we should remember that they come up in the context of what Socrates characterizes as a story told by the Muses "playing and jesting with us as it we were children" (545e).

43. Socrates says that the *epistēmē* that qualifies one as *sophos* in the relevant sense is knowledge "that doesn't judge about any particular matter but about the city as a whole and the maintenance of good relations, both internally and with other cities" (428c–d). When Glaucon asks for clarification, Socrates merely declares that this knowledge is called guardianship *(hē phulakikē)* and that it is possessed by complete guardians. What I have suggested is that the knowledge involved in guardianship is knowledge of how best to structure the social division of labor, and that achieving this knowledge requires holistic inquiry that goes back and forth between form and function in order to generate a picture of the best possible society. What it requires, in short, is the kind of ideal theory that Socrates models in the *Republic*.

§5 Philosophers as Rulers

44. We can now see why Plato thinks that the activity he calls ruling is intrinsically related to philosophy. Ruling in the relevant sense is not simply a matter of exercising power or holding office. It is rather the craft of maintaining other people's souls in good condition (§1). What makes philosophers particularly suited to this activity is their ability to guard their own souls in good condition, and therefore to resist the *pleonexia* that quickly turns ruling into exploitation (§2). The human psyche is shaped (both in childhood and in adulthood) by a wide range of sociocultural influences. To maintain their subjects' souls in good condition, rulers therefore need to shape the wider culture, and this requires exercising control over the social, political, and economic division of labor (§3). In Kallipolis this would be a matter of maintaining the city in good

---

The main point is that no matter how wise the rulers are, at some point "calculation together with sense perception" will fail them, and they will do something "at the wrong time" *(para kairon)* (546a–d). Logically speaking, this would have to be a permanent threat to Kallipolis in various domains, most obviously in warfare but also with respect to the division of labor. If this is correct, then Plato's choice of breeding as an example is rhetorical, motivated by his desire to emphasize the importance of nature and nurture, selection and education, to the health of the city. In any case, the overall point stands: the *Republic* has a place for the notion of hitting the mark temporally, and it is right at the center. On *kairos* in the *Statesman*, see Lane, *Method and Politics in Plato's "Statesman."*

order as opposed to creating a new order. But since cities are artefacts rather than living entities, maintaining them requires a degree
of engineering. Rulers therefore need to engage in the kind of philosophical reflection I discussed in Chapter 1, going back and forth
between particular things and true forms and then between true
forms and the interlocking structure of formal and final causes that
is goodness (§4). Even if ruling well does require political power in
the standard sense, then, it should not be conflated with personal
domination, bureaucratic administration, or practically wise decision
making along Periclean lines.[46] Every single one of its constitutive
elements is connected with philosophy, understood as the activity of
seeking knowledge of true forms in the sense described in Chapter 1.

45. This raises a potential problem, however. The claim that ruling
well requires philosophy might be thought equivalent to the claim
that philosophy is a means to ruling well. But if philosophy is merely
instrumental for ruling, philosophers would seem to be disqualified
from ruling, since true rulers must want not to rule (346e–347d).[47]
If the philosopher-ruler pursues two crafts, by contrast, she violates
the "one-man, one-job" principle. The only remaining option is that
ruling is actually for the sake of philosophy. This seems perverse at
first, but on reflection it makes sense.

46. The Platonic-Aristotelian approach to activities permits us to
go beyond the superficial marks and characteristics available to immediate perception in order to make distinctions based on *telē*.[48] A
craftsman who makes leather shoes might conceivably spend some
of her time fashioning raw materials into insoles, outsoles, heels, toe
caps, vamps, quarters, and tongues and the rest of her time preparing
the raw materials, for instance by cutting leather strips. Yet the cutting

---

46. See also Burnyeat, "Plato on Why Mathematics Is Good for the Soul," 56:
"The important task of ruling is not day-to-day decision-making, but establishing and
maintaining good structures, both institutional and psychological."

47. Allan Bloom claims that Plato uses the fact that philosophy and ruling are two
separate tasks to tip us off that he intends to portray idealism as "the most destructive
of human passions." See, e.g., Bloom, "Interpretive Essay," 407–410. In conversation
Gabriel Richardson Lear has suggested that the "one-man, one-job" objection is a
pseudoproblem, since philosophy is not a craft. That is certainly one way to go,
although it would need textual support.

48. See, e.g., Aristotle, *Nicomachean Ethics* I.1.

of leather strips and the putting together of the shoes do not necessarily count as two separate activities. Leather cutting might be a subactivity within the overall activity of shoemaking. This would be so if the *telos* of the leather cutting is shoemaking, such that the shoemaking gives the leather cutting its standards of success. On the Platonic-Aristotelian view, then, leather cutting and shoemaking can be two separate activities, but only if they have separate *telē*, that is, if their standards of success and completion are distinct—as they might be, for instance, in a world with a deeper division of labor than imagined in this example.[49]

47. Much as the shoemaker cannot make leather shoes without cutting leather, so a ruler cannot rule well without philosophy. We might therefore be tempted to consider philosophy a subactivity of ruling. As we have seen, however, this would disqualify philosophers from ruling. The alternative is to run things the other way around, considering ruling a subactivity of philosophy. This would explain why philosophers do not want to rule: just as a shoemaker might prefer to focus on the aesthetics of the shoe rather than the humdrum labor of cutting laces and so on, so a philosopher would view ruling as little more than a necessary chore for the sake of her true interest, philosophy.

48. Why would ruling be instrumental for philosophy? Socrates provides the answer in Book I: "The greatest punishment for being unwilling to rule is being ruled by someone worse than oneself" (347c).[50] If philosophers do not rule, they will suffer. Think of the ship-of-state analogy: when the true captain is mocked and ignored, the results are bad not only for everyone else but also for him—if the ship of state goes down, so too does the philosopher (488a–489c). Philosophy is dangerous in a corrupt city, as the historical Socrates

---

49. One might usefully compare the conception I am attributing to Plato with the *Statesman*'s discussion of what constitutes weaving as opposed to related crafts, 280a–283a.

50. We might also draw on Book IV, where Socrates gives us two different descriptions of *sophia*: knowledge of what is advantageous to oneself (442c) and knowledge of the city as a whole in its relations with its parts and with other wholes (428c–d). As Cooper points out, Socrates must suppose that these amount to the same thing. See Cooper, "Psychology of Justice in Plato," 21.

found out: if things go badly on a ship where the true captain is called a "stargazer," or in a city where philosophers are not distinguished from sophists, ridicule can quickly turn to rage.[51] The best strategy for a philosopher in a bad city is therefore to avoid politics "like someone who takes refuge under a little wall from a storm of dust or hail driven by the wind" (496d). But Socrates makes clear that this can only ever be a second-best solution. Under a suitable constitution, not only will the philosopher preserve the good condition of both the collective and the individual (*ta koina* and *ta idia*), but "his own growth will be fuller" (497a).[52] The notion of growth (*auxēsis*) is clearly connected to that of *phusis*; the idea is that to realize his true nature, to achieve his potential, a philosopher must live in the right kind of city, namely one ruled by philosophers. Philosophical rule is therefore a condition of possibility for the flourishing of philosophers.[53]

49. Commentators have often wondered what motivation philosophers would have for returning to the cave after beholding the forms.[54] But if we look at the relevant passage while keeping in mind

---

51. Much of the *Republic* can be seen as a response to the events and doctrines described in Plato's *Apology*. At 17b–18a Socrates raises the idea that the person whom people call an orator is not in fact a true orator, as in the ship-of-state analogy (cf. 40a, 41a); the understanding of courage adumbrated at 28b–29b is clearly related to that of *Republic* IV; the critique of those who focus on acquiring more and more wealth and honor without attending to the excellence of their soul, that which makes such external goods good (29d–30b), calls to mind the overall theme of the *Republic*; the image of Athens as asleep while the philosopher is awake (31a) recurs throughout the *Republic* (e.g., 476c–d, 520c, 534c); the worry that political engagement is dangerous in a bad regime (31e–32a) comes up in *Republic* Book VI (496a–e); and the city-soul analogy is hinted at in 37c–d.

52. Cf. 492e–493a, 497b–c, and 499a–b.

53. Cooper comes to the same conclusion by means of what looks like a sleight of hand: simply asserting that a philosopher's "ultimate end is to improve not just the small part of the world that is constituted by his own life, but the whole of it," he then adds a further assertion, that "the degree of one's *eudaimonia* [happiness, flourishing] is measured by how close one comes to realizing one's ultimate end," in order to draw the conclusion that a philosopher who focused only on the rational order in his own soul would by definition be less happy than one who did not ("Psychology of Justice in Plato," 26).

54. Cooper, as we have seen, claims that since "a just person is a devotee of *the* good, not *his own* good," he must desire "to advance the reign of rational order in the world as a whole," a fact that makes him "a sort of high-minded fanatic" (ibid., 24, 28). My account is similar to that of C. D. C. Reeve, "The Happiness of the Philosopher-Kings," chapter 9 of *Blindness and Reorientation*.

that ruling is a condition for the possibility of philosophers' flourishing, Plato's argument is revealed as perfectly lucid. When Glaucon
asks whether ruling will make philosophers unhappy, Socrates refers back to his earlier doctrine that the goal of a lawgiver is to bind
the city together as one by making everyone play for the team, as it
were, whether "through persuasion or compulsion" (519e; 420b–421c).
Yet it soon becomes clear that the compulsion in question is compulsion by argument, not force.[55] The passage is worth quoting in full:

> Observe, then, Glaucon, that we won't be doing an injustice to
> those who've become philosophers in our city and that what
> we'll say to them, when we compel them to guard and care for
> others, will be just. We'll say: "When people like you come to
> be in other cities, they're justified in not sharing in their city's
> labors, for they've grown there spontaneously, against the will
> of the constitution. And what grows of its own accord and owes
> no debt for its upbringing has justice on its side when it isn't keen
> to pay anyone for that upbringing. But we've made you kings in
> our city and leaders of the swarm, as it were, both for yourselves
> and for the rest of the city. You're better and more completely
> educated than the others and are better able to share in both
> types of life. Therefore each of you in turn must go down to
> live in the common dwelling place of the others and grow ac-
> customed to seeing in the dark. When you are used to it, you'll
> see vastly better than the people there. And because you've seen
> the truth about fine, just, and good things, you'll know each
> image for what it is and also that of which it is the image. Thus,
> for you and for us, the city will be governed, not like the majority
> of cities nowadays, by people who fight over shadows and struggle
> against one another in order to rule—as if that were a great
> good—but by people who are awake rather than dreaming, for
> the truth is surely this: A city whose prospective rulers are least

---

55. This passage therefore echoes the opening of the *Republic* (326e–328b), which
toys with the concepts of persuasion and compulsion as Polemarchus enjoins Socrates
to remain in Piraeus for dinner, a horse race, and the all-night festival. Like all great
writers, Plato takes immense care to begin his work as suggestively as possible.

eager to rule must of necessity be most free from civil war, whereas a city with the opposite kind of rulers is governed in the opposite way." (520a–520d)

The argument is put in terms of justice. As Socrates says right afterward, "We'll be giving just orders to just people"; the orders are just, but they also concern justice. It is only in Kallipolis that philosophers can fully realize their nature, so insofar as their nature is fully realized, they owe that to the city.[56] But this should not be understood as a one-off debt, incurred in childhood and then paid back in full by adults. Just as the city must continually be refounded and reconstituted, so must the soul; hence the debt is continually incurred just insofar as the institutions of Kallipolis continue to enable philosophers to prosper. The debt in question, then, is not the kind that encourages a Simonidean conception of justice as paying back what is owed once and for all, but rather that kind that a soccer player owes a team for enabling her to flourish as a player and hence the kind that one repays simply by continuing to play for the team rather than for oneself.[57]

50. We can now see that philosophers both do and do not want to rule. They do not want to rule in the sense that the *telos* of philosophy is not ruling; if they could achieve that *telos* without ruling, they would. Yet in another sense they do want to rule, just as a man standing in the forecourt of a gas station wants to fill up his car: as a necessary part of his journey. In the world such as we know it, Plato suggests, philosophy requires ruling.[58]

---

56. Barring the kind of divine intervention spoken of at 492e–493a.

57. One might think of a player like Ryan Giggs, who excelled for years at the club level with Manchester United but played his international soccer for Wales, where his fellow players were neither talented nor organized enough to permit him to excel to the same degree. The Giggs of Wales was therefore something like the Socrates of Athens, even if the latter's virtue was, in Plato's (somewhat dubious) view, owed to no human institution but rather to the gods alone (492e–493a).

58. Reeve makes a similar argument in "Happiness of the Philosopher-Kings" before pointing out a potential objection, namely that this interpretation would leave justice as a merely instrumental good for philosophers, which would then put them in the position of the weak people of Glaucon's Book II contract story, those who practice justice "as something compulsory, not as something good" (358c). Reeve's solution is to say that philosopher-kings aim for justice qua state of soul as a noninstrumental

51. The philosopher may long for a world in which this were not true, a world in which her full development was not dependent on the sociocultural environment. But this longing is utopian, which is why it is figured in terms of mistaking earth for heaven—believing that one has already emigrated to the "Isles of the Blessed" despite still being alive (519c). Plato seems to respect the utopian longing for a form of order of which we are by nature incapable, perhaps because he views the desire for self-transcendence as an ineliminable part of the desire for goodness. But rather than allowing this utopian longing to shape his politics or his ethics, he treats it as a form of *erōs* that is the philosophical equivalent of *pleonexia*—a state of soul against which philosophers must guard themselves, no matter how naturally it comes to them.[59]

PLATO BELIEVES THAT SOCIETY would be best ruled by philosophers—that much is clear. To see whether that proposition has anything to be said for it, we must reconstruct Plato's reasons for holding it, which can be done only if we simultaneously ask what he might have meant by it. Chapter 1 therefore asked what Plato might have meant by philosophy such that ruling could plausibly be thought to require philosophy, while this chapter has asked what he might have meant by ruling such that ruling might plausibly be thought to require philosophy.

I began with the observation that for Plato, exercising control over political institutions is neither necessary nor sufficient for ruling (§1). Just as doctors are craftsmen who aim to benefit their subjects by maintaining their bodies in good condition, so rulers are craftsmen who aim to benefit their subjects by maintaining their souls in good condition. One can hold office without aiming at this goal, and one

---

good while performing just actions instrumentally. I accept this solution and add only that on Plato's view, whatever else just actions are instrumental for, they are also instrumental for creating a just soul (443c–445b).

59. The utopian longing for self-transcendence is manifest when Socrates says that the true city is the first city (372e), for instance, and that the true soul is reason by itself (611b–612a), but these remarks are not allowed to structure the politics or psychology of the *Republic*. Note also the "true erotic love for true philosophy" (*alēthinēs philosophias alēthinos erōs*) that is said to mark philosopher-rulers (499b).

can aim at the goal without holding office. Given the influence of sociocultural environment on psychic structure—so crucial to Plato's picture of the human condition—it will be natural for rulers to want to shape that environment. And given the influence of political institutions on sociocultural environment, it will be natural for rulers to want to hold office. But for the true ruler, political power is, and can only ever be, a mere means to the end of soul shaping—if there are other ways of effectively shaping the sociocultural environment, they ought to be of equal interest to a "craftsman of temperance, justice, and the whole of citizenly virtue" (500d).

After noting this feature of Plato's position, I spent the rest of the chapter considering how philosophy, understood as the activity of asking after true forms in light of functional contexts, might bear on the type of soulcraft that operates through political institutions. What qualifies philosophers as stewards of others' souls, we saw, is not only that they do not want the attendant power for its own sake, but also that they are capable of guarding their own souls (§2). The reason is that their distinctive activity allows them to preserve their convictions about justice in the face of the forces of forgetfulness and persuasion, since they and they alone can reconstruct the arguments in favor of justice. In this respect the *Republic* might be seen as reflexive: it offers a model of the kind of reasoning that philosopher-rulers will undertake. Something similar is true in connection with the city as well. To guard the city well requires understanding that its essence is its constitution, which amounts to its social, political, and economic division of labor, and then maintaining that constitution in its optimal condition, given changing circumstances (§3). This will involve a continual process of refounding the city in thought in order to assess both whether each part is adequately serving the whole and whether the whole is adequately serving its purpose with respect to the human good (§4). Once again, the *Republic* offers a model of just this kind of reasoning in its ideal-theoretic construction of city and soul.

Having drawn that conclusion, I ended by addressing the long-debated question of what would motivate philosophers to rule, arguing that ruling ought to be understood as a necessary (if lamentable) precondition of the full development of philosophers themselves

(§5). Even philosophers, then, are vulnerable to their sociocultural environment—and given that philosophers are uniquely capable of self-guarding, this goes to show how high the stakes of government must be for every citizen. The political theory of the *Republic* is therefore no mere by-product of its investigation into ethics and psychology: it arises necessarily, as a direct result of Plato's basic way of looking at the world, and in particular as a result of his fundamental insight that individuals can never be self-sufficient with respect to the good life—that there is no such thing as answering the question of how to live all by oneself.

3

The Beautiful City

WE CAN DISTINGUISH between two senses of the word "ideal." The first refers to models—the ideal F or the ideal G—that exist in the imagination, whether as the product of deliberate reflection or as the product of acculturation. The second refers to transcendent goods, such as community or justice or beauty, that seem to organize a hierarchy of lower goods against which they cannot be traded.[1] The two kinds of ideal will inevitably shape each other. Our conception of the hierarchy of values will shape our notion of what counts as a model F, but at the same time we often seem to acquire our understanding of transcendent goods by taking certain items in the world as models, whether consciously or not.[2]

Plato was greatly exercised by this two-way process. He saw us as mimetic creatures who imitate things and in so doing form habits that eventually crystallize into characters. But we do not imitate just anyone or anything; we especially imitate things we consider valuable,

---

1. See Charles Taylor, *Sources of the Self,* 62–75.

2. The notion that we can acquire a conception of transcendent goods through taking certain items as models is compatible with various accounts of the mechanism by which this happens, from Freud's notion of introjection in *The Ego and the Id* to pragmatist, behaviorist, and neuroscientific accounts, as well as Plato's account of mimesis.

fashioning ourselves after role models and fashioning objects after model instances. And since anything we do or make can subsequently serve as a model for others, the wheel turns continually. In Plato's view, this process of imitation and emulation leaves us thoroughly and permanently exposed to the possibility of a dysfunctional social world. Humans live in accordance with their conceptions of the good life, and we tend to absorb those conceptions from our cultural environment. It follows that our prospects for flourishing depend on the existence of a healthy cultural environment. Philosophers have a greater-than-average capacity for distancing themselves from current standards, but even they will not achieve their fullest growth outside Kallipolis.[3] This is why "there can be no happiness, either public or private, in any other city" than the one whose rulers shape the cultural environment in line with dialectical investigation into city, soul, and cosmos (474e).

In Chapter 2 we saw that if philosopher-rulers are charged with guarding the social, political, and economic division of labor, it is not only because the division of labor is crucial to the ongoing existence of a society as the kind of society it is, but also because it shapes souls—both because patterns of action shape patterns of soul, so that the work we do on a daily basis molds each of us in certain ways, and because the sociocultural environment is the result, at least in part, of our combined productive activities. In this chapter we will deepen our understanding of what it means to shape the cultural environment in the interest of soulcraft.

Our starting point will be a pair of passages from Book VI that compare ruling to painting. The first passage claims that rulers need to philosophize because ruling requires establishing and preserving usages regarding what is beautiful or just or good.

> Do you think that there's any difference, then, between the blind and those who are really deprived of the knowledge *[gnōsis]* of each thing that is, and have no clear model *[enarges para-*

---

3. Note that Socrates himself confesses to having had a "sort of reverential love . . . for Homer since childhood," a love he cannot fully shake no matter how strong the counteracting drug of rational argument may be (595b–c; 497a).

deigma] in their souls—those who cannot look away, like painters, to what is most true, and cannot, by making constant reference to it and by studying it as exactly as possible, establish here on earth usages *[nomima]* regarding beautiful, just or good things when they need to be established, or guard and preserve those that have been established? (484c–d)[4]

After an extended discussion of the place of philosophy in the city—including the ship-of-state analogy—Socrates returns to the same imagery in the second passage. In and of itself, Socrates claims, philosophy is directed away from temporal human affairs: as he "looks at and contemplates things that are orderly and always the same, that neither do injustice to one another nor suffer it, being all in a rational order, [the philosopher] imitates them and tries to become as like them as he can" (500b–c).[5] But this activity of shaping one's own soul in line with models of perfect rational order can also be extended, once the philosopher is made ruler, to shaping the characters *(ēthē)* of the citizenry. The philosophical ruler is therefore a "painter of constitutions" (501c):

> I suppose that, as they work, they would look often in each direction: on the one hand, toward what is in its nature just, beautiful, temperate, and all the rest; and, on the other, toward what they are trying to put into human beings, mixing and blending pursuits to produce a human likeness *[andreikelon]*, based on the one that Homer too called divine and godly when it appeared among human beings. . . . They would erase one thing, I suppose, and draw in another, until they had made human

---

4. Using Reeve's translation but changing "conventional views about" to "usages regarding," for reasons to be discussed later.

5. I do not think this conflicts with the central claims of Chapter 1, that philosophical knowledge is of an aspect of this world and that such knowledge will include knowledge of the true form of natural and artificial entities, including humans themselves. Socrates' claim is just that philosophers are interested in these things in their eternal aspects rather than their temporal ones. That is why he emphasizes philosophers' disdain for local quarrels and disputes. Compare 517c–d on the return to the cave.

characters *[anthrōpeia ēthē]* as dear to the gods as possible. (501b–c)[6]

By the middle of Book VI, then, Socrates' claim that "cities will have no rest from evils" until philosophers rule or rulers philosophize (473c–d) has been transformed into the claim that "there is no way a city can ever find happiness unless its plan is drawn by painters who use the divine model *[paradeigma]*" (500e).

The question is what it could mean in a nonmetaphorical sense for a ruler to "paint characters"—and what it could mean to do so by "looking toward" a model or paradigm. In the first half of this chapter I will explicate the notion of "painting characters" as a matter of altering the cultural environment before showing how that relates to establishing and preserving usages *(nomima)* regarding which items and properties count as beautiful, just, and good. In the second half I will interpret "looking toward" a paradigm as a matter of constructing ideals for the purpose of dialectical investigation before showing how the dissemination of these ideals within society might generate an environment that shapes characters in the right way. In Chapter 4 I will then consider the role that ideal theory can play within nonideal societies.

§1 Shaping Characters and Establishing Usages

1. "There is [nothing] better for a city," says Socrates in Book V, "than that the best possible men and women should come to exist in it" (456e). This is the *telos* of the city, that which completes its mission. For the *archē* of the city, its principle or source, is our lack of individual self-sufficiency—"A city comes to exist . . . because none of us is individually self-sufficient, but each has many needs he cannot satisfy" (369b)—and the needs for which we require society go well beyond our daily existence: we also rely on it for our basic orienta-

---

6. Using Reeve's translation but changing "people's characters" to "human characters" to reflect the divine/human contrast present in the Greek. Reeve suggests that the Homer reference is to passages such as *Iliad* I.131, in which Achilles is referred to as "godlike" *(theoeikelos)*.

tion to the world, which is always already shaped by the time we are in a position to consciously reflect on it. Society shapes our characters, and a good society shapes our characters well. This is what enables Plato to treat true political rulers as one species of a wider kind, those who look after the souls of their subjects. The most important benefit that political rulers can bring to the ruled, in other words, is psychic. The ruled need to have their desires directed at the right objects and arranged in the appropriate order, and those who control the sociocultural environment are in a position to help with that. This is why the true ruler is described as a "painter of constitutions" (501c). Her task is to maintain her subjects' souls in optimal condition, and this involves ensuring that the parts of those souls fit together as harmoniously as possible. She is, as Socrates puts it, a "craftsman of temperance, justice, and the whole of citizenly virtue" (500b–d).

2. A craftsman is necessarily limited by her material. In Plato's conception, optimal character is a matter of the organization or constitution of one's soul, which amounts to having one's desires directed at the right objects and arranged in the appropriate order. To have one's desires directed at the right objects and arranged in the appropriate order is to have the correct conception of the good life. Those who are unabashedly appetitive are simply wrong about the relative importance of various goods and the same goes for those who view honor as the highest good: if they were able to see that the truest pleasures are those that come from understanding, they would organize their lives around its pursuit (580d–588a). But Plato does not believe that everyone can grasp the truth in this respect: genuine knowledge is available only to those who philosophize successfully, and not everyone has the cognitive gifts and motivational structure to do that. This means that philosophical soulcraft is necessarily limited: it cannot be so successful that every citizen becomes fully just in the psychological sense, such that their desires are perfectly directed and arranged. Yet something can be achieved nevertheless.

3. In fact, Socrates goes so far as to suggest that rule by philosophers would be good for spirited and appetitive people even by their own standards: over the long run, they would achieve more spirited and appetitive satisfaction in Kallipolis than in cities ruled by those

of their own ilk. The thought is that spirit and appetite are not good at discerning their own pleasure accurately, whereas reason, which inquires into the best possible condition of each thing by considering a nested series of functional contexts, can determine what is good for spirit and appetite.

> Can't we confidently assert, then, that, even where the desires of the profit-loving and honor-loving parts are concerned, those that follow knowledge and argument, and pursue with their help the pleasures that wisdom prescribes, will attain—to the degree that they can attain true pleasure at all—the truest pleasures, because they follow truth, and those that are most their own; if, indeed, what is the best for each thing is also what is most its own? . . . So, when the entire soul follows the philosophic element and does not engage in faction, the result is that each element . . . enjoys its own pleasures, the best pleasures and—to the degree possible—the truest. (586d–587a)

The metaphor of spirit and appetite following the philosophical element, or pursuing the pleasures that wisdom prescribes, is shorthand for describing the familiar process of habituation, whereby we alter our desires over time in line with an understanding of what is good for us. Philosophers are capable of doing this for themselves. They are not ascetics, but they are temperate. They "neither starve nor feast their appetites," and even if they can never fully eliminate appetites that are untethered to goodness, they know not to indulge and thereby foster them (571b–572b; 431c). This is because philosophical inquiries reveal the rational order of reality—which we have glossed as an interlocking structure of form and function—and thus disclose the fact that achieving a healthy psychic constitution requires us to imitate this order in our own lives (cf. 443c–445b, 500b–d, 353d).[7] Nonphilosophers are not capable of such self-habituation. To achieve psychic stability (to the extent possible given their natures), they require help from the outside. In an appetitive

---

7. See Gabriel Richardson Lear, "Plato on Learning to Love Beauty."

soul left to its own devices, appetite governs (580d–581e). But if an appetitive person could be persuaded to delegate rule over herself to someone fully just, Socrates suggests, her soul would then be governed by reason, if only in a derivative way (590c–d). She would act justly, more or less, and given that patterns of action shape the soul (444e; 576b), she would gradually become more just. She would experience a reduction in her unnecessary desires, and this would in turn facilitate the satisfaction of her appetites. Those who grow up in Kallipolis would benefit to an even greater extent: as Jonathan Lear puts it, they will have been "brought up to have just the appetites which the well-ordered polis can satisfy."[8]

4. Talk of being ruled by someone else's reason might raise eyebrows, especially given that Socrates describes the nonreasoner as becoming a slave (doulos) to the ruler (590c–d).[9] Elsewhere, however, it is perfectly clear that the relationship between ruler and subject is nothing like slavery; for example, the transition from Kallipolis to

---

8. See Jonathan Lear, "Inside and Outside the *Republic*," 74. "Ironically, it is because the reason in his psyche is subservient to the appetitive part that the appetitive person submits himself to the rule of reason in the polis. Just as the appetitive person will abjure junk food for healthy bread and relishes, so he will abjure junk bonds for municipal bonds. And all the while he will be telling himself, correctly, that this is the really good investment for himself and his family. This is how the appetitive person's role in a well-ordered polis looks from an appetitive perspective. On the one hand, his reason is focused on securing gain; on the other, he concludes that the best way to do this is to follow the rule of reason in the polis. So the appetitive person will be happier in Kallipolis than in other cities, even by appetitive standards, and this will secure his adherence to the constitution. This would not have been possible if he had not been brought up in such a way as to internalize appropriate cultural influences and get rid of unnecessary appetites" (74–75). See also Ferrari, *City and Soul in Plato's "Republic,"* 48: "The farmer and artisan class of Callipolis is materialistic and practical. It is well suited, then, to appreciate the rule of impartial and incorruptible officials who do not enrich themselves at the expense of the citizenry, who impose minimal taxes, maintain a stable economy, prevent the neighbour who might flaunt his wealth from becoming wealthy in the first place, promote public piety and order, and take upon themselves the entire military burden of defending their citizens' farms and families."

9. The argument clearly prefigures Aristotle's account of slavery in Book I of the *Politics*. On the reality of ancient slavery, see Finley, *Ancient Economy*, 62–94. In an unpublished manuscript, "The Relation between Liberty, Law, and Rule," Melissa Lane suggests that the day-to-day reality of slavery in the Athenian context allowed it to serve as a synecdoche for rule as such. The language of slavery might also be due to the fact that, as we will see in Chapter 4, on Plato's account even legitimate rule will appear as slavery to those corrupted by democratic ideals.

timocracy is characterized as a change away from friendship and toward a master-slave relationship (547b–c). Socrates does say that in Kallipolis "the desires of the inferior many are mastered by the wisdom and desires of the superior few" (431c–d), but the kind of mastery that is at issue (the verb is *kratein*, to hold sway or prevail) does not seem to be control over day-to-day decision making. Given that Socrates continues the "slavery" passage by saying that it is "clearly the aim of the law *[nomos]*" to make sure that everyone is "ruled by divine reason, preferably within himself and his own, otherwise imposed from without" (590d–e), it seems more reasonable to suppose that the way in which philosopher-rulers exercise control over citizens' libidinal structures, and hence their characters, is by using coercive power to structure the cultural environment. For Plato could hardly believe that nonphilosophers literally never reason. He is best understood as claiming that their reasoning is in the service of ends whose nature and value they do not interrogate. An honor lover, for example, will deliberate in light of honor, valuing a given pursuit (such as learning) only to the extent that it brings honor (581d). But her notion of what counts as honorable will be imbibed from her social environment. So if that social environment were structured in light of philosophical inquiry, we could justifiably claim that the honor lover's desires are controlled by the wisdom and desires of philosophers.[10]

5. We can now see that when the philosophical ruler is said to make "human characters as dear to the gods as possible" (501c), the point is that she will structure the cultural environment so as to ensure that citizens absorb a conception of the good life that reflects the

---

10. This interpretation finds support in Socrates' claim in Book IX that the aim of the law is the same as "our aim in ruling our children," namely, to secure their psychic constitution (590e), and in his declaration in Book IV that the auxiliaries will preserve true belief about what is genuinely fearful not because they have an account of why something is fearful, as a philosopher might, but because they have had true belief "dyed" into them from an early age. "What we were contriving was nothing other than this: That because they had the proper nature and upbringing, they would absorb the laws [or customs] in the finest possible way, just like a dye, so that their belief about what they should fear and all the rest would become so fast that even such extremely effective detergents as pleasure, pain, fear, and desire wouldn't wash it out—and pleasure is much more potent than any powder, washing soda, or soap" (430a–b).

conclusions of philosophical inquiry. The question is what it means to structure the cultural environment. Part of the answer, as we saw in Chapter 2, is making sure that citizens work together in a coherent division of labor aimed at producing an environment conducive to the good life.[11] But this leaves open the question of what such an environment would consist in. To get clearer on this, we must connect the ruler's mandate to shape her subjects' characters (500d–501c) with her mandate to "establish here on earth usages *[nomima]* regarding beautiful, just or good things when they need to be established, or guard and preserve those that have been established" (484c–d).

6. The word *nomima* is variously translated as "customs," "conventions," or "conventional views." Sometimes Socrates uses it to refer to practices: in Book IV, for instance, he gives as examples of *nomima* "the silence appropriate for young people in the presence of their elders; the giving up of seats for them and standing up in their presence; the care of parents; hairstyles; clothing; shoes; the general appearance of the body; and everything else of that sort" (425a–b). Other times, however, Socrates seems to use it to refer to beliefs, as in Book V's argument with the sight lovers, whose *nomima* about beauty are said to be unstable, rolling around between being and nonbeing (479d). This oscillation is no doubt a feature of the Greek language itself: the cognate verb *nomisdō* can mean both "to customarily practice" and "to believe something." One strategy would therefore be to translate differently according to context, so that

---

11. Note that the word that Socrates uses for "character" is *ēthos*, from which our word "ethos" derives. *Ēthos* can mean either "character" or "custom." This is not a case of mere homonymy, as with the various meanings of the word "bank." The underlying thought, as Aristotle points out in the *Nicomachean Ethics*, is that characters are bound up with practices. See Aristotle, *Nicomachean Ethics* II.1.1. For further analysis of the relationship between character and custom, including the relationship between the closely related words *ēthos* and "ethos," see Arthur B. Miller, "Aristotle on Habit and Character"; and Woerther, *Éthos aristotélicien*. Plato clearly shares this way of thinking. Book IV's argument regarding justice concludes with the observation that "fine pursuits *[epitēdeumata]* lead to the possession of virtue, shameful ones to vice" (444b–e); each citizen is said to "become not many but one" through doing one job (423d); and the tyrant's character degenerates partly as a result of his "habits" or "ways," so that "the longer he remains tyrant, the more like the nightmare he becomes" (574c–575a; 576b; 591a–b). What one does shapes who one is. This is why Socrates connects the task of "painting characters" with that of "mixing and blending pursuits" in the city (501b): the division of labor shapes both producers and consumers.

when the ruler is said to establish *nomima* regarding what is beautiful or just or good, this involves either establishing conventional views or establishing a set of practices. My strategy, by contrast, will be to use a term that retains the ambiguity of the Greek, namely "usages." For just as the ambiguity of the Greek term implies that practices and beliefs are bound up with one another, so the term "usages" covers a variety of practices that are bound up with beliefs.

7. *Nomima* is derived from *nomos*, which means "law" or "custom." One of the structuring dichotomies of ancient Greek thought was the divide between *nomos* and *phusis* (nature): *nomos* was typically viewed as variable, impermanent, and artificial in contrast to the permanence and universality of *phusis*.[12] Herodotus famously observed the hold that customs have over humans:

> If one were to offer men to choose out of all the customs in the world such as seemed to them the best, they would examine the whole number, and end by preferring their own; so convinced are they that their own usages far surpass those of all others. . . . That people have this feeling about their laws may be seen by very many proofs: among others, by the following. Darius, after he had got the kingdom, called into his presence certain Greeks who were at hand, and asked what he should pay them to eat the bodies of their fathers when they died. To which they answered, that there was no sum that would tempt them to do such a thing. He then sent for certain Indians, of the race called Callatians, men who eat their fathers, and asked them, while the Greeks stood by, and knew by the help of an interpreter all that was said, what he should give them to burn the bodies of their fathers at their decease. The Indians exclaimed aloud, and bade him forbear such language. Such is men's wont herein; and Pindar was right, in my judgment, when he said, "Custom is king over all."[13]

---

12. See, e.g., McKirahan, "*Nomos-Phusis* Debate," and Oswald, *Nomos and the Beginnings of the Athenian Democracy*.

13. Herodotus, *Histories* III.38.

Herodotus's story is open to more than one interpretation. The most obvious moral would be that the customs of a given community will always seem natural to its members, while wise, cosmopolitan judges will recognize that customs can only ever be contingent and arbitrary. This opens up a method for social critique: stripping *nomoi* of their claim to permanence and obviousness and revealing them to be arbitrary. Another interpretation, however, would be that Herodotus is subtly suggesting that although customs are always contingent in the sense of being subject to change, they are not necessarily arbitrary.[14] What divides the Greeks and the Callatians is really their respective views about what constitutes the essence of humanity: material body or immaterial soul. If our bodies are all we are, or the core of what we are, then to honor one's father after death might well involve perpetuating his existence by physically incorporating him into one's own living body; if our bodies are secondary to our immaterial souls, on the other hand, dead bodies are at best worthless and at worst prisons for the soul. If there is a truth of the matter regarding our essence, and that truth is accessible to human reason, then resolving the debate between the Greeks and Callatians might require philosophical or scientific investigation. The ultimate goal would be to settle on *nomoi* that actually reflect *phusis*.

8. Whether or not this interpretation is valid as a reading of Herodotus, it certainly reflects Plato's position on *nomoi*. Plato wishes to expose certain *nomoi* as arbitrary, but unlike the sophists or their postmodern heirs, he does so with the aim of creating *nomoi* that really do reflect *phusis*—or rather, since it might be objected that the sophists do emphasize living according to *phusis*, understood as something like the will to power, he does so with the aim of creating *nomoi* that reflect *phusis* as dialectic reveals it to be.[15] As we saw in

---

14. Leon Kass suggested this interpretation in a seminar on Aristotle's *Ethics* at the University of Chicago.

15. C. D. C. Reeve argues that Glaucon's challenge should be understood as an attempt to resist the pleonectic picture of nature, according to which, as the sophist Callicles puts it in the *Gorgias*, the natural good consists in letting the appetites grow as large as possible while having the power to serve them (491e–492a). See Reeve, "Glaucon's Thrasymachean Challenge," chapter 4 of *Blindness and Reorientation*. On the moment in the *Protagoras* when the sophist Hippias is depicted as advocating

Chapter 1, on Plato's view philosophers understand the cosmos as a teleological whole in which true forms, or natures, are bound up with functions. The natural state of something is therefore not the state to which it tends when left to its own devices, all other things being equal, but its optimal condition given its functional context. This is critical to Plato's outlook. Against Thucydides, for example, or Hobbes, Plato would not regard the way people behave during a civil war or natural disaster as revelatory of their nature. In fact, he would consider such periods unnatural, not only in the sense that they are exceptional but also in the sense that they represent fallings away from harmonious functional contexts. Whether this is the right picture of nature clearly depends on whether one accepts that goodness is the first principle of the universe. But for present purposes the important point is that Plato thinks *nomoi* ought to reflect *phusis*, where that in turn means they ought to reflect *telē*.

9. Socrates provides a clear example of such reasoning about *nomoi* in Book V when he argues that musical, athletic, and military training ought to be extended to women (452a–b). He knows this is a shocking suggestion. Aristophanes' comedy *Assemblywomen* treats the idea of women in government—as well as communal property and reforms to sexual practices, also features of Kallipolis—as so obviously ridiculous that it can serve as a kind of reductio ad absurdum of contemporary political degeneracy, and his *Thesmophoriazusae* adopts a similar strategy. Socrates does not make things easy for himself in this respect. Of all the educational practices that could become gender neutral, the one he focuses on is mixed athletic training, presumably because the idea of men and women exercising together in the wrestling school (*palaistra*) while naked, or even lightly clad, would seem especially ridiculous to most Athenians—the stuff of comedy indeed.[16]

---

nature as against convention but then immediately suggesting a new convention (337d–338b), see Lane, "Self-Knowledge in Plato?"

16. Allan Bloom claims, perversely in my view, that Socrates in fact agrees with Aristophanes, with the only difference being that Socrates' wants to present the proposal as ridiculous in a deeper sense than Aristophanes had seen: "In appearing to disagree with Aristophanes about the city, Socrates shows that only he knows the true grounds of its inadequacy." Bloom, "Interpretive Essay," 381.

10. Socrates' defense comes in three stages. First he points out that although *nomoi* regarding gymnastics may seem natural, so that any diversion from them appears ridiculous, they are in fact contingent:

> [Critics] should remember that it wasn't very long ago that the Greeks themselves thought it shameful *[aischros]* and ridiculous *[geloios]* (as the majority of the barbarians still do) for even men to be seen naked and that when the Cretans and the Lacedae-monians began the gymnasiums, the wits of those times could also have ridiculed it all. (452c–d)

But against those who would take the contingency of *nomoi* as evidence of their arbitrariness, Socrates goes on to suggest that some customs are more adequate than others. The only viable criterion of adequacy, in his view, involves relating them to their functional context.

> But I think that, after it was found in practice to be better to strip than to cover up all those parts, then what was ridiculous to the eyes faded away in the face of what argument showed to be the best. This makes it clear that it's foolish to think that anything besides the bad is ridiculous or to try to raise a laugh at the sight of anything besides what's stupid or bad or (putting it the other way around) it's foolish to take seriously any standard of what is fine or beautiful other than goodness. (452d–e)

Socrates then concludes by arguing that his proposed *nomoi* do in fact reflect *phusis* understood teleologically. His argument is pleasingly simple. The first premise goes back to the foundation of Kallipolis as a division of labor: "The same pursuits [must] be assigned to the same natures" (456b; 453b; 370c). The second premise is that where the division of labor is concerned, two people count as having the same nature just insofar as they are both naturally suited to a given activity. For instance, "a male and female whose souls are suited for medicine have the same nature" (454c–d) and should therefore both be assigned to the same pursuit.[17] If we assume a third premise, that those assigned to the same pursuit should receive the same training (451e), it follows that women suited to war should receive the same training as men suited to war, and the same for all the other occupations in the city—including ruling—no matter how far away from contemporary custom this takes us.

11. Book V proceeds by way of three proposals for overhauling Greek *nomoi*: giving men and women access to the same jobs and the same training; instituting sexual and economic communism among the guardians and auxiliaries; and mandating that rulers must philosophize. Each of these proposals brings its own "wave" of criticism and ridicule; Socrates and his interlocutors must "save [themselves] from the sea of argument *[logos]*" that threatens to drown them (453d; 457b–d; 473c). This marine imagery foreshadows the ship-of-state simile, which pictures the philosopher as the only citizen capable of reliably finding her bearings in political life and hence as uniquely qualified to rule (487e–489c). But it also foreshadows the passage at the end of Book V where Socrates is wrapping up his argument against the sight lovers: "The majority of people's many usages *[nomima]* regarding beauty and the rest are somehow rolling around between what is not and what purely is" (479d). The word translated as "rolling around" in this passage is *kulindeitai*, from a verb that Homer uses to describe the movement of waves (among other things).[18] The usages of nonphilosophers, we might say, are tossed about like a ship because they are unmoored from the fixed points of the forms. What counts as beautiful in one context is considered ugly in another, with no explanation of why that is. The implication is that linguistic usage, no less than other usages, would be overhauled in Kallipolis.

---

17. See §7 of Chapter 1 for further discussion of sameness and difference within a teleological ontology and especially as regards gender.

18. For *kulindein*, see, e.g., Homer, *Iliad* XI.307 and *Odyssey* V.296 and IX.157. Pindar uses the same verb to describe the way men's hopes are tossed about like a ship on the sea: "I entreat you, child of Zeus the Deliverer, preserve the might of Himera, Savior Fortune. For it is you who on the sea guide swift ships, and on land rapid battles and assemblies that render counsel. As for men's hopes, they often rise, while at other times they roll down as they voyage across vain falsehoods." See Pindar, *Olympian Odes* 12, trans. William H. Race.

12. Certainly Plato pays a great deal of attention to language in the *Republic*. Sometimes he seems to suggest that philosophy ought always to begin with ordinary language, as when he has Socrates ask Glaucon whether he wants to adopt their "usual procedure" for examining a topic: "We customarily hypothesize a single form in connection with each of the many things to which we apply the same name" (596a; cf. 507a–b). This extraordinary confidence in ordinary language's ability to more or less "cut nature at the joints," to paraphrase Socrates in the *Phaedrus* (265e–266a), is reflected elsewhere in the *Republic*.[19] In Book IV Socrates relies on the principle that "things called by the same name" must be like each other "with respect to that to which that name applies" in order to drive home the city-soul analogy (435a–b). In Book V he assumes that "as we have two names, 'war' and 'civil war,' so there are two things and the names apply to two kinds of disagreements arising in them" (470b). Finally, the notion of the "true ruler" is itself grounded in ordinary language— the true ruler is the ruler in the precise sense, not in a new sense. Running counter to this current, however, is a series of passages that highlight the ways in which ordinary language can mislead us. In Book VI, for instance, we learn that the masses call the sophists "wise men" (the literal meaning of *sophistai*) when they are in fact moneymakers (or "private wage earners"); the sophists reciprocate by calling the convictions of the masses "wisdom" (493a). Comparing the masses to a beast that must be flattered and appeased, Socrates says that the sophist

> knows nothing about which of these convictions or appetites is fine or shameful, good or bad, just or unjust, but he applies all these names in accordance with the great beast's beliefs— calling what it enjoys good and what angers it bad. He has no other account to give of these terms. And he calls what he is compelled to do just and fine, for he hasn't seen and cannot

19. The full quotation is "To cut up each kind according to its species along its natural joints, and to try not to splinter any part, as a bad butcher might do." Plato, *Phaedrus*, 265e, trans. Alexander Nehamas and Paul Woodruff.

show anyone else how much compulsion and goodness really differ. (493b–c)[20]

It might seem easy to resolve this apparent contradiction: after all, to argue that ordinary language tracks real distinctions is not to deny that it can sometimes be misused. But Plato seems to be alert to a further danger, which is that the whole community might go wrong in its usage. In the ship-of-state analogy, for instance, the one who is now called a useless stargazer is in fact a true captain, while the one who is called captain is in fact just the one who is clever at persuading or forcing the shipowner to let him rule (488c–d, 489c). Were the sailors to push through to the precise register and ask after the nature of the true captain, they might find themselves mistakenly declaring that the true captain is one who rules the ship for his own benefit. Indeed, this is one way of describing what Thrasymachus is doing when he declares that rulers rule for their own advantage: although he pushes through to the precise register, he remains trapped by the *nomima* of his society, which are unmoored from *phusis* as it really is.

13. If Socrates is able to challenge Thrasymachus's account of the precise sense, it is thanks to his ability to engage (however imperfectly) in genuine dialectic, connecting the nature of particular roles to the wider context of the city and ultimately of goodness. This suggests a new understanding of the passages where Plato seems sanguine about ordinary language. Words are tools, and if they have been handed down from generation to generation, it is likely that they will mark many important distinctions.[21] It therefore makes sense to begin with ordinary language. But sometimes we will find ourselves in a situation in which established usage is either deeply misleading or simply unclear. For example, Socrates says that although we apply the label "knowledge" or "understanding" (*epistēmē*) to the mathematical crafts—calculation, geometry, astronomy, and harmony—this is only by force of habit, since argument reveals that

---

20. Compare Book IV's description of the tendency of citizens of an unhealthy city to honor those who flatter their appetites (426e).

21. See Austin, "A Plea for Excuses," in *Philosophical Papers*, 181–182.

they are merely subordinate to dialectic and therefore do not constitute knowledge or understanding as such; given that they are nonetheless "clearer than opinion [or belief] *[doxa]*," we ought to invent a new name for them—*dianoia*, "thought" (533d). The name is not as important, Socrates suggests, as the underlying distinction.[22] To think about such questions is to go beyond eristic, or "disputation," which begins and ends with the marks and signs of language, to dialectic, which starts with language but goes beyond it, arguing back and forth about which things really are the same and which different, and hence about the principle of unity that each thing has, its essence or form (454a–b).[23]

14. Plato's emphasis on linguistic usage opens up a new front in his argument for rule by philosophers. For the misguided usage manifest in the ship-of-state simile might be seen as not merely symptomatic of a warped social order but also partially productive of it—it both encodes and transmits values deeply at odds with human flourishing. In a perfectly governed city, by contrast, general usage would be as close to dialectical usage as humanly possible; for example, it seems that the soldiers of Kallipolis—the only city that deserves to be called a city (422e)—will know what to call "war" and what to call "civil war," and that this will make a difference to their behavior (470a–b).[24] But how is this shaping of general usage to be achieved?

15. In Book IV Socrates declares that it is futile to legislate about usages such as the young being silent in front of their elders, standing up in their presence, and making way for them. "Verbal or written decrees," he says, "will never make them come about or last" (425b). The key is to legislate upstream, as it were, to ensure that people are well educated and therefore virtuous enough to make the right choices across a variety of circumstances: "When children play the right games from the beginning and absorb lawfulness from music and poetry, it follows them in everything and fosters their growth, correcting anything in the city that may have gone wrong before"

---

22. In the *Cratylus*, however, Plato suggests that names are important.

23. For a discussion of this, see §7 of Chapter 1.

24. Compare 347d, 422e, 443e–444a, 454a–b, and 533d with 488c–d, 489c, and 493b–c.

(425a). If the same applies to linguistic usage, the key would be for rulers to ensure that citizens are well educated in the first place. Just as the proliferation of laws regarding respect is the symptom of a decaying social order that is unwilling to address its underlying disease (425e–426b), so in a healthy city there would be no need for language police—education would have done the work already.[25]

16. If philosopher-rulers are to focus on educating their subjects to ensure correct usages, then official schooling is just the beginning. We may be more malleable as youths, but we absorb lessons from our environment our whole lives long. In the final analysis, then, the whole city ought to be considered a school, with philosophers setting the curriculum. In this connection we should note how Socrates introduces the topic of gender-neutral education at the start of Book V:

> I'm not afraid of being laughed at—that would be childish indeed. But I am afraid that, if I slip from the truth, just where it's most important not to, I'll not only fail myself but drag my friends down as well. . . . For I suspect that involuntary homicide is a lesser crime than misleading people about beautiful, good, and just usages *[nomima]*. (451a)

It is easy to skip by this as if it were mere stage setting laced with false modesty. In light of what we have just noted, however, we can see that Socrates is modeling his own account of philosophical rule. For just as a ruler should be a friend to her subjects by using her knowledge to shape their characters, so Socrates wants to be a friend

---

25. Paul Shorey and Allan Bloom translate *nomima* in 484d as "laws," i.e., "laws of the beautiful, the just and the good" (Shorey) or "laws about what is fine, just and good" (Bloom). It is hard to see what these laws would amount to, but linguistic policing is one possibility. Given that the word *nomima* has been used a few pages before as a technical term that contrasts with knowledge (479d), it seems to me that we should keep the same translation for both instances, i.e., "usages." That said, when Socrates pictures a questioner asking a citizen, "What is the fine?" toward the end of Book VII, he also pictures him answering "what he has heard from the traditional lawgiver" (538d), as if the laws did provide an account in a literal sense. This could be metaphorical, or it could imply something like the lawgiver's preamble that comes up in *The Laws*.

to his pupils by using his knowledge to shape their characters. And just as the ruler's soulcraft will turn out to involve shaping usages (*nomima*) concerning beauty, justice, and goodness, so too does Socrates'.[26] What makes Socrates nervous is just that he lacks the knowledge required to carry out this task reliably—all he can offer is hypotheses (506c, 533a). Philosopher-rulers, by contrast, will be able to set the curriculum by "looking toward" the forms, like painters who look off at their subjects and then back down toward the canvas. It is to this image that we must now turn.

§2 Constructing Ideals

17. As we have seen, Socrates twice compares rulers to artists. At the start of Book VI he speaks of them as being able to "look to what is most true, make constant reference to it, and study it as exactly as possible" and then look back at the city in order to establish and preserve usages regarding beautiful, just, and good things (484c–e). And then toward the middle of Book VI he speaks of the rulers as "painters of constitutions" who "look often in each direction: on the one hand, toward what is in its nature just, beautiful, temperate, and all the rest; and, on the other, toward what they are trying to put into human beings" (500e–501b). What does it mean to "look to what is most true"? On the face of it, the phrase would seem to suggest a picture of philosophical knowledge as a kind of ineffable perception, with philosophers directly cognizing, or "intellecting," special objects known as forms that somehow enable them to shape their subjects' souls. I have been trying to offer an alternative to interpretations that build such a deep mystery into the notion of rule by philosophers. In Chapter 1 I argued that even if forms are nonsensible, they are nevertheless an aspect of this world and its objects; knowledge of forms requires holistic investigation of everyday objects in light of

---

26. Socrates' attention to the usages of his interlocutors comes across most strikingly in what must surely be the first instance of academic political correctness. When Glaucon says that Socrates has "produced ruling men *[tous archontas]* that are completely beautiful," Socrates responds thus: "And ruling women *[tas archousas]*, too, Glaucon, for you mustn't think that what I've said applies any more to men than it does to women who are born with the appropriate natures" (540c).

goodness understood as the harmonic order of formal and final causes. On the basis of this reading we might offer a deflationary reading of Socrates' perceptual language. The language humans use to describe cognition tends to be riddled with perceptual images, from the visual ("See my point?") to the auditory ("You're not hearing me") and even the tactile ("You feel me?"), and there is rarely any reason to take these images literally. Just as one could speak of rulers "looking to the past" without implying any kind of direct perception of the past, so too we might speak of "looking to the forms" without implying any kind of direct perception. This approach seems right to me for the most part: to look to the forms is just to engage in dialectic. But what I will argue in this section is that there is a little more to the perceptual imagery than the deflationary reading would suggest. For when Socrates says that what enables guardians to look back and forth between their subjects and their canvases is the presence in their souls of "a clear model" (*enarges en tei psuchei paradeigma*; 484c), it seems to me that he is telling us something important about the cognitive process involved in dialectical inquiry.

18. We can distinguish between two kinds of models: excellent instances and theoretical ideals. An excellent F will be an actually existing entity that instantiates the form of F to an exceptional degree, while an ideal F will be a theoretical entity that fully instantiates the form of F. Both excellent instances and imagined ideals can serve important cognitive functions. In mathematical education, for instance, we might explain certain geometrical facts with reference to an existing triangle or by asking the student to imagine a perfect triangle. It is important to see that Socrates uses the word *paradeigma* in both senses. Sometimes he speaks of models that are out there in the world; other times he speaks of models that are theoretical constructs.

19. Let us begin with models that are out there in the world, that is, excellent instances. In Book VII Socrates says that in studying relative motion "we should use the ornaments in the heavens as models" on the basis that they display "the most beautiful and most exact motions that such things can have." He goes on to note, however, that the stars are imperfect models which true astronomers

would have to leave behind for the sake of rigorous investigation (529c–530c). At this point, presumably, we would have to turn to theoretical models of relative motion that are immune to the imperfections of the sensible world—mathematical constructs of the kind attributed to geometers at the end of Book VI (510a–511d). But the burden of that passage, with its image of the divided line of cognition, is that genuine understanding *(epistēmē)* requires us to derive these constructs from the first principle that is goodness. In this respect goodness can serve as an actually existing model for our cognition, much as Socrates suggests at the end of Book VII when he says of philosopher-rulers that "once they have seen goodness itself, they must use it as their model and put the city, its citizens, and themselves in order throughout the remainder of their lives, each in turn" (540a–b).[27]

20. As I put it in Chapter 1, goodness is not an object of any kind but rather the harmonic structure of forms that serves as their formal and final cause. I distinguished between substantial forms, such as the form of the cobbler or the couch, which concern the true natures of ordinary things, and structural forms, such as beauty and justice, which concern the proportion and harmony that substantial forms must manifest, both individually and in relationship to one another. Since goodness is the beautiful, just, rational order of forms, the structural forms are the properties of goodness. This is what allows Socrates to switch between saying that philosophers will use goodness as their model when they are shaping cities and souls, as in the Book VII passage under discussion, and saying (as in Book VI) that they will use "the divine model" of "what is in its nature just, beautiful, temperate, and all the rest" (500e–501b). These statements are equivalent.

21. Although goodness is an existing model, it is obviously not available to sensory perception in the way an existing triangle would be.

---

27. It follows that not all actually existing models are imperfect, contra Danielle Allen, who argues that all models fall short of the Forms. See *Why Plato Wrote*, appendix 1: "Although paradigms provide visualization of the truths embodied by the Forms, they also contain not-F properties. They participate in the F properties but not as reliably as the Forms themselves. In this sense, they both 'participate' in the Forms and are 'less real' than the Forms" (152).

When philosopher-painters look away from their canvases and toward goodness, what then is the object of their perception? One answer, as we have seen, is deflationary: there is no one perceptual object to which they look. To look toward the past, rulers would have to speak to eyewitnesses, consult historiography, and dig up old documents; to look toward goodness, they would have to engage in dialectical investigation, working out the form of a given object in light of its place within a chain of parts and wholes. This response is a useful corrective to interpretations that assume Socrates is referring to a mysterious sixth sense by which philosophers directly "intellect" the forms, but it misses the role that theoretical models can play in dialectical investigation. For when we speak of goodness as a perfect harmonic order, a cosmos, we do thereby picture it in a certain sense: we construct a theoretical ideal that is visible to our mind's eye. If all goes well, we will have what Socrates calls a "clear model in our souls" (484c).

22. Although this mental picture is by no means equivalent to the thing itself, we can make cognitive progress by investigating it and thereby testing our understanding. When we try to picture goodness, for instance, we discover that our ideal has a fractal quality: the harmonically ordered cosmos contains microcosms of rational order, such as the perfectly just city and the perfectly just soul. If we are right to model goodness in this way, then investigation of one microcosm ought to be able to guide investigation of another. This might lead us to inquire into justice in the soul by first inquiring into justice in the city (368c–369a). And if that procedure were to fail, we would have reason to revise our picture of the macrocosm that is goodness.

23. Generalizing from this case, we can say that theoretical models allow us to visualize our understanding and thereby test and expand it. This is not to remain within the realm of sense perception. To work out what X really is, in a teleological view, requires that we work out what it is to be a good X.[28] To assess whether our understanding is adequate, we would need to engage in dialectic as I outlined it in Chapter 1. The true form of X will be that order or

---

28. In a certain sense there is therefore no distinction in Plato and Aristotle between ethics and ontology: finding something's virtues is doing its ontology. The radical separation between practical and theoretical concerns that Annas assumes—and then charges Plato with ignoring—misses this point. See Annas, *Introduction to Plato's "Republic,"* 260–266.

arrangement of its parts or material that best allows it to serve its purpose within the functional whole of which it is a part, where that whole must in turn be judged as part of a wider whole. If the functional context itself is not good, the goodness of a part that does its job as well as possible will only be relative.[29] But if the functional whole is as good as it can be, then a part that does its job as well as possible will be absolutely good. Dialectical reasoning of this kind is central to the *Republic*, but for present purposes the important point is that it can sometimes involve the construction of theoretical objects, or ideals, that visualize our understanding by perfectly exemplifying the true form of X as we currently conceive it.[30] Ideals in this sense are answerable to dialectical reasoning, not the other way around; those who fail to realize this will be cut off from the highest level of cognition, as the image of the divided line makes clear. But even if ideals have no independent justificatory weight, they can nevertheless make an independent contribution to our learning process.[31]

24. Understanding the educational value of theoretical models is crucial for understanding Plato's political theory.[32] For the just man and the just city, the timocrat, the oligarch, the democrat, the tyrant, and their correlative regimes—all these are theoretical models in the sense I have been outlining. Socrates and his interlocutors construct images of the just man and the just city in order to aid their reasoning regarding what cities and souls are, and how they can best be. The other models are not exemplary but rather serve to manifest

---

29. For instance, Aristotle seems to think that in most regimes the ideal citizen—the one who best serves the constitution—will not be the same as the ideal human being. See Aristotle, *Politics* III.4.

30. For a contrasting view, see Morrison, "The Utopian Character of Plato's Ideal City," 245, which argues that forms are themselves models: Socrates' portrait of Kallipolis, for instance, would be of no use to philosopher-kings in Kallipolis, on Morrison's view, since the latter would look directly to forms as *models*.

31. Although our accounts are different, the thoughts in this paragraph have much in common with those of Danielle Allen in *Why Plato Wrote*: "Images in the domain of thought work . . . as *visualizations* that provide access to those independently imperceptible concepts" (43). Allen's account is certainly consonant with mine, even if, unlike her, I think that not only the consumer but also the producer of the visualization can learn from it, a view that Allen seems to oppose (52).

32. On Kallipolis as a model, see Burnyeat, "Utopia and Fantasy," 298; and Sedley, "Philosophy, the Forms, and the Art of Ruling."

defective form and thereby set true form in relief. As Socrates puts
it in Book V:

> It was in order to have a model that we were inquiring into the
> nature of justice itself and of the completely just man, supposing
> he could exist, and what he would be like if he did; and simi-
> larly with injustice and the most unjust man. We thought that
> by seeing how they seemed to us to stand with regard to happi-
> ness and its opposite, we would also be compelled to agree about
> ourselves as well: that the one who was most like them would
> have a fate most like theirs. (472c–d)

The same goes for the city: the goal of the "discussion *[logos]* of a
good city," Socrates says, was "to produce a model" (472d). These
models are produced through discussion rather than simply discovered: they are theoretical ideals, not actually existing exemplars.[33]
As such, their function is to enable the interlocutors to test and
thereby refine their understanding of cities and souls.

---

33. It might be objected that Socrates does speak of an actually existing model of
the city at the end of Book IX: "There may perhaps be a model laid up in the heavens
for anyone who wishes to look at it and to establish himself on the basis of what he
sees" (*en ouranoi isōs paradeigma anakeitai toi boulomenoi horan kai horōnti heauton
katoikisdein;* 592b). It is not entirely obvious that Socrates is claiming that what is laid
up in the heavens is a model *of* the city as opposed to a model *for* the city—that is, a
model of the rational order that a city should manifest. It could be that the heavenly
firmament, despite its imperfections, is supposed to serve as an exemplar of rational
order and hence as a model for the city (cf. 529c–530b). Or it could be that the rational
cosmos of forms is supposed to serve as such an exemplar, as when Socrates speaks of
soul-shaping philosophers using as their model "things that are orderly and always the
same, that neither do injustice to one another nor suffer it, being all in a rational order
[kosmoi de panta kai kata logon echonta]" (500c). That said, on balance there is reason to
suppose that Socrates is in fact referring to a model city: for one thing, the word I
translated as "laid up," *anakeitai,* is frequently used in connection with the dedication
of statues, which are models of a certain kind; for another, the next sentence concerns
whether the city exists or will exist anywhere, which implies that the subject of its
predecessor was the city. But this does not affect my argument in any case, for just as
looking to the forms seems to involve engaging in the back-and-forth of dialectic
rather than any kind of direct perception, so it is perfectly plausible that our only
mode of access to the model of the city is through dialectical discussion. The
argument would then be that dialectic involves the construction of theoretical models
to test and expand our understanding, and that the city created by Socrates and his
interlocutors is an example of such a model.

§3 Ideals and Utopias

25. It is no accident that the model city is described as *hē kallipolis*, "the beautiful city" (527c). True form involves the harmonious, proportionate order of parts within functional wholes; models of true form must therefore be harmonious and proportionate. Within Plato's conceptual scheme, this means they must be beautiful. This conclusion has epistemological value for the dialectician because it sets up a criterion for assessing whether something really is ideal. What is not beautiful cannot be ideal. When we construct theoretical models, we must therefore pay special attention to whether the parts cohere into a harmonious whole. Socrates illustrates this combination of aesthetic and ideal theory toward the start of Book IV in response to the charge that the guardians' living arrangements will make them unhappy:

> Suppose, then, that someone came up to us while we were painting a statue and objected that, because we had painted the eyes (which are the most beautiful part) black rather than purple, we had not applied the most beautiful colors to the most beautiful parts of the statue. We'd think it reasonable to offer the following defense: "You mustn't expect us to paint the eyes so beautifully that they no longer appear to be eyes at all, and the same with the other parts. Rather you must look to see whether by dealing with each part appropriately, we are making the whole statue beautiful." (420c–d)[34]

No part can be considered fully beautiful unless the whole of which it is a part is also beautiful: we cannot assess the beauty of the eyes without assessing the role they play in the beautiful order of the whole statue. By the same token, however, the statue will itself be part of a wider whole, such as a monument. So we cannot finally decide what counts as a beautiful statue until we have considered what counts as a beautiful monument. This monument will in turn be part of a wider whole, such as a temple, that we can assess in the

---

34. Cf. 361d, 540c.

same way, and this process will then be iterated until we get to the widest whole of all, namely the interlocking, harmonic structure that is the cosmos. Ideal theory, like dialectic, is therefore necessarily holistic.

26. The statue analogy has a further payoff. Socrates' point is not simply that a statue will be less aesthetically appealing if the eyes are painted purple, given the overall balance of colors. Even if it did produce an attractive effect in that sense, eyes are simply not the kind of thing that can be purple. Something similar goes for the beautiful city: if we were to "clothe the farmers in purple robes, festoon them with gold jewelry, and tell them to work the land whenever they please," Socrates says, then "a farmer wouldn't be a farmer, nor a potter a potter, and none of the others would keep to the patterns of work that give rise to a city" (420e–421a). Just as a statue with purple eyes is not a statue of a human but rather of some imaginary being, so a city in which citizens didn't have to work would not be a human city but rather a utopia.

27. Whatever its reputation, the *Republic* is not a utopian work. Plato is fully cognizant of the line between ideal and utopian theory, and although he respects the utopian longing to transcend the bounds of our given natures, he never permits it to infect his political philosophy. Indeed, some of the structuring features of Kallipolis are best understood as attempts to ensure its natural possibility. As we saw in Chapter 2, for instance, it is utopian to think that philosophers could achieve their full growth outside a healthy social order; the existence of such an order requires them to rule, so rule they must. Likewise, it is utopian to think that philosopher-rulers will be so successful at self-guarding that they can be exposed to the temptation of private gain; hence they must be denied all access to property.[35] Plato's concern with natural possibility also explains the generation of Kallipolis as against the first city described by Socrates, since it is utopian to think that the latter could ever be a stable social order for humans.

---

35. See Thakkar, "Moneymakers and Craftsmen."

28. The first city does initially appear to answer the foundational demand to provide those goods that humans cannot provide for themselves outside a society (369b–c). There will be basic goods such as food, clothing, and housing, but also more sophisticated ones like couches and festivals and singing and sex; in response to Glaucon's prompting, Socrates allows his putative citizens a variety of delicacies, such as salt, olives, cheese, boiled roots, vegetables, figs, chickpeas, beans, and—in what is apparently a sexual pun—permission to "roast myrtles and acorns before the fire" (372a–c).[36] But although Socrates calls this the true city *(hē alēthinē polis)* and the healthy city (372e), this should be regarded as a provocation rather than a conclusion; after all, it is not the first city that the just man is said to consider "his own" at the end of Book IX, but Kallipolis (592a). Certainly the first city does model the qualities that Plato considers essential to a good polity: unity, peace, health, and the capacity for stable self-reproduction. Its citizens will "live in peace and good health, and when they die at a ripe old age, they'll bequeath a similar life to their children" (372d). In that sense it is a beautiful city whose parts form a coherent and harmonious whole. Yet this beauty is only apparent since it depends on an unrealistic conception of what citizens could be. What makes the first city inadequate for Socrates' theoretical purposes is that it has no need for justice (371e). But the reason that there is no need for justice in this city is that it is a utopia in which citizens' desires are uniformly adapted to their environment, as if by nature. Justice, by contrast, is a virtue pertaining to beings whose desires are shaped by their conceptions of the good life, and hence their imaginations. Such beings are vulnerable to peculiar forms of dissatisfaction caused by *pleonexia* and *amour-propre*, and this makes them vulnerable to peculiar forms of conflict.[37] Since this is the kind of being that we ourselves are, our ideal city must be constructed accordingly, on pain of becoming a mere utopia. That is not to deny that the utopian city, with its unity, peace, health, and stable

---

36. The footnote in the Grube and Reeve translation says, "Myrtle *(murton)* and acorn *(phēgos)* are common slang terms for the female and male genitalia respectively."

37. See Rousseau, *Discourse on the Origin and Foundations of Inequality among Men,* in *The Basic Political Writings,* 60–64, 73–74.

self-reproduction, ought to serve as an inspiration for us—but in that respect it is no different from the constellation of heavenly bodies, which also provides a model of rational order composed of superior material.[38]

29. Even if Kallipolis is deliberately contrasted with the utopian city, we might still wonder whether it is itself supposed to be possible. Certainly it would have been so far removed from Athenian political actuality as to seem politically unfeasible to Plato's readers, and there is therefore a sense (to go back to §2 of the Introduction) in which we could call it practically impossible in the Athenian context. But Book V's discussion of models might seem to suggest the stronger conclusion that Kallipolis is not even supposed to be humanly possible:

> Then it was in order to have a model [paradeigma] that we were trying to discover what justice itself is like and what the completely just man would be like, if he came into being, and what kind of man he'd be if he did, and likewise with regard to injustice and the most unjust man. We thought that, by looking at how their relationship to happiness and its opposite seemed to us, we'd also be compelled to agree about ourselves as well, that the one who was most like them would have a portion of happiness most like theirs. But we weren't trying to discover these things in order to prove that it's possible for them to come into

---

38. For a similar account, see Reeve, *Philosopher-Kings*, 176–178. See Morrison, "Utopian Character of Plato's Ideal City," for a radically different account, according to which the city of pigs really is the best city, on Socrates' view, and possible too. What would make it possible, Morrison says, would be if all citizens were temperate like Socrates, in other words, if the whole city were full of philosophers, for example, if the ruling class of Kallipolis were to depart and set up a new colony. This is a reasonable suggestion, but if even philosophers are vulnerable to their psychic environments, as Plato surely thinks they are, such a city would in fact be unstable without the educational institutions of Kallipolis. Morrison argues that we should not assume that Socrates' description of the city of pigs was complete when Glaucon interrupted it; Socrates might have gone on to explain how intemperate desires were to be controlled in the city. This is a strange argument to make, since Socrates clearly suggests that the city is complete (371e) before Glaucon pushes him to introduce delicacies or relishes. See also Hyland, "*Republic*, Book 2, and the Origins of Political Philosophy," in *Finitude and Transcendence in the Platonic Dialogues*, 35–58.

being. . . . Do you think that someone is a worse painter if, having painted a model of what the finest and most beautiful human being would be like and having rendered every detail of his picture adequately, he could not prove that such a man could come into being? (472c–d)

It is easy to read this passage as suggesting that *paradeigmata* are not in fact subject to any constraints regarding possibility, and hence that Kallipolis is deliberately utopian. But what Socrates actually says is that proof of possibility is not an intrinsic criterion for the success of an ideal theory in the way that beauty is. We have already seen that the ascription of beauty carries with it the notion of natural possibility: to paint the most beautiful human being, it is necessary still to paint a human being. Given that Socrates clearly believes Kallipolis is as beautiful as it could be, it follows that he believes it does not violate the laws of natural possibility. His real point becomes clear in what follows.

Then what about our own case? Didn't we say that we were making a theoretical model of a good city? . . . So do you think our discussion will be any less reasonable if we can't prove that it's possible to found a city that's the same as the one in our theory? Is it possible to do anything in practice the same as in theory [literally, "as it is spoken"]? Or is it in the nature of practice to grasp truth less well than theory does, even if some people don't think so? . . . Then don't compel me to show that what we've described in theory can come into being exactly as we've described it. Rather, if we're able to discover how a city could come to be governed in a way that most closely approximates our description, let's say that we've shown what you ordered us to show, namely, that it's possible for our city to come to be. (472d–473a)[39]

---

39. It is worth noticing as well that until the last clause Socrates' point is really about how the city can come into being, not whether it can exist tout court.

Socrates' goal here is to remind us that Kallipolis is a "city in theory" or a "city in words" (369a, 592a).[40] As an imagined entity, an abstraction, Kallipolis is of a different ontological order from a real city.[41] This does not imply that it depends on unrealistic assumptions about human capacities, only that like all theoretical constructs it abstracts from various features of actuality. Some of these features may matter for practical purposes, just as a hikers' map may abstract from topographic features like hedges that do bear on the activity at hand. But the construct will have succeeded if its abstract lines track the core truths regarding a situation, including those having to do with possibility. As Socrates puts it in Book VII, "The things we've said about the city and its constitution aren't altogether wishful thinking. . . . It's hard for them to come about, but not impossible" (540d).[42]

§4 Disseminating Ideals

30. This chapter began with two passages in which Socrates compares rulers to painters who have to shift their attention back and

---

40. Grube and Reeve's translation, "city in theory," highlights the fact that although from one perspective Kallipolis comes into existence for the sake of its citizens, from another it is actually created in answer to Socrates' needs, in order to explain the nature and value of justice, such that its extent is delimited by that task. The tension between these perspectives marks the whole political philosophy of the *Republic* and arguably helps explain various notorious features, such as the absence of any discussion of education for the lower classes.

41. Burnyeat makes a similar point: "Kallipolis is a perfect but imaginary particular exemplification of justice" ("Utopia and Fantasy," 298). As such, it is in the wrong metaphysical category to be realized, so the question of possibility is really the question whether a reasonable approximation to it is possible, given various human obstacles.

42. Does the gap between model and real cities mean that Kallipolis can only ever be imperfectly realizable? It might be useful to think once again of soccer. Suppose a tactics sheet spells out a team's formation in pure, ideal form. An actual team will have no option but to behave in ways not specified within the narrow remit of the tactics sheet because a real match is more complex than the sheet could allow. But that just means that there is more than one way of fully implementing the plan. Of course, it may well be true that every team will also fall away from its formation at some point over the ninety minutes. But if at any moment the team is perfectly disciplined, it will surely be manifesting the relevant formation perfectly at that moment. What is beyond human possibility, however, is for such arrangements to last forever. "It is hard for a city composed in this way to change," declare the Muses whom Socrates has conjured in order to explain the demise of Kallipolis, "but everything that comes into being must decay" (546a).

forth between a model and a canvas. The two passages give ostensibly different accounts of the aim of this activity, with the first focusing on the need to establish and preserve "usages regarding just, beautiful and good things" and the second focusing on the need to "make human characters as dear to the gods as possible." In §1 we saw how these tasks are bound up with each other. To ensure that citizens are the best they can be, rulers need to shape linguistic and cultural usages so that the whole city becomes a kind of school designed to inculcate true belief regarding the good life. In §2 we turned away from the canvas and toward the models that philosopher-rulers are said to look toward. We saw that there are two kinds of models—actually existing exemplars and theoretical ideals—and that in some cases we will need to construct the latter in order to gain cognitive access to the former. Among the models of rational order that philosophers will look to in shaping souls are surely their ideals of the just man and the just city, both constrained by the requirements of natural possibility (§3). Putting these thoughts together, we can see that the ideal of Kallipolis ought to play an important role within Kallipolis itself. In the ideal city, that is, rulers would construct a model of the ideal city—a model in which the rulers would construct a model of the ideal city, and so on. This makes Socrates himself the model of a future philosopher-ruler: although he does not know the forms, he is nevertheless able to model the activity of holistic, dialectical inquiry involving the construction of theoretical ideals against a teleological horizon. But the reflexivity does not end there. As we will see, theoretical ideals such as the model of Kallipolis will guide not only the rulers of the just city but also its citizens.

31. In the famous image with which Book VII begins, Socrates speaks of nonphilosophers as trapped in a cave, with their necks and legs fettered so that they can only look directly in front of them. Far above the prisoners, and behind them, lies a fire that provides the only source of light in the cave. Between the fire and the prisoners sits a man-made wall, and just behind that wall (on the side of the fire) walk a group of people who talk among themselves and carry statues and artefacts that project above the wall. The prisoners would gain a kind of secondhand knowledge of this activity through the echoes and shadows bouncing off the wall of the cave, and not knowing

any better, they would take these echoes and shadows "for true reality" (515c). This epistemic condition would then support a social structure in which there are "honors, praises and prizes" for grasping the patterns created by the shadows (516a). Socrates compares this situation to a puppet show (514b).

32. But who are the puppeteers behind the wall? Given the theatricality of the situation, one's thoughts inevitably turn to the poets castigated elsewhere in the *Republic*. Two objections present themselves immediately. First, one might reasonably assume that artists would themselves be prisoners in the cave, given their epistemic and psychological condition. Second, Socrates gives no indication that those behind the wall deliberately project shadows or echoes; they appear to be simply going about their business. Neither point is fatal for the interpretation. The fact that those behind the wall go about their business blindly, without any effort to leave the cave, suggests that they are themselves trapped in some respect—not necessarily by some external force but more likely by their own desires, given that the prisoners' bonds turn out to be fastened to them by "feasting, greed, and other such pleasures . . . which, like leaden weights, pull [one's] vision downwards" (519a–b). If the poets are in the same epistemic and psychological condition as their audiences, being both unwilling and unable to look toward the truth, there would be two senses in which they do not deliberately project shadows or echoes on the wall of the cave. They do not recognize the power they have vis-à-vis the citizenry but rather pursue professional success blindly; and they are incapable of recognizing shadows as shadows or echoes as echoes in any case. We might therefore imagine the poets occupying two positions simultaneously—considered as producers, they are behind a wall that is high above the audience; considered as consumers, they are among the crowd at the bottom of the cave.

33. Although the statues carried along the wall of the cave are initially said to be "of people and other animals" (514c–515a), a few pages later we hear of the philosopher who returns to the cave being forced into arguments concerning "the shadows of justice or the statues of which they are the shadows" (517e). This transition, from physical distortion to ethical distortion, comes up time and again in

the *Republic*.[43] Art may distort our perception of physical objects, as with the mimetic painting discussed in Book X (597e–598c; 602c–d). But such examples are merely propaedeutics to prepare us for the real point, which is that artworks can distort our perception of the good life.[44] Socrates notes, for instance, that Homer is widely credited with the ability to "educate people and make them better" and to "benefit people and make them more virtuous," so that people think they should arrange their whole lives in accordance with his teachings despite the fact that he has no claim to epistemic or ethical superiority (600c–e; 606e).

34. The importance of art to ethical life is one of the great themes of the *Republic*. Toward the beginning of Book II, after Glaucon has challenged Socrates to provide an argument against the view that justice is valuable only for those too weak to reliably get their own way (358e–359b), Adeimantus observes that Glaucon's cynical account is entirely consonant with the lessons transmitted by Athenian culture. Although Athenian fathers do teach their sons to be just, they do so by referring to the rewards that follow from a reputation for justice, such as political offices and good marriages. And in this respect they are simply imitating famous poets such as Homer and Hesiod, whose stories depict a transactional relationship between gods and men in which just behavior is a way to secure favors from the gods. Given that another way to secure such favors is to offer plentiful sacrifices, the logical conclusion is that unjust people can be favored by the gods so long as they are rich and powerful (362e–365a). A youth capable of articulating the lesson these stories convey regarding "what sort of person he should be and how best to travel the road of life" would sum it up as follows, Adeimantus concludes: "I should create an

43. See Fine, "Knowledge and Belief in *Republic* V–VII," 233: "When Plato says that most of us are like the prisoners . . . he does not mean that most of us literally see only images of physical objects; we are [like them] in our moral beliefs (not in our physical object beliefs)."

44. I believe this would be clearer to readers if we thought of Greek sculpture instead of Greek painting, since classical sculpture clearly aimed at conveying a certain kind of ideal of human life. Admittedly, Socrates refers to painting, but this may be because the notion of physical distortion is easier to grasp than that of distortion at the level of ideals. In any case, sculpture does come up a great deal in the *Republic*, as we will see shortly.

illusionistic painting *[skiagraphos]* of virtue around me to deceive
those who come near, but keep behind it the wise Archilocus' greedy
and cunning fox" (365a–c).[45] The challenge facing Socrates is therefore not only to refute the cynical account of justice but also to find a
"device" *(mēchanē)* to ensure that even the richest and most powerful
honor justice rather than finding it laughable (366b–c). As Adeimantus suggests, this will involve cultural instruction from earliest
youth onward—and hence, one would assume, the reconfiguration
of artistic production (367a). This paves the way for Socrates' discussion of art in Books II and III, where he suggests regulating the
form and content of stories and music.

35. It is easy to get lost in the details of Plato's treatment of art,
but the most important point has already been made. Artists are educators. They influence our perception of the world, orienting us
toward a conception of what is beautiful, just, and good. As a result,
they shape our desires. And this makes them rulers in Plato's sense.
As we saw in Chapter 2, ruling is a craft that does not necessarily
involve holding office. A true ruler is someone who benefits her
subjects by maintaining their souls in optimal condition. This involves education, whether through direct instruction, as in the
household or the school, or through indirect instruction via the cultural environment. On Plato's understanding, artists are engaged
in just this activity. This is why Socrates speaks of those who revere
Homer as "the poet who educated Greece" and believe that "for
the management of human affairs and education in them, one
should take up his works and learn them and live guided by this
poet in the arrangement of one's who life" (606e). The trouble is
not with mimetic poetry as such, but with poets who "imitate images of virtue and of all the other things they write about, and have
no grasp of the truth" (600e), and therefore proceed blindly, without
knowing "in what way [the imitated] thing is good or bad" (602b).
These poets are in the condition of the sight lovers of Book V, whose

---

45. Compare the *prostasis* (facade of dignity) presented by the tyrant at 576d–577a
and the illusionistic painting described at 602d, as well as the *Gorgias*'s reference to
"flattery" or "pandering" *(kolokeia)* as the pseudo-craft that puts on the *mask* of a given
craft (464c–e).

usages regarding beauty roll around unstably—with the difference
that the poets are in a position to shape everyone else's usages.[46]
From Plato's perspective, the results are inevitably disastrous. Like
the philosopher-ruler, the poet is characterized as a painter of constitutions. But unlike the philosopher-ruler, the poet "arouses,
nourishes and strengthens [the appetitive] part of the soul and so
destroys the rational one" and therefore "puts a bad constitution
in the soul of each individual" (605e). The challenge for philosophers is therefore to replace poets as educators and thus as rulers.

36. To see what this involves, let us return to the cave. The group
carrying statues behind the wall, I said, could be artists qua producers; the rest of the population, including artists considered qua
consumers, then takes the shadows cast by these statues to be indica-
tive of the truth about the world, including the truth about justice.
But what are the statues? My suggestion is that they are models in
the sense of *paradeigmata*. The centerpiece of Socrates' discussion
of storytelling in Books II and III is the notion of imitation (*mimēsis*),
and imitation is intertwined with models. If stories transmit usages
regarding just, beautiful, and good things—a conception of the
good life, in short—it is not only because they depict the world as
constituted according to certain rules (so that it is possible for unjust
people to be happy, for instance) but also because they offer models
for imitation. Put simply, works of art tend to portray heroes, and
heroes are those whose traits we want to emulate; and since action
shapes souls, in straining to imitate heroes we end up shaping ourselves. So stories can provide models in the sense of imagined exemplary instances, and those models can play a crucial role in our ethical
development.

37. To bolster this interpretation, note that the image that Plato
most frequently uses to describe theoretical models is the statue. The
just man and the unjust man were created as models (*paradeigmata*)
to enable the interlocutors to assess the relative happiness of the two
lives in response to Glaucon's challenge, says Socrates (472c–d)—and

---

46. In fact, I would go so far as to say that they are the most important sight lovers;
recall that in Chapter 1 we saw that the sight lovers come into the picture because they
are rivals to philosophical rule.

when Glaucon first presented that challenge, Socrates described his descriptions of the just and unjust life as being like statues purified (the verb is *ekkathairein*) for a competition (361d). At the end of Book VII Glaucon returns the compliment, describing Socrates as "like a statue-maker" for having produced rulers who are beautiful in every way. Meanwhile, Kallipolis is also compared to a statue, both at the start of Book IV (420c), in the passage concerning the color of the eyes, and at the moment of its inception, which is described as a process of purifying *(kathairein)* the luxurious city, an image that would call to mind a sculptor whittling away imperfections even if it did not echo Socrates' earlier invocation of purification (399e). Finally, the word *plattein*, meaning "to mold" or "to sculpt," comes up repeatedly in connection with the construction of theoretical models: Socrates and his interlocutors are described as sculpting a city (374a, 420c), and in Book IX Glaucon is asked to sculpt a new image of the soul (588b–d).[47]

38. Given the connection between models and statues within Plato's symbolic order, as well as the fact that works of art provide models for imitation, it seems reasonable to conclude that the statues whose shadows are projected on the wall of the cave are models provided by artists—models that are taken as exemplary despite being created by people ignorant of true form.[48] If this is right, then ideals in the sense of models are the vectors of damage to ideals in the sense of highest values. Assuming there is no way out of the cave for most citizens, the only way for philosopher-rulers to give citizens true belief about beauty, justice, and goodness would be to replace the poets' statues with ones of their own making. Where once Homeric heroes like Achilles seemed to make divine form and true virtue manifest on the human stage, in Kallipolis the stage will be popu-

---

47. Philosopher-rulers are also said to mold the souls of their citizens (377b–c, 500d). This connects the image of philosopher-rulers as painters with the image of them as sculptors; given that statues were painted, this may be an anachronistic distinction in any case. On another note, Allen points out that Plato uses the word *plattein* more often than any other fourth- or fifth-century Greek author. See Allen, *Why Plato Wrote*, 44.

48. Allen, *Why Plato Wrote*, 76–77.

lated with heroes like Socrates.[49] And the master statue, one might suppose, will be the model of the beautiful city itself—the story of a harmonious and stable social order that knows itself as such.[50]

§5 Making the City Beautiful

39. Philosophers cannot shape the sociocultural environment by themselves; they depend on the division of labor. For it is not only statues whose shadows are projected onto the wall of the cave, but "artefacts of all sorts" (*skeuē pantodapa*). The word *skeuē* also features prominently in Book III's discussion of crafts, with its peculiar claim that philosophers ought to supervise craftsmen to ensure that painting, weaving, embroidery, architecture, and the manufacture of implements or furnishings (*skeuē*) do not "represent—whether in pictures, buildings, or any other works—a character that is vicious, unrestrained, slavish, and graceless" (400e–401b). One might wonder how it is possible for a building to represent a character. The clue is that the Greek verb translated as "represent," *empoiein*, suggests not imitation but rather building in. The idea appears to be that material artefacts come with a picture of human life built into them, such that their mere presence in our environment helps brings that vision into being.

40. To make sense of this proposition, it might help to connect it with a powerful argument made by a contemporary theorist of ideology, Sally Haslanger. Haslanger, drawing on the work of William Sewell, suggests that social structures are constituted by a combination of "schemas and resources."[51]

> [Schemas are] intersubjective patterns of perception, thought and behavior . . . embodied in individuals as a shared cluster of open-ended dispositions to see things a certain way or to

---

49. For an allusion to Homer in this connection, see 501b. On Socrates as hero, see Allen, *Why Plato Wrote*, 72.

50. On the cave and the self-image of society, see Burnyeat, "Culture and Society in Plato's *Republic*," 240–243.

51. Haslanger, "But Mom, Crop-Tops *Are* Cute!," in *Resisting Reality*, 413–417. The reference is to Sewell, *Logics of History*.

respond habitually in particular circumstances. Schemas encode knowledge and also provide scripts for interaction with
each other and our environment.[52]

A schema is a shared orientation to the world, not necessarily present
to consciousness, that shapes our perceptions and actions. For this
orientation to constitute a social structure, as opposed to a mere psychological generality, it must be embedded in the material world
somehow, so that the world "pushes back" when we try to think differently. This is where resources come in: they "provide the materiality of social structures."[53] Resources are anything that can be used
to enhance or maintain power, from strength and skill to inanimate
objects. For example, the schema of two sex categories is built into
toilet facilities in terms of both their design and their labeling, so
that people who try to adopt a different schema will find the material world pushing back against them. Once we see that material objects can both encode a way of looking at the world and provide
scripts for interacting with one another, it begins to dawn on us that
the entire human landscape is structured in this way: "Towns, city
halls, churches, universities, philosophy departments, gyms, play-
grounds, homes, are schematically structured and practice-imbued
material things."[54] As Plato thought, then, artefacts are normatively
laden. They bring with them a picture of human life, and they play
a part in making that picture a reality. No less than the models
we emulate, they cast shadows on the wall of the cave.

41. The question that Haslanger takes up is how we can critique
beliefs that depend on "schematic materiality," given that they are
clearly tracking something that is objective in the sense of being out
there in the world rather than up to us as individuals. Plato's answer
would involve repairing to a higher form of inquiry in which we consider what the true form of a craft object would be, given its function in society, where that in turn depends on the true form and
function of the soul.

---

52. Haslanger, "But Mom, Crop-Tops Are Cute!," 415.
53. Ibid., 415.
54. Ibid., 417.

42. We can see this if we consider a third passage in which the word *skeuē* plays a prominent role, namely Book X's treatment of the metaphysics of crafts (596b–e, 601d–e). Socrates begins by saying that craftsmen who make manufactured items do so by "looking towards the forms" of the couch or the table or whatever else they are making (596b). Later he says that it is the users of craft objects, not their makers, who have knowledge *(epistēmē)* of the qualities that make them good or bad and are therefore in a position to "prescribe how [those products] should be made," thereby giving craftsmen correct belief *(pistis orthē* or *doxa orthē)* on the subject (601d–602a). These two statements appear to contradict each other: in the first, craftsmen receive guidance by looking toward the forms; in the second, they receive guidance by asking users about the qualities that make an object good or bad. For the statements to fit together, it must be the case that for a craftsman to look toward the form of the object she produces just is for her to ask its user about which qualities would make it good or bad. This is surprising. In Books V–VII knowledge of forms was hard to come by, to say the least—certainly being experienced *(empeiros)* in a practical domain, as the users of Book X are said to be, was not sufficient. On the other hand, in Chapter 1 we saw that for Plato, philosophy is just the activity of posing certain kinds of questions, principally questions about how things fit together into functional wholes. In a sense this is what the users of Book X have to be doing when they reflect on what makes objects of a certain kind good or bad, since they cannot answer that question without asking themselves what the objects in question are for. To pose this question seriously requires discipline and dialectic. We would have to inquire whether a flourishing culture requires, say, couches, and, if so, what kind of couches they ought to be, given that different kinds of couches might conduce to different kinds of activity. To do this, we might imagine a world without couches and then ask whether their introduction would serve a genuine need. We might go back, in other words, to Book II of the *Republic*, to the founding of a city in words—to ideal theory.

43. It is hard to imagine any ordinary user of craft objects reasoning along these lines. But just as Book X's examples of art misleading our senses are merely simple propaedeutics to help us see that

art misleads us regarding the good life, so the experienced user of
Book X is only a propaedeutic to help us see that the ultimate user
of craft products is the city as a whole, with philosopher-rulers reasoning on its behalf. To illustrate this point, it might be helpful to
think of the beginning of the *Nicomachean Ethics*, where Aristotle
draws a picture of a whole economy tied together by reflection on
what it is for individuals and collectives to flourish. Every human activity seeks some good, and some activities control the ends of other
activities. Bridle making falls under horsemanship; horsemanship
falls under generalship; and generalship falls under the political craft,
which is the expertise "that sets out which of the expertises there
needs to be in cities, and what sorts of expertise each group of people
should learn, and up to what point," with its guiding end being
"the human good" *(tanthrōpinon agathon).*[55] This is Plato's picture as
well. In Chapter 2 we saw that the rulers of Kallipolis will direct the
division of labor according to a conception of the form and function
of city and soul. Now we can see that this will involve instructing
craftsmen as to the role of their products in society and hence as to
what would make those products good and bad.

   44. The couches of Kallipolis will therefore be different from the
couches of Athens. Those who make them will receive instruction
from philosophers, who act on behalf of the ultimate user, the city as
a whole, to "weave together" different activities so as to generate and
maintain a sociocultural environment conducive to human flourishing.[56] This means that the couches will embody, or "build in," a philosophically informed ideal of the human soul and the human city. As
Myles Burnyeat observes, recognizing Plato's interest in material culture allows us to comprehend the unity of his political philosophy and
his philosophy of art, and therewith the unity of the *Republic* itself:

> The ideal city is ideal because its entire culture—material,
> moral, and musical—is pervaded by the right values, thanks to
> the philosopher-rulers' understanding of the Forms, including
> the Forms of Couch and of Table. Book X's positing of these

---

55. Aristotle, *Nicomachean Ethics* I.1–2.
56. The image of "weaving" comes from *Statesman* 279a ff.

two Forms indicates that Plato wants to claim there is an objectively correct answer to the question how the city should make
use of couches and tables and all the other apparatus of civilized
gatherings. By an objectively correct answer I mean one that is
rooted in human nature, so that in the ideal city human nature
achieves the best cultural expression it can aspire to. . . . The
correct way to design and use a couch is . . . determined by its
function, to help turn the impressionable young into worthy
citizens. . . . The long discussion of musical poetry in *Republic*
II–III can be read as Plato's account of the objectively best way
to use couches and tables for the education and fulfillment of
human nature.[57]

45. Through our productive activities, we build a world for ourselves.[58] This world embodies certain self-understandings, and the
resulting schematic materiality, to use Haslanger's phrase, serves to
further entrench these self-understandings.[59] In an ideologically
unified society, every single object therefore serves as a model of a
certain kind. A given couch may not be perfect, but to the degree that
its form is tailored to its intended purpose, it will bespeak a picture
of the human good, however warped that picture may be.[60] It therefore serves as an invitation to those who interact with it; it invites us
to think a certain way and to act a certain way. In Haslanger's terms,
it provides a script for interaction with each other and with our
environment. In Plato's terms, it casts shadows on the wall of the
cave.

46. In the two passages with which this chapter began, philosopher-
rulers were said to shape citizens' characters, as well as their usages
(*nomima*) regarding just, beautiful, and good things. The two are

---

57. Burnyeat, "Culture and Society in Plato's *Republic*," 245–246.
58. See Arendt, *Human Condition*, 79–174, for an attempt to distinguish between
"work," which builds a world, and "labor," which aims only at self-reproduction. I do
not accept this distinction, but the notion of world building is still helpful. Marx's
Economic and Philosophical Manuscripts of 1844 is still the locus classicus for this topic.
59. Here Haslanger and Sewell are drawing on Giddens, *Constitution of Society*.
60. In Chapter 7 I will consider production that is warped by the logic of
moneymaking.

related because shaping characters involves shaping conceptions of the good life and hence shaping conceptions of what counts as just, beautiful, and good. We can now understand what it means to say that philosopher-rulers turn the whole city into a kind of school: control over the division of labor allows them to create an environment permeated with ideals and models, from the just man and the just city to the right kind of couch and the right kind of shoe.

47. If the social environment educates its citizens adequately, they will have true belief about what counts as just, beautiful, and good. Although this would not amount to knowledge, it would be beneficial in two ways. First, it would enable each citizen to flourish to the highest degree possible, given her psychological type. Honor-loving people would pursue things that are truly honorable, for instance, and appetitive people would neither indulge nor develop destructive appetites. Second, it would stabilize the social order itself. For although most citizens will not understand why Kallipolis is the best city, they will believe it just, beautiful, and good. In this respect we might fruitfully compare Plato's ideal society to Rawls's—but whereas for Rawls the disposition critical to social stability over time is the sense of justice, Plato emphasizes the sense of beauty.[61]

48. "Perhaps much of what we are saying, since it is contrary to custom [para to ethos], would incite ridicule if it were carried out in practice as we've described," says Socrates of his idea that men and women should strip down for exercise together (452a). The first stage of his response, we saw earlier, is to point out that "it wasn't very long ago that the Greeks thought it shameful [aischros] and ridiculous [geloios] (as the majority of barbarians still do) for even men to be seen naked" (452c). Ridiculousness is an aesthetic category in the sense that it is rooted in perception (aisthēsis): one seems to simply see

---

61. It is worth noting that the *nomima* (usages) at issue in the argument against the sight lovers concern beauty in particular. The contrast is between those whose understanding (*epistēmē*) allows them to reliably discriminate between beautiful and ugly things (whether tokens or types) on the basis of an account of forms, giving them some cognitive moorings as they encounter the flux of material life, and those whose usages are rolled hither and thither by each passing wave of change because they remain untethered to any higher standard. Socrates makes clear that this applies to more than just beauty, but beauty is a particularly apt example. For Rawls's views on the sense of justice, see Rawls, *Theory of Justice*, pt. 3.

something as ridiculous. Yet however obvious or immediate the ridiculous appears to be, standards of ridiculousness are always cultural or conventional. That is why Socrates is able to say that "what was ridiculous to the eyes faded away" once Athenians became accustomed to the new practice of stripping for exercise (452d). But although standards of ridiculousness vary from society to society, some are better than others. The criterion is goodness:

> It's foolish to think that anything besides the bad is ridiculous or to try to raise a laugh at the sight of anything besides what's stupid or bad or (putting it the other way around) it's foolish to take seriously any standard of what is fine or beautiful other than goodness. (452d–e; cf. *Gorgias*, 474d–475a)

As this passage makes clear, for Plato, ridiculousness is an aesthetic category in a second sense as well: to perceive something as ridiculous just is to perceive it as ugly or shameful (held together in Greek as one concept, *to aischron*) as opposed to beautiful or noble (held together as *to kalon*). Our standards of ridiculousness, in other words, derive from our standards of beauty. The reconfiguration of *nomoi* concerning exercise is therefore at the same time a reconfiguration of *nomima* regarding what counts as beautiful and therefore noble or worthy of pride. And this is just one part of a larger aesthetic reorientation designed to stabilize the social order.[62]

49. Aesthetic education would also prepare the way for genuine knowledge among those capable of it, namely philosophers. "Truth is akin . . . to what is proportionate," we hear in Book VI, so a true philosopher will need "a natural sense of proportion and grace, one whose innate disposition makes it easy to lead to the form of each thing which is" (486d). This "natural" sense is as much the product of second nature as of first nature; in Book IV Socrates tells us that "good education and upbringing, when they are preserved, produce

---

62. This may affect the production and consumption of artworks: Aristophanes' *Clouds* and *Assembleywomen* may no longer be considered funny, for instance. Note the use of *kōmōidein* at 452d—Plato seems to have real *kōmōidoi*, such as Aristophanes, in mind when he has Socrates speak of those who will find his new customs ridiculous. See also the discussion of comedy in Book X, 606a–c.

good natures" (424a).[63] The educational program of Books II and III is obviously concerned with giving prospective philosophers the right beliefs, but it is also concerned with inculcating sensitivity to true form. This is why stories must follow the right pattern *(tupos)*, and why weavers, embroiders, architects, and so on must produce works that manifest "gracefulness"—*euschēmosunē*, literally, well-formedness (377b–c; 400e–402a).

> Anyone who has been properly educated in music and poetry will sense it acutely when something has been omitted from a thing and when it hasn't been finely crafted or finely made by nature. And since he has the right distastes, he'll praise fine things, be pleased by them, receive them into his soul, and, being nurtured by them, become fine and good. He'll rightly object to what is shameful, hating it while he's still young and unable to grasp the reason, but, having been educated in this way, he will welcome the reason when it comes and recognize it easily because of its kinship with himself. (401d–402a)

Here we see the importance of aesthetic education for establishing true belief, on Plato's view. The idea is that if we grow up with the right kind of patterns around us, we will imbibe a nontheoretical, perceptual sense of beauty and well-formedness that will allow us to register when something is out of place or otherwise lacking in harmony.[64] The wool will be dyed, as it were, and no amount of washing will be able to remove the color (429c–430b). To develop this true belief about beauty into knowledge, the budding philosophers of Kallipolis will eventually engage in dialectic, considering particular questions in light of a "unified vision" *(sunopsis)* that brings together all

---

63. Thanks to M. M. McCabe for drawing my attention to this passage, which represents yet another instance in which the *Republic* turns out to contain what is usually thought to be a distinctively Aristotelian doctrine.

64. As we saw in §3 of Chapter 2, the image of things slipping by without our noticing recurs time and again throughout the *Republic*, both in connection with the interlocutors and in connection with the rulers—it is crucial to guardians that they watch over the city relentlessly.

forms of inquiry (537b–d). And then, when the time comes, they will cast their own shadows on the walls of Kallipolis.

IF KALLIPOLIS IS THE BEAUTIFUL CITY, it is because its rulers, who are repeatedly compared to sculptors and painters, actively make it so. Their goal is to ensure that their subjects are the best they can be in terms of psychic order and therefore—since beauty is a matter of proportion and harmony—as beautiful as they can be, given the limitations imposed by their natural endowments. To paint the constitutions of their citizens, they must paint the constitution of the city. They must ensure that customs and usages reflect natural truths, and this requires them to turn the city into an environment replete with models of rational order. To do this they must watch over the division of labor to ensure that craft products build in an accurate vision of the good life. This can be achieved either directly or indirectly. Since the city is the ultimate user of craft products, philosopher-rulers (or their auxiliaries) will hold craftsmen to account for their work. But philosophers will also produce something of their own, namely models of the good city and the good person. For philosophical inquiry into city and soul will often involve the construction of such models for the purposes of testing and expanding understanding, and these models can then be disseminated throughout society as part of the effort to engender true belief about what counts as just, beautiful, and good. If this process is successful, ordinary citizens will naturally orient their labors toward the production of a healthy cultural environment. Once again, then, we can see that ideal theory will play a crucial role within the ideal city. To rule well, rulers will need to construct an ideal of their own society and continually work to refine it. But they will also need to propagate that ideal via stories and speeches so that each citizen comes to recognize the social order as beautiful and noble and hence as worth defending. The ideal city is therefore beautiful in three different ways: in the harmony of its constitution; in the texture of daily life; and in the fractal, self-reflexive way it reflects on itself.

4

Plato and Athens

POLITICAL IDEALISM, as I have defined it, consists in a commitment to orient oneself with respect to a vision of the best possible form that one's society could take. This commitment will shape both the way one acts and the way one thinks. On the theoretical side, it will involve repeated attempts to consider how one's society might best be and then to perceive its current condition in light of that potential. On the practical side, it will involve acting so as to close the gap between the actual and the potential.

There is reason to be skeptical of grand claims concerning the value of political idealism, whether positive or negative. Certainly it is possible for political idealism to be pointless or dangerous. An ideal might be of little use in charting and navigating the world as it actually is. It might lead us to misperceive the situation by, as we say, "idealizing" it. Or it might serve to protect the status quo by directing our attention away from the messy and the unpleasant and toward the precise and the pure, dispersing dissatisfaction that might otherwise boil up productively. These are genuine possibilities. But it is surely also possible for political idealism to be salutary and transformative. In disposing us to consider the full range of political possibility, idealism might disclose actuality more truly. And by protecting us from the mental torpor that elides feasibility and possibility, it might enable us to transform our world for the better.

Again, these are genuine possibilities. It therefore looks as though the abstract question regarding the appropriate role of political idealism in political life ought really to dissolve into a concrete question regarding the appropriate role of a given kind of idealism in a specific situation. A specific ideal—say, John Rawls's theory of justice—may function as radical in one decade and ideological in the next. To correctly assess its practical and theoretical value may require sound judgment rather than abstract philosophical argument.[1] If the abstract form of the question is indeed intractable, the most we can do at the general level is to arrive at a list of ways in which idealism can go well or badly. To have dissolved the abstract question in this way might represent a gain in clarity and perhaps self-knowledge.[2] But philosophical inquiry would have no further contribution to make.

That does not seem to be Plato's position. Political idealism comes up in two ways in the *Republic*. It is essential to the functioning of the ideal society, as Chapters 2 and 3 have shown. Rulers must be philosophers, and that entails, I have claimed, that they must orient themselves, both practically and theoretically, with respect to a vision of the best possible form their society could take, as well as ensuring that the cultural environment is replete with models that orient the citizenry with respect to the good life. But the *Republic* also contains a wealth of reflection concerning the role of political idealism in nonideal societies, as this chapter will show. We can therefore say that the *Republic* as a whole does offer an answer to the question of political idealism in its general form, if only disjunctively: it inquires into the appropriate role of political idealism in both ideal and nonideal societies, and hence in all societies.

---

1. One of the ironies of recent political philosophy is that those who have (as a matter of metaphilosophy) emphasized the ineliminable need for theorists to address themselves to specific contexts have tended not to ask themselves what their own context might call for. As I wrote in the Introduction, my hunch is that contemporary politics stands in need of both a hardheaded look at power structures *and* a dose of idealism.

2. Compare Wittgenstein, *Philosophical Investigations*, §127: "The work of the philosopher consists of assembling reminders for a particular purpose."

In Book VI Socrates seems to suggest that wise citizens will keep well away from political life in a nonideal city. Having "seen the insanity of the masses and realised that there is nothing healthy, so to speak, in public affairs, and that there is no ally with whose aid the champion of justice can survive," the wise citizen "keeps quiet and does his own work, like someone who takes refuge under a little wall from a storm of dust or hail driven by the wind" (496c–d). This thought is repeated at the end of Book IX, where Socrates says the wise man will "take part in the politics of [Kallipolis] alone, and of no other [city]" (592b). If we take this to represent Plato's own position, the question naturally arises: what then is the point of sketching the outlines of Kallipolis? Is the goal simply to provide a model on the basis of which to constitute our own souls, as the end of Book IX (592b) appears to suggest? Or does the sketch achieve some kind of political work? If the latter, is the idea to provide a blueprint just in case a king should ever become a philosopher or vice versa?[3] Or to disabuse philosophers of their idealistic illusions and to encourage them to abandon politics altogether?[4] Or is there some more subtle relationship between the ideal presented in the *Republic* and the day-to-day realities of nonideal politics?

A growing body of scholarship focuses on the relationship between Plato's political theory and its Athenian context.[5] One thing seems clear: publishing the *Republic* was a political act.[6] Interpretations of the dialogue differ greatly, but it is beyond dispute that the *Republic* invites Athenians to think differently about political life in general and democracy in particular. So Plato cannot have meant to advocate complete quietism on the part of philosophers in nonideal socie-

---

3. On the notion of a blueprint, see above all Popper, *Open Society and Its Enemies*, 157–168.

4. See especially Strauss, *City and Man*, 50–138, as well as Allan Bloom's "Interpretive Essay" in his edition of the *Republic*, 307–436.

5. Some important examples are Ober, *Political Dissent in Democratic Athens*; Monoson, *Plato's Democratic Entanglements*; Allen, *Why Plato Wrote*; and Lane, "Antianarchia."

6. On reading works of political philosophy as speech acts within particular political contexts, see above all Skinner, "Meaning and Understanding in the History of Ideas."

ties, a life of philosophy as opposed to politics—or at least he cannot have done so consistently, given the example he himself set.

Beyond that, however, the space for interpretation remains surprisingly open. Historians have an easy time interpreting the speech act represented by, say, Bertholt Brecht's play *The Resistible Rise of Arturo Ui:* it is clearly a satire on the rise of Adolf Hitler. We know a lot about Brecht's political commitments from his other writings; we have a good picture of his intellectual milieu (what he was reading, who his peers and rivals were, and which phrases and images were common); we know he wrote the play in 1941; we know enough about the history of the period to recognize that every single scene is based on an actual event; and (as that goes to show) the play is not particularly subtle in its aims or execution. When we turn to the *Republic*, most of these elements are missing. We cannot fix Plato's political commitments in advance by looking to his other writings, since they are no less debatable than the *Republic* and in any case may reflect different phases in his development. Our knowledge of his intellectual milieu is limited since it depends on the partial and most likely unrepresentative selection of texts that have found their way down to us across the generations. Since there is little consensus on the relative ordering of the different dialogues, let alone their dates of composition, we cannot be sure how many allusions to recent occurrences will forever elude us. And to cap it all, the *Republic* is an extraordinarily complex piece of writing, both philosophically and rhetorically.

Given these difficulties, the most promising avenue for grasping the political act constituted by the *Republic* may in fact turn out to be close reading informed by (historically sensitive) philosophical reconstruction. In this chapter I use the interpretive resources developed in Chapters 1, 2, and 3 to uncover Plato's way of thinking about the role of political idealism in nonideal societies. I begin from the idea of poets and philosophers as political rivals. If philosophers in Kallipolis are to replace poets' statues with their own, there is no reason that philosophers in other cities cannot fight the same battle. This suggests a way of interpreting the contribution of the *Republic* to Athenian politics: by introducing models of the just man and the just city, the *Republic* aims to change the way Athenians perceive their own city. As Danielle Allen puts it, "Plato's dialogues were so many seeds sown broadly under the hot Athenian sun to implant culturally and politically salient changes in the democracy's system of value, that is, its constitution. Plato wrote to re-order the symbol garden of Athenian culture."[7] Once we see that Plato aims to alter Athenians' self-understanding, we can bring in a dimension of philosophical rule that we have not yet discussed, namely the dissemination of images that are strictly speaking inaccurate. This chapter therefore discusses the *Republic*'s myths—the myth of Er in particular—and also its caricatures, especially its caricature of democracy. The goal is to uncover the relationship between Plato's political idealism and what we might call his critical theory—that is, his attempt to effect political change by chipping away at the ideological underpinnings of Athenian society.[8]

§1 Rule without Office

1. Plato's conception of rule is idiosyncratic, as we have seen. To rule people is to exercise control over their souls; to rule them well is to maintain their souls in the best possible condition. To rule a population effectively, it is best to have control over political institutions so that one can make enforceable decisions pertaining to the constitution of society and hence the composition of the sociocultural environment. But political power is not an essential feature of rule. The key is control over souls—over characters and usages, that is, and so over conceptions of the good life.

2. A resigning minister once said of the British government of the day that it "gives the impression of being in office but not in power." Plato might have said something similar of the statesmen of his day—for the real rulers of Athens, he thought, were the poets. Clearly poet-rulers like Homer do not hold office: they exercise power over

---

7. Allen, *Why Plato Wrote*, 68.
8. Whether this counts as a critical theory will depend, of course, on the definition we use. Here I am using the term to denote a form of social inquiry that is at once descriptive and normative and that seeks to undermine the contemporary social order in some way. In this sense, critical theory goes beyond its Hegelian instantiation in the Frankfurt school. For more on the question of how to define critical theory, see Chapter 7.

the imagination rather than the state, but in so doing, they shape citizens' ideals and hence their souls. This power is so great that not even Socrates can escape it. For all the many arguments he marshals against poetry, he admits that "the love of [it] has been implanted in us by the upbringing we have received," with the result that the best he can achieve in the face of its pleasures is continence: when poetry tempts him to neglect justice and the rest of virtue, he says, he can only "behave like people who have fallen in love with someone but who force themselves to stay away from him, because they realize that their passion isn't beneficial" (607e–608b; cf. 595b).

3. The baleful influence of poets has a silver lining. If ruling does not require holding office, then philosophers do not need to wait for the one fine day when "political power and philosophy entirely coincide" (473d) in order to begin taking power in their cities. Certainly Kallipolis will come about only if "philosophers come to power in a city" (540d); and "there can be no happiness, either public or private, in any other city" (473e). But this does not entail that non-Kallipolean cities are all in the same condition: some engender virtue better than others. Nor does the fact that a philosopher will refuse to "take part in the practical affairs" of those cities (592a–b) entail that he must refuse to play any role whatsoever in improving their wider culture. So if ruling is a matter of shaping souls, philosophers can exercise a form of rule in nonideal societies just by teaching young people, as Socrates himself did. Aristotle makes much the same claim toward the end of the *Nicomachean Ethics* (X.9):

> It is best, then, if the community attends to upbringing, and attends correctly. But if the community neglects it, it seems fitting for each individual to promote the virtue of his children and his friends—to be able to do it, or at least to decide to do it. From what we have said, however, it seems he will be better able to do it if he acquires legislative science *(nomothetikē)*.

In a nonideal society, Aristotle suggests, individuals must do the best they can to promote the virtue of their friends, a category that on his view includes one's fellow citizens and even, it seems, one's fellow

human beings in general.[9] This will involve seeking to acquire legislative expertise and to exercise it, as far as possible, daily. As so often,
Aristotle both inherits and schematizes Plato's position. For Plato,
as we have seen, shaping souls requires shaping the cultural environment, both by controlling the division of labor and by molding
society's image of itself and its aims—the "social imaginary," as it is
sometimes called.[10] Philosophers ought to do this in ideal and nonideal societies alike, and for much the same reasons: in order to act
justly and so maintain their internal psychic order by performing
their social work, but also in order to contribute to the creation of
a sociocultural environment in which their own growth, and that
of philosophy, will be fuller. By exercising influence over the social imaginary, philosophers in nonideal societies will create a better
environment both for their fellow citizens and for themselves.

4. This helps explain what Plato is up to in the *Republic*. Consider
the ship-of-state simile, for instance, which Socrates introduces in
response to Adeimantus's charge that his arguments regarding the
political value of philosophy are belied by the fact that those who
take up philosophy generally become useless cranks (487b–d). Presumably a precondition for rulers coming to philosophize would be
the existence of a culture in which philosophy is not misunderstood

---

9. On friendship with fellow citizens and human beings in general, see Aristotle,
Nicomachean Ethics VIII.11.

10. On the notion of a social imaginary, see Castoriadis, *Imaginary Institution of
Society;* and Charles Taylor, *Modern Social Imaginaries.* Castoriadis writes, "Every
society up to now has attempted to give an answer to a few fundamental questions:
Who are we as a collectivity? What are we for one another? Where and in what are
we? What do we want; what do we desire; what are we lacking? Society must define its
'identity', its articulation, the world, its relations to the world and to the objects it
contains, its needs and its desires. Without the 'answer' to these 'questions', without
these 'definitions', there can be no human world, no society, no culture—for everything would be an undifferentiated chaos. The role of imaginary significations is to
provide an answer to these questions, an answer that, obviously, neither 'reality', nor
'rationality' can provide. . . . Of course, when we speak of 'questions', 'answers', and
'definitions', we are speaking metaphorically. These are not questions and answers that
are posed explicitly, and the definitions are not ones given in language. The questions
are not even raised prior to the answers. Society constitutes itself by producing a de
facto answer to these questions in its life, in its activity. It is in the doing of each
collectivity that the answer to these questions appears as an embodied meaning; this
social doing allows itself to be understood only as a reply to the questions that it
implicitly poses itself" (146–147).

and despised, so if Socrates is to persuade Athenians that rulers should philosophize, he needs to shift the way they imagine philosophers. The image he offers is complicated, but roughly speaking, the invitation is to compare the city to a ship whose owner (the demos) is cognitively limited and easily persuaded. The sailors quarrel over who should captain the ship, even though none of them have learned the craft of captaincy (or even recognized its existence). Anyone skilled at persuading or forcing the shipowner to let him rule gets praised as a skilled captain, while the true captain—the one who recognizes the importance of the seasons, the stars, and the winds, for example—is dismissed as a stargazer or a useless babbler. Transposed back to the city, this leaves us with the image of a society that has lost the concept of ruling as a craft and so cannot recognize the importance of philosophy. The image of philosophers as stargazers calls to mind Aristophanes' *Clouds*, which mocked Socrates in more or less those terms and thereby shaped Athenian perceptions of Socrates in ways that became crucial at his trial.[11] There is reason to believe, then, that the ship of state is an image of democratic Athens in particular. This impression is reinforced a few lines later, when Socrates tells Adeimantus to "teach this image *[eikōn]* . . . to the person who is surprised that philosophers are not honored in cities" (489a–b)—for if Adeimantus is to teach the simile to others, he must surely do so within his own city, which is democratic Athens. To speak in the *Republic*'s own idiom, we can say that Socrates is instructing Adeimantus to project the image of the ship of state onto the wall of the Athenian cave with the goal of transforming the way Athenians conceive of philosophers.

5. Bernard Williams made a helpful distinction between the listener and the audience of a work of political philosophy.[12] The listener is the person purportedly addressed by the text or by a given portion of it—a prince, say, who is being advised on how to conduct himself. The audience, on the other hand, consists of the group of people expected to learn from the text—the wider public or some subset of it. The literary nature of the *Republic* complicates this

---

11. See Plato, *Apology* 19c.
12. Williams, "The Liberalism of Fear," in *In the Beginning Was the Deed*, 56–58.

distinction without erasing it. In the case of the ship of state, for
instance, there is an immediate listener, Adeimantus, and there are
also secondary listeners in the form of all those in attendance, namely
Glaucon, Thrasymachus, Polemarchus, Lysias, Euthydemus, Char-
mantides, and Clitophon. The primary audience, meanwhile, in the
sense of those expected to learn from the dialogue, is presumably
the members of Plato's Academy, with a secondary audience being
the wider Athenian demos. In asking Adeimantus to propagate the
ship-of-state simile, then, Socrates is effectively appealing to acade-
micians to share the image with their fellow citizens.

6. If the ship-of-state image were disseminated widely, and if it
somehow took root in the Athenian imaginary so that parents cited
it to their children much as they were wont to cite Homer's images—
"shepherd of the people" being replaced by "captain of the people,"
perhaps—it might alter the way Athenians conceived of the relationship
between philosophy and politics. They might become more skeptical of rhetoric, for instance, and more respectful of philosophy, and
this shift in what they considered worthy of honor might in turn
affect their ambitions. If this were the case, then Plato would have
succeeded in shaping the characters of his fellow citizens. He would
have ruled them.

7. Once we recognize this possibility, a new aspect of the *Republic*
comes into view. For the ship of state is just one of many educational
images in the *Republic* and hence just one of many statues to be placed
on the wall of the Athenian cave—indeed, the image of the cave is
another, along with the sun, the line, the just man, and the just city.
Suitably internalized, any of these images might serve to reorient the
Athenian social imaginary and thereby shift conceptions of the good
life and perceptions of the present situation.

8. But that is not all, for the *Republic* is itself a model of a certain
kind. It is a highly sophisticated literary object, for one thing: a narrative dominated by dialogue that contains various subsidiary narratives and dialogues; a coherent whole that links its parts through
techniques of ring composition; and a work that reflects on its own
nature and purpose.[13] At its best, the *Republic* is therefore a kind of

---

13. On the notion of ring composition, see Barney, "Platonic Ring-Composition
and *Republic* 10." It is sometimes claimed that Socrates' narration disobeys his own

microcosm: a rational, harmonious order in which each part plays a role, with each part being a whole itself composed of parts. As such, it is the kind of craft object whose production serves to educate its user in standards of beauty and thereby to shape characters and usages.

9. The *Republic* also models dialectical inquiry, as we have seen repeatedly. In Chapter 1 we saw that Book IV's philosophical psychology provides a model of dialectical inquiry as holistic investigation that goes back and forth between concrete particulars and a set of nested functional contexts. In Chapter 2 we saw that Books II–IX provide a model for the inquiry a true guardian would have to pursue in order to guard herself, justifying from scratch the belief that psychic and political justice are both beneficial for more than their simulator-accessible consequences, and we also saw that Socrates' theoretical construction of the ideal city provides a model for the rulers' regulation of the social division of labor. Finally, in Chapter 3 we saw that Socrates' attention to the usages of his interlocutors concerning just, beautiful, and good things provides a model for the rulers' attention to the usages of their citizens. These are only provisional models, to be sure—Kallipolis is designed to ensure that philosopher-rulers far surpass what Plato himself can achieve—but provisional models are still models. So the *Republic* models dialectical inquiry for an Athenian audience, showing how holistic investigation into form and function might go. And the master model in this respect is the figure of Socrates, elevated above ordinary mortals as a paragon of intellectual and ethical virtue, a restless seeker of knowledge and an incorruptible teacher of his fellow citizens.[14]

---

prohibitions regarding mimesis, and hence that Plato must be intending to deliberately undercut the coherence of his work. I find this implausible, not only because the work tends toward glorifying coherence, both rhetorically and philosophically, but also because Socrates' prohibitions are directed at the young and impressionable. In Book X Socrates makes clear that he himself has already been educated by Homer and company, which implies that any attempt on his part to follow the prohibitions would come too late; he also says that mimesis will not corrupt those who have "knowledge of what it is really like as a drug to counteract it," which implies that the prohibitions are irrelevant to mature philosophers (595b–c).

14. Not that Socrates is perfect, of course, either ethically or intellectually—he is just a provisional model, to be replaced in due course.

10. By the terms of Plato's account, then, the *Republic* constitutes an attempt to exercise a kind of rule over Athens. As we saw in Chapter 3, Plato thinks that artists shape our ideals in the sense of our conceptions of the good life, and that they do so by propagating ideals in the sense of models for emulation. In his view, the influence of models on human development is unavoidable; even philosophers, who are capable of reforming their conceptions of beauty, justice, and goodness in light of dialectical inquiry, remain to some extent shaped by their cultural environment. The key is therefore to disseminate models that reflect true form and thereby make characters and usages as good as they can be. To do this is to convert the harmful rule of poets into the beneficial rule of philosophers. And although this is best done by those who hold office, some progress can be made by philosophical citizens. In that sense, at least, the *Republic* represents Plato's attempt to be an Athenian philosopher-king.

§2 The Shadow of Death

11. Plato wants to influence the Athenian imaginary by sculpting a series of statues that cast shadows on the wall of the cave, leading some to turn toward the light and others to absorb a sense of what counts as good and true. Pride of place would be given to paradigms of true form, such as the just man and the just city. But there would also be room for models of deficient form, such as the oligarchic man and the oligarchic city, as well as images whose surface meaning is false, but whose deeper meaning is true.

12. Allen shows that Plato draws a distinction between two kinds of images (*eikones*), namely those that make forms manifest, which get called models (*paradeigmata*) or types (*tupoi*), and those that mislead the understanding, which get called phantasms (*phantasmata*) or idols (*eidōla*).[15] Socrates is willing to propagate images of the latter kind—ones that are strictly speaking misleading—so long as they instill true belief in the souls of their consumers.

---

15. See Allen, *Why Plato Wrote*, 148. Allen notes that although *eikōn* is used of both groups of images, it is most often used in a restricted sense to mean paradigms and types. On this she cites Naddaff, *Exiling the Poets*, 80.

13. The myth of metals, or "noble falsehood" *(gennaion pseudos)*, is the perfect example.[16] Citizens are to be told that they were born and raised inside the earth and must now deliberate on its behalf, defend it against attack, and regard one another as siblings. Each has had a particular metal mixed into their soul. Those with gold in their souls should rule; those with silver should be auxiliaries; those with iron should be farmers; and those with bronze should perform other crafts. Since metals are imperfectly transmitted between generations, however, educational testing is required to determine which metal is within which soul, and hence which roles are to be assigned to which people.

14. Socrates calls the myth a "device" or "contrivance" *(mēchanē)* designed to make guardians "care more for the city and for each other" (414b; 415c–d). His choice of words makes clear that he is implicitly answering Adeimantus's challenge at the start of Book II, which was to provide a "device *[mēchanē]* [to] get someone with any power—whether of mind, wealth, body, or family—to be willing to honor justice, and not laugh aloud when he hears it praised" (366b–c). Citizens who believe the myth of metals will honor justice in the political sense: they will believe they should be allotted to the social role appropriate to their natural capacities, and they will obey and revere those whom they should obey and revere. As Allen puts it, the noble falsehood will therefore be "pragmatically efficacious for the whole citizenry, implanting principles and rules for action that could just as well have flowed from the metaphysical beliefs that Socrates propounds but which he is unable to bring a whole citizenry to see through dialectic."[17]

---

16. Allen points out that the introduction of the noble-falsehood passage at 414b–c refers us back to 382a–d, where Socrates uses the term *eidōlon* to refer to useful falsehoods (*Why Plato Wrote*, 184n17). She also points to 443c–d, where Socrates says that the image of a just shoemaker was a useful *eidōlon*—in reality, one is just in virtue of one's internal state and not in virtue of one's behavior, so the image was, strictly speaking, misleading. But it was a vital part of the process that led Glaucon to the right belief about justice, and therefore, it was pragmatically justified (53). In my view, we can speak of just shoemakers so long as we are clear that we are speaking about justice in the political sense rather than justice in the psychological sense, and that the latter is primary. See notes 40 and 43 in Chapter 2.

17. Allen, *Why Plato Wrote*, 66.

15. It is tempting to conclude that Socrates is willing to spread falsehoods within the city whenever their acceptance would produce good consequences for social stability or aggregate well-being.[18] But there are some falsehoods whose dissemination Socrates will not countenance. In Book II he draws a distinction between "falsehoods in words" and "true falsehoods" (382a–e). A true falsehood—the genuine article—is a falsehood told "to the most important part" of oneself concerning "the most important things." Given the rest of the *Republic*, we can infer that the most important part of oneself is reason and the most important thing is goodness. A true falsehood would therefore involve being fundamentally misoriented vis-à-vis goodness. As Socrates says in Book VI, "No one is satisfied to acquire things that are *believed* to be good. On the contrary, everyone seeks the things that *are* good" (505d). To be mistaken regarding the good life is to live in falsehood concerning the most important things; and this sort of falsehood, Socrates repeats, is hateful to gods and humans alike. A falsehood in words, by contrast, is "not an altogether pure falsehood" in that sense—it can help instill good behavior and true belief and thereby, counterintuitively, ensure that people live in the truth. We can conclude that falsehoods should be spread in the city only to the extent that they enable people to live as they would if they were capable of dialectic.

16. The noble falsehood illustrates this well. Although the content of the story is false, strictly speaking, since humans were not fashioned in the earth of four different metals, at the level of pattern it is actually true: on Socrates' account there really are four kinds of people; each really should stick to his own job; each really is the product of a common parent (the city); and this really does create special obligations (414b–415d).[19] At the level of pattern or type (*tupos*), then,

---

18. This is what Allen suggests: "On the example of Socrates' own *eidola*, then, the requisite resemblance of a useful falsehood to the truth resides not in the meaning of the words uttered in the lie in comparison to those in the true statement, but instead in the consequences that flow from believing each" (ibid., 66–67). Allen credits Plato with a "pragmatist approach to truth," where internalizing a true belief means internalizing a useful rule for action, where what counts as useful is given by philosophy, and calls his pragmatism "ultimately very cynical" (20).

19. This is why I prefer to say "noble falsehood" rather than "noble lie": a lie involves the intention to persuade someone to believe something one knows to be

the noble falsehood is true. It seems to me that all the images in the *Republic* are intended to convey some cognitive truth, as opposed to merely practical truth, whether it be by modeling true form, as with ideals, or by modeling bad form, as with caricatures, or by conveying a truth through allegory (*huponoia*, 378c–d), as with myth. They may be "falsehoods in words," but since they bring nonphilosophers closer to having truth in their souls about the most important things, they should not be called "true falsehoods."[20]

17. If the rulers of Kallipolis are to disseminate images that are false on a surface level but nevertheless convey deep truths regarding goodness, then by the terms of §1's argument we should expect Plato to attempt the same vis-à-vis Athens. As with the noble falsehood in Kallipolis, the goal would not be to convince adults of the truth of these fictions—as Glaucon suggests, that would be impossible (415c)—but rather to get them to teach their children accordingly. The myth of Er is particularly interesting in this respect.

18. The myth might seem a peculiar ending to the *Republic*—Annas calls it "lame and messy," "a painful shock" whose "vulgarity seems to pull us right down to the level of Cephalus, where you take justice seriously when you start thinking about hell-fire"—but read allegorically it turns out to be a fitting capstone.[21] The story is of a

---

false, whereas the myth allows the rulers to persuade people to believe something that they themselves take to be true. See Jonathan Lear, "City Prefect"; and Lear, "Allegory and Myth in Plato's *Republic*."

20. The hardest case for this interpretation to handle concerns the breeding arrangements of Book V (458d–461e). The best men should mate with the best women and only the best children should be allowed to survive. The former arrangement is to be masked by a rigged lottery, and the latter by communal nursing and the use of every possible device (*mēchanē* again) to ensure that mothers will not recognize their offspring, with a system of religious sanctions to discourage disobedience. Are these true falsehoods? Certainly by modern standards, someone who goes on supporting a regime that has, unbeknownst to her, killed her child would be living in falsehood concerning the most important things. But that just begs the question against Plato, for whom the family is subordinate to the city. We do not need to accept Plato's claim about the family to see that by his own lights, at least, the breeding arrangements of Book V do not involve the dissemination of true falsehoods. And that is all I need for my interpretation, according to which Plato rules out the dissemination of true falsehoods. The question whether belief in such falsehoods could ever have good consequences, which would certainly occur to contemporary philosophers, is never raised by Plato, so any answer on my part would be purely speculative.

21. Annas, *Introduction to Plato's "Republic,"* 349, 353.

man named Er who comes back from the dead and recounts what he saw of the afterlife; his account involves intricate descriptions of the physical architecture of the afterworld and, more importantly, of an elaborate scheme that organizes the reincarnation of souls by a combination of lottery and choice. Socrates does not explicitly call this story an *eidōlon*, but he does suggest something along those lines by introducing it with an elaborate pun whose meaning Reeve glosses as follows: "It isn't a tale that shows strength of understanding that I'm going to tell but one that shows the strength of the Muse of storytelling."[22] Yet despite the expectations this sets up and the pages of fiction that follow, the myth conveys the central propositions of the *Republic* rather well.[23]

19. The core of the myth, once we get past the promise that justice and injustice will be rewarded and punished in the afterlife (614b–616a), is that after death individual souls will be reincarnated into the lives that they themselves have chosen (617d–618b). There will be a lottery to decide who gets first choice among the various models or ideals of lives (*ta tōn biōn paradeigmata*; 618a), followed by the choice itself; whichever ideal one chooses, one is then bound to it for the next life.[24] It is easy to get bogged down in the details of how the lottery or the reincarnation process are supposed to work, but it is worth remembering that Socrates himself sometimes admits to having no knowledge regarding the afterlife.[25] As with Dante's *Inferno*, another great myth of the afterlife, it may be more rewarding to concentrate on what the myth of Er tells us about this life.[26]

---

22. Reeve's translation, note to 614b. Reeve explains that the Greek pun is on *Alkinou apologoi*, the tales of Alcinous from Books 9–11 of the Odyssey, and *alkimou*, which means brave. *Alkinou* might be taken as a compound of *alkē* (strength) and *nous* (understanding) and *alkimou* as a compound of *alkē* and *Mousa* (a Muse).

23. Allen suggests a similar interpretive strategy, but she calls the myth a "model," which seems mistaken to me, at least if models are to be understood as metaphysically accurate in the way in which Socrates' model of a just man or just city is. What we have in the myth, as with the noble falsehood, which it should be remembered is itself a myth, is rather an allegorical structure in which the surface meaning is, strictly speaking, false but the underlying meaning is true. See Allen, *Why Plato Wrote*, 75.

24. One will also choose one's own *daimon* or guardian spirit (617d–e).

25. *Apology* 40c–42a; cf. *Republic* 427b–c and *Phaedo* 63b–c.

26. Despite calling the myth "a painful shock" and accusing it of "vulgarity" and "childishness," Annas goes on to propose such a "demythologizing" interpretation,

20. The most obvious point of the lottery story is that one will live well only to the degree that one is capable of recognizing and valuing virtue. If this is the case, then the most important pursuit for humans will be philosophy.

> The soul is inevitably altered by the different lives it chooses. . . . Each of us must neglect all other subjects and be most concerned to seek out and learn those that will enable him to distinguish the good life from the bad and always to make the best choice possible in every situation. He should think over all the things we have mentioned and how they jointly and severally determine what the virtuous life is like. That way he will know what the good and bad effects of beauty are when it is mixed with wealth, poverty, and a particular state of the soul. He will know the effects of high or low birth, private life or ruling office, physical strength or weakness, ease or difficulty in learning, and all the things that are either naturally part of the soul or are acquired, and he will know what they achieve when mixed with one another. And from all this he will be able, by considering the nature of the soul, to reason out which life is better and which worse and to choose accordingly, calling a life worse if it leads the soul to become more unjust, better if it leads the soul to become more just, and ignoring everything else. (618b–e)

Note that this passage makes no reference whatsoever to the afterlife. Taken out of context, it could easily fit into the passages on philosophical self-constitution in Books IV and VI (443c–445b; 500b–d). This suggests that Socrates' goal with the myth, as with the noble falsehood, is to convey an underlying message that stands

---

arguing that the myth "serves merely to dramatize what is at stake in one's choices *now*" (*Introduction to Plato's "Republic,"* 351). Given that she realizes this interpretive possibility and even defends it, it is unclear why she is so dismissive regarding Plato's deployment of the myth. On Dante, the idea would be to read *Inferno* against the background of Boethius, whose (Neoplatonic) notion was that vice was its own punishment; this strategy may work less well for *Purgatorio* and *Paradiso*, of course.

even if its overt content is false, strictly speaking. This would explain his repeated references to "this life":

> We have seen that this is the best way to choose, whether in life or death. Hence, we must go down to Hades holding with adamantine determination to the belief that this is so, lest we be dazzled there by wealth and other such evils, rush into a tyranny or some other similar course of action, do irreparable evils, and suffer even worse ones. And we must always know how to choose the mean in such lives and how to avoid either of the extremes, as far as possible, both in this life and in all those beyond it. This is the way that a human being becomes happiest. (618e–619b)

But if the myth is aimed at instructing us regarding this life, why is it framed in terms of the next one?

21. The answer is that as a shaper of souls, the ruler cannot afford to ignore what Annas calls "the level of Cephalus." As Jonathan Lear observes, the *Republic* begins with Cephalus "describing the structure of a traumatic cocktail."[27] When asked to say what he thinks the greatest benefit of accumulating wealth has been, Cephalus responds by citing his increased capacity to ward off fears arising from childhood stories of the afterlife:

> What I have to say probably wouldn't persuade most people. But you know, Socrates, that when someone thinks his end is near, he becomes frightened and concerned about things he didn't fear before. It's then that the stories we're told about Hades, about how people who've been unjust here must pay the penalty there—stories he used to make fun of—twist his soul this way and that for fear they're true. And whether because of the weakness of old age or because he is now closer to what happens in Hades and has a clearer view of it, or whatever it is, he is filled with foreboding and fear, and he examines himself to

---

27. Jonathan Lear, "Allegory and Myth in Plato's *Republic*," 28–29.

see whether he has been unjust to anyone. If he finds many injustices in his life, he awakes from sleep in terror, as children
do, and lives in anticipation of bad things to come. (330d–331a)

This is an astonishing passage. Cephalus has organized his life
around the pursuit of money. His justification is that wealth enables
him to pay off his debts and therefore to sleep soundly at night. That
justification is in turn grounded in a picture of the afterlife imbibed
as a child, a picture that mixes a terrifying picture of retributive justice with a conception of justice as paying back what is owed. As
soon as Socrates begins to question that conception of justice, Cephalus departs. The reason he gives is that he needs to "look after the
sacrifice" (331d)—in other words, to rid himself of one more debt. If
Socrates is right to doubt Cephalus's conception of justice, that sacrifice may be unnecessary. But Cephalus is set in his ways, and those
ways are the product of childhood myths.

22. Given that the *Republic* begins with a character whose conception of justice, and indeed whole life, is oriented by stories concerning the afterlife—the kind of stories that Adeimantus highlights
as setting the wrong tone for Athenian society (362e–367a)—it is
surely not accidental that it ends by offering a new conception of the
afterlife.[28] But there is more to the myth than simply inculcating
the sense that what matters most is the capacity to "determine what
the virtuous life is like" (618c) rather than paying back what is owed. It
is also worth paying attention to the fact that this lesson is couched
in terms of reincarnation.

§3 Self-Reproduction

23. If the reincarnation story were true, it would follow that our
current life is the product of a choice that has already been made.
We might therefore say that the myth dramatizes our uncanny sense

---

28. For more on ring composition in the *Republic*, see Barney, "Platonic Ring-
Composition and *Republic* 10." For a different suggestion of what is at issue in the
mirrored beginning and ending of the *Republic*, see "Cephalus, Odysseus, and the
Importance of Experience," chap. 3 of Reeve, *Blindness and Reorientation*.

that we have always already made a decision on how to live, or even that the decision has somehow been made for us. At any given point we might be able to specify our overriding ambitions and goals, but where they came from remains mysterious. It does not seem quite right to say we chose them—they are at least partly owed to our families, institutions, and cultural surroundings—yet we still feel responsible for them in some way. The myth might therefore be said to express our sense of what Heidegger calls "thrownness" (*Geworfenheit*).[29] But it is also about moments of choice, since at the end of a given cycle one is released from one's body and is obliged to decide what kind of life to lead next. If we transpose the whole cycle of reincarnation to this life and this life only, we get the idea that within a given lifespan one must repeatedly choose what kind of life to lead, projecting oneself into the future in response to cycles of change and opportunity. Just as ruling requires refounding, given changing circumstances, so too does leading a life: we must continually reconstitute ourselves as the kinds of people we are—as parents, teachers, students, and citizens, for example—by our choices in the face of shifting situations. And just as rulers must refound the city in light of an ideal of the good society, so we must reconstitute ourselves, the myth suggests, in light of an ideal of the good life.[30]

---

29. Heidegger, *Being and Time*, chap. 5.

30. There is a clear affinity between the notion that human life involves continual self-reconstitution and the thrust of both Heidegger's *Being and Time* and Korsgaard's *Self-Constitution*. See also Halliwell, "Life-and-Death Journey of the Soul," 469: "The motif of a prenatal life choice can be interpreted as a stark emblem of the inescapably self-forming consequences of ethical agency, a magnified image of how at every moment ("always and everywhere") the individual soul/person is intrinsically responsible for what matters most about its existence. Every action, we might thus say, brings with it its own 'afterlife'. Every choice makes us what we are; when we choose, we activate (and become) something, and therefore cannot simply pull back from *ourselves*, as the greedy soul would like to do—a graphic exemplification of Book 9's idea of the tyrant as peculiarly enslaved by, and imprisoned in, his own desires" (577d–e; 579b). Halliwell also reminds us that the myth's "densely allusive texture yields a surplus of possible meanings that cannot be adequately encompassed by any single interpretation" (445) and that "we should not expect to find a definitive key to the reading of any Platonic myth" (455). I agree, but I nonetheless believe that we can isolate the feature of the myth that makes it particularly apt to serve as the *Republic*'s capstone.

24. The first thing Socrates says to Cephalus is this: "I enjoy engaging in discussions with the very old. I think we should learn from them—since they are like people who have travelled a road that we too will probably have to follow—what the road is like, whether rough and difficult or smooth and easy" (328d–e). Socrates' immediate interest concerns the nature of old age, but his remark resonates beyond that, for what it brings into view is the question of how to live (cf. 352d). One of the characteristic theses of Greek ethics from Solon to Aristotle is that if we are to think about happiness, or how to live, we need to consider whole lives.[31] And what is distinctive about the very old is that they are in the unusual position of having a vantage point from which to reflect on their whole lives, near enough. Talking to them therefore teaches us to view whole lives as the appropriate objects of ethical reflection. This is what Glaucon does with his "statues" of the just and unjust in Book II (361d); and it is also what the myth of Er has us do with its models of lives (ta tōn biōn paradeigmata; 618a). These are sketches of lives, biographies in the literal sense. The first such sketch in the Republic is of Cephalus, and it repays close attention.

25. Cephalus was a real historical figure, a resident alien (or "metic") who was renowned as one of the richest men in Athens.[32] Plato has him tell Socrates that he organized his life around money in order to assuage his fears regarding Hades, as we have already seen, but also in order to benefit his sons by leaving them "a little more than I inherited" (330b). Plato's readers would have known that the inheritance did not go smoothly: Polemarchus, the eldest son, whom Cephalus describes as his "heir in everything" (331d), was famously executed in 404 by the oligarchy that seized power after Athens's defeat at the hands of Sparta in the Peloponnesian War.[33] And as Mark Gifford observes, there is a real sense in which that *was* his inheritance. For Cephalus was an arms manufacturer, the largest shield

---

31. Herodotus, *Histories* I.31–33; Aristotle, *Eudemian Ethics* II.1; and *Nicomachean Ethics* I.10.

32. Nails, *People of Plato*, 84–85.

33. Cephalus died sometime between 421 and 415, according to Nails, *People of Plato*, 84. For Polemarchus's fate, see ibid., 251; and Lysias, *Against Eratosthenes*, in *Lysias*, trans. S. C. Todd.

producer of his day, and it is not much of a stretch to imagine that as a resident alien he sold these arms to the Athenian polis without worrying too much about whether they would end up facilitating Athens's self-destruction. We can rephrase by saying that Cephalus gave weapons to a deranged friend (Athens) simply because they were owed by contract—which is more or less the example that Socrates gives to refute his definition of justice (331c).[34] The immediate result of Cephalus's action was an exacerbation of his friend's madness, and the final result was the death of his son. Of course, the causal chain was neither so direct nor so simple. But it does not seem unreasonable to suggest, following Gifford, that the *Republic*'s opening exchanges are suffused with the kind of tragic irony we find in Arthur Miller's *All My Sons*.[35]

26. Aristotle has a thorny discussion of whether judgments about one's happiness can be affected by what happens to one's children after one dies, concluding that "the dead do seem to somehow be affected when their loved ones do well, and similarly when they do badly, but in such a way and to such an extent as neither to render the happy unhappy nor do anything else of the sort."[36] Plato seems to agree that the good life is at least partly dependent on the fate of one's children.[37] Throughout the *Republic* we come across scenes of parents trying to pass on a way of life to their children, both successfully, as in Book II's impossible city, whose citizens "live in peace and good health, and when they die at a ripe old age . . . bequeath a

---

34. See Mark Gifford's insightful essay "Dramatic Dialectic in *Republic* Book 1." Gifford points out that the term Socrates uses at 331c for what is to be handed back is *hopla*. This is plural, counterintuitively: we tend to remember the example as involving handing back a single weapon rather than an arsenal. It is also a word whose narrow meaning refers to shields in particular. Both elements seem to point to Cephalus's profession. See also Thakkar, "Moneymakers and Craftsmen."

35. See Gifford, "Dramatic Dialectic in *Republic* Book 1," 37–52. Note also that Cephalus's other sons, Lysias and Euthydemus, half brothers of Polemarchus, are both present, albeit silent, throughout the conversation of the *Republic* (328b).

36. Aristotle, *Nicomachean Ethics* I.10–11, trans. Sarah Broadie and Christopher Rowe.

37. This would seem to tie in loosely with Diotima's picture in the *Symposium*, according to which our longing for immortality finds its most basic, animal satisfaction in bodily reproduction (207d–208b) and a more advanced satisfaction in giving birth to certain kinds of soul (208e–209e). We might also think of the various discussions within the Platonic corpus of whether virtue can be taught (and therefore reliably passed from one generation to the next), e.g., in the *Protagoras* and the *Meno*.

similar life to their children" (372d), and unsuccessfully, as with the many broken families of Books VIII and IX, as well as the children in Book VII who lose respect for their parents when they are exposed to argument prematurely (537d–539d). What happens when we allow whole lives to come into view, then, is that whole families come into view. But families are attempts at self-reproduction, and the success of that self-reproduction depends on the cultural environment. So once we allow whole families to become an object of thought, we are quickly forced to contemplate whole societies. And once we have societies in view as self-reproducing systems, we are in a position to begin political philosophy in the Platonic sense.[38]

27. The scene with Cephalus embodies exactly this pattern of thought: the portrait of a whole life opens out into a portrait of a whole family, which in turn opens out into a portrait of a whole society—democratic Athens, whose turmoil created the conditions for Cephalus's career in arms dealing and Polemarchus's eventual execution. The suggestion is that our projects and plans are dependent on society, both in the sense that our ambitions are always shaped by the cultural environment and in the sense that their fulfillment depends on social stability. This prepares the reader for the argument that a stable social order directed toward the good life requires rule by philosophers.

28. During the Peloponnesian War, political instability frequently led to shifting fortunes for individuals and families. Regimes came and went as the war ebbed and flowed. Whenever oligarchy replaced democracy or democracy replaced oligarchy, the rights and duties of law-abiding people, whether citizens or metics, also changed dramatically. Partisans of the previous regime often suffered harsh punishments. This was the context for Polemarchus's execution under the so-called Thirty Tyrants, who seem to have killed around 1,500 prominent citizens in just thirteen months, but it was also the context for the murder case that his brother Lysias famously constructed

---

38. See Jonathan Lear, "Inside and Outside the *Republic*," for an argument that the political instability depicted in Books VIII and IX is bound up with the psychological instability depicted in the same books because each generation internalizes the externalizations of the previous one.

against one of the Thirty after the restoration of democracy.[39] In such tumultuous periods it becomes impossible to reliably take one's moral and political bearings from society at large; "thick" ethical concepts like courage and civility lose their content.[40] To anchor oneself on fixed moorings, philosophy is needed. Socrates, for example, was able to gain a measure of independence from the prevailing winds through reflecting on the nature of justice, piety, and courage, finding grounds to refuse both the democratic stampede to illegally try ten generals after the battle of Arginusae and the oligarchic command to bring Leon back from Salamis to Athens by what we might nowadays call "extraordinary rendition."[41] But even Socrates could not gain complete independence: in 399 he was tried and put to death. Likewise, the philosophical man in a badly governed city—the one who keeps to himself, "concentrating his mind on his own thoughts"—finds himself incapable of passing his values on to his son, who becomes an honor lover (549c–550b; cf. 496a–e, 591e–592b). Vulnerability to our sociocultural environment is part of the human condition; and Plato's suggestion is that no one will flourish stably unless that environment is placed in the hands of people capable of maintaining it in good condition across changing circumstances—philosopher-rulers.[42]

---

39. On the death toll of the Thirty, see Aristotle, *Constitution of Athens* 35. For Lysias' speech, see *Against Eratosthenes*, trans. S. C. Todd. We have Lysias's speech, but we do not know whether or in what form the case ever took place—as a metic, Lysias would not have been able to deliver the speech himself, but it is written in the third person. It is possible that the text was simply circulated in order to shift public opinion. See Todd's introduction and notes.

40. On the question of what happens when thick ethical concepts like courage lose their content in times of change, see Jonathan Lear, *Radical Hope*.

41. *Apology* 32a–d.

42. This interpretation might help us to resolve a notorious scholarly crux concerning the dramatic date of the conversation depicted in the *Republic*. According to Debra Nails, Book I appears to have been composed as a separate dialogue "set in May–June 424 or perhaps 421," when Glaucon and Adeimantus were only children and Cephalus was still alive; yet from Book II onward, the two are said to have participated in the battle at Megara (368a), which suggests a dramatic date of 408–407, by which time Cephalus was long dead. Nails summarizes the scholarly literature by saying that we have a "prosopographically scrambled dialogue . . . consistency for the family and friends of Cephalus in the first book, and also for Plato's brothers in the second, but an uncomfortable fit for the dialogue as a whole" (*People of Plato*, 325). Plato must have known that this would create an odd effect for the Athenian reader, given that Cephalus and his family were famous figures. Even if there were pragmatic reasons for

29. The myth of Er presses home much the same point. Nonphilosophers must rely on the understandings they pick up from the surrounding culture and its usages. In bad cities these understandings will be false; in good cities they will amount to true belief. But even true belief is not enough when circumstances change radically. The myth dramatizes this point in stunning fashion through its depiction of the fate selected by a decent but nonphilosophical man who gets to pick between lives:

> The one who came up first [in the lottery] chose the greatest tyranny. In his folly and greed he chose it without adequate examination and didn't notice that, among other evils, he was fated to eat his own children as a part of it. When he examined at leisure the life he had chosen, however, he beat his breast and bemoaned his choice. And, ignoring the warning of the Speaker, he blamed chance, daimons, or guardian spirits, and everything else for these evils but himself. He was one of those who had come down from heaven, having lived his previous life under an orderly constitution, where he had participated in virtue through habit *[ethos]* and without philosophy. (619b–d)[43]

This is the most shocking moment in the *Republic*. The unreflectively virtuous man is sometimes prized as a paragon; Plato has him eating

---

composing one large dialogue out of two, three, or even four smaller pieces, the composition clearly aims at a kind of unity, so why leave this loose thread hanging? My suggestion is that putting an incongruous cast of characters on stage in Book I allows Plato to give the impression that the conversation is somehow indeterminately placed within the tumult of the Peloponnesian War. If Nails is right, then the conversation with Cephalus ought really to take place in 424 or 421, between the great Athenian success at the Battle of Sphacteria in 425 and the Peace of Nicias of 421, which appeared to settle the war in Athens's favor. Given the presence of Glaucon and Adeimantus, however, the conversation should take place in 408–407, during a period of democratic victories after the colossal failure of the pleonectic expedition to Sicily in 415–413 and the oligarchic revolution of 411–409, but only a couple of years before the final reverse and the dictatorship of the Thirty Tyrants. Oscillating between these different political contexts gives something of the effect of tragic irony: just as we might hear Cephalus's words about Polemarchus's inheritance in light of our knowledge of his future execution, so we might view the whole period of Cephalus's speech, a period of democratic self-confidence, in light of our knowledge of democracy's subsequent failures.

43. Cf. *Phaedo* 81d–82c.

his own children.[44] Plato's point is not that someone like this will necessarily choose a bad life—and hence a bad soul, the two being inseparable (618b)—but rather that there is nothing to prevent his doing so. Without a reflectively stable account of the good life, we cannot recognize what each course of life entails, structurally speaking, and we are therefore left vulnerable to the understandings and usages we imbibe from our cultural environment. And since customs vary from society to society, this leaves us exposed to the winds of fortune.[45]

30. Given that the *Republic* begins with Cephalus and Polemarchus, it is no accident that the myth of Er figures our vulnerability to sociocultural conditions in terms of the risk of inadvertently harming our children.[46] Cephalus is a good example of an unreflectively virtuous man. Old age has not changed the basic orientation of his soul, but it has liberated him from excessive appetites, giving him at least a measure of virtue (329a–d).[47] As we hear in Book VI, however,

---

44. Ironically, in *War and Peace* Tolstoy goes so far as to name the unreflectively virtuous man after Plato himself: Platon Karataev.

45. My account thus tallies with John Cooper's account of Book IV; Cooper argues persuasively that Book IV shows that true belief about the good is not enough for justice or any of the virtues ("Psychology of Justice in Plato," 19–20).

46. Sarah Broadie provides an alternative reading of the myth that also accounts for its emphasis on children: "The point is not that an individual in the grip of one of those false ideas cannot be genuinely virtuous in his life, but that his virtue is much less likely to propagate itself across the generations. His virtue is a set of habits which, where it really exists, operates independently of his ideology. But with a false ideology circulating and the moral establishment giving it their blessing, the young understandably find it simply irrational that their parents, when it comes to particular situations, balk at the moral corner-cutting glanced at earlier. Thus through changes of standards one generation's out-of-reach object of fantasy becomes another's practicable option or even ruling aim. Perhaps the myth of Er is intended in part to remind us of this possibility, whatever other truth we are also meant to find in it, so that the identical soul stands, in successive reincarnations, first for an innocent but philosophically foolish father, then for his ruthless and hateful son. The son's life spells out in concrete reality the father's 'merely recreational' conception of *eudaimonia*. The content of the conception is transmitted across the generations as if it were a single soul living on from father to son. Between lives, that soul can see—prophetically too late—how the father by feeding his own life on fantasy will have devoured his children's chance of *eudaimonia* in theirs. The right reflective attitude to virtue is required, then, not for possession of virtue by individuals, but for its inculcation in the next generation." Broadie, "Virtue and Beyond in Plato and Aristotle," 108–109.

47. The fact that Cephalus is still appetitive is revealed in the haste with which he departs the scene as soon as the serious philosophical discussion gets under way

"Those who express a true opinion without understanding are [no] different from blind people who happen to travel the right road" (506c). The image of traveling a road (*hodos*) ought to put us in mind of Book I's description of Cephalus as having "travelled a road that we too will probably have to follow" (328d–e).[48] And as we have seen, Cephalus's increased moderation was not enough to prevent him from eating his own children, figuratively speaking.

31. The big difference between Cephalus and the man depicted in the myth of Er is that the former lived in democratic Athens, whereas the latter "lived his previous life under an orderly constitution, where he had participated in virtue through habit [*ethos*]." The paradigm of an orderly constitution, of course, is Kallipolis, in which appetitive and honor-loving individuals are habituated into living as excellently as possible given their natures. As we saw in Chapter 3, our appetitive and honor-centered desires can be altered through habituation so as to maximize their chances of long-term satisfaction. But since the lower parts of the soul are not capable of accurately discerning their own pleasure (586d–587a), the optimization of appetitive and honor-centered pleasure requires the rule of reason, which uses inquiry into goodness to set standards for what counts as genuinely pleasurable. The problem is that for appetitive and honor-seeking people, reason is the slave of the passions; it serves a merely logistical function, assessing means to pregiven ends (580d–581e). If those ends are to be shaped by rational inquiry into goodness, it must be someone else's reason that does the work. This is the role of law within a good city: to instill a "wise ruler" within every citizen, so that "we are all captained by the same thing" (590c–591a). We might

---

despite having told Socrates of his "desire for conversation and its pleasures" just moments before (329c–d; 331d). The kind of conversation that Cephalus has in mind is surely philosophical, given that he brings it up in connection with the thought that Socrates should visit him more often. In a seminar Jonathan Lear pointed out parallels with the democratic man's shifting desires, including for philosophy, as depicted in Book VIII (561c–d)—which is not to deny that Cephalus is more of an oligarchic personality than a democratic one. For a more optimistic account of Cephalus's old age, see Reeve, *Blindness and Reorientation*, chap. 3, "Cephalus, Odysseus, and the Importance of Experience."

48. See also Adeimantus's remarks about the lessons Athenian culture teaches to the young concerning "what sort of person they should be, and of how best to travel the road of life" (365a–b).

call those whose souls are governed by reason in this derivative way "quasi-reasoners" because they will often behave no differently from genuine reasoners. As the myth puts it, they will participate in virtue through habit. But this excellence is fragile since it depends on the ability of true reasoners to regulate the cultural environment by propagating beneficial images and watching over the division of labor. When the social order changes, quasi-reasoners are no better off than nonreasoners.

32. This suggests that the myth of Er might play a role within Kallipolis itself, alongside the noble falsehood and so on, as a device to bolster the social order. Appetitive and honor-loving people are not set up to reconstruct the argument for Kallipolitan institutions for themselves. They need to be persuaded by other means—by statues on the wall of the cave. This is where models of the ideal city and the ideal life enter into political life, as well as myths that convey deep truths despite being superficially false. With its depiction of the terrible fate of the virtuous man shorn of philosophy's protection, the myth of Er illustrates the hellish consequences that would come from deposing philosopher-rulers. For in a certain sense everything that the myth of Er implies regarding the fate of the individual might also be said of the city. Cities too must reconstitute themselves in the face of changing circumstances, and this reconstitution must be performed in light of a reasoned account of the good life. If the ruling class is awake and keen sighted in its refounding, the city as a whole will be too; if not, it will be blind and hence liable to stumble and fall.[49] If the myth of Er were widely disseminated and internalized, its terrifying depiction of what happens when one makes choices without wisdom might give the Cephalus of Kallipolis a different kind of nightmare from that of his Athenian equivalent: rather than waking up in horror at the prospect of unpaid debts, his terror would be directed at the prospect of living in a city where philosophers no longer rule.

33. There is an obvious objection to including the myth of Er among the stories that rulers are to project on the wall of the cave: unlike the noble falsehood, it is not introduced as part of Socrates'

---

49. Cf. 544d–e, 428e, 520c.

construction of Kallipolis—its target is rather Glaucon, who still needs to be persuaded that justice must be loved "both because of itself and because of its consequences" (358a). Why, then, should we assume that the myth will be propagated within Kallipolis? Certainly there is no hard evidence. The claim can only be that the hypothesis allows us to make more sense of the *Republic* than would otherwise be the case, showing how it hangs together as a harmonious whole.

34. In any case, if the argument of §1 holds, the *Republic* aims to alter the Athenian social imaginary. "The pragmatic efficacy that Socrates hopes for from his symbols," writes Allen, "lies in [their] capacity to shift the landscape of someone's imagination, whose contours define what that person takes to be real, possible, and valuable."[50] If Plato is trying to achieve something similar, as I have argued that he is, then the myth of Er might be directed at an Athenian audience. Recall that Adeimantus's challenge revolved around the lessons taught to Athenian youth, not the youth of Kallipolis. A response might therefore conceivably involve generating a "device" that could get Athenians to "be willing to honor justice, and not laugh aloud when [they] hear it praised" (366b–c). Earlier we saw that when Socrates asks Adeimantus to propagate the ship-of-state image, we can read this as an instruction from Plato to the reader, and hence perhaps to his students at the Academy, to teach the simile to their fellow citizens. When Socrates teaches the myth of Er to Glaucon, we might imagine something similar: although adults will never believe such a myth, the intended audience is the children of Athens, who cannot yet "distinguish what is allegorical from what is not" (378d; 415c).[51] This might seem like a small payoff, but in the Platonic-Aristotelian picture the most important task of rulers is always to shape the next generation. Rulers aim to foster citizens of excellent character; character is bound up with beliefs about the good life; and as Socrates declares in Book II, and the example of Cephalus shows, "the beliefs [children] absorb at that age are difficult to erase and tend to become unalterable" (378d–e). If their bedtime

50. Allen, *Why Plato Wrote*, 58.
51. See Jonathan Lear, "Allegory and Myth in Plato's *Republic*."

stories concerned the decent man who ended up eating his own children, Athenians might grow up terrified of ignorance concerning the good life and fully persuaded of the need for regulation of the cultural environment by philosophers.[52]

§4 Caricatures and Grotesques

35. Let us take stock. The goal of this chapter is to recover Plato's way of thinking about the role of political idealism in nonideal societies. The *Republic* seems to advocate quietism vis-à-vis the maelstrom of nonideal politics: just as the wise citizen "keeps quiet and does his own work" rather than fighting for honors and offices, so Odysseus turns out to be the hero of the myth of Er, his clever deliberations now leading him to "[look] for the life of a private individual who did his own work" (496d; 620c; 592b). But there is more to political life than honors and offices; indeed, on Plato's view the sphere of politics in the ordinary sense is merely epiphenomenal relative to the real center of gravity in the polis, which is the sphere of cultural production. Politicians, no matter how powerful, choose their actions in light of conceptions of the good life imbibed from the surrounding culture; the real rulers (*archontes*) are therefore those

---

52. For Glaucon's benefit, Socrates phrases the moral this way: "Here, it seems, my dear Glaucon, a human being faces the greatest danger of all, and because of that each must, to the neglect of all other subjects, take care above all else to be a seeker and student of that subject which will enable him to learn and discover who will give him the ability and the knowledge to distinguish a good life from a bad, so that he will always and in any circumstances choose the better one from among those that are possible" (618b–c). This is a peculiar passage; it suggests that to overcome the greatest danger of all—picking the wrong life—one must become a seeker and student not of the subject that teaches you how to distinguish a good life from a bad, but of the subject that teaches you who can teach you that. This may simply be an infelicity on Plato's part, but the repeated pleonasm in the passage ("seeker and student," "learn and discover," "the ability and the knowledge," "always and in any circumstances") suggests that the composition is deliberate and controlled. The effect of the construction is to frustrate our desire to get straight to the subject matter and to interpose the necessary medium of a teacher. The narrow purpose is to warn the young that dialectic requires discipline and guidance, as well as maturity (cf. 537e–539d), but the broader purpose is surely to suggest the need for deference to philosophers in society more generally.

who instill first principles *(archai)* in their fellow citizens.[53] In Plato's view, rule in this sense is best carried out by philosophers, since doing it well requires dialectical inquiry into formal and final causes. So if doing one's own work means sticking to the task through which one can best contribute to society, given the situation and one's abilities, then the work of philosophers—their social function, that is, rather than the entirety of their life activity—will be to shape the cultural environment so that conceptions of the good life are as accurate as possible. This will be true in both ideal and nonideal societies. What differ, obviously, are the available means. Ideally philosophers would hold office, since this would enable them to generate healthy conceptions of the good life by controlling what is produced through the division of labor (from couches to stories). In a nonideal society, they would have to influence the culture from below, as it were, as private individuals who keep out of politics in the ordinary sense. Once we grasp this, it becomes possible to interpret the *Republic* as a model of philosophical production in a nonideal city—a work designed to recalibrate Athenian culture by disseminating both "metaphysically accurate and pragmatically efficacious images and models, among which masses of democratic citizens, whether intelligent or not, might graze and thereby assimilate new rules for action in line with the principles of justice."[54] We have seen that the *Republic* offers models of good order, such as the just man and the just city; models of bad order, such as the ship of state and the various defective regimes and personality types; and images that are superficially false but convey deep truths, such as the noble falsehood and the myth of Er. All these images can be understood as attempts to influence the Athenian cultural environment in light of a vision of the best possible society, and therefore as political in what Plato would consider the deepest sense. But the story does not end there. In Chapter 3 we saw that philosopher-rulers would aim to recalibrate aesthetic sensibilities, where that means not only the sense of

---

53. Compare 425a–427a on the epiphenomenal character of legislation as compared to education. In Steven Lukes's terms, true rulers exercise the "third dimension of power," shaping beliefs and preferences even before agendas are set (the second dimension) and specific decisions are made (the first dimension). See Lukes, *Power*, 29.

54. Allen, *Why Plato Wrote*, 68.

beauty and ugliness—which models of good and bad order might touch—but also the sense of what counts as honorable and shameful and hence worthy of pride and contempt.[55] If the argument I have been making is correct, we should expect the *Republic* to attempt something similar with respect to Athens. This expectation is borne out by the way Socrates treats democracy.

36. The most famous tribute to Athenian democracy comes in the funeral oration that Thucydides has Pericles give in his *History of the Peloponnesian War*. Pericles, explicitly addressing himself to both citizens and foreigners, sets out to describe the "constitution and way of life which has made [Athens] great" and which in turn makes it a model (*paradeigma*) for others (2.36–2.37).[56] He praises Athenian democracy as a system in which power is not restricted to a minority; everyone is equal before the law; what counts is ability rather than wealth; public and private life are free and open, with citizens tolerant and noncensorious yet respectful of the law and public authorities; valor is achieved without heavy discipline and the life of the mind without softness; beauty is found in public and private spaces alike; wealth is used for public benefit; poverty is not despised; political discussion is universally appreciated and productive of sound decisions; and international relations are governed by a spirit of friendship rather than self-interest. All in all, declares Pericles, "our city is an education to Greece" (2.41). Foreigners should emulate it and citizens should protect it: "You should fix your eyes every day on the greatness of Athens as she really is, and should fall in love with her" (2.43).[57]

---

55. It is worth noting that the word "ridiculous" (*geloios*) and its cognates appear fifty-six times in the *Republic*, according to the index in Reeve's translation.

56. Thucydides, *History of the Peloponnesian War*, trans. Rex Warner.

57. In Chapter 3 we saw that one of the elements that makes Kallipolis a stable social order is the fact that it knows itself as such: the ideal plays a role within the ideal. Pericles appears to be aiming at something similar for Athens: to stabilize the social order by getting citizens to behold it as exemplary. Whether or not Plato was influenced by Thucydides in this respect is a matter for speculation, but there is certainly an elective affinity.

37. How we should interpret Pericles' speech is a matter of endless controversy.[58] Certainly his words are not those of a disinterested political scientist. He is offering Athenians an ideal to fight for, but also to live up to—and the very fact that he sees the need to call citizens to their higher selves suggests they are not always as exemplary as he pretends. The real author of the speech, of course, is Thucydides, who makes perfectly clear that the speeches in his history are his attempt to evoke "the sentiments proper to the occasion" (1.22). The funeral oration came early in the Peloponnesian War, before the plague that would give the lie to claims of Athenian public-spiritedness and the Sicilian expedition that would do the same for claims of wise democratic deliberation. In the context of the whole narrative, then, Pericles' words may be ridden with proleptic irony. Furthermore, the very preeminence of Pericles—manifest on this occasion as on so many others—suggests that his Athens may have been a democracy in principle but an aristocracy in practice.[59] We can set aside these complexities for present purposes, however, since none of this rhetorical chicanery would work unless the funeral oration succeeded in capturing the Athenian self-image.

38. Whereas Pericles urges the Athenians to take pride in their city, contemplating its greatness every day—the verb he uses is *theaomai*, to behold, from which *theōria* is derived—the *Republic* teaches them to view it critically. As Sara Brill notes, the text is suffused with imagery concerning the search for new and better points of view:

---

58. For a particularly helpful interpretation, see Ober, *Political Dissent in Democratic Athens*, 83–89.

59. See 2.65 for this suggestion: "Pericles, because of his position, his intelligence, and his known integrity, could respect the liberty of the people and at the same time hold them in check. It was he who led them, rather than they who led him, and, since he never sought power from any wrong motive, he was under no necessity of flattering them: in fact he was so highly respected that he was able to speak angrily to them and to contradict them.... So, in what was nominally a democracy, power was really in the hands of the first citizen." This assessment ought to be read in conjunction with Pericles' repeated denigration of words by comparison with deeds (a denigration that in turn casts a shadow both over his own speech and over democratic institutions, which rely on speeches).

Dominated by a landscape of peaks and valleys, ascents and descents, winding paths, dense thickets, caves, plains and plateaus, the *Republic* presents to its readers a rugged and varied terrain. . . . This is to say that the *Republic* is in many ways a dialogue about vision and the terrains that afford it; it is deeply concerned with generating logoi that gain purchases, points of view and privileged perspectives.[60]

We should remember, for example, that the conversation of the *Republic* takes place outside and below Athens, in Piraeus, while its most famous image, the cave, takes the reader outside and above the city. Our view of Kallipolis, meanwhile, comes from the elevated perspective of the guardians, whose encampment is chosen precisely in order to allow them to watch over the city (415d–e). But the most important shift of perspective is achieved through an expansion of the reader's political imagination. For the deeper the reader enters into the imaginative exercise of constructing a theoretical ideal of the city from first principles, as a functionally coherent division of labor aimed at fostering the good life, the more she absorbs a way of thinking whose effect is to make her own city appear alien and strange. This distancing movement, by which the reader is gradually placed farther and farther outside Athens, is accompanied by an evaluative movement whereby democracy is demoted in the hierarchy of constitutions. Put together, these two movements result in the reader's looking down at Athens from the elevated vantage point of Kallipolis. Brill therefore suggests we see the *Republic* as offering a "critical theory" of Athenian democracy:

Plato's *Republic* develops a robust critical theory: *theory* in that it aims at a viewing, a *theōria*, of the city; *critical* in that it presents this vision for the sake of the critique of a particular city; *Plato's* because it operates by way of a radical image-making facility, one which forms an inextricable part of its philosophical enterprise. The theoretical lens Plato employs in his critique of

---

60. Brill, "Plato's Critical Theory," 236.

Athenian democracy hinges upon the creation of linguistic and conceptual images that are designed to provide critical purchase on the polis as such and on Athens in particular.[61]

Whether the *Republic* offers a critical theory in the post-Hegelian sense—one that criticizes the present from the standpoint of its un-actualized potential—is debatable, but it does seem fair to credit Plato with aiming to liberate his readers from the dominant ideology so that they come to see that "it is not Kallipolis that is the dream-world, but Athens."[62] Pericles suggests that Athenians who take time to contemplate their city will fall in love with it and fight to preserve it; Plato suggests that those who take time to contemplate Kallipolis will fall out of love with Athens and fight to change it. This reconfiguration of the political imagination will amount to a kind of internal emigration, with readers coming to think of Kallipolis, rather than Athens, as the city they should call their own (592a–b).

39. This interpretation allows us to solve a puzzle concerning Socrates' portrayal of democracy in Book VIII. He pictures each regime type as characterized by a particular constitutive principle, or highest value, the insatiable pursuit of which generates instability (562b). The good around which timocracies are organized is honor (547c), and they are undermined by their structural tendency not to consider what is truly worthy of honor; when wealth comes to be prized above virtue, the regime starts to collapse (550d–551a). The good around which oligarchies are organized is wealth (555b; 562b), and they are undermined by their structural tendency to promote intemperance and class division and to erode military strength by sapping any sense of the common good (551c–552a; 555c–557a). The good around which democracies are organized is individual freedom (557b; 562b–c), and they are undermined by their structural tendency to avoid relations of rule, so that the authority of their magistrates and laws is flouted (562c–d, 563d–e). All this is clear enough on a schematic level, but the question is how it relates to empirical

---

61. Ibid., 233. On *theōria*, see Nightingale, *Spectacles of Truth in Classical Greek Philosophy*.
62. Brill, "Plato's Critical Theory," 235.

reality.[63] Socrates' description of democracy is especially question-able, as W. G. Runciman rightly notes, since it blatantly distorts reality in crucial ways:

> Socrates' exchange with Glaucon at 562c–563c certainly reads as if they have in mind the here and now. Plato might, accord-ingly, have been expected to justify his dislike by showing that the vesting of judicial and executive power in the Athenian as-sembly [ekklēsia] has given rise to the inconsistencies in policy making, the compulsive litigiousness, the excessive license in manners and mores, the popular envy of riches, the contempt for learning, and the mutual sycophancy of demagogues and populace which make harmony and order unattainable. But he does not do this. Instead, he presents the democratic *polis* as one in which (he says) there is freedom for the individual citizen to rule or be ruled, to keep the peace or break it, and to flout the rules (if there are any) about eligibility for political or judicial office (557e–558a). This is so far at variance with the actual state of affairs in any democratic *polis* as to make the reader wonder what Plato can be getting at.[64]

Socrates does make clear that his portraits of regime types are theo-retical abstractions designed to bring out critical features: each is an "outline sketch" rather than an "exact account" since "it would be an incredibly long task to discuss every constitution and every char-

---

63. It is also true that the precise mechanism whereby democracy collapses into tyranny remains tenuous—the claim seems to be that class conflict grows no less in democracy than in oligarchy, thanks to general permissiveness, but is more dangerous in the former since the poor are empowered to confiscate the wealth of the rich (564c–565d).

64. Runciman, *Great Books, Bad Arguments*, 46–48. See also Annas, *Introduction to Plato's "Republic,"* 300–301: "Plato presents democracy as defined by tolerant pluralism, but Athens was a populist democracy, with a clearly defined way of life separating those with power from those without, and about as tolerant of openly expressed nonconformity as McCarthyite America." Another example would be Socrates' claim that democracy gives the poor an equal share in the constitution with the rich. As Melissa Lane points out, existing democracies sometimes had a property qualification for citizenship and often had a property qualification for holding particular offices. See Lane, "From History to Model."

acter without omitting any detail" (548c–d). The trouble is that Socrates goes well beyond omitting details for the sake of theoretical clarity—he also adds spurious details of his own, such as the alleged freedom of democratic citizens to accept or reject rules as they see fit (557e–558a). His sketch of democracy therefore seems less ideal type than straw man.

40. The obvious conclusion is that Plato's portrait of democracy is skewed by the requirements of his systematic theory. As Annas puts it, "Democracy has to be, for Plato, a permissive free-for-all with no, or weak, sense of overall unity, because it is a further stage of breakdown of the ideal state's unity."[65] Plato's account of the various constitutions certainly is guided by a systematic logic within which the notion of unity is crucial. Socrates says that constitutions are to be treated only insofar as they have a distinctive form (eidos), which is why various intermediary regimes are not discussed (544c–d)—and for Plato, as we have seen, something's form is its principle of unity. Each of the constitutions aims to unify society around a given goal, and there is a clear hierarchy between them in terms of their success at generating genuine unity and hence stability.[66]

41. One way of defending Plato would therefore be to say that the label "democracy" is beside the point: the underlying goal is to isolate and to criticize a form of social organization organized around the promotion of individual freedom, which it "defines as the good" (562b–c, 557b), whether or not this corresponds exactly to Athens. If

---

65. Annas, Introduction to Plato's "Republic," 300.

66. On top of this, the decline story is clearly formulaic, designed to reveal different structures rather than to predict constitutional developments—Plato must have been aware that democracy was capable of changing into oligarchy, for instance, given that this happened more than once within his lifetime. In this respect we might compare the decline story with stories of origins like the one found in the first few chapters of Genesis or those found in social-contract narratives, which are also best understood as attempts to reveal ontological structure rather than attempts at causal explanation. (On Genesis, see Kass, Beginning of Wisdom.) For a contrasting suggestion of how to read the decline story in the Republic, see Lane, "From History to Model." Lane helpfully suggests that Plato is developing an account of the logic of social change by outlining one possible future, the goal being to show that constitutions break down when the group holding the offices become divided (545c–d) since they no longer take the good of the ruled as their proper object. I believe this account, which focuses the mechanism by which deficient regimes collapse, is ultimately compatible with my own, which focuses on the reasons for their underlying instability.

this is right, then perhaps he should simply have called the regime something like "anarchy" rather than "democracy"—perhaps he simply lacked a suitable term for it.

42. This interpretation does not seem tenable. To begin with, Plato is perfectly happy to invent neologisms where they are required, "timocracy" being a prime example (545b; cf. 533d). Moreover, the word "anarchy" already existed in Greek *(hē anarchia)*—indeed, Socrates uses it twice (562e; cf. 558c)—and although it was standardly used to refer to a situation in which the offices of government stood vacant, as opposed to a situation of complete lawlessness, Plato would have been perfectly capable of repurposing it.[67] If Socrates calls the regime organized around individual freedom "democracy," it is surely because Plato wanted to connect it to the Athens of his day.

43. Plato's distortion of democracy makes sense only if we assume that he was actively trying to surprise and shock the reader. It is hard to believe that he would not have anticipated his readers reacting with befuddlement when Socrates says, for example, that "there is no compulsion to rule in this city, even if you are qualified to rule, or to be ruled if you do not want to be; or to be at war when the others are at war, or to keep the peace when the others are keeping it, if you do not want peace" (557e). And that is just the beginning. Socrates goes on to claim that democracy eliminates a whole range of (supposedly) natural hierarchies: those between father and son, citizen and non-citizen, teacher and student, young and old, master and slave, man and woman, and, finally, humans and animals. By this point the reader might reasonably be expected to smell a rat. "Horses and donkeys are accustomed to roam freely and proudly along the streets," Socrates declares, "bumping into anyone who doesn't get out of their way" (563c). "You're telling me what I already know," responds Adeimantus. "I've often experienced that sort of thing while travelling in the country" (563d). This is clearly deadpan comedy. No one could seriously claim that democracy is characterized by horses and donkeys

---

67. See Ober, "Original Meaning of 'Democracy,'" 4n3, 6. Examples of references to *anarchia* include Herodotus, *Histories* 9.32; Thucydides, *History of the Peloponnesian War*, 6.72; and Xenophon, *Hellenika*, 3.1.3. These references are drawn from Kasimis, "Recovering a Theory of Performativity in Plato's Mimesis."

roaming the streets freely and proudly. This is a comedic moment comparable to Aristophanes' caricature of Socrates in *Clouds* as a mad professor, floating high in the sky so as to "make exact discoveries of the highest nature."[68] Just as Aristophanes was able to make Athenians see Socrates as both dangerous and ridiculous—a blasphemous sophist with his head in the clouds—so Plato hopes to change the way they perceive democracy.

44. This is by no means the only caricature in the *Republic*. There is also the image of the self-styled cognoscenti charging around town "as if their ears were under contract to listen to every chorus" (475d); the image of the sophist as "a little bald-headed tinker who has come into some money and, having been just released from jail, has taken a bath, put on a new cloak, got himself up as a bridegroom, and is about to marry the boss's daughter because she is poor and abandoned" (495e); and the image of appetitive people as "always looking downward like cattle . . . [that] feed, fatten, and fornicate . . . [and] kick and butt with iron horns and hooves, killing each other, because their desires are insatiable" (586a–b). The goal in each case is to take a familiar phenomenon and invite us to see it as ridiculous, so that a new scale of values becomes integrated into our day-to-day perception.

45. Caricature is not argument, of course—but as with Plato's other rhetorical techniques, the goal is to convey truths. The democrat is therefore perfectly entitled to ask what Plato's critique of democracy would look like if stated soberly. Socrates claims that the most salient characteristic of democracy vis-à-vis other constitutions is its elevation of the "license . . . to do whatever one wants" into the organizing principle of society, the goal that ties its various activities together (557b). But this obsession with freedom is downstream from a mistaken picture of equality: democracy allows "a sort of equality to both equals and unequals alike" (558c). For Plato, as for Aristotle, equality should be proportionate rather than arithmetical in any simple way—equal shares should be given to those who are equal, and unequal shares to those who are unequal. What is at issue here is equality of authority rather than resources. In the natural

---

68. Aristophanes, *Clouds*, trans. Peter Meineck, 217–234.

order of things, Socrates suggests, parents should have authority over children, citizens over resident aliens, teachers over students, the old over the young, masters over slaves, males over females, and humans over animals. These are relations of rule, and the antonym of rule is freedom: this is why it makes sense to call democracy, which flattens these distinctions, a constitution organized around individual freedom.[69] Socrates' portrait of democracy is therefore really a reductio ad absurdum of the refusal to recognize the necessity of relations of rule.

46. There is an obvious sense in which democracies do recognize the necessity of rule: equality and freedom need to be enshrined in law; the whole point of a democratic assembly is to legislate; and democratic laws are generally upheld and enforced. This might seem to refute Socrates' claim that democratic citizens are free to do as they please, regardless of what the law enjoins (557e–558a). But we should not take Socrates literally. His real meaning becomes clear in what follows, when he characterizes the city's tolerance or leniency (sungnōmē) as primarily a matter of its "utter disregard" for the education of its citizens (558a–b). This goes together with his claim that in a democracy "each person would arrange his own life in whatever way pleases him." The result of this educational free-for-all is that democracy ends up as a "supermarket of constitutions" (pantopōlion politeiōn, 557b–d)—like a bazaar in which psychological types are displayed side by side with no hierarchy among them. The contrast with Kallipolis is clear, since the goal of philosopher-rulers is precisely to "establish a constitution" in each citizen, and especially in those who will exercise political power (590c–591a; 501c). What democracy does not recognize the necessity of, then, is rule in Plato's sense—shaping souls by watching over usages and beliefs.[70] This is

---

69. Note that before Socrates turns to humans and animals, he claims that in democracy "males and females bought as slaves are no less free than those who bought them" (563b).

70. There may also be a sense in which it is blind to the fact that ruling in the standard sense is necessary. Melissa Lane, noting that democracy is described as anarchos at 558c, places this description in the context of a wider story in Book VIII regarding the nature of office: in democracy the link between the capacity to rule and the duty to do so has been severed (557e), so that "there is an absence of rule in the sense of an absence of any stable constitutive connection between office and rule." In

what licenses Socrates to say that democracy is *anarchos* (558c): from a Platonic point of view, it lacks rulers altogether, and that fact flows from the very essence of a system that considers political equality the highest value. So although Socrates is clearly exaggerating when he says that democracies permit their citizens to flout their institutions at will, his caricature brings out a serious point. A society will be stable only if it fosters individuals willing to sustain its institutions. Given its refusal to concern itself with soul shaping, democracy in its pure form lacks the resources to maintain itself as a stable social order.

47. Cultural education does happen in democracies, of course—just not as a result of conscious deliberation concerning individual and collective flourishing. Those who shape citizens' conception of the good life do so blindly: they are entrepreneurs who simply provide what sells in the marketplace without thinking about how that affects the wider culture. In Chapter 3 we saw that every single craft product plays its part in constituting the cultural environment and hence in shaping the social ethos, and that the most important of the statues on the wall of the cave are those placed by poets. Poetry, Socrates says, "nurtures and waters [the appetites] and establishes them as rulers in us when they ought to wither and be ruled" (606d), so that in any city that allows it—a set that must include all democracies—"pleasure and pain will be kings . . . instead of law or . . . reason" (607a). Plato's ambition is to dethrone pleasure and pain in favor of law and reason, and to do this he must do battle with poets over the Athenian social imaginary.

48. But although poetry sets the tone of society, given its capacity to shape usages concerning what counts as just, beautiful, and good, the more immediate enemy for philosophy is sophistry:

> Not one of those paid private teachers, whom the people call sophists . . . teaches anything other than the convictions that the majority express when they are gathered together. Indeed,

---

Lane's account, it is therefore no accident that the terms "rule" and "office" do not come up at all with respect to tyranny, the stage that comes after democracy in Plato's decline story. See Lane, "From History to Model."

these are precisely what the sophists call wisdom. It's as if
someone were learning the moods and appetites of a huge, strong
beast that he's rearing—how to approach and handle it, when
it is most difficult to deal with or most gentle and what makes
it so, what sounds it utters in either condition, and what
sounds soothe or anger it. Having learned all this through
tending the beast over a period of time, he calls this knack
wisdom, gathers his information together as if it were a craft,
and starts to teach it. In truth, he knows nothing about which
of these convictions or appetites is fine or shameful, good or
bad, just or unjust, but he applies all these names in accordance
with the great beast's beliefs—calling what it enjoys good and
what angers it bad. He has no other account [logos] to give of
these terms. (493a–c)

The demos as beast and the sophist as trainer: this is one of the great
images of the *Republic*. The demos does not think of itself as being
reared or taught, and hence ruled in the Platonic sense, by anyone—
that would imply inequality or unfreedom. Yet its usages are being
shaped regardless, not by philosophers but by those who (having no
dialectically defensible account of beauty, goodness, and justice) are
on the same cognitive level as their pupils and therefore have nothing
more to take their bearings from—or "look away to"—than their
own desire for power.[71] This image of democracy connects to another "image in words" presented by Socrates, namely Book IX's
image of the soul as composed of a human being, a lion, and a "mul-
ticolored beast with a ring of many heads that it can grow and change
at will" (588b–588d). If the demos is a beast, it is because it is led by
those who appeal to the beast within each citizen. Yet even that does
not do justice to the situation. For these are leaders who do not even
know themselves as leaders. This takes us back to the puppeteers of

---

71. In this connection it is worth noting that Thrasymachus, the most fleshed-out
example of a sophist in the *Republic*, is clearly portrayed as a spirited personality, full
of shame and anger, engaging in argument for the purpose of winning praise. See
especially 336b, 337a, 338a, 350d.

the cave, who project their statues unwittingly—the blind blindly leading the blind.

49. The image of the demos as beast is part of a battery of images designed to jolt the Athenian reader out of Periclean self-congratulation. Like Socrates' portraits of the just man and the just city, as well as the rulers' models of city and soul, these images are sketches or outlines rather than complete pictures (cf. 500d–501c, 548c–d). And just as models of good form should be beautiful and noble, so models of bad form should be ugly and ridiculous.[72] To a nonphilosopher, Socrates suggests, democracy might appear the most beautiful of all constitutions since it allows for all kinds of experiments in living: "Like a coat embroidered with every kind of ornament, this city, embroidered with every kind of character type, would seem to be the most beautiful" (557c). Philosophers, by contrast, understand that beauty is a matter of proportional harmony among the parts of a whole, so that a constitution will be truly beautiful only if citizens carry out specific roles within a coherent division of labor organized toward the production of genuine goods (420c–421c). The *Republic*'s caricatures are designed to make this insight palpable to nonphilosophers without relying on dialectical reasoning: democracy's claim to beauty is simply ridiculed.

50. Plato is therefore practicing what Socrates preaches: calibrating citizens' sense of the ridiculous *(to geloion)* in light of dialectical inquiry into goodness (452c–e; 457a–b).[73] In Book V the ridiculous is lined up on the side of the ugly and the shameful *(to aischron)* against the beautiful and the honorable *(to kalon)*. Our sense of the ridiculous is therefore bound up with our sense of pride and hence with *thumos* or spirit—the drive for honor but also (perhaps more fundamentally) the drive to protect and promote what is one's own.[74] In Kallipolis the rulers must ensure that citizens take the city itself as

---

72. The "should" here is both logical, given the relationship between goodness and beauty, and psychological, given the need to appeal both to reason and to spirit.

73. With echoes at 451a, 452a, 454c–d, 463e, 467, and 474a.

74. The precise nature of *thumos* is open to debate: it has to do with the drive for honor and recognition (581a–b), but it also has to do with courage in battle (375a–b), as well as the capacity to feel anger (439e–440e); and in all of this it is responsive to reason, especially with respect to considerations of what one is owed (440c–d). It seems to me that we can tie all of this together by interpreting *thumos* as the drive to

their primary object of pride, and this involves propagating the image of the city as beautiful.[75] In caricaturing Athenian democracy, Plato is engaging in the same activity, namely recalibrating the reader's sense of what is ridiculous in order to recalibrate his sense of what is his own, only for different purposes. The goal is not to stabilize the social order but to alienate the reader from it—to make it seem ugly and unlovable and therefore distant and foreign. If the model of Kallipolis is to be placed above the wall of the cave as an ideal whose shadows serve to orient and inspire, the model of democracy is to be placed alongside it as a gargoyle or grotesque whose function is to generate disgust at the status quo and a longing for something better.

51. With this in mind, we can see how directly political the *Republic* is, given its conception of politics. For Plato, ruling in the full sense is guarding both the city and the souls of the citizens who compose it. This entails both supervising the division of labor and shaping conventional views concerning beauty, justice, and goodness, and this latter task requires propagating ideals, myths, and other images. Given that he depicts democracy as a free-for-all with respect to rule in this sense, and given that throughout the *Republic* Plato is himself propagating ideals, myths, and other images, both negative and positive—including, by the way, the characters that he sketches, especially Socrates, Cephalus, and Thrasymachus but also Glaucon and Adeimantus—we might therefore say that the *Republic* represents Plato's attempt to guard Athens to the degree possible for a philosopher in his day. The question must therefore arise whether Plato might have been trying to do Athenian democracy a service by correcting its excesses. This is perhaps too speculative from a scholarly

---

protect and promote what is one's own, with reason feeding in a conception of what actually is one's own (cf. 433e).

75. Thucydides' Pericles seems to be up to the same thing in his funeral oration, as we have seen. On Kallipolis as the beautiful city, see Chapter 3. Of course, Socrates also suggests that the abolition of family structures among guardians and auxiliaries will be crucial in recalibrating *thumos* (463b–464d).

perspective, but as a strategic possibility it is worth keeping mind in the chapters to follow.[76]

THIS BOOK AIMS to open up a new way of thinking about the role of political idealism in contemporary political life, where idealism is understood as a commitment to orient oneself toward a vision of the best possible society. Plato's *Republic* offers a sophisticated way of thinking about political idealism in this sense. Once we understand the metaphysics of the *Republic* as having to do with formal and final causes, we can understand what it means to say that rulers should be philosophers: ruling is a matter of guarding one's subjects' souls in good condition, and doing this well requires holistic, dialectical inquiry into formal and final causes. Such inquiry involves the production of ideals in the sense of models, so the argument that philosophers should rule is also the argument that ideal theorists should rule. Moreover, the ideal society will itself be suffused with ideals, since models of good form should be disseminated throughout society in order to shape citizens' characters. But as we have seen in this chapter, ideal theorists can also shape citizens' perception of their social world by propagating myths that convey deep truths to the young, as well as caricatures that invite citizens to view their own world critically. In reorienting the social imaginary, then, political idealism can play an emancipatory role, inching nonideal societies closer to the ideal. The question, of course, is what any of this has to do with the present—and it is to this that we must now turn.

---

76. Given that democracy in Plato's sense is an ideal type, we may wonder whether the lesson of his account is just that any existing democracy needs to be infused with principles from a different social order for the sake of its own stability. (In Book V of his *Politics*, 1309b–1310a, Aristotle argues that oligarchies, although defective, can be rendered more stable by an infusion of democratic principles, and vice versa in the case of democracies.) If so, then institutionally speaking, the debate would be over introducing nondemocratic elements into Athenian democracy or retaining those that already exist—the diminished role of the Areopagus after 462 was much debated, for instance, and generals were elected rather than being chosen by lot, which is what permitted Pericles to serve as "leader" for over thirty years. For an interpretation that emphasizes the complexity of Plato's relationship with Athenian democracy, see Monoson, *Plato's Democratic Entanglements*.

5

Historical Possibility

CAN PLATO'S POLITICAL theory have any purchase in today's world? The prospect seems remote. We have seen that the notion of philosopher-rulers depends on distinctive conceptions of philosophy and rule; once these conceptions are properly understood, the theory is revealed as coherent. But even if the notion of philosopher-rulers is coherent, it seems straightforwardly incompatible with the practices and tenets of liberal democracy. Political Platonism might therefore seem ripe for the dustbin of history.

The rest of this book will argue against that conclusion. I begin by restating the principal elements of my reading of the *Republic*. Next I develop a notion of "historical possibility," according to which even if we suppose that Plato's theory was possible in ancient Athens, it may no longer be possible in Western societies deeply committed to liberal democracy. Finally I outline the strategy that I propose to take in response to this fact, namely to modify Plato's view whenever it comes into conflict with liberal democracy. In Chapter 6 I carry out the surgery in question, showing that what remains is both compelling and distinctively Platonic: the thought is that excellent citizens of a liberal democracy ought to be idealists, both in the narrowly political realm and in their wider social lives. In Chapter 7 I show how this conception might reshape our perception of the contemporary social order and thereby provide a critical theory of sorts.

§1 The Story So Far: Political Platonism

1. As we saw in the Introduction, "ideal" is a term with various possible meanings. Some speak of principles as ideals, so that an idealist is one who sticks to her principles; others speak of ideals as transcendent goods in terms of which a hierarchy of lower goods is ordered or organized; still others speak of "regulative ideals" as ends that give sense to our activities despite the impossibility of our ever fully realizing them. The term is so multivocal that any philosophically productive usage is likely to be stipulative, fixing the meaning for analytical purposes. Although I have spoken of ideals in the sense of highest values, for the most part I have been using "an ideal" to signify "an imagined perfect case," where "perfect case" in turn means "best possible instance of a given kind." This usage entails that ideals are unrealizable in one sense but not in another. Ontologically speaking, they belong to the domain of the imaginary, so in that sense they are not such as to be realized. But we can nevertheless draw a distinction between ideals and utopias. Both are imaginary entities, but whereas ideals are constrained by possibility, utopias are not.

2. Plato deploys a distinctive philosophy of language in the *Republic*, and this reflects an even more distinctive metaphysics. A predicate such as "ruler" has its ordinary use—or misuse—and its "precise sense"; the precise sense is not so much a departure from ordinary language as a realization of its inner possibility. The conceptual structure Plato has in mind can be seen in sentences of the following form: "He may be on the Supreme Court, but he's no judge." A certain kind of ordinary-language philosopher might maintain that such remarks transgress the bounds of sense. After all, it seems natural to suppose that the extension of a term like "judge" can be dictated only by the conventions of a given society, and in the United States these conventions clearly specify that being appointed to the post of judge according to the correct procedure and under the appropriate conditions is sufficient warrant for calling someone a judge. But Wittgenstein himself might well have seen propositions like "he may be on the Supreme Court, but he's no judge" as exemplifying an integral part of our conceptual grammar. For if "essence is expressed in grammar" and "grammar tells us what kind of object

anything is," as Wittgenstein says in §317 and §373 of the *Philosophical Investigations*, then might not such peculiar phrases, with their recognizably distinct and iterable grammar, point to the fact that the essence of "judgehood" is given by normative standards? Plato would say yes, in any case, as a result of what we might call his "ontological perfectionism."

3. Let ontological perfectionism be the view that for a given range of objects, the true F is the perfect F. Plato seems to believe that ontological perfectionism holds of everything that can properly be said to be an object. For something to count as one and only one object, as opposed to either a mere heap or two objects, it must have a principle of unity that serves as its criterion of identity. This principle of unity is its form, the principle by which its parts are organized. But we can make sense of the organization of parts only if we understand them as organized for some end. Form is therefore necessarily related to function. For any given end, some forms will achieve the end better than others. Those that achieve it perfectly we can call "true forms." The true form of F is therefore that organization which allows an F to be the best F it can be, that is, the perfect F. And if we recall that the form of an entity serves not only as its principle of unity and organization but also as its criterion of identity, that which makes it the kind of thing it is, it follows that possessing the true form of F allows an F not only to be the best F it can be but also to count as an F in the fullest sense. Hence an imperfect judge is not a judge in the fullest sense.[1]

4. If Plato believes that ontological perfectionism holds of anything that could count as an object, he must also believe that it holds of the polis, or society.[2] For him, only the perfect society would

---

1. When Plato speaks of "forms" in the *Republic*, he generally means "true forms." But he does reserve space in his conceptual scheme for principles of organization that are not as good as they might be. This is what makes sense of Socrates' reference to inferior species of city and soul as distinct forms (*eidē*) in Book VIII (544c–d).

2. The term *polis* is typically translated as "city." In Chapters 1 through 4 on Plato I often kept to that translation for the sake of simplicity, but as I said in Chapter 1, I prefer the term "society" from a conceptual point of view—whereas "city" connotes an urban area of a certain size, the ancient Greek polis contains both rural and urban areas, its boundaries tracking those of what we would now call a given "society."

count as a society in the fullest sense. Society is therefore an aspiration, not a given; it can be achieved but not assumed. So it is an open question to what degree any of the entities we currently call "societies" are truly deserving of the name, and indeed whether there has ever been such a thing as a genuine society.

5. What differentiates a society from a mere heap of people? For Plato, the answer is its constitution. A constitution is a society's form, its principle of unity and criterion of identity. For a society to be constituted as a society is, in the first instance, for its citizens to pull together to create and sustain a collective body; and the scheme by which the citizens achieve this is the constitution, which governs the distribution of offices and tasks. By this definition most of the entities we call societies do in fact count as societies in some sense; having some form, they are not best categorized as mere heaps. But Plato would probably accuse them of being badly constituted and hence of being bad at being societies. Notice, first of all, that Plato's understanding of a constitution makes a society's metaphysical criterion of identity into an observable causal force; a society whose unity is questionable from a metaphysical point of view, one whose citizens are not pulling together in the appropriate fashion, will ipso facto also be vulnerable to external and internal threats. But the ultimate function of society is to enable its citizens to lead the best lives they can, and a society might have sufficient unity to maintain itself in existence while nonetheless failing at this.[3] In Plato's view, flourishing requires having one's soul in the right order, which is to say having one's drives (and therefore one's desires) directed at the appropriate objects and organized into the appropriate hierarchy. But the structure of one's soul is not entirely up to oneself. It is arrived at through a combination of nature and nurture; and nurture includes education and habits, both of which require the right kind of society. The true society will therefore have a constitution that enables its citizens to flourish as far as possible, given

---

3. In response to an anonymous reader for the press, I should clarify that I do not mean to imply that such failure must be due simply to lack of unity—it could also be due to the misdirection of a fully unified society. This ties in with the distinction between dysfunctional and malfunctional societies in Chapter 7.

their natural endowments. Given his understanding of what it would be to have one's soul in the right order, Plato would almost certainly think that even if contemporary Western societies do count as societies in some sense, they are nonetheless bad at being societies and so cannot be called societies in the fullest, or precise, sense.

6. A society, as opposed to an elk or an oak tree, is not the kind of entity that has an innate impulse toward acquiring or retaining its true form. Although it can certainly come into existence spontaneously, as conventions evolve in response to practical problems, on Plato's view a society will achieve its full potential only if we think of it as an artefact of a peculiar kind, one whose good order needs to be consciously maintained by craftsmanship that imposes form on citizenly material. A craftsman of the relevant kind operates by giving laws and shaping ideology, and doing this well requires her to seek wisdom.

7. As we have seen, the ruler's first task is to maintain her society in existence. But this requires that she have some basic metaphysical knowledge—she must know that the essence of a society, that which must be preserved through all other change if it is to perdure, is its constitution. Imagine that this metaphysical fact was unknown to the rulers of, say, Sparta, who instead assumed that the essence of a society was its territory. If Spartan territory were to come under threat, the rulers would then be mandated to do all they could to preserve it, even if that meant turning Sparta from an aristocracy into a tyranny. But if Plato is right, such a decision might actually mean the death of Sparta. Even if people went on applying that name to the territory in question, in reality Sparta would no longer exist. This example is somewhat fraught since it admits of an alternative interpretation according to which the Spartan aristocracy might not continue to exist, but Sparta itself would. Certainly there are easier examples of societies going out of existence when their constitutions are abandoned or dismantled: the dissolution of Yugoslavia and the USSR spring to mind.[4] But the Sparta example is more interesting

---

4. These examples raise their own questions: it might be, for example, that genuine guardians would in any case encourage the dissolution of societies that are too large to maintain the necessary affective ties between citizens.

because it highlights one of the central features of ontological perfectionism, namely the idea that an imperfect F is not fully F. If Sparta's constitution changes for the worse, it will become less of a society; and at some point it will no longer count as a society at all. Here one thinks of "failed states" that are unable to ensure the provision of basic goods such as security.

8. The job of the ruler is to guard society, and to guard society is to guard its essence, that is, its constitution. But a constitution—even in the loose sense that Plato imagines, as opposed to a written constitution like that of the United States—necessarily requires interpretation to apply it to particular, changing circumstances. Consider this remark of G. K. Chesterton:

> All conservatism is based upon the idea that if you leave things alone you leave them as they are. But you do not. If you leave a thing alone you leave it to a torrent of change. If you leave a white post alone it will soon be a black post. If you particularly want it to be white you must be always painting it again; that is, you must be always having a revolution. Briefly, if you want the old white post you must have a new white post.[5]

Chesterton was wrong to portray himself as damning conservatism rather than refining it, but his point still stands: to conserve a white post, it is necessary to continually repaint it. The same holds of a constitution: if it is to be maintained in existence, it must be continually applied to new circumstances. We might be tempted to conceive of this as a merely administrative task, albeit one that requires a high degree of practical wisdom; in that case there would be a sharp contrast between lawgiving, which would require philosophy, and ruling, which would not. But for Plato the practical wisdom required to apply a constitution to new circumstances is dependent on philosophical understanding. To continue with Chesterton's analogy, with constitutions there is always a genuine question concerning what "white" amounts to—what *was* the constitution? To answer this question, the ruler must understand the constitution's underlying logic, which

---

5. Chesterton, *Orthodoxy*, 194. Compare Locke, *Second Treatise on Government*, §§157–158.

means understanding the function toward which its organization of tasks and offices is aimed. But to match the form of society to its function is the lawgiver's task. To rule a society therefore entails permanently refounding it.

9. There are constitutions and there are constitutions, and to create and maintain a true constitution the ruler must organize society so that it carries out its ultimate function, which is to allow citizens to lead the best lives they can, given their natural endowments. This requires her to understand both optimal and deficient forms of the human soul. As a heuristic device for working out the true form of F, Plato suggests constructing ideals, that is, visions or models or paradigms of the perfect F. By constructing a "society in speech," for instance, arguing back and forth over whether our vision is as good as it can be, we can arrive at an ideal entity that maximally exemplifies the true form of a society. Ideals of society and soul permit the ruler to regulate the division of labor so that individual talents are deployed optimally and what is produced is genuinely beneficial. These models can then be disseminated among the citizenry by means of craft objects, including stories, in order to ensure that citizens have true belief about what counts as good and bad.

10. In sum, the *Republic* advances a distinctive way of thinking about the role of idealism in political life. On the ontological level, only a perfect society counts as a society in the fullest sense. To think about what a society is, we therefore must think about what a perfect society would be. So ideal theory, which constructs models of the perfect society, is an inquiry into the nature of things. On the political level, to construct such models is to develop a picture of the different tasks that need to be performed if citizens are to constitute a society that fosters the good life. Ideal theory is therefore essential for the regulation of the social division of labor and hence for ruling well, where ruling is understood as the task of shaping souls. On the cultural level, models of good form can influence conceptions of the good life as well as perceptions of the present situation. Ideal theory can therefore affect the prevailing culture by reorienting the moral and political imagination. Putting these dimensions together, we can say that political idealism—understood as

the activity of working out and orienting ourselves toward visions of the best possible society—should play an important role in both ideal and nonideal societies. Genuine rulers should be idealists, but in nonideal societies genuine rulers must rule from below, shaping the culture by disseminating models of both good form and bad form. In that sense ideal theory and critical theory ultimately come together as two sides of the same coin.

§2 Historical Possibility

11. Some ideal theorists permit themselves to deny any interest in practical questions. They take themselves to be simply seeking the truth about the nature of certain values (such as justice) and see no need to concern themselves with the subsequent question of how their work might be relevant for political actors. In a certain sense they are therefore invulnerable to the accusation most naturally thrown at them, that their work is incapable of guiding action—they simply don't care, or at least not officially.[6] But my goal is to show that Plato's political theory can be useful for political life today. If I fail to show that Platonism can guide action in today's world, I will have failed by my own standards.

12. The idea that societies are best governed by philosophers would have sounded ridiculous in Plato's day, as Socrates repeatedly acknowledges, and it will surely seem even more absurd today. Are we to imagine world leaders taking time off from steering the ships of state in order to pore over competing treatments of the trolley problem or the metaphysics of possible worlds? We might respond by insisting on the interpretations of "philosopher" and "ruler" worked out in Chapters 1, 2 and 3, namely that a philosopher is one who works out the true forms of things by constructing ideals of parts and wholes, and that a philosopher-ruler is someone who looks to these ideals in order to shape society and souls. But talk of shaping souls only makes matters worse to a liberal ear, since it evokes the specter of theocracy and totalitarianism. We seem, then, to be caught

---

6. See Estlund, "What Good Is It?"

in a dilemma: either Platonism is too far-fetched to be taken seriously, or it is such a clear and present danger that we must do everything to guard against it.

13. A genuine ideal must be both good and possible; if Plato's theory is bad or impossible, it is not an ideal at all. But it would be hard to make the case that Plato's candidate ideal is straightforwardly bad without begging the question. Suppose we want to say, for instance, that the idea of soul shaping infringes our autonomy since it seems to depend on censorship, and hence that it fails to accord each citizen due respect. Plato might respond by accusing us of having a warped notion of autonomy; although he may not have used the term, his ultimate political ambition might well be described as the fostering of true autonomy (as opposed to enslavement to the appetites).[7] There is nothing intrinsically incoherent in Plato's notion of autonomy, which he shares with a whole tradition that sees "positive liberty" as the fundamental goal of politics.[8] Isaiah Berlin, who made the distinction between negative and positive liberty famous, never denied that positive liberty is a genuine, objective value—he merely noted that its pursuit must come at the detriment of negative liberty, and hence that tragic choice was unavoidable.[9] To make the case that positive liberty ought to be sacrificed in favor of negative liberty, we would most likely have to draw on our intuitions, at least to some degree.[10] But by the terms of Plato's theory our intuitions are deeply suspect because we have not grown up in Kallipolis. That argument could run both ways, of course, for although we would

---

7. See Korsgaard, *Self-Constitution*, chaps. 7–9 for a stimulating comparison between Plato and Kant in this respect.

8. I am not claiming that Plato uses the word "liberty" *(eleutheria)* to express a positive conception (although 395c may be read that way, given the parallel with 500d) but only that he endorses the underlying idea. In my view, he clearly believes, for instance, that those who are slaves to no man can nevertheless be slaves to their appetites, and that this form of slavery ought to be of paramount importance to politics. See, e.g., 519a–b and 574d–575a.

9. For Berlin, the underlying point is that no social system can express every genuine value. See Berlin, "Two Concepts of Liberty," Part VIII.

10. I do not mean to imply that intuitions are simply raw data in philosophy, as some seem to assume. But even if we think of them as "considered judgments" in Rawls's sense, the same worry emerges: what if our considered judgments simply reflect the shadows cast on the wall of the cave?

have to rely on our intuitions to reject Plato's view that our intuitions are corrupt, we would also have to rely on them to accept his own view. Ultimately, then, the point is simply pragmatic: it will be harder to make a definitive case that Plato's theory is wrong than to show that it is not possible.

14. But what do we really mean when we call a political proposal impossible? Clearly much that gets called impossible in everyday life is not literally impossible. We might say that "it is impossible for Arnold Schwarzenegger to become president," yet there is a clear path to that eventuality, involving a massive surge in his popularity and an amendment to the U.S. Constitution to permit foreign-born candidates to stand for the office, that in no way contravenes the laws of logic or of nature. We can therefore imagine a sliding scale of likelihood along the following lines:

Logical necessity	Natural necessity	Space of natural possibility	Natural impossibility	Logical impossibility
If P, then Q; P, therefore Q	A is mortal	A does or does not become president	A grows wings	P and not-P exist at the same time in the same respect

Plato's theory is intended to fall within the space of natural possibility, and it does. But that space, as it stands, is unvariegated. I believe we can draw a distinction within it between the practically possible and the practically impossible.[11] To dismiss claims like "it is impossible for Arnold Schwarzenegger to become president" as conceptual sloppiness or simple exaggeration risks missing a distinction that ordinary language makes within the realm of human possibility, between the merely unlikely and the practically impossible. When we call a political eventuality such as Schwarzenegger's

11. See also Holly Lawford-Smith's analysis of what she calls "feasibility" in "Understanding Political Feasibility."

presidency "impossible," we mean something relatively specific, namely that it is so unlikely that it fails to be action guiding in any meaningful way. The threshold for practical impossibility will depend on the discursive context. Republican strategists deciding how best to win the next presidential election might reasonably consider Schwarzenegger's candidacy practically impossible, given the courses of action available to them. If the conversation were somehow to involve the entire American electorate, by contrast, the judgment of practical impossibility would not make sense, since the electorate as a whole could in fact undertake actions designed to make Schwarzenegger president. At what point a given possibility fails to be genuinely action guiding is of course a matter of judgment, and self-deception is a serious risk. But that does not make the concept useless: the fact that dusk exists does not mean there is no such thing as night or day.

15. There are various ways in which a putative ideal might be thought so unlikely as to have crossed the threshold into the realm of the non-action-guiding and hence utopian. Two of them depend on historical change and so might constitute a distinct category within the sphere of the practically impossible, namely the "historically impossible." First, an ideal might depend on various external background conditions; removal of these conditions might render it so unlikely as to be practically impossible. For instance, suppose that the ideal intellectual was once a Renaissance man. The realization of this ideal has become less and less likely over time as the division of intellectual labor has deepened, and we may now have reached the point where the amount of work needed to keep up with each academic discipline makes it humanly impossible to be a Renaissance man. If this is the case, the Renaissance ideal no longer makes sense; to pursue it would be utopian or quixotic, ridiculous at best.[12] This example points to the fact that we may not even be aware of the background conditions necessary for the cogency of an

---

12. See Weber, "Science as a Vocation," 7–8. Perhaps we ought to reserve the term "quixotic" for utopian action as opposed to utopian thought. It would then refer to action aimed at bringing about that which is impossible—the vain attempts of Cervantes' Don Quixote to revive chivalry being the paradigm example.

ideal until they break down. So one way in which Platonism might have been possible in ancient Greece but impossible today would be if it tacitly depends on certain background conditions regarding the size of societies and the possibility of insulating them from outside influences.[13]

16. An ideal might also become utopian if over the course of history our deepest institutional and evaluative commitments come into conflict with it. For instance, if a political ideal—to take an extreme example, let us say Aristotle's theory of slavery—clashes unavoidably with our society's commitments, it might then be considered historically impossible. In the case of slavery we might simply say that we have discovered that the so-called ideal was in fact bad; it would be odd to describe the institution as merely impossible today, as if it could in principle be the subject of utopian longing. But in cases where it is hard to be so confident about our own judgments, we can always retreat to the language of practical possibility for practical purposes. For whatever the philosophical merits of a putative ideal, it is less likely to be accepted to the degree that it diverges from extant institutional or evaluative commitments. And if its likelihood is thereby greatly diminished, it may cross the threshold into practical impossibility. So a second way in which a theory can be historically impossible is by being too distant from contemporary

13. This brings into view a reason for taking history seriously in political philosophy that Jonathan Floyd, in his otherwise exhaustive attack on that doctrine, ignores: an ideal theory is a theory of an ideal X, but historical changes might make it the case that what we take to be an X is in fact a Y, so to speak. In other words, it might be that the theory of the ideal polis is no guide to the theory of the ideal industrial democracy in much the same way in which the theory of the ideal canoe is no guide to the theory of the ideal submarine. See Floyd, "Is Political Philosophy Too Ahistorical?," as well as Collingwood, *Autobiography*, 64. If the political philosophy of the polis really does require the possibility of insulating the polis from outside influences, one might conceivably make the case that Plato's ideal was already impossible in ancient Athens because of its maritime trade. That would give special resonance to the fact that the conversation of the *Republic* takes place at the house of a foreigner—Cephalus—and in the port of Piraeus. But this does not mean that the ideal was necessarily impossible in the Greek world more generally. In the *Laws* the Athenian Visitor is careful to specify that the ideal city should be a certain distance from the sea to make it less vulnerable to corruption through commercial intercourse, and given the history of Greek colonization, there is no reason to believe that founding a city in such a location would have struck the reader as impossible or even unlikely. See Plato, *Laws* 705a–b.

commitments. If Platonism turns out to depend heavily on certain background beliefs that are no longer widely shared, for instance concerning the nature of the universe or the possibility of reaching knowledge about ethical matters, we might therefore have to count it as historically impossible.[14]

17. To sum up, the space of human possibility is whatever is not governed by logical or natural necessity. This space is divided into the practically possible and the practically impossible, where the latter is a threshold concept. And one species of practical impossibility is historical impossibility, where something is made impossible by the presence or absence of background conditions or commitments. The reason why all of this matters is that I have used the notion of possibility to demarcate ideals from utopias. And the reason why that matters is that my goal is to show that Plato's theory can be action guiding in today's world.

§3 Four Approaches to the Gap between Plato and Ourselves

18. To what extent does Plato's theory rely on background conditions and commitments that no longer hold? This question may be impossible to answer in the abstract, since we can hardly provide a full charter of Plato's presuppositions, let alone our own. My ap-

---

14. It is an interesting question whether we can always redescribe instances of historical impossibility in terms of goodness. For instance, we could conceptualize the two senses of historical impossibility in terms of an argument made by David Estlund about goodness. Sometimes, argues Estlund, the goodness of (a) depends entirely on its being conjoined with (b). In these cases, even though the best-case scenario would be to have (a) and (b), if (b) is not present, then it will not be good for us to have (a). The presence of (b) is a necessary condition on the goodness of (a). So being a Renaissance man can be good only if it is also true that we can master a number of different disciplines, and Aristotle's ideal of slavery can be held good only if we also deny the individual's right to dispose of his body as he pleases. So it is at least often the case that in speaking of ideals, questions of possibility can be reframed as questions of goodness. Is this in fact always the case? And might the reverse also be true? Insofar as one of the necessary conditions on something's being held good is always going to be that it does not clash too strongly with our other commitments, it would seem that something is held good if and only if it is also historically possible. This chimes in with the thought that a utopia is not "best but impossible" but "impossible and so not best." See Estlund, "Utophobia: Concession and Aspiration in Democratic Theory," in *Democratic Authority*, 263–271; and Estlund, "What Good Is It?," 397–399.

proach in Chapter 6 will therefore be to pose a series of objections to instituting Platonism today. This will allow the gap between Plato and ourselves to emerge—and then we can consider how to bridge it.

19. Before getting started, it is worth outlining four possible strategies we could adopt in response to whatever gap emerges between Plato and us. First, we could simply dismiss Plato's theory. For many this will be the natural reflex—after all, why on earth would we need to invoke Plato in the twenty-first century? To some extent this question could be asked of any attempt to use a past thinker to illuminate a contemporary problem: if an argument is to stand, it must stand on its own merits. Granted, investigating the views of past thinkers might always bring some reward. Uncovering the structure of alien views might lead us, for instance, to recognize—and so potentially own—commitments we hold only tacitly. And if those views are part of our own tradition (which need not exclude their being alien to us) then bringing them to light will help us grasp our own historical position. But this does not imply that we should accept the theory in question.

20. The second possible strategy would be the reverse: we could double down on behalf of Plato, arguing that his views are true and ours false. This strategy presents two difficulties: first, winning the argument without begging any questions would be extremely difficult; and second, even if the theory is left standing after nine rounds, it will most likely still be historically impossible, given its distance from current commitments. We will be left with a romantic utopianism that might serve as an excuse for tragic cynicism about political life.[15]

---

15. For a criticism of such "Augustinian" political philosophy, see David Miller, *Justice for Earthlings*. One might wonder whether the distance of Kallipolis from contemporary Athenian commitments licenses us to call it utopian from a practical point of view, even if it is not beyond the bounds of human nature. As with practical possibility more generally, the answer will depend on the discursive context. From the perspective of any given individual, Kallipolis was surely practically impossible. But alternative modes of political organization, especially that of Sparta, did seem to play an important role in the Athenian political imagination. So in that sense Kallipolis can be understood as amplifying certain contemporary values at the expense of others and hence as historically possible. In this respect Hegel's treatment of the *Republic* in his *Lectures on*

21. The third strategy would be to show that any discrepancy between Plato's views and our own is only superficial, and that the two are in fact compatible. But this is likely to prove impossible, and if we take it as the standard of success, we are likely to tempt ourselves into intellectual dishonesty. If we want to *learn* from a thinker, we must render her views as strong as possible. But if we want to learn *from* a thinker, we must not conflate her views with ours. Plato's political thought is illiberal and antidemocratic, and to pretend otherwise is special pleading.

22. My own strategy will be to minimize the distance between Plato and ourselves by modifying his theory whenever it seems to conflict with what I take to be the foundational commitments of contemporary Western society. This will involve making Platonism compatible with some form of liberalism. Although contemporary voices are by no means united in praise of liberalism, Western institutions clearly embody liberal presuppositions in various ways and to varying degrees. They tend to grant the individual certain rights, whether de facto or de jure, against both fellow citizens and the state; they allow democratic election for major offices; and they permit some form of pluralism concerning the question of the best way to live. Clearly these principles are all debatable, and Plato would certainly want to debate them. A whole literature has developed in support of political perfectionism, the view that the state cannot and should not be neutral with respect to the good life, and Plato would obviously be on the perfectionists' side.[16] Something similar is true of epistocracy, the view that political power should be given only to experts.[17] If we presume the failure of perfectionist and epistocratic

---

the History of Philosophy remains remarkably insightful. Thanks to Jenna Spitzer for pushing me to address this question.

16. On perfectionism in politics, see Arneson, "Liberal Neutrality on the Good"; Galston, *Liberal Purposes*; Haksar, *Equality, Liberty and Perfectionism*; Hurka, *Perfectionism*; Kraut, "Politics, Neutrality and the Good"; Macedo, *Liberal Virtues*; Raz, *Morality of Freedom*; Sandel, *Democracy's Discontent*; Sher, *Beyond Neutrality*; Wall, *Liberalism, Perfectionism and Restraint*; and Wenar, "Political Liberalism."

17. The term "epistocracy" comes from Estlund, *Democratic Authority* and "Why Not Epistocracy?" Kasper Lippert-Rasmussen discusses Estlund's objections to it in "Estlund on Epistocracy." See also Brennan, *Against Democracy*, 204–230.

arguments, we may end up cutting more out of Plato than we need to. That said, there are good reasons to pursue this strategy. The first is intellectual hygiene: bracketing perfectionist and epistocratic considerations allows us to see whether there are other ways in which Plato's political theory might bear on the present. The second is practical: just as a philosophical theory is stronger to the degree that it relies on fewer controversial premises, so a political proposal is more likely to be taken up to the degree that it is compatible with a variety of views on matters beyond its central concern.

I began this brief chapter by outlining what I take to be the core of Plato's political theory as expressed in the *Republic*, which counts as idealist on three levels: it focuses on ruling well as opposed to avoiding misrule; it suggests that ruling well will involve producing ideals or models; and it maintains that only the perfect society counts as a true society. Since my goal is to arrive at a theory that can guide action in today's world, I needed to ask whether and in what sense Plato's theory is possible today. I therefore constructed an account of "practical possibility" according to which a theory is practically possible only if it manages to stay on the right side of a threshold of sufficient unlikelihood whose location is determined by asking when a natural possibility is so remote that it can no longer play a meaningful role in practical deliberation. "Historical impossibility," I argued, is a species of practical impossibility wherein the distance between a given proposal and the institutional and normative commitments of contemporary society makes it a possibility so remote as to be practically impossible. By this measure Plato's political theory seemed at first to be historically impossible and hence utopian.

In response, I have outlined a concessive strategy that will modify Plato's theory wherever it strongly conflicts with contemporary commitments. I will deliberately construe those commitments as awkwardly as possible for Plato, insisting on a form of liberalism according to which the state must maintain some form of neutrality with respect to the good life and hence denying myself the ability to draw on various pertinent critiques of such neutrality—whether perfectionist or epistocratic—in my defense of Platonism. This is largely a matter of being clear about which argument is being made at which time and hence allowing ourselves to see which arguments bear which loads. But it is also true that my theory will be more valuable to the degree that it can find a place deep in liberal territory, both practically and theoretically.

6

Philosopher-Citizens

THIS CHAPTER ARGUES that the central claim of political Platonism—
that those who govern should engage in philosophical reflection—
is both attractive and true. This may seem absurd: as I said in the
Introduction, few would want to replace Churchill with Wittgenstein or Obama with Parfit. But the point is not that those who are
typically called rulers should undertake what is typically called
philosophy.

Ruling in the Platonic sense is the activity of shaping people's
characters; doing this well requires shaping the cultural environment;
doing that well requires shaping the social division of labor; and that
in turn requires having control over institutions. Philosophy, meanwhile, is the activity of considering phenomena in light of the underlying, interlocking structure of parts and wholes that constitutes
goodness. Doing this well requires a holistic back-and-forth between
our understandings of particular things in their current states and
in their best possible states, and that requires a holistic back-and-
forth between our understandings of the best possible states of individual things and of the wholes of which they are parts. What it
requires, in short, is ideal theory.

If we accept Plato's way of conceiving ruling and philosophy, it is
not hard to see why he thought that philosophers should rule. Those
who shape people's characters should do so in light of an ideal of

human flourishing; this requires understanding actual humans in light of their highest potential; and that requires understanding the place of humanity in the cosmos. Those who shape the social division of labor, meanwhile, should be able to see how different activities could best cohere into a scheme that sustains the good life; and this too requires reflecting on how parts and wholes can best fit together.

Merely understanding what led Plato to think that philosophers should rule will not lead us to share his way of thinking, of course. A succession of liberals have argued convincingly against giving anyone the power to refashion society on the basis of claims to expertise about the good life, while the scientific revolution has largely done away with the teleological picture of nature that is supposed to support those claims in the first place. Yet I shall argue that political Platonism ought to be attractive even to those who hold firmly to liberal democracy and the scientific revolution.

There are four sections to this chapter. The first canvasses liberal objections to Platonism. I begin with Karl Popper's famous accusation that Kallipolis is totalitarian. This is an exaggeration, but it allows us to locate a more durable charge, namely that Plato's vision is essentially paternalistic. With this in mind, I move on to an account of Rawlsian political liberalism, which would seem at first sight to rule philosophers out of court completely. The remainder of the chapter challenges that perception. In the second section I set out and defend a Platonic theory concerning institutions, namely that they should be governed with an eye to their functional coherence and their effects on citizens' characters, and hence that they should be governed by ideal theorists. In the third section I show that this argument in no way depends on rejecting the modern scientific worldview, and that it is perfectly compatible with political liberalism. In the fourth and final section I set out and defend a Platonic theory of citizenship. The fundamental idea is that since we rule ourselves through everyday actions that shape the cultural environment and hence our characters, and ruling ought to be undertaken in light of philosophical reflection, each citizen ought to philosophize to some degree. This notion promises to enrich political liberalism, but also to take us beyond it. In an ideal society, I conclude, citizens would be idealists.

§1 The Liberal Challenge

1. As we saw in Chapter 2, Plato conceives of society as a kind of team constituted by and for its members. Teams come in different forms. In a tug-of-war, everyone carries out the same task; in soccer, individuals carry out differentiated roles. Sports teams compete against other teams; mountain-rescue teams compete against no one. But what all teams have in common is cooperation. By cooperating with others, a set of individuals becomes more than the sum of its parts. Like a class, then, a team has members—but whereas a class is constituted by the properties of its members, a team is constituted by their activity. It makes perfect sense to look at a group of eleven soccer players, all wearing the same kit and playing in the same direction, and to declare that they are no team. Teamhood is the product of a certain kind of work, namely teamwork. The word "product" is clumsy, however, since teamhood is not separable from teamwork in the way that a product is from the act of production. A group of players engaged in teamwork just is a team—or, to put it another way, to be united in teamwork is to be united by teamwork. What makes a player's activity count as teamwork is that it aims at the good of the team, and that it does so as part of a coherent division of labor. From these facts about teams, it follows that a team requires both discipline and oversight. The division of labor will work only if each member sticks to their allotted task. But some schemes are better than others. If the team is to function well, tasks need to be assigned in light of the goal of the team, the relative abilities of each member, and the specifics of the present situation. In the normal case, the person who carries out this task is the manager.

2. Like a team, a society is constituted by the work of its members. In order to constitute a genuine society, citizens need to perform what we might call their social work: activity that aims at the good of society as part of a coherent division of labor. It follows that a society will also require both discipline and oversight. Citizens

need to stick to their tasks in the division of labor, thereby manifesting the virtue of justice in the political sense.[1] But if a society is to flourish, tasks must be allotted in light of an understanding of the good life, the relative abilities of each citizen, and the specifics of the present situation. This is why those who manage society ought to be those who seek wisdom (*sophia*), the ability to reliably judge what is good for society as a whole in both its internal and external relations (428b–e). So those who occupy the highest offices should engage in philosophy—and everyone else should obey them.

3. Although the idea of citizens pulling together to achieve the good life is appealing, Plato's picture of society is obviously illiberal and antidemocratic. In *The Open Society and Its Enemies*, Karl Popper argues that Plato's whole approach is back to front. Plato assumes that a political theory should specify how a society could be ruled well as opposed to how it could avoid being ruled badly.[2] He therefore fails to consider the limits we need to impose on the scope of rule if we are to guard against corruption and cruelty on the part of rulers. In the absence of explicit rules, Popper suggests, power is unchecked. This might not present a problem if we could ensure that only the virtuous rule; indeed, that is exactly why Socrates proposes a complex scheme for selecting, educating, and maintaining the guardians. But even if this scheme were realizable, it could never be completely efficacious. Some bad apples would sneak in; some good apples would rot. Popper concludes that Plato's theory lends itself to the ideological needs of oppressive elites who pose as philosopher-kings and try to "wipe [the slate] clean," in Plato's own damning phrase.[3] If Plato had been more concerned about the realities of

---

1. As in Chapter 2, a qualification is in order: we are talking here about individual justice in the political sense as opposed to in the psychic sense (which Plato thinks is primary). See notes 40 and 43 of Chapter 2.

2. Popper, *Open Society and Its Enemies*, 1:121–123, 157–168. To support this line of thought, one might also invoke Judith Shklar's reflections on "the liberalism of fear." See Shklar, "The Liberalism of Fear," in Rosenblum, *Liberalism and the Moral Life*, 21–38.

3. Plato, *Republic* 501a; see also 540d–541b. In this vein a critic might plausibly argue that Plato's tripartite class structure is as much an instance of "ideological" utopianism as Aristotle's theory of slavery in the *Politics* or the theory of property acquisition in Robert Nozick's *Anarchy, State and Utopia*, 150–182. Given the difficulty of discovering people's true nature, the argument would go, Plato's justification of an

political power, Popper suggests, he would have insisted that any social engineering be merely "piecemeal" as opposed to total, and he would have seen the value of democracy—understood by Popper not as rule by the people, a formulation that itself raises questions about the limits of rule, but rather as a system of accountability that permits the ruled to dismiss their rulers.[4]

4. Popper's objection to Platonism might have held at any stage in history—it has much in common with classical republicanism, for example, which seeks to reduce or eliminate arbitrary power through checks and balances, mechanisms of accountability, procedures of appeal, and the general rule of law—but it gains its urgency from the catastrophes of twentieth-century totalitarianism, which decisively demonstrated the need to limit top-down power.[5] On Plato's view, a genuine society is capable of acting as one entity and this will be achieved only if citizens pull together by fulfilling their allotted roles in a coherent division of labor. Popper thinks such organicist imagery generates a "totalitarian ethics" according to which the good of the individual is to serve the state:

> Plato recognizes only one ultimate standard, the interest of the state. Everything that furthers it is good and virtuous and just; everything that threatens it is bad and wicked and unjust.

---

aristocratic class structure will only serve to further entrench the existing position of established elites.

4. Popper, *Open Society and Its Enemies*, 1:125: "Seen in this light, the theory of democracy is not based upon the principle that the majority should rule; rather, the various equalitarian methods of democratic control, such as general elections and representative government, are to be considered as no more than well-tried and, in the presence of a widespread traditional distrust of tyranny, reasonably effective institutional safeguards against tyranny, always open to improvement, and even providing methods for their own improvement." Popper thinks that any theory that recommends a particular regime based on arguments from sovereignty faces the paradox that whichever group is made sovereign can thereby choose to have some other group rule; e.g., the majority can elect a tyrant. On accountability as a feature of ancient Greek political thought and practice, see Lane, "Popular Sovereignty as Control of Officeholders."

5. For classical republicanism see, e.g., Book VI of Polybius's *Histories* and Books II and III of Cicero's *Republic*. For the inheritance of this way of thinking by the American founders, especially Madison, see *The Federalist Papers*, especially nos. 9, 10, 47, 48, 49, and 51, in Wootton, *The Essential Federalist and Anti-Federalist Papers*. For a contemporary treatment of republican themes, see Pettit, *Republicanism*.

Actions that serve it are moral; actions that endanger it, immoral.[6]

Popper accuses more charitable interpreters of lapsing into "idealization of the great idealist."[7] Where I used the analogy of a team to explicate Plato's view, for example, Popper prefers to speak of a machine with cogs:

> The cogs in the great clockwork of the state can show "virtue" in two ways. First, they must be fit for their task, by virtue of their size, shape, strength, etc.; and secondly, they must be fitted each into its right place and must retain that place. The first type of virtues, fitness for a specific task, will lead to a differentiation, in accordance with the specific task of the cog. Certain cogs will be virtuous, i.e. fit, only if they are ("by their nature") large; others if they are strong; and others if they are smooth. But the virtue of keeping to one's place will be common to all of them; and it will at the same time be a virtue of the whole: that of being properly fitted together—of being in harmony. To this universal virtue Plato gives the name "justice."[8]

5. Popper clearly goes too far in suggesting that Kallipolis is totalitarian. To begin with, he fails to acknowledge that the ultimate goal of rulers in ensuring that society acts as one is to enable individuals to lead the best lives they can: citizens are cogs in a machine designed to facilitate the good life for *them*. Moreover, he translates *polis* as "the state," which connotes a peculiarly modern phenomenon in which relatively autonomous elites exercise what Michael Mann calls "despotic" and "infrastructural" power over the forces of civil society.[9] This is what allows him to view Kallipolis as continuous with the totalitarian administrative states of the twentieth century. But Socrates makes perfectly clear that the laws that ordinary citi-

---

6. Popper, *Open Society and Its Enemies*, 1:108.
7. Ibid., 1:87–88.
8. Ibid., 1:107–108.
9. Mann, "Autonomous Power of the State," 188–189.

zens must obey leave a wide realm of "negative" freedom in Isaiah Berlin's sense (that is, noninterference).[10] Indeed, Socrates goes so far as to suggest that as a rule of thumb the number of laws in a society will be inversely proportional to its health; if the right kind of ethos is in place, there will be little need for detailed laws (425a–426e). It is hard to reconcile this with images of the secret police knocking at the door.[11] That said, there is no doubt that Plato's theory is deeply paternalistic: ordinary citizens have no say over the structure of the social order or the character of the cultural environment. This may not be totalitarian, but it certainly seems illiberal.[12]

6. Liberalism is by no means a single, stable doctrine; like many political terms, its valence and extension change depending on the context.[13] But it seems fair to say that liberals tend to object (in varying ways and in varying degrees) to the notion that elites should tell ordinary people how to live. In John Stuart Mill's formulation, "Neither one person, nor any number of persons, is warranted in saying to another human creature of ripe years, that he shall not do with his life for his own benefit what he chooses to do with it."[14] Or as Kant puts it, "No one can compel me (in accordance with his beliefs about the welfare of others) to be happy after his fashion; instead, every person may seek happiness in the way that seems best to him, if only he does not violate the freedom of others to strive

---

10. See Berlin, "Two Concepts of Liberty," 194–195.

11. One might reasonably charge that Socrates is idealizing away dissent and misbehavior, but that is simply to return to Popper's earlier accusation, that Plato's whole approach to political life is back to front. In the *Laws*, which moves into nonideal theory, we do see some consideration of punishment.

12. To put it another way, the appropriate twentieth-century comparison would be postrevolutionary Iran rather than the Soviet Union. Readers looking for a fuller treatment of Popper's totalitarian charge should consult C. C. W. Taylor, "Plato's Totalitarianism."

13. As Joseph Raz remarks, liberalism is best understood "as a historical phenomenon identified by lines of historical development, by cross-references that express the appeal that some writers had for others, and often by a common temperament." Raz, "Comments on the Morality of Freedom," 4. We might be tempted to characterize the "common temperament" of which Raz speaks in terms of a cluster of value commitments—an emphasis on freedom and equality, for instance. But since liberals disagree on how to characterize these values, we cannot conclude that they are all committed to the same values, even if they do tend to appeal to the same words. See also Freeden, *Liberalism*; and Ryan, *Making of Modern Liberalism*, chap. 1.

14. Mill, *On Liberty*, chap. 4.

toward such similar ends as are compatible with everyone's freedom under a possible universal law."[15]

7. Mill's objection to paternalism comes down to the proposition that it is unlikely to do much good. Each of us tends to know more about our own interests and circumstances than anyone else, and in any case one of our core interests consists in exercising our capacities for deliberation and self-determination.[16] Plato and Mill are not as far apart as they may seem, however. Plato would agree that self-determination is necessary for a human life to be fully valuable.[17] He just considers it a rare achievement. Those who are incapable of getting their own desires in order stand in need of a cultural environment that does at least some of the job for them. And an environment of that kind would be best stewarded by those who are not slaves to their passions. This is paternalism for the sake of increasing autonomy—a possibility that Mill himself countenances when he speaks of prohibiting individuals selling themselves into slavery.[18]

8. A stronger objection to Platonic paternalism would invoke deontological arguments regarding what agents owe to one another. Many liberals have argued that for coercive structures to be legitimate, they must be justifiable to each citizen. On this view, a given law will be legitimate only if moral equals would have good reason to agree to impose it on one another. We can therefore make progress in political philosophy, we are told, by framing questions of institutional design in terms of a hypothetical social contract whereby citizens give up certain freedoms in exchange for others. And in many versions of this story, citizens would not agree to coercive interference from wise elites in the name of their own happiness. According to Kant, for instance, political power can never legitimately be deployed in the service of substantive conceptions of the good life, since

---

15. Immanuel Kant, "On the Proverb: That May Be True in Theory, but Is of No Practical Use," in Kant, *Perpetual Peace, and Other Essays*, 72.

16. On the importance of being able to deliberate for ourselves, see Mill, *On Liberty*, chap. 3.

17. C. C. W. Taylor is nevertheless right to observe that Plato simply never considers the idea that an agent's self-direction in accordance with a scheme of values that she endorses might be a necessary condition on her life's having any value at all. See C. C. W. Taylor, "Plato's Totalitarianism," in *Plato 2*, 295.

18. See Mill, *On Liberty*, chap. 5.

creatures capable of freely setting their own ends are rationally required to permit one another the greatest degree of free choice
consistent with the freedom of others, regardless of whether the
choices they make render them more or less happy.[19]

9. The most influential theory of this general kind may be that
presented by Rawls in *Political Liberalism*.[20] Rawls argues that for certain kinds of coercion to be legitimate, they must be justified in
terms of "public reasons" that do not depend on controversial conceptions of the good life.[21] A Catholic judge, for example, must not
reach decisions on the basis of sectarian dogma; the reasons she offers
ought to be grounded in considerations native to the realm constituted
by rules of fair cooperation between free and equal citizens.[22] The
same would also apply to a Platonist: when she enters the courtroom,
she should leave her arguments regarding human flourishing at the
door. Given that Rawls's restrictions extend to anyone acting in a
public capacity, from legislators and administrators to candidates
and even voters, it seems fair to say that "political liberalism," as
Rawls calls this doctrine, rules philosophers out of court.

10. Political liberalism is a bitter pill to swallow. The idea that polities should never be organized around a specific vision of the good
life entails the abandonment of many people's deepest political aspirations. Within the confines of our churches, mosques, and temples,
we are entitled to preach that our rivals are mistaken and even damned;
but where the exercise of state power is at issue, we have a "duty of civility" to set aside our commitments and treat other worldviews with

---

19. Kant does allow that laws can sometimes be directed toward the happiness of
citizens, but only as a means of securing the legitimate state against its enemies. See
"On the Proverb: That May Be True in Theory, but Is of No Practical Use," 78.

20. It is debatable whether Rawls's view is in fact deontic at bottom—it does not
seem to me to be so—but the Kantian inspiration is clear.

21. See Rawls, *Political Liberalism*, passim; and, for a helpful overview, Leif Wenar's
entry on Rawls in the *Stanford Encyclopaedia of Philosophy*. See also Ronald Dworkin,
"Liberalism," in *Public and Private Morality*, 127: "Political decisions must be, so far as
possible, independent of any particular conception of the good life, or of what gives
value to life."

22. Although a public official may legitimately deploy Catholic language and
imagery for rhetorical purposes, her judgments must be independently justifiable in
terms of values native to the public sphere. See Rawls, "The Idea of Public Reason
Revisited," reprinted in *Political Liberalism*, 435–490.

respect. This restriction seems to condemn us all to living amid, or at least alongside, what we consider to be untruth. At some level that is unavoidable, of course: the social world is never quite as any of us would wish. But many have conceived of the good life as an inescapably collective matter such that individuals can thrive only if the whole community is on the right track. The God of the Old Testament tends to smite whole cities rather than sparing the righteous few, for instance, while in Plato's view, as we have seen, there is no substitute for a healthy cultural environment fostered by wise laws.

11. Rawls acknowledges this cost, writing that "the hope of political community must indeed be abandoned, if by such a community we mean a political society united in affirming the same comprehensive doctrine."[23] But in his view that hope already died with the Reformation, in whose wake the central problem of political life became how to create a stable and just society among those of conflicting faiths that each claim the mission of saving souls by expanding throughout the world.[24] Since human reasoning is beset by ineluctable epistemological barriers, which Rawls calls "the burdens of reason," we should not expect the passage of time to bring convergence on a single doctrine regarding the human condition and the nature of the good life.[25] The only way to bring about convergence would be for the state to use coercive force to repress dissenting views, but this would be illegitimate since it is impossible to see how citizens conceived as free and equal would agree to a social structure that permitted such repression. Some form of tolerance for ideological pluralism is therefore a constraint on any viable political

---

23. Rawls, *Political Liberalism*, 146. On the distinction between a political community and a political society, see ibid., 40–43, 201–206; and Rawls, *Justice as Fairness*, 3, 21, 198–202.

24. Rawls, *Political Liberalism*, xxi–xxvi.

25. On the alleged "burdens of reason," see ibid., 54–66. For a cogent critique of the idea that these should figure in our explanation of reasonable pluralism, see Nussbaum, "Perfectionist Liberalism and Political Liberalism." A stronger explanation of pluralism would be Isaiah Berlin's thesis that the normative world is fundamentally tragic in that there exists a plurality of competing but nonetheless objective values, with no possibility of an overarching or harmonious reconciliation. See, e.g., Berlin, "Two Concepts of Liberty," Part VIII.

ideal in the modern world.[26] Rawls insists that this constraint is in no way to be regretted: pluralism is simply "the natural outcome of the activities of human reason under enduring free institutions," so to see it as a disaster would be "to see the exercise of reason under the conditions of freedom itself as a disaster."[27]

12. From a Platonic perspective, the question would be whether a pluralistic society could ever be stable—one thinks, for instance, of Socrates' depiction of democracy as falling apart for lack of a robust normative core. Rawls argues that the success of liberal institutions since the Reformation has disproved the assumption that "social unity and concord require agreement on a general and comprehensive religious, philosophical or moral doctrine."[28] On his view, the liberal order will be stable if its major institutions are supported by what he calls an "overlapping consensus" among citizens regardless of their other disagreements.[29] The thought is that each citizen might come to endorse the terms of political cooperation as a "freestanding module" within a larger outlook. Religious people, for example, could endorse freedom of religion for reasons internal to their religion, and atheists could endorse it for reasons internal to their doctrines.[30] If such endorsements were sufficiently widespread, society would achieve "stability for the right reasons." It would be a psychologically and normatively coherent order.[31]

---

26. As Rawls puts it in *Justice as Fairness*, 197, contemporary political ideals must accommodate themselves to the "historical and social conditions of modern democratic societies," namely "(i) the fact of reasonable pluralism and (ii) the fact of its permanence, as well as (iii) the fact that this pluralism can be overcome only by the oppressive use of state power." Charles Larmore adverts to the same considerations in justifying what he calls "procedural neutrality." See Larmore, *Patterns of Moral Complexity*, 48.

27. Rawls, *Political Liberalism*, xvi, xxiv–xxv. Rawls seems to draw his account of the inevitable results of the free exercise of human reason from Madison. See *Federalist* no. 10, in Wootton, *The Essential Federalist and Anti-Federalist Papers*, 168–169.

28. Ibid., xxv; and Rawls, *Justice as Fairness*, 197. Rawls credits those who advocated and instituted ideological pluralism with "the discovery of a new social possibility."

29. Rawls, *Political Liberalism*, xlv and Lecture IV.

30. Rawls points to the Second Vatican Council as a crucial example in this regard: the Catholic Church endorsed religious freedom as grounded in the dignity of the human person. See *Political Liberalism*, 476–477.

31. For legitimacy to be achieved, by contrast, social institutions need only have the potential to be the object of an overlapping consensus.

13. The image of political principles as a "freestanding module" is worth pondering. Imagine an American citizen who is perfectly willing to abide by the laws of the United States, but only as a compromise with reality: ideally, she wishes for the establishment of sharia law. She accepts liberal institutions as a modus vivendi rather than endorsing them as fundamentally desirable. What Rawls requires, by contrast, is for her belief system to undergo a kind of organ transplant: the theocratic module is removed, and in its place goes the liberal module. If the new organ is not to be rejected by its host, the host must have its reasons for accepting it. But these are hardly obvious. Groups who view each other as infidels will have to come to view each other as equally in need of having the basic structure of society justified to them. It seems unlikely, however, that such groups could ever view one another as equally worthy of respect and concern. Rawls's solution is to say that we should adopt the relevant notion of equal status not because it corresponds to some fact of the matter, but rather because it allows us to arrive at terms of social cooperation that can become the object of an overlapping consensus: it is a "normative and political" conception of the person as opposed to one that is "metaphysical or psychological."[32] The reason that our hypothetical Muslim might accept the proposed transplant, in other words, is that liberal society permits her to enjoy certain goods that might otherwise be unavailable or unstable: the goods of mutual recognition, designing and executing a plan of life, and cooperating with others on terms that each can consider fair.[33] But even supposing that her religious convictions do in fact give her reason to value these goods—which might not be true in every case— they might also give her reason to value the possibility of living in a society where what she considers the correct conception of the good life is backed up by law. If the first set of reasons outweighs the

32. The way Rawls puts it is that political liberalism regards every citizen as passing a threshold level with respect to "two moral powers," the capacity for a sense of justice and the capacity for a conception of the good, which together fit them to be considered free and equal. The conception of citizens as possessing the two moral powers is also supposed to be implicit in the "public political culture of a democratic society." See Rawls, *Justice as Fairness*, 18–19; and Rawls, *Political Liberalism*, 201–204.

33. See Rawls, *Political Liberalism*, 201–204.

second, political liberalism can regard her as a loyal citizen. If not, it must regard her as deficient qua citizen—"unreasonable," as Rawls puts it.[34]

14. From a Rawlsian point of view, Plato's political theory will look no less unreasonable. Plato considered ideological pluralism a sign of a badly ordered society. If rulers fail to understand their role, he thought, they will permit artists and orators to feed people what they want to hear rather than what is good for them, and this will lead to a certain kind of anarchy. In a well-ordered society, by contrast, rulers will disseminate a unified ideology that orients citizens toward goodness. What qualifies rulers to exercise such power over everyone else is their capacity for the kind of patient reasoning that leads to bad ideas being refuted. Even if there are "burdens of reason" that affect all humans, in other words, they do not affect us all equally. To put it more starkly: some are worthier of respect than others and to pretend otherwise is ruinous.

15. Rawls does not offer much of an argument against Plato or other "unreasonable" thinkers. As we have seen, political liberalism will be attractive only to those who value the goods of liberal society more highly than other goods. Those who do not accept this move at the "ethical" level will have no reason to rise to the "political" level at which ethical considerations are subsequently bracketed. Yet Rawls refuses to make the case that the goods of liberal society are central to human flourishing, stating merely that they are central to the "political conception of the person," which is just a framework adopted for the purpose of arriving at political agreement.[35] This seems circular at best. A true grounding of political liberalism, one might think, would require an ethical argument for the priority of goods

---

34. For a powerful critique of the Rawlsian treatment of nonliberals as "unreasonable," see Finlayson, *Political Is Political*, chap. 2. For helpful considerations of similar questions from a liberal point of view, see Scanlon, *Difficulty of Tolerance*, chap. 10; and Macedo, *Liberal Virtues*, chap. 2.

35. Relevant passages here are Rawls, *Political Liberalism*, 202–203, on the reason that political society is good for citizens, and 156, on the nature and purpose of political conceptions. In the first of those passages Rawls flirts with making the ethical case for political liberalism before retreating to the language of the political conception; in the second we see that political conceptions are adopted for the purpose of reaching agreement rather than for the purpose of reaching the truth.

such as mutual recognition over other possible goods. But that would return us, at least temporarily, to some version of what Rawls calls "comprehensive" liberalism.[36] It would therefore entail accepting that political liberalism, no less than Platonism, imposes a controversial conception of the good life on its citizens.[37]

16. Let us assume for the sake of argument that Rawlsians can in fact show that the goods of liberal society are worth privileging over other goods, and that the best way to achieve those goods is by demanding public reasons, as political liberalism suggests. It might seem to follow that political Platonism is nothing more than an unhelpful fantasy that threatens to undermine liberal democracy. What I want to show in the rest of this chapter, however, is that the Platonic way of thinking about governance has the potential to enrich contemporary political life even on the assumption that political liberalism is necessary.

§2 Institutions and Wisdom

17. Following Geoffrey Hodgson, we can usefully distinguish between two senses of "institution." In the broad sense, institutions are "systems of established and embedded social rules that structure so-

---

36. For the kind of account that Rawls treats as "comprehensive," see Raz, *Morality of Freedom*, as well as the liberalisms of Kant and Mill. For a critique of that label, see Gaus, "Diversity of Comprehensive Liberalisms," 100–114: "It should be clear that the label 'comprehensive' liberalism is misleading: it includes everything from truly comprehensive liberalisms as wide-ranging secular philosophies to Kantian liberal theories of political justice that seem consistent with a wide range of notions about value, social knowledge, and conceptions of selfhood."

37. Rawls's view seems to be that although the ethical grounds of political liberalism are philosophically controversial, they are implicit in the public culture of modern democracies and so can be assumed as a starting point for constructivist political philosophy. See "Kantian Constructivism in Moral Theory," reprinted in Rawls, *Collected Papers*, 303–358. The problem with this account is that insofar as there are some citizens who do not share the relevant value judgments, the liberal state will not be able to claim that its arrangements are justifiable to everyone unless it also claims that those value judgments are simply true, which would open up a gap between people's sense of what is justified and the truth about what is actually justifiable. That would solve the problem, but only at the expense of giving up the pretense of an ethically and metaethically neutral foundation. For a helpful collection of essays on these questions, see Wall and Klosko, *Perfectionism and Neutrality*. See also Macedo, *Liberal Virtues*, chap. 2, and Galston, *Liberal Purposes*.

cial interactions," where rules can mean norms of behavior and informal conventions just as much as codified injunctions.[38] Examples of institutions in this broad sense include languages, monetary systems, funeral customs, and family structures. In the narrow sense, by contrast, the term refers to organizations, understood as "special institutions that involve (a) criteria to establish their boundaries and to distinguish their members from nonmembers, (b) principles of sovereignty concerning who is in charge, and (c) chains of command delineating responsibilities within the organization."[39] Where organizations are at issue, in other words, the complex of rules that structures social interactions also generates explicit roles and responsibilities and therefore explicit power relations. Examples of institutions in this narrow sense include companies, schools, churches, and states.

18. Despite the fact that institutions in this second sense clearly involve relations of governance, political theorists have not generally paid much attention to the question of how they should be organized. The governance of state institutions has been of enduring interest in the liberal and republican traditions, of course, since the exercise of coercive power raises questions concerning justice, legitimacy, and freedom. And theorists cognizant of the relationship between state power and corporate power have certainly brought into focus the governance of business corporations.[40] But from a Platonic perspective these inquiries stop short of what is required for a full vision of social life. For there is more to life than justice, legitimacy, and freedom. If our concern is the good life more generally, we should also be thinking about the governance of universities, hospitals, sports clubs, choirs, and other institutions. After all, by enabling certain kinds of action and proscribing others, these institutions will inevitably shape characters to some degree. They also make available, or at least regulate, forms of cooperation that yield distinctive goods. The activities of academic inquiry, artistic production, sporting competition, religious worship, and civic deliberation all open up

---

38. Hodgson, "What Are Institutions?," 18.
39. Ibid., 18.
40. See, e.g., Ciepley, "Beyond Public and Private"; and Anderson, *Private Government*.

distinctive possibilities for action and expression and hence for self-development and self-fulfillment. These activities are all structured by institutions in one way or another. So if we want to construct a vision of the best possible society, we need a theory of institutional governance that covers local associations just as much as business corporations and organs of state.

19. On Plato's view, as we saw in Chapter 1, to understand the way things really are, one must understand the way they would best be ordered. The whole cosmos is pictured as a kind of team in which every genuine entity has a distinct role and, in virtue of that role, an optimal way of being organized. This cosmic version of the "one-man, one-job" rule ought to apply, we might infer, to institutions. If this is right then the Platonic position would be that for something to count as a genuine institution, it must have a distinct role within society and, in virtue of that role, an optimal way of being organized. If it is not unified around a particular pursuit, it will not be one thing at all. It will either be more than one thing—like a soul or society that is not one but many—or else it will be a mere heap of activity. A genuine institution, like a genuine soul or a genuine society, will be one whose parts constitute a coherent whole directed toward a particular function.[41]

20. This line of thought leads to a distinctive picture of institutional governance. As an artificial entity, an institution must be consciously regulated if it is to reach or retain its optimal organization. But this true form is not always obvious to governors. To grasp it, they must engage in ideal-theoretic reasoning about form and function. First they must ask how the institution might best fit into the whole of which it is a part. Then they must work out how its own parts might best be organized into a whole that can reliably carry out the function in question. In other words, they must construct an ideal not only of the institution but also of the context into which it fits. Yet since that context will be part of a wider whole, this chain of rea-

---

41. Roughly speaking, the function of the soul is to furnish the good life for an individual human being, and the function of society is to furnish the good life for a collection of human beings. See especially *Republic* 353d–e and 369b–c, bearing in mind the interpretation offered in Chapters 2–4. For the society that is not one but many, see 422e–423c; for the soul becoming one rather than many, see 443d–e.

soning will not be complete until governors arrive at a picture of the whole cosmos. In the Platonic picture, then, institutional governance requires ideal theory of the broadest kind. Rulers should be philosophers.

21. Plato's vision of the cosmos as a kind of team in which each entity ought to play a definite role depends on the essentially speculative premise that goodness is the first principle of the cosmos, and that we can know it as such. This thought may not have been alien to the ancient world. The Greek word *kosmos* means "order," so that it can be used in phrases such as *kata kosmon*, "as order requires," or to refer to a beautiful ornament, such as a piece of jewelry.[42] Neither Plato nor Aristotle seems to have doubted the capacity of human reason to grasp the cosmic order; they seem to have thought of reason as the divine element within us and hence as unimpeachable in itself. Bernard Williams suggests a fundamental "ditch" between those ancients who subscribed to this belief, such as Plato and Aristotle, and those who did not, such as Sophocles and Thucydides. But however widespread it may have been in the ancient world, the notion that the universe is a good and knowable order is apt to strike the modern mind as wishful thinking. Since the scientific revolution of the seventeenth century, most (though by no means all) moderns have come to see goodness and fundamental ontology as unrelated. As Christine Korsgaard puts it, "the world has been turned inside out. The real is no longer the good. For us, reality is something *hard*, something which resists reason and value, something which is recalcitrant to form."[43]

22. It is hard to see how we could offer any argument in favor of the proposition that goodness is the first principle of the universe. It

---

42. The point about the word *kosmos* has been made by many, but my phrasing echoes that of Geuss, "Wisdom of Oidipous and the Idea of a Moral Cosmos," in which he also discusses the remarks of Bernard Williams alluded to later in this paragraph, which come toward the end of *Shame and Necessity*, 163. See Plato, *Philebus* 28c–30d, and pretty much the whole of the *Timaeus*.

43. Korsgaard, *Sources of Normativity*, 4. Neo-Aristotelians exist, of course, but even they recognize that their arguments go against the grain of contemporary *doxai*. And where the *doxai* do seem to entail that goodness and ontology are related, as I will claim is the case with institutions, it is not because of any facts about fundamental ontology or substance in general.

seems to be an article of a faith that is no longer widely shared (even if it does undergird some of the more refined forms of Christianity).[44] But if goodness is not the first principle of the universe, there seems to be no reason to believe a priori that institutions have definite functions waiting to be discovered. The historical record, meanwhile, seems to refute any a posteriori claim, as Nietzsche and Foucault famously show in their respective genealogies of punishment: even if institutions do sometimes come into being for a definite purpose, they soon get recruited and combined for other purposes, and in the process they typically become messy composites that have no real coherence.[45] This might seem fatal for the notion of rule by philosophers. For if institutions do not have discrete functions, they will not have true forms either, and hence there will be no reason to believe that ideal theory is essential to governing well. Once we remove the connection between goodness and ontology, political Platonism seems to collapse like a house of cards.

23. This conclusion is too hasty. Although Plato certainly considered his political theory inseparable from his ontology, there is reason to believe that he was wrong. The political proposition that those who govern institutions should engage in ideal-theoretic reasoning concerning form and function could be supported by a metaphysical claim to the effect that each institution has a distinctive function within the wider cosmos. But it could also be founded on a normative claim to the effect that institutions should have discrete functions within their wider contexts. On this view, which we might call "normative functionalism," the claim is just that institutions are better, other things being equal, when they cohere around a single goal.[46] If normative functionalism can be justified, then political Platonism need not share the fate of cosmic teleology. Nor would Nietzschean arguments regarding institutional genealogy speak

---

44. See, e.g., Augustine, *Confessions* VII.xii (18); see also Johnston, *Saving God*.

45. See Nietzsche, *On the Genealogy of Morality*; and Foucault, *Discipline and Punish*.

46. Just to be clear: I do not mean to endorse "normative functionalism" in the sense in which that term was used by Talcott Parsons and his followers, which refers to a functionalist explanatory framework in which social norms play a central role. See, e.g., Parsons, *The Social System*.

against it, absent a further argument to bridge the gap between "is" and "ought."

24. Normative functionalism is arguably implicit in our ordinary reasoning about institutions.[47] We can all think of institutions that are to some degree incoherent. Sometimes the work of one department is duplicated by another; sometimes two units counteract one another; sometimes each expects the other to act, so that neither does. We tend to label such institutions "dysfunctional." In so doing, we take it for granted that institutions ought to be functionally coherent. Each unit ought to have a clear remit of its own within a division of labor designed to ensure that work is never duplicated or wasted. This allows the institution to be efficient in whatever it does. It also generates clear standards for decision making by managers. Those who manage the institution as a whole have to make sure that each unit is clear about its responsibilities and fit to carry them out, and that the division of labor is optimized with respect to the goals of the organization. Those who manage individual units then have the same task with respect to the branches beneath them. Different institutions will be run differently, of course, and some will view middle management as unnecessary or inefficient, preferring that order emerge more spontaneously. But if order does not emerge, so that work is duplicated or wasted or neglected, that always seems to represent a failure of sorts.

25. This is not to say that functional coherence is the only good for an institution. A thriving institution can have multiple ambitions. A university, for instance, may reasonably aim at giving undergraduates a rigorous education, training graduate students to be productive scholars, enabling faculty members to teach and research to the best of their abilities, maintaining relations with alumni, benefiting the local community, and ensuring its own survival. If the university is to be coherent, all these activities must be understood as serving

---

47. This might go some way toward explaining the persistence of explanatory functionalism in social science. Rather than being a puzzling and unjustified holdover from premodern metaphysics, such explanatory functionalism might represent an attempt to grapple with a realm in which human normativity shapes the facts that are the object of scientific inquiry. Thanks to David Holiday for helping me see this point. See also Seumas Miller, *Moral Foundations of Social Institutions*.

an overarching goal, such as promoting academic excellence. But it may well be that a mildly dysfunctional university would bring about more good in the world than a completely functional one. Suppose, for example, that it is possible to benefit the local community by granting access to the university's sports facilities at certain times. The university's justification for building and maintaining these facilities might ultimately revolve around academic excellence, given some kind of "sound-body, sound-mind" principle. But it is hard to see how their use by people outside the academic community could be justified in the same way. One might think that no justification is required, since the costs are trivial. But let us assume that the more people who use the facilities, the faster the equipment will need to be replaced. The question then becomes: why spend the university's resources this way? It is hard to see how the answer would involve academic excellence. We could say that the university's mission is to serve the local community, but then the question would arise of how academic excellence is related to that goal. It seems more plausible just to admit that there are occasions where some form of incoherence turns out to be desirable.[48] The claim that normative functionalism makes should therefore be understood as essentially limited: it is just that functional coherence makes an institution in one way better. This dimension of value may be outweighed by others within our all-things-considered judgments, but it will never be entirely erased.[49]

---

48. Compare Clark Kerr's concept of a "multiversity" in *The Uses of the University*, 14–15: "The multiversity is an inconsistent institution. It is not one community but several—the community of the undergraduate and the community of the graduate; the community of the humanist, the community of the social scientist, and the community of the scientist; the community of the professional schools; the community of all the nonacademic personnel; the community of the administrators. Its edges are fuzzy—it reaches out to alumni, legislators, farmers, businessmen, who are all related to one or more of these internal communities. . . . A community, like the medieval communities of masters and students, should have common interests; in the multiversity, they are quite varied, even conflicting."

49. For the notion of something's being in one way better, see Parfit, "Equality and Priority," 210–211. In the present case the idea would be to distinguish between something's being of overriding value and something's having a distinct kind of normative force.

26. Clarity of purpose furnishes governors with a standard by which to guard and reform their institutions; it also furnishes stakeholders with a standard by which to judge governors. Suppose a university president is deciding whether to issue special scholarships for talented athletes. If her institution is constituted around the goal of fostering academic excellence, she must ensure that its various departments and programs fit together in the service of that goal. So although there might turn out to be a place for athletic scholarships within such a scheme, the case for them would have to be articulated in terms of academic excellence, and the same would be true with regard to the subsequent question of how many resources to devote to the program. There is no substitute for practical wisdom in such cases, but at the same time we can imagine institutional structures whereby the president might be made to account for her reasoning before various stakeholders. "If a university devotes more and more of its resources to sports," she might say to faculty, students, alumni, and trustees, "there comes a point where it is no longer a university at all."

27. Institutional goals are never entirely self-evident, of course. In cases where there is no official mission statement, the governors of an institution will have considerable freedom in determining its goals. There is a sense, for example, in which the University of Chicago's famous decision to scrap its American football program and build a state-of-the-art library in place of its stadium actually created a new self-understanding rather than merely reflecting an old one. But even when there is an official mission statement or founding charter, important decisions still need to be made. Constitutions must be interpreted not only to apply general principles to particular cases but also to take account of the way the institution and its surroundings have developed over the course of time.[50] What it means to honor and promote "academic excellence" may change as social conditions change, for instance. To work out how best to interpret it at a given time, our putative president would have to think

---

50. It may be reasonable for governors to treat their tenure as part of a chain novel, where each consciously attempts to build on the work of her predecessors, in order to maintain the unity of their institutions over time. For a proposal of this kind regarding jurisprudence, see Dworkin, *Law's Empire*, chaps. 6 and 7. I will return to Dworkin's notion later in this chapter.

in terms of the university's role within some wider context. Other institutions will also be pursuing academic excellence, so one question will concern the distinctive contribution that this particular university can make to research and teaching in general, given its current strengths and weaknesses and those of its peers. But it will also be necessary to consider what we mean by excellence in research and teaching, and to do this properly will require reflection on the role of those activities in bringing about (or perhaps constituting) the good life. For although we might begin by assuming certain accepted criteria for excellence, such as citation indexes, there will always be a question whether those criteria are truly appropriate. To work out what the appropriate criteria for academic excellence would be, we have to ask what research and teaching are for. And this demands that we think about the nature of the good life.

28. On the view I have been outlining, those in charge of institutions have a *pro tanto* duty to make them functionally coherent, both internally and externally. They need to ensure that the various units are all pulling in the same direction so as to avoid institutional dysfunction. But they also need to decide what that direction should be, on pain of what we might call institutional malfunction, whereby an institution succeeds in cohering but does so to ill effect. All else being equal, it would therefore be best for governors to be good at reasoning back and forth between visions of wholes and visions of parts, and hence at reflecting on the place of various goods within human life. It would be best, in other words, if they were both good at ideal theory and disposed to engage in it. As the *Republic* suggests, then, those who govern should also philosophize.[51]

29. One might question whether governors really need to consider best possibilities in order to reason successfully. As Amartya Sen ar-

---

51. As Socrates puts the point in speaking of Kallipolis, rulers need to exercise wisdom (*sophia*), the form of knowledge that "does not deliberate about some particular thing in the city, but about the city as a whole, and about how its internal relations and its relations with other cities [i.e., its external relations] will be the best possible" (428d). Plato thought that such reflection must ultimately open out into questions concerning the nature of the cosmos, so that governing well would require holistic inquiry into form and function at the broadest possible level. He also thought that this holistic inquiry—which he called philosophy—would be successful only if it disclosed mind-independent reality. My account is less demanding on both counts, as I will explain.

gues, we can make pairwise comparisons between possible states of affairs without any reference to best possibilities.[52] There is no need to know what an ideal society would look like in order to make a rational decision whether to devote newfound resources to education or to famine relief, for instance. Likewise, we might think, governors do not need to have a worked-out vision of a perfectly functional institution in order to make a rational decision between two policy proposals. If this is right, then it looks as though ideal theory may be otiose.

30. The appropriate response would be to question the strict separation between ideal and nonideal theory. Unlike utopian theory, ideal theory is constrained by possibility. But as we saw in Chapter 5, the criteria for what counts as impossible can vary according to context. There is a clear sense in which it is possible for Arnold Schwarzenegger to become president of the United States of America despite having been born abroad: this eventuality would contravene no logical or natural laws, and the relevant human laws can be changed. Yet there is also a clear sense in which Republican strategists would be right to declare a Schwarzenegger presidency impossible for their purposes: it would require a dramatic shift in public opinion concerning both the candidate and the Constitution, followed by a prolonged battle to propose and ratify an amendment in the various American legislatures, and our hypothetical strategists would have no reason to believe they could achieve this. But our judgments of possibility and impossibility in this practical sense can only ever be relative to a given context. For certain purposes, it will make sense to treat certain facts—such as public opinion or institutional rules—as fixed, whereas for others, it will make sense to treat them as malleable. In many cases the choice will depend on the relevant time horizon: over a ten-year period, for example, it may be possible to change facts that we should treat as fixed in the short term.

31. The flip side of all of this is that ideal theory—understood as the process whereby we work out visions of the best possible F—need not be a matter of blue-sky thinking. What counts as the best possible

---

52. See Sen, *Idea of Justice*, 15–18.

F will depend on our conception of possibility, and that in turn will depend on our purposes. For some purposes, we may want to imagine societies or institutions that bear little or no relation to existing arrangements. For others, we may want to imagine societies or institutions that are very close to existing arrangements. We might therefore imagine a spectrum of ideals in which a given ideal is less down to earth to the degree that it depends on assumptions that are further away from actuality.

32. To return to Sen's argument, the thought would be that ideal theory can itself involve pairwise comparisons between imperfect states of affairs. We may sometimes have reason to work out a vision of the best possible human society all told. But we may also have reason to work out a vision of the best possible *us*, and built into that "us" are certain imperfections that we may treat as more or less given depending on the time horizon. The pertinent question for a university president, for example, is how *this* university might best be. But although this reflection is necessarily tied to a particular time and place, present circumstances can enter into her ideal-theoretic reflections to different degrees. She might ask herself how the university should ideally be, given the way it currently is and the limited resources (such as time, money, and energy) available for changing it. But she might also vary the facts, as it were, asking how the university would ideally be if certain things had already been changed—for example, if certain funds were to have been raised. We might be inclined to say that the former vision is less ideal than the latter in that it "idealizes away" from fewer facts. But both are attempts to work out visions of the best possible F, and therefore both count as ideal theory in my sense. Furthermore, if the president is reasoning along the lines suggested earlier in this section—focusing on institutional coherence in light of a reasoned conception of the good life—then she will also be seeking wisdom in the Platonic sense.[53]

---

53. This broadly Deweyan picture of locally situated ideal theory certainly departs from Plato's own picture. As we saw in Chapter 1, on Plato's account, philosophy is a dialectical process in the sense of being holistic: we go back and forth between our understanding of the way things actually are and our understanding of the way things might best be, as well as between our understanding of parts and our understanding of wholes. The big difference between full-blown Platonism and the picture I have been

33. In any case, there is a second way of making the case for Platonic governance of institutions that is both independent of the arguments just given and far quicker. Philosophers as diverse as Plato, Aristotle, Marx, and Dewey have shared an empirical premise to the effect that the way we behave shapes the way we think. Action shapes character, in other words. If we accept this premise, then the fact that institutions are constituted by rules that structure social interactions ought to be of serious interest to us. For what it implies is that every institution shapes souls to some degree. Those who exercise power within those institutions, framing and interpreting their rules, are therefore ruling in the Platonic sense. Whether consciously or not, they are shaping characters. The Platonic argument would be that it would be better for them to do so in light of an ideal of the good life won from serious reflection on the human condition than to do so accidentally and haphazardly. Obviously the first criterion for selecting the conductor of an orchestra or the manager of a boxing club should not be the candidate's vision of the human condition. But on the Platonic view, a truly excellent candidate would have such a vision. Once again, then, those who govern should seek wisdom.[54]

§3 Compatibility with Liberalism

34. There need be nothing illiberal about this line of thought. For one thing, the picture that I have been sketching might justly be described as procedural rather than substantive. Whereas Plato's theory presupposes that excellent governors will eventually converge on the same account of the good life, mine claims only that they should seriously reflect on what the good life might amount to and that stakeholders should hold them accountable for those visions. This

presenting, which I have called normative functionalism, is that Plato insists that rulers ought to inquire into the nature of the cosmos itself, and hence into goodness itself. It follows that Plato expects rulers to engage in maximally idealized ideal theory, wherein one asks how the whole cosmos would best be. But given the holistic nature of the process, it seems to me that he might also expect rulers to engage in the kind of local or situational ideal theory that I have been outlining. For Dewey's attempt to reconcile idealism and local action, see *Human Nature and Conduct*, 259–264.

54. For an idea of how this might work with respect to sports, see Thakkar, "Hail Mary Time."

implies that the card-carrying Platonic philosopher-governor, equipped with doctrines concerning human psychology and the nature of the cosmos, will be only one species of a wider genus. Social unions will be organized around a multitude of differing ideals, and well-organized institutions will therefore shape people in very different ways. A church might try to create parishioners whose works express their faith; a university might try to create students who think critically and independently. This pluralistic vision is disappointing in a way, since it forecloses the possibility of a certain kind of unified community—but that is just the liberal condition.

35. In a liberal society the institutions of civil society are perfectly entitled to promote controversial conceptions of the good life so long as they do not violate citizens' basic rights—as Rawls puts it, "While churches can excommunicate heretics, they cannot burn them."[55] But philosophical governance will also have a place at the level of the state. This is true even under political liberalism. For the demand for public reasons—and hence for a certain kind of neutrality regarding the good life—applies first and foremost to constitutional essentials and matters of basic justice, such as who has the right to vote, which religions are to be tolerated, and who is to be economically privileged. But Rawls himself acknowledges that "many if not most political questions do not concern these fundamental matters."[56] Where the environment, the arts, and the economy are concerned, it seems that democratic decision making will necessarily involve battles between competing conceptions of the good life. Failure to license such battles would turn liberalism into libertarianism.[57] The libertarian, of course, would argue that there is no

---

55. Rawls, *Justice as Fairness*, 11.

56. Rawls, *Political Liberalism*, 214. As examples, Rawls cites "much tax legislation and many laws regulating property; statutes protecting the environment and controlling pollution; establishing national parks and preserving wilderness areas and animal and plant species; and laying aside funds for museums and the arts."

57. In truth, Rawls is regrettably unclear about this. Shortly after the passage just quoted, he declares that although citizens may deliberate about political questions however they like when they are in the private realm, "the ideal of public reason does hold for citizens when they engage in political advocacy in the public forum, and thus for members of political parties and for candidates in their campaigns and for other groups who support them" (ibid., 215). He also suggests on the same page that "it is usually highly desirable to settle political questions by invoking the values of public

way of stopping this slide: liberalism properly understood and impartially applied just is libertarianism. Those who reject this claim ought to be open to a form of political Platonism. To the extent that democratic deliberations necessarily involve thick value judgments, it is surely better for those judgments to be open to view. Lawmakers should think about how a proposed policy might best fit together with other policies, and to do that they should form an idea of how their society currently is and how it might be improved. Sometimes they will find that a given policy is normatively overdetermined: there are many different reasons to ensure access to clean drinking water, for example. But often their conceptions of the good life will make a difference to their decision making, and in these cases, the Platonist will suggest, they ought to think seriously about what the ideal society would be. Ordinary citizens, meanwhile, ought to use public forums to hold their representatives to account for all these conceptions.

36. So Platonism can provide a useful supplement to political liberalism, offering an account of good governance that applies both to the institutions of civil society and to certain activities of the state. But it can also enrich political liberalism itself. To see this, it helps to recall Socrates' caricature of democracy as a regime that lacks any and all relations of rule. His real point, we saw in Chapter 4, was about rule in Plato's distinctive sense. Any society that refuses to watch over the usages and beliefs of its citizens, Socrates suggests, will be fundamentally unstable. In the long run it will be as if the regime did not care about whether its laws were obeyed, since laws mean very little in the absence of a supporting ethos. Now Rawls would agree with Plato that a social order will be stable only if its citizens endeavor to support is institutions. While citizens do not have to affirm the same comprehensive doctrine, he says, they do have to "share one very basic political end, and one that has high priority:

---

reason." This does not seem to follow. The restriction on political advocacy certainly makes sense where constitutional essentials and matters of basic justice are being discussed, and Rawls may also be right that citizens should consider only public reasons when they are voting on such questions. But deliberations concerning other matters will necessarily involve thick value judgments. It is surely better for those judgments to be explicit, and so open for debate and assessment, than for them to be covert.

namely, the end of supporting just institutions and giving one another justice accordingly."[58] With this in mind, the state can legitimately engage in what Plato would have thought of as the shaping of souls, with the constraint that the only virtues that can be legitimately inculcated are the "political virtues" appropriate to a liberal regime, such as tolerance, respect, civility, and fairness.[59] This might seem fairly uncontroversial, but it certainly involves relations of rule in Plato's sense, whereby one group is permitted to educate another. (Imagine an advertising campaign urging citizens to be tolerant in certain situations. Just as cinemas sometimes screen ads against drunk driving before the show begins, so we would have ads illustrating the dangers of intolerance. Those who were already "reasonable" might view these short films as little more than reminders, but those whom political liberalism counts as "unreasonable" would surely experience them as paternalistic impositions.) As both Rawls and Plato saw, however, political regimes must accept this form of hierarchy or invite their own annihilation.

37. With this in mind, it is easy to see how political Platonism might enrich Rawlsian liberalism. Those in charge of a state institution should ensure that its various activities cohere so that the institution becomes a functional whole that performs its role within the wider whole of which it is a part, namely the liberal state. This will require them to reflect on the nature and purpose of political liberalism. And in assessing the role that a given institution ought to play in sustaining the liberal state, they will have to take into account not only its primary task—enforcing tax codes, say—but also how it might contribute to fostering a liberal ethos.[60] In some cases this

---

58. Ibid., 202.

59. See Rawls, *Justice as Fairness*, 116–118, 195–202; and Rawls, *Political Liberalism*, 191–206. On the importance of the liberal virtues, see Galston, *Liberal Purposes*; and Macedo, *Liberal Virtues*, 256–263.

60. That is not necessarily to deny the central claim of normative functionalism, that institutions are better (all else being equal) when they are organized around one goal. It is often possible to unify apparently disparate activities by interpreting them as all aiming at one overarching goal. There may turn out to be a description of the IRS's task (perhaps in terms of upholding the Constitution or serving the government to be the best of its ability, given its resources) that allows us to interpret soul shaping as a subsidiary part of its mission. But even if this kind of argument cannot be made, so that charging the IRS with soul shaping introduces an element of incoherence, the

contribution might be fairly direct. The education department might mandate citizenship classes for pupils of a certain age, for example, or it might review the curriculum to make sure that certain topics are included. In other cases the responsibility might be far weaker. The Internal Revenue Service (IRS) might discharge it, for instance, simply by treating people equally regardless of sectarian affiliations. But the point remains: excellent governors would take responsibility for the soul-shaping effects of their institutions—for the message that they send, as we ordinarily put it. To do this well, they would need to think seriously about what good citizenship involves. And to do that well, they would have work out an ideal of liberal society.

38. Obviously there are limits to liberal soul shaping. In Plato's view, rulers ought to leave no stone unturned in their quest to produce the right kind of cultural environment. They must design and supervise educational programs that cover the physical, musical, and intellectual aspects of human development all the way from the early play of children to the final formation of the fifty-year-old philosopher-ruler. They must also supervise the division of labor to ensure that every single craft is optimally directed toward the maintenance of a healthy cultural environment. The upshot is the paradigmatically illiberal requirement to create stories that promote virtue and to censor artworks that do not. Clearly the soul-shaping ambitions of political liberalism cannot reach that far. Rawls takes freedom of speech, association, and choice of occupation to be "constitutional essentials" for a liberal regime. These are basic rights, in other words, that limit the exercise of political power for any purpose whatsoever, no matter how benign.[61]

39. This might seem to imply that liberal governors can shape souls only through certain kinds of public education and messaging. But this is too quick. As we have already seen, institutions can shape people in subtle ways. Their rules shape behavior and expectations and hence beliefs and norms. Furthermore, the decisions that

---

decision to do so would not involve rejecting normative functionalism. It would imply only that the value of institutional coherence needs to be weighed against other values in our all-things-considered judgments, which we already know.

61. Rawls, *Political Liberalism*, 227–230.

institutions make may also serve to generate a particular kind of environment. To take an obvious example, a national radio station might broadcast explicit calls for toleration and civility, but it might also have an effect on citizens' characters just through its selection of topics and speakers, which may shape what listeners take to be normal and natural. The same might be true, as I suggested earlier, of a mundane institution such as the IRS: insofar as it ignores sectarian differences in determining tax obligations, the IRS contributes to an environment in which certain liberal presuppositions are taken for granted.[62]

40. Let us take a step back. In §1 I canvassed the most important liberal objections to Plato's ideal of society as a kind of team working together to achieve the good life under the wise direction of philosophers. Popper objects to Plato's scheme on the grounds that it gives too much power to rulers and lacks mechanisms for holding them to account. The Rawlsian objection, by contrast, has to do with justice and legitimacy: any society characterized by free institutions will also be characterized by disagreement over the good life, and if citizens are conceived as equal, it will not be fair or legitimate for some people to force others to abide by their conception. What we have seen in this section is that these objections are by no means fatal for political Platonism. As a general matter, institutions would be best governed by those who seek wisdom in the relevant sense—that is, an understanding of what the good life is and how harmonious order can bring it about. Governors of this kind would put their institutions in order in light of inquiry into the place of various goods in human life, paying attention to the way in which habits shape character. None of this need alarm liberals. Where voluntary associations are concerned, governors are perfectly entitled to make decisions in light of their conception of the good life so long as their actions remain within the law. Where the state is concerned, the picture is a little more complicated. In some domains governors are fully entitled to make decisions in light of their conception of the good life but restrained by democratic accountability and the rule of law. In

---

62. Whether the present IRS actually does this is obviously beside the point.

others they must be able to offer public reasons that are neutral with respect to controversial conceptions of the good life. But even here, in the central redoubt of political liberalism, governors ought to seek (a restricted form of) wisdom, reflecting on the nature and purpose of liberal institutions and on the requirements of excellent citizenship. They should then order their institutions on the basis of these inquiries, keeping in mind that a liberal state needs to engender a liberal ethos among the citizenry.

§4 Philosophical Citizenship

41. One of the foundational premises of the liberal-democratic ideal is that citizens should rule themselves. What self-rule should amount to is the subject of much debate. The assumption tends to be that citizens rule themselves insofar as they have some kind of control over the power exercised over them by the state. In Rousseau's view, for instance, self-rule requires a legislature in which every single citizen votes on every single law and an executive that is then answerable to the legislature. Other democratic theorists permit representation but insist that electoral systems be designed so that each citizen has an equal opportunity to influence the result. A small minority proposes that representatives be chosen via lotteries in the much the same way as juries currently are.[63] Whichever theory of democracy we endorse, one thing seems clear: just as there are better and worse rulers, so there can be better and worse self-rulers. There are various criteria for excellent democratic citizenship, but if the argument of §2 holds, one of them will be the willingness to form a conception of how one's society might ideally be. Just as governors of state institutions should make decisions in light of serious reflection on the good life—bearing in mind that the scope of this reflection will vary depending on the issues at hand, given the constraints of political liberalism—so citizens should do likewise when acting in

---

63. This is not the place for a survey of the literature on democracy, but readers interested in representation might consult Urbinati, *Representative Democracy;* those interested in "lottocracy" might begin with Guerrero, "Against Elections." For Rousseau's views, see *On the Social Contract,* especially Book III, in *The Basic Political Writings.*

the same capacity (however indirectly). If rulers should be philosophers, in short, then so should citizens.

42. The thought that citizens ought ideally to engage in some kind of philosophical reflection is arguably implicit in some of the canonical works of liberal-democratic political theory. In the introduction to Book 1 of his *Social Contract*, for instance, Rousseau explains his project as follows: "Since I was born a citizen of a free state and a member of the sovereign, the right to vote is enough to impose upon me the duty to instruct myself in public affairs, however little influence my voice may have in them." In this respect Rousseau seems to be offering himself as a model for others. Few citizens will go as far as Rousseau, of course, but he does seem to imply that democratic citizens should engage in some kind of philosophical reflection. For if his substantive arguments are correct, laws will be alien impositions unless citizen-legislators vote for what they think will bring about the common good rather than what they think will benefit themselves or their allies.[64] The question is what might lead citizens to vote in this manner. Part of the answer, Rousseau suggests, will lie in a "civil religion" that promotes belief in the "sanctity of the social contract and of the laws" and thereby generates a sturdy civic ethos.[65] But unquestioned dogma, no matter how powerful, cannot suffice. On Rousseau's theory, we will experience ourselves as free only if we can consciously endorse the political order whose laws bind us. And to do that, we need to understand the ideal of democratic self-government—which is, of course, where Rousseau's own work comes in. We might therefore say that philosophical citizenship is part of the Rousseauvian democratic ideal.[66]

43. Philosophical citizenship also seems to be part of another ideal of self-rule, namely Rawlsian political liberalism. Noting that an ideal society must be able to maintain itself over time, Rawls claims that a society will be stable for the right reasons—as opposed to being

---

64. See especially Rousseau, *On the Social Contract*, Book IV, chap. 2, in *The Basic Political Writings*.

65. See ibid., Book IV, chap. 9.

66. To make this case more rigorously, we would, of course, have to take into account Rousseau's other writings, especially *Émile* and *Reveries of a Solitary Walker*.

stable thanks to the balance of power at a given time—only if citizens are able to justify its basic structure to one another so that each person can endorse it from their own point of view.[67] In an ideal society, in other words, stability and legitimacy come together. As with Rousseau, then, the thought is that the social order should be such that citizens can reconcile themselves to its constraints rather than viewing them as alien impositions.[68] But if citizens are to be able to justify social arrangements to one another, three conditions must hold: "Everyone accepts, and knows that everyone else accepts, the very same political conception of justice"; the basic structure is publicly known to satisfy the relevant principles of justice; and citizens each have a "sense of justice" that enables them both to understand those principles and to act in accordance with them.[69] The placid, repetitive quality of Rawls's prose is liable to obscure just how ambitious this vision is. Together, these conditions imply that a society will not be legitimate, and thus stable for the right reasons, unless citizens are able to understand the principles that animate its major institutions. But to truly understand such principles,

---

67. Rawls, *Political Liberalism*, 391, cites Jeremy Waldron's remark concerning the liberal demand to justify the social world in a manner acceptable "at the tribunal of each person's understanding." See Waldron, *Liberal Rights*, 61. This aspiration is central to the social-contract tradition in general. Locke, for example, begins his *Second Treatise of Government* by suggesting that his goal is to explain the conditions under which political power might be legitimate such that individuals have a standing reason to submit to it regardless of the balance of forces in society. As with Rawls, then, the thought is that the social order will be truly stable only if citizens recognize it as legitimate, and that political philosophy is therefore required on both sides of the equation—both for governments and for citizens, in other words. See Locke, *Second Treatise of Government*, preface and chapter 1.

68. See Rawls, *Justice as Fairness*, 3: "Political philosophy may try to calm our frustration and rage against our society and its history by showing us the way in which its institutions, when properly understood from a philosophical point of view, are rational, and developed over time as they did to attain their present, rational form"; and Rawls, *Political Liberalism*, 391–392. On the relationship between Rawls and Rousseau, see Brooke, "Rawls on Rousseau and the General Will." On the relationship between Rawlsian and Hegelian reconciliation, see also Rawls, *Justice as Fairness*, 38, 115, 180–202; Schwarzenbach, "Rawls, Hegel, and Communitarianism"; Bercuson, *John Rawls and the History of Political Thought*; and Lange, "Reconciliation Arguments in John Rawls's Philosophy."

69. See Rawls, *Justice as Fairness*, 8–9; and Rawls, *Theory of Justice*, 114–116, 453–512. For an account of what it would mean to apply the principles of justice in one's own life, see Titelbaum, "What Would a Rawlsian Ethos of Justice Look Like?"

on Rawls's account, requires testing them against rival principles in the court of reflective equilibrium. And if Rawls is right, the best way of doing that is to engage in ideal theory. Rawlsian liberalism is therefore surprisingly reflexive. In the ideal society, each citizen would know that their society is ideal: "Understanding how to conduct oneself as a democratic citizen," for example, "includes understanding an ideal of public reason."[70] Something similar would also be true of excellent citizens in nonideal societies, since in Rawls's view we have a "natural duty" to resist unjust institutions and to create just ones, and discharging this duty to requires us to figure out the correct principles of justice.[71] In Rawls's ideal of liberal democracy, then, political philosophy ought to be part of everyday life.[72]

44. Both Rousseau and Rawls picture ideal theory as a necessary component of the ideal society. The obvious analogy with Plato is of more than merely taxonomic interest, since it opens up the possibility of using Plato's way of thinking to enrich liberal democracy from within. Accounts of liberal-democratic self-rule tend to take for granted that ruling is a matter of exercising power through the machinery of state. Once this is assumed, it seems obvious that for citizens to rule themselves, they must have some kind of control over the power exercised over them by the state, whether through demo-

---

70. Rawls, *Political Liberalism*, 218.

71. See Rawls, *Theory of Justice*, 114–116, 333–394.

72. Stephen Macedo raises an interesting objection to this way of thinking about liberalism, namely that a liberal regime that insists on public justification might fail to generate allegiance from enough citizens. We can imagine a situation in which illiberal citizens go along with a liberal regime without really thinking about whether they endorse liberal values and then gradually develop liberal convictions through force of habit. The question is whether that situation is more desirable than one in which liberal citizens openly confront illiberal citizens with philosophical arguments without succeeding in convincing them. Macedo rejects that view on the basis that "public justification is a form of respect for persons" and therefore central to the liberal ideal. Liberals should therefore avoid "driving a wedge," Macedo concludes, "between critical reflection and political practice." Macedo, *Liberal Virtues*, 67, 69. This seems right to me, but in any case it is worth pointing out that this question concerns how best to transition to a just and legitimate society rather than what such a society would look like. And on Rawls's view, it seems to me, for a liberal society to be stable for the right reasons, it would need a philosophical citizenry. For Macedo's discussion, see *Liberal Virtues*, 64–69.

cratic institutions or through liberal protections, and that excellent self-rule is a matter of exercising this control well. As we saw in Chapter 2, however, a different conception of ruling is possible. In Plato's view, the deepest sense of ruling involves shaping other people's souls, where that means something like shaping the hierarchy of their beliefs and desires. My hypothesis is that citizens in a liberal democracy should be ruling themselves in this sense as well as the others, and that this will once again require them to engage in ideal-theoretic reasoning.

45. On Plato's account, true rulers ensure that the cultural environment fosters the good life. To do this, they must regulate the division of labor to ensure that each profession, from poetry to carpentry, plays its part in creating and sustaining a healthy environment. To do that, they must exercise two forms of power. They must pull and push on the usual levers of government, legislative and executive, but they must also fashion and disseminate images and models that serve to shape citizens' understandings of themselves and their social world. This second mode of power is available even to those who hold no legislative or executive office. This is what allows Socrates to suggest that poets are the hidden rulers of democratic Athens: wittingly or not, they shape the social imaginary, using ideals in the sense of models to shape ideals in the sense of values. It is also what allows us to understand Plato's own activity as an attempt to exercise philosophical rule without holding office, and hence to construct a Platonic account of philosophical citizenship.

46. Platonic philosopher-citizens carry out the same thought process as philosopher-kings. They begin by working out an ideal of the good life and an ideal of the social division of labor that would foster it. They then assess the social situation in order to select the best available means for moving individuals and society closer to that ideal. Sometimes this involves exercising coercive power. Sometimes it involves propagating images and models that convey truths about the good life. But other times it may involve tasks that are even further from philosophy as commonly understood: fighting in wars, for example, as we know that Socrates did when necessary. Any activity could fit the bill so long as it represents the best deployment of one's talents at the time, given the goal of creating and sustaining a cultural

environment conducive to psychic health. Each of our actions shapes the environment to some degree, and that environment in turn shapes habits, desires, beliefs, and expectations. In the background is Plato's picture of humans as mimetic creatures that naturally orient themselves toward exemplars. Although some of our education takes place through explicit instruction, much of it takes place through imitation. The models we imitate can be people, such as parents or teachers, but they can also be objects or actions. From stories and sculptures to jokes and salutations to tables and chairs, each of our works is apt to be imitated by others, known or unknown. And each of them is apt to communicate, and hence to spread or reinforce, certain assumptions about the social world and the human good. It follows that each and every one of us is a steward of the social imaginary. Whether we know it or not, that is, we are all rulers in the Platonic sense—we shape one another's souls. But ruling well, Plato argues, requires patient philosophical discussion concerning the nature of the good life and the division of labor required to bring it about. It would therefore be better, in principle, if each citizen were to engage in philosophical reflection. But in Plato's view that is a utopian dream, like a city without conflict or a soul without appetites. In the real world, only a small minority will ever be willing or able to think and act like philosopher-rulers. The ideal scenario—as opposed to the utopian one—is for that minority to hold office. Philosophical citizenship, by contrast, is not part of the ideal. It can only ever be an attempt to make a bad situation better.[73]

47. Plato's elitism is certainly antithetical to the liberal-democratic ideal. In Rawls's version of that ideal, every citizen is to be regarded as having the capacity to understand, apply, and act from a public conception of justice.[74] The thought is not that we are all equally

---

73. Although for Plato, membership of the philosophical class is restricted to those with outstanding cognitive capacities and a specific psychological constitution, we saw in Chapter 3 that he does suggest that in Kallipolis ordinary citizens will endorse the social order at some level. Philosophers will disseminate ideals in the form of stories and images, and one of those ideals will be that of the beautiful city itself. Ordinary citizens will therefore feel proud of their city and will be ready to defend it, but they will not understand why it is ideal.

74. See Rawls, *Political Liberalism*, 19.

capable of grasping the ins and outs of political philosophy, of course, but only that we are all sufficiently capable that we can consciously endorse the liberal social order. Whether or not this "political conception of the person" counts as a "noble falsehood" in the Platonic sense—that is, a belief that is false if taken literally but which orients citizens toward deeper truths concerning the good life—there is no doubt that something like it is fundamental to the liberal-democratic self-image.[75]

48. For present purposes, however, the fact that Plato views philosophical citizenship as a second best is immaterial. The important point is that his theory offers to enrich our understanding of what such citizenship might entail—and thereby to enrich the liberal-democratic ideal. In §3 we saw that the liberal state needs to engender a liberal ethos among its citizens. Now we can see that citizens need to do likewise. The Platonic thought, in other words, would be that each individual ought to play their part in creating and sustaining a culture that is maximally conducive to the liberal virtues—and that they can do this through their day-to-day activities, including their ordinary labors. Such activity goes beyond what the liberal state can achieve by itself. The state cannot legitimately order ordinary citizens to produce artworks promoting religious toleration, for example. But virtuous citizens can and should motivate themselves to produce such works. So although the liberal state may not have license to mandate that citizens produce certain goods or take up certain occupations in order to bolster the liberal culture, it does have license to foster an ethos in which citizens make this demand of themselves. Answering this demand involves grasping the liberal ideal, thinking seriously about how one's own activities can best promote it, and carrying out the work in question. In sum, it amounts to exercising wisdom and justice in the Platonic sense for the sake of bringing about justice and freedom in the liberal sense.

49. Yet this is not the only role that philosophical citizenship can play in a liberal society. Let us take a step back and recall, once again, that as a vision of social life, political liberalism is far from complete.

---

75. See Charles Taylor, *Modern Social Imaginaries*.

What it provides is a theory of how a society's most fundamental arrangements might become just and legitimate. But as I noted in §2, justice and legitimacy are by no means the only goods that humans aim to realize together in social life. A whole host of collective endeavors, from religious worship and academic inquiry to sports and crafts, open up possibilities for action and expression, and thus self-development and self-fulfillment, that would otherwise be unavailable to individuals. Concerning these irreducibly social goods, political liberalism says nothing except that justice and legitimacy must always come first. This restriction is by no means trivial: it makes it impossible for any of those other goods to play an architectonic role in political life, and this in turn rules out many ideals of the best possible society. But the story should not end there. For we still have reason to care about these goods, as well as the practices associated with them, even if we accept that there are limits on how we can protect and promote them. If a given activity changes its character or dies out completely, for instance, that might greatly impoverish us. At the limit, it might even represent a kind of cultural devastation, with parents unable to pass on a way of life to their children. But individuals cannot maintain social practices by themselves: this is a collective task. It seems natural to think of this task as crucial for the overall health of a society and hence as an important topic for political philosophy.

50. It was this line of thought that led to the discussion of voluntary associations and their governance in §2. But for all that local institutions can contribute to creating and sustaining a cultural environment conducive to human flourishing, it is important to recognize the extent to which their powers are limited in a liberal society. Individuals will always have one foot within a given institution and one foot in the wider culture; and the teachings of the wider culture will never be fully in line with one particular vision of the good life. Since local associations are voluntary, moreover, it will always be possible for individuals to withdraw from them at will. This introduces what we might call the problem of deference. Those who sign up for a voluntary association thereby sign up for some form of deference to the rules of that association, including the rules specifying who makes which decisions. In a liberal society, however, individuals are free to

choose which associations to join and hence whom to obey—and it is tautological to say that individuals who are unwise are unlikely to choose wisely. Insofar as citizens are "spirited," to use Plato's term, they are likely to shop around until they find an association whose governor flatters their pride; insofar as they are "appetitive," they might look for excitement. It is perfectly possible, in other words, that citizens will gradually sort themselves into associations that simply mirror their existing dispositions. Associations that preach disciplined self-transformation, by contrast, will be fighting an uphill battle.[76]

51. Toward the end of *After Virtue*, Alasdair MacIntyre urges right-thinking people to stop trying to achieve nationwide transformation and focus instead on "the construction of local forms of community within which civility and the intellectual and moral life can be sustained through the new dark ages which are already upon us."[77] Plato would have rejected this stance. Granted, he does acknowledge that a form of quietism may be prudent for those living in imperfect societies: mindful of the historical Socrates' fate, in Book VI of the *Republic* he has his Socrates suggest that the philosopher in an unjust society will avoid public affairs, keeping quiet and doing his own work "like someone who takes refuge under a little wall from a storm of dust or hail driven by the wind" (496d). But Plato makes clear that in his view this strategy, optimal though it may be in some circumstances, solves nothing in the end. The quietist shows up again in Book VIII, only this time he is depicted as a father incapable of transmitting virtue to his son (549c–550b). Although he scrupulously "avoids honors, political office, lawsuits, and all such meddling in other people's affairs," his son ends up "a proud and honor-loving man." Only in a healthy society, Plato seems to suggest, can excellence be securely transmitted from generation to generation. The Platonic response to MacIntyre would therefore be to deny that local communities can keep the flames of civilization

---

76. It must be admitted that the "marketplace of ideas" picture leaves out the way many of us enter local associations, namely through our parents' choice. The picture would therefore be a distortion of reality if taken too literally; I consider it a useful abstraction and nothing more.

77. MacIntyre, *After Virtue*, 263. For a more recent version of this claim, see Dreher, *Benedict Option*.

burning by themselves. After all, we are not talking about isolated monasteries any more. In a liberal society local institutions are only ever partial and porous, their influence and meaning always vulnerable to wider cultural trends. Try as we might to batten down the hatches, they will remain stubbornly open. The only stable solution is to prevent the storm at its source. And that requires constructing an environment hospitable to human flourishing.

52. This is what leads Socrates to say that "until philosophers rule as kings in cities or those who are now called kings and leading men genuinely and adequately philosophize . . . cities will have no rest from evils" (473c–d). Unless the cultural environment is stewarded by those who think seriously about the good life, going back and forth between ideals of parts and wholes, it will gradually decay. In the example from Book VIII, for instance, what undermine the quietist father in his attempt to "nourish the rational element" of his son's soul are social structures of esteem and honor that are unmoored from rational standards: "Those who do their own work in the city are called fools and held to be of little account, while those who do not are honored and praised" (550a–b). But honor will only be awarded appropriately, Socrates suggests, if society's "leading men" genuinely and adequately philosophize.

53. In a liberal democracy, there is a sense in which we are all "leading men"—and as such, I want to argue, we should all philosophize. We have already seen that philosophical citizenship ought to be part of the ideal of political liberalism. Ideally speaking, each citizen ought to do their bit to foster a culture that manifests and encourages liberal virtues such as tolerance and civility. This involves acting in light of a lifelong inquiry into the nature of justice, not only by supporting just institutions and opposing unjust ones but also by considering how one's day-to-day activities might help sustain the right kind of ethos. We can now see that something similar will also hold with respect to the vast domain of social life that lies beyond the purview of political liberalism. Stated abstractly, the thought would be that citizens ought to exercise both justice and wisdom in the Platonic sense of those terms. They ought to reflect on the nature of the good life and the social division of labor that might best bring it about, and then act in light of those ongoing re-

flections by carrying out the work that seems to fall to them given the situation at hand.[78] This need not contravene any liberal principle. To take a seemingly trivial example, concern for the beauty of the social environment ought to lead householders to paint their properties in light of how their neighbors have already painted theirs. Neighbors will disagree on the appropriate colors and shades, of course. But absent special circumstances (such as the existence of a previously agreed policy), each individual clearly has license to act as they see fit in this domain without needing to worry about the specter of illegitimacy or injustice. The Platonic claim would be that such activity is not simply permissible but eminently desirable, and that this should affect our understanding of good citizenship. For just as a good society is a beautiful society, a Kallipolis in which each object both encodes and transmits a vision of the good life, so a good citizen plays her part in making the social world more beautiful. Even if the liberal state is not entitled to promote a particular conception of the (extrapolitical) good life, then, it should nevertheless ask each citizen to advance their own.

54. The ideal of philosophical citizenship would transform public education, but it would also transform the way we conceive of career choice. Freedom of occupation is central to liberal political theory as against certain forms of socialism.[79] The thought is that each of us has an inalienable interest in formulating and executing our own life plans, and that our careers will be central to those life plans. But the fact that individuals should be left to decide their own life plans—subject to the usual liberal provisos—does not imply that that there cannot be better or worse life plans, or that one of the standards by which life plans can be better or worse is that of good citizenship. Excellent liberal citizens will, as we have seen, tailor their activities so that they contribute to a just order. But since justice is not the only social good, excellent citizens will also tailor their activities so that they contribute to the social good more generally.

---

78. I offer a deontic argument for this conclusion based on the nature of joint action in Thakkar, "Neo-socialism"; the overall line of thought was first explored in Thakkar, "Socialism We Can Believe In."

79. For an internal critique of liberalism on this score, see Stanczyk, "Productive Justice."

This will require them to form a conception of how their society could reach its full potential and how they could bring it closer to that condition, given the situation and their own talents along with the need to develop specialized skills over time. This will guide their choice of career, as well as their choices within a given career—their choices of which particular skills to develop, for example, but also their choices of what to produce and exchange.

55. If citizens are wise and just in the Platonic sense, they will shape their activities in light of their conception of the common good and of the division of labor that would promote it, assigning themselves to roles that seem to fit their talents. How they should do this is a matter for practical wisdom—there is no algorithm. Many ways of contributing to the common good will be fairly uncontroversial: baking bread, healing the sick, and teaching mathematics are hard to gainsay. There will be legitimate questions whether, say, running an opera company or a lumberyard contributes to the common good, but it is not hard to see how they might. Patent trolling, by contrast, would be impossible to justify as the best use of one's talents; the same would go for ticket scalping. When it comes to oft-scorned activities like tabloid journalism or high-frequency trading, the debate might revolve around how we should conceive of the common good. In almost every situation, it should be said, there will be considerable vagueness concerning which options are merely beneficial and which are truly optimific. Attempts to provide objective answers in the manner of the so-called effective altruism movement are likely to beg the most important questions.[80] Rather than trying to specify in advance which decisions will be correct in which circumstances, we should content ourselves with an account of which kinds of reasons should figure in our deliberative processes in which situations. My claim is simply that our status as citizens of a given society gives us a standing reason to think about how our labors might best serve the common good, and hence to engage in ideal-theoretic reflection. This reason must then be weighed against our other reasons in order to form all-things-considered judgments about what to do.

---

80. On effective altruism, see McKaskill, *Doing Good Better*; and the website 80000hours.org.

56. The most obvious objection to the notion of philosophical citizenship that I have been outlining concerns pluralism. Clearly citizens can differ enormously in their conceptions of the good life, and these differences do not seem to disappear through reflection and debate. This proposition is crucial to political liberalism: if a society's core institutions and arrangements need to be justifiable to all its citizens, and those citizens disagree about the good life, then the justifications in question might need to abstract as far as possible (which is not to say all the way) from controversial conceptions of the good life. That is not the issue in the present case, since individual attempts to promote a certain vision of the good life are perfectly permissible even under political liberalism. But normative disagreement does seem to present a distinctive problem for the kind of liberal Platonism that I have been advocating. To return to the relatively trivial example of house painting, the worry is that if our conceptions of the appropriate color scheme diverge, our individual efforts to promote a beautiful environment may result in an ugly mess. To take a more serious example, one person might stand on a corner preaching the Gospel while another tries to drown her out with the Koran. Something similar might take place on the economic plane: if citizens assign themselves to careers on the basis of their assessments of social needs, that might lead to huge shortages of labor in one sphere and massive oversupply in another—too many "creatives" and not enough refuse collectors, perhaps. The concern, in short, is that philosophical citizenship will produce little more than incoherence and dysfunction. And for a theory that pictures a good society along the lines of a harmonious team, that would be an important failing.

57. There is no question that full coherence will be extremely unlikely in a liberal society. That is simply the price we pay for liberalism, as Rawls concedes when he says that "the hope of political community must indeed be abandoned, if by such a community we mean a political society united in affirming the same comprehensive doctrine."[81] We should not overstate the problem, however. Given

---

81. Rawls, *Political Liberalism*, 146.

that we are presuming a background of liberal institutions, there is no question of one group coercing another in the name of a sectarian vision. Insofar as we are also presuming the liberal virtues, we must also be presuming that citizens oppose each other respectfully, with an eye to maintaining a liberal ethos.[82] Many professions contribute to the common good in fairly uncontroversial ways in any case—the controversy will often be over whether a given activity is truly optimific rather than merely beneficial. Moreover, in assigning themselves to roles, citizens will have to take into account the needs of the present situation, and this will involve paying attention to what others are already doing. If enough people have already set out to paint the neighborhood in reddish hues, those who would have preferred blue should obviously not go their own way with dogged intransigence. Likewise, if there is a glut in a given area of the job market then it might be best to turn one's attention elsewhere. We might think in this connection of Ronald Dworkin's ideal of constitutional interpretation as taking the form of a chain novel, with each new generation trying to add a new chapter that advances the narrative in a particular direction while nevertheless remaining consistent with the previous chapters.[83] We might also go back to the team analogy, thinking this time of a team without a manager: each player has to form her own conception of the appropriate team strategy, given the match situation, and then adjust the way she executes that strategy in light of her teammates' actions, which reveal their conceptions of how the team should be working together. To put the point more abstractly, one of the social goods at which philosopher-citizens would aim is coherence itself, and sometimes other goods must be traded off in favor of it. This will not entirely solve the problem: if one group thinks the other represents the devil, they will want to erase their chapter of the chain novel rather than to build on it. But

---

82. This is admittedly an idealizing assumption, but again the question under discussion is what makes for excellent citizenship. There is no suggestion that real-life laws and policies should be written for angels. They should, however, make it easier for ordinary human beings to become excellent citizens. And that makes it important to think about what excellent citizenship entails.

83. See Dworkin, *Law's Empire*, chaps. 6 and 7.

on balance it seems fair to say that philosophical citizenship stands to make society more coherent than it would otherwise have been.

58. In sum, then, Platonism can enrich liberal democracy by enlarging our conception of what excellent citizenship entails. A fairly standard liberal-democratic thought is that citizens rule themselves to the degree that they reliably exercise control over both the actions and the overall shape of the state.[84] To do this excellently, we saw, they need to develop an understanding of how the state might best be, and hence to engage in some kind of ideal theory. On the Platonic view, however, citizens will not fully rule themselves unless they also take part in the process whereby their own beliefs and desires are shaped. This is partly a matter of voting in certain ways and making certain kinds of argument in the public sphere, but it is also a matter of consciously playing one's part in the creation of a healthy environment. For as Plato suggests, the dissemination of ideology is by no means limited to artists and philosophers—on the contrary, every human artefact, whether a poem or a play or a house or a chair, both bespeaks and promotes a vision of the good life, so that what we produce affects whether we "crop and graze" in a "meadow of bad grass" or "live in a healthy place" where the environment benefits us like "a healthy breeze from wholesome regions" (401b–402a). Not that there is any reason to limit ourselves to artefacts: work comes in many forms, and having a word with someone can have just as much of an effect on the environment as crafting a clay pot. Success in this regard is a scalar concept, not a threshold one—it comes by degrees. Just as one day of pollution from one small factory can make a difference to a given natural environment, so our every action can contribute to the social environment.[85] What success does require, on the Platonic view, is serious reflection on the nature of the good

---

84. There are complications, of course. Most obviously, Rawls thinks of the relevant object of control as being "the basic structure of society," i.e., "the way in which the major social institutions distribute fundamental rights and duties and determine the division of advantages from social cooperation." See *Theory of Justice*, 6. This does not affect the point at hand, however.

85. This analogy leads Melissa Lane to introduce the helpful concept of "eco-production": we are coproducers of the environment, hence eco-producers. See Lane, *Eco-Republic*, 126.

life and how one's society could work together to achieve it. Each of us, that is, needs to philosophize. This vision can happily feed into the Rawlsian notion of a liberal ethos, but it can also transcend it. For political liberalism offers a partial vision of social life. What it insists is that liberal values must always trump others where conflict arises—but that leaves open the question of what we should do when there is no danger of liberal values being trumped. On the Platonic view, we should work to bring about the common good as we see it. This is not a moral demand but a political one. The claim is about citizenship: excellent citizens will work out an ideal of how their society might best be and orient themselves toward this ideal in their day-to-day labors. In so doing, they will gradually bring that ideal into being, if only by the smallest increments.

THE PURPOSE OF THIS chapter has been to show that the central claim of political Platonism, that those who govern should engage in philosophical reflection, should be both compelling and attractive even to those firmly committed to liberal democracy. No doubt Plato's own theory is vulnerable to many of the critiques mounted by Popper and other liberals: it grants an unaccountable elite sweeping powers to thoroughly reshape society in line with a particular conception of the good life, and even in the best-case scenario the results include censorship and eugenics. But even if we assume a form of liberalism that is maximally hostile to such paternalistic elitism, namely the political liberalism of Rawls, we still have good reason to hew to the Platonic conception of governance. For all other things being equal, it is better for institutions to cohere both internally and externally—and the only way to reliably achieve such coherence, I suggested, is for governors to think about how the various parts and wholes of society might ideally fit together. What is more, since institutions inevitably shape people's habits and hence their beliefs and desires, it is also better (all other things being equal) if they are governed with an eye to an ideal of human flourishing. This conception of governance is compatible with political liberalism. Those who govern the liberal state ought to make sure that it is coherent and that it shapes people in the right ways; they simply have to make sure that their purposes can be accounted for in terms of public reasons wherever basic rights and privileges are at issue. Those who govern local institutions, meanwhile, have relatively free rein in any case, so long as they are good liberal citizens in the sense of playing their part in sustaining a liberal culture. But in a liberal democracy citizens should also be understood as rulers in the Platonic sense—through their daily activities, they play a part in shaping their own souls as well as those of their fellow citizens. Excellent citizens will take responsibility for this process by acting in light of reflections on the nature of the good life and the social division of labor that might foster it. The ideal society will therefore encourage its citizens to be idealists.

7

Moneymaking and Malfunction

THE OVERARCHING GOAL of this book has been to show that Plato's *Republic* can provide us with a fresh approach to a problem that taxes contemporary political philosophers and haunts contemporary political life: what is the proper place of idealism and ideal theory in society? Philosophers tend to assume that Plato's theory is so antithetical to liberalism that one must choose between the two, and for the most part that has rendered Platonic politics little more than an object of curiosity. But my claim is that even if we hold liberalism lexically prior to Platonism, so that every time Plato's theory entails something illiberal, we reject that element, and even if we draw our criteria for what counts as liberalism from the most anti-Platonic form possible—Rawlsian political liberalism, which abhors the use of "comprehensive doctrines" to justify state action—something remains that is both distinctively Platonic and fundamentally compelling.

Liberalism, in other words, is a genus that permits of many species—and the same is true even of political liberalism. In Chapter 6 I argued that it is possible to have a form of political liberalism that retains Plato's guiding ambitions. This theory would replace philosopher-kings with philosopher-citizens who rule from below, or, in the case of those who govern the institutions of civil society, from the middle. If citizens engage in ideal theory, con-

274

ceiving of the social division of labor as they see fit and then carrying out the tasks that seem most appropriate for them, they may constitute what Plato would have considered a genuine society. This ideal is, of course, unlikely to be fully realized, but it remains a coherent aspiration that can and should guide individual action.

One of the criticisms of ideal theory that I canvassed in the Introduction was Geuss's charge that it has nothing to say about the way the world actually is, beyond the fact that it falls short. The flip side of that objection is that a successful political philosophy would have to address "the actual institutional, economic, and political reality of the world into which [it] is trying to allow us to intervene."[1] The purpose of this chapter is to show that the ideal of philosophical citizenship can satisfy this criterion. To be more specific, I believe that a revived Platonism can breathe life into the Marxian critique of capitalism.

The word "capitalism" can cause eyes to glaze over. Like many terms in political life, it can seem at once too vague and too loaded to be of any analytical use. Yet the fact remains that most if not all of today's liberal democracies can justly be described as capitalistic, and any attempt to wrestle with our political possibilities will have to come to grips with that fact. Capitalism is indeed said in many ways, often by the same theorist. But by connecting Plato with the archetypal theorist of capitalism, Karl Marx, we can isolate one sense of the word that has clear meaning and normative import: an economic system that causes society to systematically "malfunction" relative to a teleological norm.[2] This notion of a malfunctioning society, I will argue, allows us to interweave critical and ideal theory and thereby open up new avenues both for political discourse and for political practice.

I begin this chapter by drawing out the implications of the ideal of philosopher-citizens for economic life. In particular, I show that Plato's distinctive views on the phenomenon of "moneymaking"

---

1. Geuss, *Outside Ethics*, 36 (cf. 38); Geuss, *Philosophy and Real Politics*, 9–18, 93–94.

2. I arrived at this term after reading R. H. Tawney's *Acquisitive Society*, in which he contrasts "functional" with "acquisitive" society. I connect Tawney's socialism with Plato's critique of moneymaking in my two-part article "Socialism We Can Believe In."

suggest a stance on economic life that contrasts with the position famously advocated by Adam Smith. If Plato's arguments hold, moneymaking activity will produce a *dysfunctional* society that fails to satisfy social needs in any stable way. I then turn to Marx's critique of capitalism, arguing that it can be both illuminated and bolstered by the Platonic ideal of economic life. More specifically, the thought is that on Marx's account capitalism entrenches moneymaking in the Platonic sense, building it into the logic of our institutions so that society degenerates beyond merely contingent dysfunction into systematic *malfunction*. In the final section I show that Marx's rationale for dismissing self-standing normative theories as empty need not apply to the ideal of philosophical citizenship, which can therefore play a useful role in a contemporary "critical theory." I then end the chapter by offering a few suggestions concerning the practical implications of this combination of Platonic and Marxian thought, using journalism as a focal case.

§1 Plato and Smith on Moneymaking

1. Modern economic thought has been fundamentally shaped by Adam Smith's invisible-hand argument. Smith argued that in a well-ordered society the general welfare will be best served if everyone pursues their own private interest rather than aiming directly at the common good.

> By directing [domestic] industry in such a manner as its produce may be of the greatest value [a businessman] intends only his own gain, and he is in this, as in many other cases, led by an invisible hand to promote an end which was no part of his intention. Nor is it always the worse for the society that it was no part of it. By pursuing his own interest he frequently promotes that of the society more effectually than when he really intends to promote it. I have never known much good done by those who affected to trade for the public good.[3]

---

3. Adam Smith, *Inquiry into the Nature and Causes of the Wealth of Nations* (hereafter cited as *Wealth of Nations*), IV.2.9.

To pursue one's own interest in economic affairs is not only acceptable, in Smith's view, but desirable. Whereas those who try to work for the public good end up being ineffectual, in a competitive marketplace those who try to serve themselves will inevitably end up serving others. If people want a given good, there will be an incentive to produce it; if they don't, there won't. "It is not from the benevolence of the butcher, the brewer, or the baker, that we expect our dinner, but from their regard to their own self-interest," Smith famously writes. "We address ourselves, not to their humanity but to their self-love, and never talk to them of our own necessities but of their own advantages."[4]

2. Smith was certainly not the cheerleader for self-interest he is sometimes supposed to be. He did not think we should always act selfishly, or even that we are inclined to. His psychological theory accords a central place to feelings of sympathy, including our natural interest in the plight of others; his economic theory accords a central place to institutions that prevent self-interest from going beyond its proper bounds; and his political theory accords a central place to justice, without which he considers society impossible.[5] But his most influential argument remains the claim that in a well-regulated market egoistic economic agents will raise productivity, creating a "universal opulence which extends itself to the lowest ranks of the people."[6] Whatever our highest ends may be, from alleviating misery to building opera houses in the jungle, this opulence can only serve them. And if it turns out to be less than universal, Smith's left-liberal followers have tended to think, we can always redistribute.

3. Plato would say that the tradesmen Smith mentions in his famous example are not butchers, brewers, or bakers at all, but rather

---

4. Ibid., I.2.2. Friedrich Hayek expressed much the same thought in his critique of socialism: "Profit is the signal which tells us what we must do in order to serve people whom we do not know. By pursuing profit, we are as altruistic as we can possibly be, because we extend our concern to people who are beyond our range of personal conception." See Ebenstein, *Friedrich Hayek*, 313.

5. See, e.g., Rothschild, *Economic Sentiments*; and the essays collected in Hanley, *Adam Smith*.

6. Smith, *Wealth of Nations*, I.1.10. For Smith, beneficence is an "ornament which embellishes" the social order rather than one of its basic components; Smith, *Theory of Moral Sentiments*, II.2.18.

"moneymakers"—and moneymaking, in his view, represents a powerful threat to society. This position may seem outlandish at first, but on closer inspection there is much to be said for it. To get the measure of it, we first need to juxtapose two passages of the *Republic* that are rarely read together.[7]

4. The first comes in Book II. "A city comes to exist, I believe, because none of us is individually self-sufficient *[autarkēs]*, but each has many needs he cannot satisfy," says Socrates. "Or do you think that a city *[polis]* is founded on some other principle *[archē]*?" (369b). The principle of society, what impels it, is individual need.[8] Note that Socrates does not specify which kinds of need are at issue here. The point is perfectly abstract: the final cause of society, that for the sake of which it first comes into existence and is then maintained in existence, is the satisfaction of needs that we can satisfy only by cooperating, whatever they may turn out to be—let us call them our "social needs." This is the foundational proposition of Plato's philosophy of the polis, by which I mean both his social ontology and his normative political philosophy.[9] From this seed the ideal of Kallipolis will eventually grow: "Let's, in our discussion, create a city from the beginning. But its real creator, it seems, will be our need" (369c). For although the proposition implies no particular conception of social needs, it does imply a further proposition regarding social ontology, and this in turn has normative implications.

5. We can already see that on Plato's view, a society must be more than a set of individuals living contiguously; it must consist of individuals cooperating to satisfy their social needs. Socrates confirms this immediately:

---

7. This section covers some of the same ground as my article "Moneymakers and Craftsmen."

8. I should remind the reader that I take *polis* to be best translated as "society" rather than "city." The term "city" does have the advantage, however, that it is naturally correlated with the word "citizen."

9. Compare Rawls, who also begins his political philosophy with an assumption in social ontology, namely that "a society is a cooperative venture for mutual advantage." See John Rawls, *Theory of Justice*, 4; and Pettit, "Rawls's Political Ontology." For a criticism of the way in which philosophers like Plato and Rawls think about social ontology, see Oakeshott, *On Human Conduct*, 112–119, although see Rawls, *Political Liberalism*, 42n., for a disclaimer.

Then because we have many needs, and because one of us calls on another out of one need, and on a third out of a different need, we gather many into a single settlement *[oikēsis]* as partners *[koinōnoi]* and helpers *[boēthoi]*. And we call such a shared settlement a city. (369b–c)

Notice the language used to describe society and its members. The city is figured as a kind of household, an extended *oikos*, where that means not simply a dwelling but also, and more importantly, a shared project or *koinōnia*. This project will depend for its existence on citizens' work. Since this work aims at satisfying our social needs, let us call it our "social work." Society can therefore be said to depend on its members' social work—without "the patterns of work that give rise to a city" (421a), there is no city.[10]

6. It does not follow that each citizen needs to carry out the same amount of social work, or that certain individuals cannot free ride on the social work of others.[11] But it does follow that there will come a point where the failure of those who live contiguously to work together as partners and helpers makes it the case that there is no longer any ground for calling their co-dwelling a society at all. Ontologically speaking, then, a society is not just a set of individuals living in the same place.[12] Nor is it bound together by collective intentions or speech acts or decision procedures, along the lines of some recent arguments in social ontology.[13] Rather it is like a team, something that can come in and out of existence depending on the work of its members. It is therefore an aspiration, a task; it can be achieved but never assumed.[14]

---

10. Using Grube and Reeve's translation, which admittedly may be rather loose at this point.

11. See also Geuss, *World without Why*, x.

12. Compare Rousseau in *On the Social Contract*, bk. 1, chap. 6: "The true meaning of [citizen] has been almost entirely effaced among the moderns; most take a town *[ville]* for a city *[cité]*, and a townsman *[bourgeois]* for a citizen *[citoyen]*. They do not know that the houses make the town but the citizens make the city." Rousseau, *Rousseau's Political Writings*, 93.

13. See, e.g., Searle, "Social Ontology"; and List and Pettit, *Group Agency*.

14. To put it in Aristotelian terms, the *energeia* or being-at-work of a society depends on the being-at-work of its members.

7. So the foundational proposition of Plato's philosophy of the polis, that the *archē* of society is individual need, turns out to imply a particular social ontology, according to which society depends for its existence on citizens' labor. This has normative implications. We can see this just by following the logic of the argument for ourselves. Since society has a function, it contains within it a constitutive normative standard.[15] Just as a good knife is one that cuts well, the function of a knife being to cut, so a good society will be one that is good at satisfying social needs.[16] The property in virtue of which a society can do its job well is its members' cooperative activity. It follows that a good society will be one in which citizens cooperate well, playing their parts in a division of labor oriented to social needs.

---

15. On constitutive standards, see Korsgaard, *Self-Constitution*, 27–34. Obviously the idea of constitutive normativity is hardly uncontroversial, but to defend it would go beyond the scope of this chapter.

16. With this in mind, we might understand the difference between Socrates' first and second cities as depending on different understandings of what the needs in question amount to. For all that Glaucon calls the first city a "city of pigs" (372d), it is not quite right to say that it deals only with our "animal needs." Pigs and other animals do not "recline on couches strewn with yew and myrtles and feast with their children, drink their wine, and, crowned with wreaths, hymn the gods" (372b). But the first city might be considered inhuman insofar as it presupposes citizens whose needs are naturally in harmony with their environment, and hence a conception according to which those needs are in important ways finite. If our needs were finite, we could indeed "produce no more children than [our] resources allow, lest [we] fall into either poverty or war," "drink in moderation," and "live in peace and good health," and "when [we] die at a ripe old age, [we would] pass on a similar sort of life to [our] children" (372b–d). But human needs are not like this. They are capable of expanding infinitely; they are potentially "multifarious" (*pantodapos*), meaning "of every shape and origin." This is why we need guardians—first to limit the damage that our *pleonexia* can wreak, since it can cause us to fight wars both against one another and against other cities, and then to shape our souls from childhood onward so that we will achieve as much harmony between our needs and our environment as is possible, given our natures. In other words, the second city comes about because Socrates supplements the foundational proposition of his social philosophy—(1) that the final cause of society is the satisfaction of those needs that we cannot satisfy by ourselves—with two further propositions: (2) that those needs include the need for our needs to be regulated in various ways and (3) that social institutions can achieve this. But (1) does not entail either (2) or (3). It would be possible, for instance, to go from (1) to a Hegelian proposition (2a) that the needs we cannot satisfy by ourselves include the need for recognition and (3a) that the institutions of society can supply this. So in itself the foundational proposition is compatible with various conceptions of needs—and hence, we might note, with various conceptions of the good life.

Hence Plato's social ontology implies a political philosophy whose primary concern will be labor.

8. This sequence of argumentation turns out to be mirrored in the progression of the dialogue: having laid down the *archē* of the city, and hence its ontology, Socrates takes his next task as founder to be working out a division of labor sufficient for meeting the primary needs of citizens. This quickly leads him onto normative considerations regarding labor. More specifically, he is led to a principle concerning what kind of work each citizen should be doing, the so-called principle of specialization.

> SOCRATES: You see, it occurred to me while you were speaking that, in the first place, we are not all born alike. On the contrary, each of us differs somewhat in nature from the others, one being suited to one job *[ergon]*, another to another. Or don't you think so?
>
> ADEIMANTUS: I do.
>
> SOCRATES: Well, then, would one person do better work if he practiced many crafts or if he practiced one?
>
> ADEIMANTUS: If he practiced one.
>
> SOCRATES: And it is also clear, I take it, that if one misses the opportune moment *[kairos]* in any job, the work is spoiled.
>
> ADEIMANTUS: It is clear.
>
> SOCRATES: That, I take it, is because the thing that has to be done won't wait until the doer has the leisure *[skolē]* to do it. No, instead the doer must, of necessity, pay close attention to what has to be done and not leave it for his idle moments *[parergon*—literally, as a sideline or by-product].
>
> ADEIMANTUS: Yes, he must.
>
> SOCRATES: The result, then, is that more plentiful *[pleiōn]* and better-quality *[kallion]* goods are more easily produced, if each person does one thing for which he is naturally suited and does it at the opportune moment, because his time is freed from all the others. (370a–c)[17]

---

17. An alternative translation for the first part of this sentence might be "more things are produced, and better and more easily, when each person."

Socrates insists that in this first city there is neither justice nor in-justice (371e–372a).[18] But this claim should not distract us from the obvious fact that the principle just stated—that each person should practice only the craft for which he is best suited—represents the first iteration of the "one-man, one-job" principle (423d; 433a) that will in turn ground the *Republic*'s main thesis regarding justice in the political sense, namely that being a just citizen consists in "doing one's own work" (433a–b; 433e–434c).[19] As Socrates says in Book III, "Everyone in a well-regulated society has his own work *[ergon]* to do" (406c). So there is a clear progression in the dialogue from social ontology to the division of labor to a principle regulating the division of labor to a thesis about the nature of excellent citizenship. This is not just a sequence; it is an structure of argumentation whereby political philosophy is grounded in social ontology. Socrates confirms this in Book IV, remarking that "right from the beginning, when we were founding the city, we had, with the help of some god, chanced to hit upon the origin and pattern *[archē* and *typos]* of justice" (443b–c).[20]

9. If the first of our passages leaves us with the thought that citizens should do their own work, the second explores what it would be to fail by that standard.[21] It comes in Book I, in the midst of

---

18. I take that to be a function of the conception of needs presupposed by the first conception, as per my remarks in note 16.

19. I say "justice in the political sense" because the *Republic* is centrally concerned with justice in the psychological sense, which has to do with having each part in one's soul do its own work. How psychological justice bears on being a just citizen is an important exegetical question, but I do not address it here. See Kosman, "Justice and Virtue," 125, as well as Chapter 2, notes 40 and 43.

20. Compare also 432d–433b, especially this: "It seems, blessed though you are, that the thing has been rolling around at our feet from the very beginning, and yet, like ridiculous fools, we could not see it" (432d). One might reasonably treat this as an admission that Socrates has built his conclusions into his premises. The question, of course, is whether that is as problematic as it first seems, or whether it simply confirms that "reflective equilibrium" is as far as philosophical argument can ever take us with respect to politics. See Rawls, *Theory of Justice*, 19–21, and especially Scanlon, "Rawls on Justification."

21. To my knowledge, the connection between these passages has not been noticed before. The reason is probably that the second passage comes before the first, and it comes in an odd context, namely during Socrates' debate with Thrasymachus in Book 1. One piece that hints at the connection between the two passages without actually discussing it is Schofield, "Plato on the Economy," 77, 79–80.

Socrates' debate with Thrasymachus over whether justice amounts to whatever is in the interests of those in power. After Thrasymachus claims that the ruler in the precise sense decrees only what is best for himself (340c–341b), Socrates makes a distinction between true craftsmen and those he calls moneymakers *(chrēmatistai)*.[22] His example is medicine. "Is a doctor in the precise sense," he asks Thrasymachus, "a money-maker or someone who treats the sick?" (341c). Thrasymachus concedes that the true doctor is not a moneymaker. This is puzzling. Why can't doctors treat the sick *and* make money? Must a true doctor really sacrifice herself with no reward?

10. The distinction becomes clearer if we attend to what follows. Socrates makes clear that he is working with a normative conception of crafts, according to which they are not just skills but structured activities that aim at producing social goods.[23] Each genuine craft aims to provide a distinct good, and this aim is what distinguishes it from other crafts. The craft of piloting, for instance, aims at getting people safely and efficiently from port to port (346a). This is not to say it provides no other benefits: spending time at sea may be good for one's health, for example. But the reason that piloting is not medicine, no matter how good it is for the health, is that health is not what it essentially aims to produce—it is only an incidental benefit (346b).

11. The notion of a constitutive aim may appear a little vague, but we can make it more concrete by thinking in terms of the standards of success and failure internal to each craft. If a pilot fails to make anyone healthy during a voyage, she has not thereby failed qua pilot; if her boat runs aground, she has. A true craftsman—the craftsman

---

22. The following few pages draw heavily on material published in Thakkar, "Moneymakers and Craftsmen."

23. The conception of crafts I am attributing to Plato differs from the Aristotelian usage according to which a craft is a two-way rational capacity, or skill, so that the craft of medicine is exercised as much in intentional poisoning as it is in intentional healing. Socrates does make use of this conception in his refutation of Polemarchus (333e7–334b), but only as part of a series of reductios that serve to bring Polemarchus toward the fundamentally different conception in which genuine exercises of a craft (as opposed to a mere skill) are necessarily directed at the good for the sake of which the craft exists. On Aristotle's notion of a two-way rational capacity, see Aristotle, *Metaphysics* 9.2 and 9.5; and Makin, "Aristotle on Modality."

in the precise sense, the craftsman qua craftsman—is therefore a worker who deliberates in light of standards of success internal to her craft, and hence with an eye to the benefit that craft characteristically produces and its function within the social whole. By deliberation I do not mean something that has to take place interpersonally; nor do I mean something that might in principle be purely internal, with no external manifestations. Rather, I am following Aristotle in thinking of deliberation as the process whereby we select means to our ends.[24] On this picture, our actions embody our practical reasoning rather than being separable from it. In any given case, it is possible that a worker who deliberates in light of standards of success internal to her craft will produce exactly the same results as a worker who deliberates with different goals in mind. As Aristotle puts it, "The products of a craft determine by their own qualities whether they have been produced well; and so it suffices that they have the right qualities when they have been produced."[25] Over time, however, deliberative processes will produce different results since they "control for" different ends (to use Philip Pettit's phrase).[26] To return to Plato's example, we can imagine two pilots, one whose primary aim is to get people safely and efficiently from port to port and another whose primary aim is to keep fit. Over a vast range of cases, the two pilots may make the same decisions. But when a storm arrives, as surely it must, the difference in priorities will become manifest. This is deliberation in action, and it clearly has concrete effects.

12. Socrates' argument with respect to moneymaking is that wages stand to medicine as health stands to navigation: they amount to an incidental benefit that plays no role in making the craft what it is. As such, they ought to play no role in the deliberations of a true craftsman. Socrates accepts, of course, that a true doctor may seek wages—but

---

24. Aristotle, *Nicomachean Ethics* III.3. It is worth noting that one way of being a means to an end on Aristotle's view is to be partly constitutive of the end, so means and ends are not always separate.

25. Ibid., II.4.

26. Pettit, *Robust Demands of the Good*, 4. This means that in any given case the actions differ modally even if they do not differ in actuality.

he denies that she does so qua doctor.[27] Insofar as an individual aims at earning wages, she thereby engages in a distinct craft, namely wage earning (*misthōtikē*; 346a–347a).[28] So the doctor in the precise sense is no moneymaker.

13. At this stage an objection might arise. For Socrates' point has been limited to craftsmen qua craftsmen rather than qua human beings. But why should anyone engage in a craft in the first place? On this point Socrates says something that might seem to negate his previous position. Given the contrast between a true doctor and a wage earner, we might expect him to enjoin altruistic self-sacrifice on the part of individuals—doctors living off alms and suchlike. Yet he turns out to accept that people will require wages to motivate them to engage in a given craft (346e–347a). This raises a problem: Why is moneymaking not the master craft standing above all particular crafts? After all, a craft should be able to incorporate subordinate crafts. The craft of shoemaking might include the craft of lace cutting, for instance, insofar as the latter is disciplined toward the former and hence guided by its standards of success.[29] So if we engage in medicine for the sake of money, isn't medicine simply a subordinate activity within the master craft of moneymaking? And doesn't that destroy the distinction between doctors and moneymakers?[30]

14. At times Plato does seem to equate craftsmen with moneymakers. In Book IV, for example, Socrates speaks of someone "who is by nature a craftsman *[dēmiourgos]* or some other kind of moneymaker" as if the two are equivalent (434a; cf. 547d). Yet in Book VI he also speaks of the philosophical ruler as a "craftsman *[dēmiourgos]* of temperance, justice, and the whole of citizenly virtue" (500d;

---

27. We might think of wages as a *parergon*, a by-product, to use the term deployed by Socrates at 370c in reference to the principle of specialization, a principle that clearly depends on the idea of differentiating activities by their aim.

28. There is a real question whether wage earning can in fact count as a craft, given Socrates' apparent understanding of crafts: it does not seem to be "set over" some object that is deficient unless that object is one's wallet; and if it belongs to some other type of craft—in particular, one that benefits the craftsman—then Socrates' argument against Thrasymachus will fail. See Barney, "Socrates' Refutation of Thrasymachus," 52.

29. Cf. Plato, *Statesman* 281d ff., and Aristotle, *Nicomachean Ethics* I.1 and X.4.

30. Allan Bloom raises a somewhat similar objection. See Bloom, "Interpretive Essay," 332–333.

cf. 395c, 421c, 455a)—and surely the philosopher-king is not a moneymaker. It is therefore important to distinguish between the times when Socrates is thinking of craftsmen as a particular class within Kallipolis and the times when he is using the word to refer to all those engaged in structured activities aimed at satisfying specific social needs. In the Book VI passage just quoted, this latter sense is clearly the one that is at issue, and the same would seem to be true of the Book I passage we have been considering (e.g., 342c, 346a).[31]

15. In any case, the question still remains: if we require wages to motivate us to engage in particular crafts, as Socrates accepts that we do (346e–347a), how can we maintain a distinction between an activity like medicine and the master activity of moneymaking? Won't medicine become part of moneymaking? The way out of this knot is to distinguish between money and wages (the word is *misthos*, which we might also translate as "recompense" or "reward"; cf. 363d). Strictly speaking, what Socrates conceded was not that craftsmen are all moneymakers, but rather that they are all wage earners. And he goes

---

31. Note that this represents a significant departure from our own concept of craft, which tends to imply production by artisans in small workshops: we would not normally think of nurses and teachers and farmers as craftsmen, but it seems that Plato would, and I will follow his usage. The broader concept of craft also represents a significant departure from the standard Greek usage of *technē*, according to which neither agriculture nor ruling would count. Plato needs to expand the concept because he thinks of work and citizenship as going together. As Socrates says, attributing the thought to Asclepius but also clearly endorsing it, "Everyone in a well-regulated city has his own work *[ergon]* to do" (406c). The flip side of this is that those who do not direct their labors toward providing social goods ought to be considered pseudocraftsmen and hence pseudocitizens, regardless of what they are usually called. This might go for the "thieves . . . and pickpockets, temple robbers, and craftsmen of all such sorts of evil" mentioned at 552d. It might also go for moneymakers. Against this interpretation one might cite 552a, where it does seem that moneymakers are regarded as part of the city in the relevant sense. As we will see, however, Plato's thought seems to be that in Kallipolis good governance can ensure that moneymakers act as if they were genuine craftsmen and so genuine citizens. Outside Kallipolis this will not be true. Stepping back, we can say that the move to conceive of everyone in the city as having some *ergon* on pain of being outside the community of citizens is reminiscent of, and potentially as radical as, Henri Comte de Saint-Simon's move to cast those who consume without producing, the *fainéants*, as either robbers or beggars— just as Saint-Simon effectively criminalizes the unproductive, so Plato declares them undeserving of medical care (405c–408b). This also seems to bear on Plato's discussion of "drones" in Books VIII and IX: at 564b, the drones are described as *argos* (*a-ergos*, i.e., idle, without work). See Saint-Simon, *Selected Writings*, 103, 158, 173.

on to argue that money is just one form of wage. The second kind of wage is honor: someone who becomes a doctor out of the desire for honor is therefore an honor seeker, not a moneymaker. The final kind of wage is more complicated. Socrates frames it as the avoidance of a penalty or punishment, but also as "the best people's kind of wages" (347a). The best kind of people are motivated to rule, for example, by the fact that their not doing so would lead to disaster—specifically, to the disaster of the task's being carried out by lesser people (347c).

16. Socrates stops here because his dispute with Thrasymachus has centered on ruling, but in principle his argument would seem to extend to other crafts. Every doctor is a wage earner before she is a doctor, yet different kinds of people seek different kinds of wage. Some pursue medicine for money; others pursue it for honor; but the best pursue it because they don't want lesser people to carry out the task. This might seem a strange motivation at first, but on reflection it makes perfect sense. A society is a cooperative scheme that comes about in order to satisfy our needs. The scheme will work better—and our needs will be better satisfied—to the degree that each person performs the task for which she is best suited.[32] The best kind of people are therefore motivated to engage in a particular craft by the desire to see citizens deploy their talents appropriately within a division of labor constituted for the sake of the common good. And when these are the wages in question, there is no conflict between being a wage earner and being a true craftsman.

---

32. On my reading, someone whose strength would in most societies dispose him toward jobs that involve lifting and similar physical tasks might assign himself to a different role in a society of bodybuilders. Greco, "On the Economy of Specialization and Division of Labour in Plato's *Republic*," distinguishes between performing the task for which one is best suited and serving society as best one can on the basis that only the latter entails David Ricardo's law of comparative advantage, which holds that "the individual with the lower opportunity cost for producing a particular output should specialize in producing that output" (57). If A is better than B at both *x* and *y*, he should be assigned to the task at which the degree of his relative advantage is greatest. This is true even if in absolute terms he is better at the other task. Greco correctly points out that this is different from the proposition that each citizen should perform the task for which he is best suited. From this she draws the conclusion that efficiency is not the guiding principle of Plato's division of labor, if efficiency is understood as "a function of *quantity* of output, given the desired level of quality" (58). I can accept this because what I mean by "serving society as best one can" is not necessarily producing the greatest quantity of goods: as Plato says, it is a matter of both quality and quantity (370c).

17. But the corollary of this proposition is that neither money-makers nor honor seekers can be true craftsmen. If one craft is engaged in for the sake of another, deliberation within the subsidiary activity will be governed by standards of success derived from the master activity. This is harmless in the case of lace cutting and shoe-making. But where moneymaking or honor seeking is the master activity, the subsidiary activity is likely to be distorted. The goal of medicine is to restore the patient to health. But what if an opportunity arises for a doctor to enrich herself at the expense of the patient by prescribing needless and dangerous surgery? Qua doctor, she should resist; qua moneymaker, she should accept; qua honor seeker, she should weigh the prestige that might be gained through additional wealth against the chances of incurring dishonor by getting caught. What this example shows (on Plato's account) is that the moneymaker and the honor seeker can only ever masquerade as, or imitate, genuine doctors: in the final analysis, benefiting the patient can only ever be an incidental goal to them, pursued just insofar as the incentives line up.[33]

18. From Smith's perspective, the Platonic position will seem moralistic and naïve. Who cares whether a craftsman has your best interests at heart? Doesn't a moneymaking concern like Breguet make pretty good watches? And if we are thinking of honor lovers, why not take the character played by Toshirô Mifune in Akira Kurosawa's *High and Low*, a shoemaker who just wants to make the best shoes he can, regardless of how little profit he makes? The reason for this dedication, it would seem, is that quality craftsmanship affords him the possibility of genuine self-respect; to lower his standards would

---

33. One might plausibly object that the subordination of medicine to wage earning is destructive of the craft even when the wages in question are "the best people's kinds of wages"—after all, Socrates holds that in Kallipolis some people will be denied medical treatment (405c–408b). In my view this merely illustrates a distinctive feature of crafts in Plato's account, namely that their proper bounds can be determined only by those with an understanding of the good of the city (and its citizens). So in Plato's view a doctor who attempted to heal "naturally sick and intemperate people" would in fact be departing from, and corrupting, the craft of medicine properly understood: Asclepius "invented the craft of medicine for people whose bodies are healthy in nature and habit, but have some specific disease in them" (407c–d).

be to bring dishonor on himself. Does this really make him less of a craftsman?

19. The first thing to say is that Plato never denies that the wise can care about honor, so long as what is considered honorable is decided by wisdom. Mifune's character could therefore be understood as a true craftsman along those lines. But if we understand him as an honor seeker in the precise sense, then the Platonic account would be that he grew up in a society that was well ordered with respect to crafts, one that attached honor to skilled craftsmanship and shame to shoddiness. Practically speaking, there will often be no difference between the work of people like this and that of true craftsmen in Plato's sense. But the two groups are still not identical: when times change, as in the postwar Japan depicted by Kurosawa, members of the first, not being led by reflection on the needs of society, may have no way of adapting their sense of what is honorable.[34] The story is much the same with respect to Breguet. It is not that its watches aren't excellent: its executives have a strong financial interest in producing watches of the highest quality, since they trade on Breguet's reputation as a luxury brand. But if it turns out that no real needs are served by the manufacture of luxury watches, that fact will not affect their decision making except insofar as it affects the demand for their products. The standards of success guiding their activity are not essentially related to social needs, and that is what differentiates them from true craftsmen. Just as a sailor produces health only incidentally, so a moneymaker satisfies social needs only incidentally.

20. We are now in a position to connect the Book I passage on moneymaking with the Book II passage on the nature of society. As we saw earlier, the latter passage and the ensuing train of thought give pride of place to citizens' labor, both politically and ontologically. Like a team, a society is an entity whose full existence depends on its members' activity. Just as we might say of eleven soccer players who wear the same colors but fail to work together that they thereby

---

34. As it happens, Gondo (Mifune) does seem capable of adapting to the situation, unlike the old man who serves as chairman of National Shoes at the start of the film. This might be a reason to think of Gondo as a true craftsman.

fail to constitute a team, so we might say of a group of people who live in the same place but fail to work together that they fail to constitute a society. This explains why justice is the central virtue of the *Republic*'s politics. Justice is the virtue of doing one's own work within the division of labor—or, to put it another way, of playing for the team. Injustice, by contrast, is the vice of failing to play for the team or of failing to consider one's work as social work. We can put more flesh on the bones of this account now that we have Book I's distinction between craftsmanship and moneymaking at our disposal. The just worker corresponds to the true craftsman: it is in directing her labors toward the production of genuine goods, goods that serve social needs, that she "does her own work." The moneymaker, in contrast, is an unjust worker: the sense in which she does not do her own work is that her labors are not optimally deployed for the sake of serving social needs but are instead directed toward the production of goods that will bring her money. The implication, once we put everything together, is that if citizens comport themselves as moneymakers, society's very existence will be threatened.[35]

21. This fate may seem merely metaphysical—why should we care about living in a "society" as opposed to a "shmociety"?[36] Yet the point is far more practical than it first seems: the claim is that in order to flourish, we need certain goods that we cannot provide except through cooperation, and that over time these goods will be produced only by citizens who deliberate in light of social needs. To the degree that citizens are moneymakers, they will perform their social work only haphazardly, and society will therefore satisfy its citizens' social needs only haphazardly. Just as a blunt knife will not fulfill

---

35. I focus on moneymaking from here on, as opposed to honor seeking, because in a well-ordered society one's sense of honor will track the social good, such that the honor seeker will be closer to the just person than the moneymaker. For more on this point, see Brennan and Pettit, *Economy of Esteem*, 24, which quotes Thomas Hobbes in this connection: "Few except those who love praise do anything to deserve it." See Hobbes, *On the Citizen*, 23. Having said that, I do think that individuals and institutions that are primarily oriented toward prestige are unlikely to consistently track the social good in the long run.

36. The term "shmociety" alludes to David Enoch's parallel objection to Christine Korsgaard's claims about agency in *Self-Constitution*. See Enoch, "Agency, Shmagency"; and Enoch, "Shmagency Revisited."

its function, so a society of moneymakers will be a dysfunctional society.

22. Casting Plato's point in practical terms simply opens up a new line of criticism, however. Following Bernard Mandeville, Smith argued that so long as policy makers design institutions appropriately, concerns about moneymaking will be beside the point from a practical perspective. For in a system where producers are incentivized to satisfy the needs of consumers—that is, a competitive marketplace—self-interest will induce a medical moneymaker, for instance, to heal patients more efficiently than a true doctor ever would. In a similar vein, Friedrich Hayek argued that a society of moneymakers will allocate social resources far more efficiently than a society of craftsmen ever could, thanks to the astonishing capacity of the price system to collate and convey information about local conditions and needs.[37] And Smith and Hayek seem to have been proved right. As Deirdre McCloskey points out, living standards have shot up since moneymaking begun to be perceived as a respectable activity: in 1800 the global average income was just $3 a day (in today's money); now it is $30, and in Norway it is $137. Whether or not we are now wiser than before, we are certainly healthier and wealthier.[38]

23. If the ideal of philosopher-citizens is to have any force in the modern world, it must avoid becoming a moralizing fantasy. Few who scoff at wealth would wish for a return to premodern living standards, toothache and all; honesty requires that we acknowledge the power of Smith's insight. It is true that within a well-functioning market, the behavior of profit-seeking individuals can lead to an efficient and mutually beneficial allocation of social resources, including labor. But this by no means removes the need for individuals to exercise justice and wisdom, since markets will be dysfunctional without such an ethos.[39]

---

37. See, e.g., Hayek, "The Use of Knowledge in Society"; and note 4 of the present chapter. For Mandeville, see *Fable of the Bees*.

38. McCloskey, *Bourgeois Dignity*, 1–2. See also the concluding remarks in Nagel, "Getting Personal."

39. See Lane, *Eco-Republic*, 43: "The present purpose is rather to argue that the current Western social model can be saved from itself, by moderating it with a set of

24. To illustrate this point, we can distinguish between true moneymaking and what we might call circumscribed moneymaking.[40] If Smith is right, a just and wise citizen could conceivably consider her talents best deployed in profit seeking within a well-regulated market against a background of redistributive state institutions. But such a citizen would engage in moneymaking activities only to the extent that she could reasonably believe them to be the best way for her to contribute to social welfare. And the idea that market incentives will always map onto social needs is patently utopian. To begin with, not all marketplaces are fully competitive—as a matter of fact, few are. To the extent that monopolies and oligopolies exist, along with asymmetries of information and other barriers to competition, customer satisfaction will be disincentivized. In any case it is hardly obvious that customers' preferences are equivalent to their needs; to the extent that they are not, to satisfy someone's preferences is not necessarily to attend to their needs. When incentives and social needs are misaligned, it will matter a great deal whether producers are moneymakers proper or moneymakers in the circumscribed sense. If the situation evidently incentivizes the production of goods that are substandard or even useless, moneymakers in the circumscribed sense will revert to deliberating in terms of social needs as they perceive them. True moneymakers, by contrast, will simply no longer serve social needs—and the 2007–2008 financial crisis is but the most glaring example of what can result.

25. So Plato's argument against moneymaking survives even if we accept Smith's point regarding aggregate productivity. Citizens who orient their work by deliberating in light of social needs can sometimes engage in a circumscribed form of moneymaking. But this is really a form of craftsmanship in Plato's sense, with money as a proximate goal pursued only insofar as it is the best means to the real end. Moneymakers in the precise sense, by contrast, have money as the object of their productive activities. They therefore completely

---

ideas against which it was forged but in light of which it can be reinvigorated. (Compare the way that Aristotle argues, in *Politics*, Book 5, 1309b–1310a, that each kind of distorted regime can be improved and saved by infusion of principles from an opposite kind.)"

40. This paragraph covers some of the same ground as my article "Neo-socialism."

fail to deliberate in light of social needs, and over time this will mean that certain needs go unsatisfied. As a result, moneymaking prevents society from functioning optimally.

§2 From Dysfunction to Malfunction

26. The proposition that citizens ought to assign themselves to roles on the basis of reflection on social needs may seem contemptibly idealistic to some, and perhaps especially to those influenced by Marx, who wrote in volume 1 of *Capital* that "my standpoint, from which the development of the economic formation of society is viewed as a process of natural history, can less than any other make the individual responsible for relations whose creature he remains, socially speaking, however much he may subjectively raise himself above them."[41] Marx did not deny that ideals can influence human behavior, but he did believe that our ideals are fundamentally shaped by what we do on a daily basis, and that the most important thing we do on a daily basis is to make a living from the world by transforming it in various ways.[42] It follows, he thought, that we should focus on understanding the logic of our economic institutions rather than arguing about what individual economic agents should or should not do. What I want to argue in the rest of this chapter, by contrast,

---

41. See Marx, *Capital*, vol. 1, 92, as well as Engels, "Socialism: Utopian and Scientific." For one expression of this line of thought, see Leiter, "Marxism and the Continuing Irrelevance of Normative Theory"; for an older one, see Alasdair MacIntyre's unkind review of R. H. Tawney's life and work ("cliché-ridden high-mindedness . . . a monument to the impotence of ideals"), "Tawney, Tawneyism and Today," reprinted in *Against the Self-Images of the Age*, 130–154.

42. The primacy of productive activity in human life is a theme that recurs throughout Marx's works; the locus classicus is *The German Ideology* (cowritten with Engels), Part I of which is reprinted in the *Marx-Engels Reader*, edited by Robert C. Tucker, 146–200. In *Capital*, for example, Marx writes that "through this movement [man] acts upon external nature and changes it, and in this way he simultaneously changes his own nature" (vol. 1, 283). This statement reiterates one of the main themes of Marx's *Economic and Philosophical Manuscripts of 1844*. Marx even goes so far as to assert that the reason that the ideal of human equality has become part of our social ethos is that capitalist institutions assume the equal value of human labor time, and this affects our practices. See *Capital*, vol. 1, 151–152. The relationship between day-to-day action and patterns of thought has also been the subject of much discussion in the tradition of American pragmatism. See, e.g., John Dewey, *Experience and Nature*.

is that Marx's account of capitalism is best understood against the background of a Platonic ideal of craftsmanship.

27. There are several different strands in *Capital*, Marx's masterwork. The most famous concern the structure of exploitation under capitalism, the propensity of the economic system to generate crises, and the inevitability of revolution, but there are also analyses of the ideological character of social science, the origins of capitalism, the temporal structure of lived experience, and much more besides.[43] What I want to focus on, by contrast, is a line of thought that is so global that it is liable to go unnoticed, not least because Marx is content to leave it largely implicit. On Marx's view, I will argue, capitalism institutionalizes moneymaking in the Platonic sense and thereby leads the social division of labor to systematically malfunction.

28. We can begin by noting that although Marx is often thought of as a quintessentially modern, Enlightenment thinker, among the most important sources for his critique of capitalism is in fact Plato's pupil Aristotle.[44] Moreover, what Marx found most rewarding in Aristotle were those passages, especially in the *Politics*, where he takes up and develops Plato's attack on moneymaking. Aristotle argues that property acquisition (*ktetike*) is by nature—and hence should only ever be—a subordinate component of the wider task of securing the good life for individuals and communities, namely household or political management. In Book I of the *Nicomachean Ethics*, he explains that to flourish fully, humans require "external goods" such as money, good looks, and fortune—for although these are less important than virtuous rational activity, they are sometimes necessary for it.[45] Property acquisition therefore helps secure such

---

43. For the point about time, which may be less well understood than the others, see Postone, *Time, Labor, and Social Domination*, 186–225, 286–306.

44. Much has been written on the relation between Marx and Aristotle, including two books and one edited collection by George McCarthy: *Marx and the Ancients*; *Marx and Aristotle*; and *Dialectics and Decadence*. See also Meikle, "Aristotle and Exchange Value"; and Meikle, *Essentialism in the Thought of Karl Marx*. To my knowledge, however, no one has thus far gone on to make the connection between Marx and Plato with respect to moneymaking (as opposed to communism, for example).

45. Aristotle, *Nicomachean Ethics* I.8, X.8.

goods (*chrēmata*—useful things) as are necessary for leading the good life. Properly understood, then, property (*ktēmata*) and riches (*ploutos*) are merely tools (*organa*) for the use of household and political managers and should therefore be pursued only to the degree that they contribute to human flourishing.[46]

29. Out of this natural practice of property acquisition there can arise a perversion, Aristotle thinks: the idea of accumulation as an end in itself and hence as a distinct craft (*chrēmatistikē*).[47] What makes this perversion possible is the nature of exchange. Exchange, however healthy, will always require the use of a given good not as the good that it itself is, but as an equivalent. For example, although the primary or proper (*oikeios*) use of a shoe—that for the sake of which it comes into being—is to protect the feet, in barter a pair of shoes might be used as equivalent to, say, half a pillow. In order to make exchange more convenient, Aristotle hazards, humans begin to use one particular commodity, such as silver or gold, as a general measure of the exchange value of other goods. This commodity becomes the currency (*nomisma*).[48] At this point the possibility of a perversion arises: it becomes possible to think of currency itself as wealth. This is mistaken, conceptually speaking, because even the richest man can still die of hunger; properly understood, riches constitute wealth just to the extent that they help us achieve the good life.[49] But apart from being a mistake, it also perverts exchange. For when property acquisition is decoupled from the requirements of household and political management, it becomes a craft unto itself. Even if it makes use of the same articles as natural property acquisition, it disciplines them toward a new *telos*: accumulation. The means has become the

---

46. Aristotle, *Politics* 1256b27–40; and *Nicomachean Ethics* IV.1–2.
47. Aristotle, *Politics* 1256b40–1257b40.
48. Ibid., 1257a6–14, 1257a32–41. Stefan Eich has an unpublished manuscript, "Between Justice and Accumulation," which provides an illuminating account of the role that currency plays in Aristotle's political thought more generally, as a "medium of civic commensurability," as a "measure of political justice," and as the condition of possibility of various virtues.
49. Ibid., 1257b8–31; Aristotle uses the Midas legend as a figure for this thought.

end. And as an end in itself, the acquisition of money becomes a boundless task.[50]

30. Adam Smith was not one for citations, but he owed a great deal to Aristotle—so much so that Joseph Schumpeter claimed the first five chapters of *The Wealth of Nations* were "but developments of the same line of reasoning" found in the *Politics* and *Nicomachean Ethics*.[51] Certainly Smith shares a great deal of Aristotle's framework, from the distinction between use value and exchange value to the treatment of money as arising when one particular commodity starts to be used as a metric for exchanges. But in his economic writings Smith shows no interest in Aristotle's normative arguments concerning economic life.[52] Whereas Aristotle distinguishes two senses

---

50. One might reasonably question whether Aristotle wants to highlight the corrupting effect of money in particular *(nomisma)* as opposed to assets in general *(chremata)*, given that the name he uses for the craft of accumulation is *chrēmatistikē*; and since Plato uses the same term for what I have been calling "moneymaking," the objection threatens to ramify. It is true that Aristotle does not impugn all forms of monetary exchange, but he does say that the craft of accumulation came into existence as a result of the invention of money (*Politics* 1257b1–5); that it is primarily concerned with making money rather than other forms of wealth (*Politics* 1257b5–6, 1257b22–23); that this aim is what allows its operations to become boundless (*Politics* 1257b23–31); and that all those engaged in it try to increase their monetary holdings infinitely (*Politics* 1257b34). In any case, in the *Nicomachean Ethics* (1119b26–27) Aristotle defines *chrēmata* as "anything whose worth is measured by money," so the opposition between the accumulation of assets *(chrēmata)* and the accumulation of money *(nomisma)* may turn out to be a distinction without a difference. With respect to Plato, finally, although it is true that Socrates' Book I critique of moneymaking *(chrēmatistikē)* does not mention currency *(nomisma)* per se, his prohibition on guardians' owning private property does so twice (417a), and in my view this prohibition follows directly from the critique of moneymaking: it is precisely because ruling is the most important craft that guardians must be prevented from owning (and *a fortiori* accumulating) money. On this latter point, see section 4 of Thakkar, "Moneymakers and Craftsmen." Thanks to Stefan Eich for pressing me to consider this objection.

51. Schumpeter, *History of Economic Analysis*, 60. Smith had rather less time for Plato, claiming that Aristotle "appears to have been so much superior to his master in everything but eloquence"; Smith, "History of Ancient Logics and Metaphysics," 122n. Both references are drawn from Pack, *Aristotle, Adam Smith and Karl Marx*, 47–48. The argument I make in the next few pages is indebted to Pack.

52. In *The Theory of Moral Sentiments*, Smith suggests that most people seek wealth for the sake of status, not for its own sake: "From whence, then, arises that emulation which runs through all the different ranks of men, and what are the advantages which we propose by that great purpose of human life which we call bettering our condition? To be observed, to be attended to, to be taken notice of with sympathy, complacency, and approbation, are all the advantages which we can propose to derive from it. It is the vanity, not the ease, or the pleasure, which interests us" (I.III.16).

of exchange, depending on whether the *telos* is to accumulate money or to secure what is necessary for the good life, Smith ignores this qualitative distinction altogether, replacing it with a quantitative one: anyone who has to exchange in order to supply his needs, Smith asserts, necessarily "becomes in some measure a merchant" and hence part of a "commercial society."[53] The second important difference is that whereas Aristotle focuses on exchange, Smith focuses on production. It is in this connection that he introduces the idea of capital, wealth that one uses in order to gain more wealth. A producer can use capital to buy raw materials, tools, and labor; the combination of these can result in a return on the original capital; the newly augmented stock of capital can then be used to buy greater quantities of raw materials, tools, and labor, leading to even greater profits; and so on.

31. Marx combines Smith's concept of capital with Aristotle's critique of moneymaking. On Marx's account, what distinguishes capital from mere money, and the capitalist epoch from previous commercial societies, is precisely the inversion of means and ends deplored by Aristotle. "The simple circulation of commodities—selling in order to buy—is a means to a final goal which lies outside circulation, namely the appropriation of use-values, the satisfaction of needs. As against this, the circulation of money as capital is an end in itself. . . . The movement of capital is therefore limitless."[54] Just like Aristotle, then, Marx argues that when the accumulation of money becomes an end in itself, a new activity is born—moneymaking or capitalism—and that since this activity is not bound by a higher purpose (securing the good life or satisfying needs) it is in principle limitless. Marx also

---

53. Smith, *Wealth of Nations*, I.IV.1. Pack claims that Smith is engaged in an implicit debate with Aristotle, and that his strategy of argumentation is to keep on insisting that the institutions of commercial society are "natural" as against Aristotle's insistence on moneymaking as a perversion of nature. This seems implausible to me, not least because such an argument would be transparently bad—Aristotle means the word "natural" to have normative force, such that something natural must be good, whereas Smith does not use the word in the same sense, so Smith could only be engaging in sophistry if he were making the argument that Pack attributes to him. See Pack, *Aristotle, Adam Smith and Karl Marx*, 62–64.

54. Marx, *Capital*, vol. 1, 253.

follows Aristotle in noting that moneymaking can be hard to distinguish from need-related exchange on descriptive or empirical
grounds alone, since the same objects (goods and money) are used
in both. The real way to distinguish the two, Marx and Aristotle
agree, is by their *telē*. Simple exchange has the form C-M-C¹, Marx
explains: one useful item (C) is sold, that is, converted into money
(M), so that another (C¹) can be bought. Capitalist exchange, in contrast, has the form M-C-M¹: money is converted into a useful item
only for the sake of acquiring more money. Any given transaction—the
purchase of a drill, for example—might fit into either form. The
point is not to make judgments about particular cases, however,
but to isolate two different *telē* that exchange might have. In simple
exchange, money is a means to satisfy human needs; in capitalist
exchange, the satisfaction of human needs is only a means to generate
more money.

32. Unlike Smith, Marx acknowledges his debt to Aristotle, calling
him "the greatest thinker of antiquity," "the great investigator who
was the first to analyse the value-form, like so many other forms of
thought, society and nature," and citing him repeatedly.[55] But if
Marx were simply regurgitating Aristotle, that would scarcely justify his claim to a theory of modernity. The first thing Marx adds is
an account of the role that economic institutions play in engendering
moneymaking activity. For even though Aristotle would no doubt
have acknowledged that moneymaking is more common in commercial societies like Athens than militaristic ones like Sparta, he still
seems to treat it as a kind of cognitive error or subjective mistake.
Marx's claim, on the other hand, is that in the modern world moneymaking has objective standing: its logic is built into the institutions
that shape our social world, such that its structures become strictures
that govern the productive process whether we like it or not. As he
puts it in explaining how the blinkered outlook of capitalists creates
"the physical and mental degradation, the premature death, the tor-
ture of over-work" of the nineteenth-century industrial economy,
"Looking at these things as a whole, it is evident that this does not

---

55. See ibid., vol. 1, 151, 152, 532.

depend on the will, either good or bad, of the individual capitalist. Under free competition, the immanent laws of capitalist production confront the individual capitalist as a coercive force external to him."[56] In Marx's view, then, capitalist institutions make it seem to individual capitalists as though critical decisions—such as whether to make workers stay longer each day, or whether to close a given factory—are no longer up to them. And there is a sense in which this is true: if individual capitalists do not obey the "laws" of capitalism, such as the imperative to continually increase productivity, they will eventually lose their status as capitalists altogether. Qua capitalists, then, they have to obey.[57] This is what licenses Marx to claim that his concepts have objective standing in modernity—such that they are actually operative in the world—while at the same time using them as ideal types. When he speaks of a "capitalist," for instance, he means to isolate what a capitalist in the precise sense would do rather than to faithfully describe the actions of particular people. The capitalist acts qua capitalist only insofar as he takes M-C-M^1 as the guide for his actions.

As the conscious bearer *[Träger]* of this movement, the possessor of money becomes a capitalist. His person, or rather his pocket, is the point from which the money starts, and to which it returns. The objective content of the circulation we have been discussing—the valorization of value—is his subjective purpose, and it is only in so far as the appropriation of ever more wealth in the abstract is the sole driving force behind his operations that he functions as a capitalist, i.e. as capital personified and endowed with consciousness and a will. Use-values must therefore

---

56. Ibid., vol. 1, 381. Cf. vol. 1, 169: "The categories of bourgeois economics . . . are forms of thought which are socially valid, and therefore objective, for the relations of production belonging to this historically determined mode of social production, i.e. commodity production." See also Postone, *Time, Labor, and Social Domination,* for an account of how the "abstract domination" of capitalist logic constrains capitalists just as much as it does proletarians.

57. Marx makes clear, both in the famous section (1.4) on the fetishism of the commodity and elsewhere, that the laws of capitalism are in fact mutable, but only if we recognize them as our own political productions (which is not to imply that the realm of politics is autonomous relative to economic life).

never be treated as the immediate aim of the capitalist; nor must the profit on any single transaction. His aim is rather the unceasing movement of profit-making.[58]

The fact that not all factory owners actually act like this is beside the point from Marx's perspective. To use the Hegelian jargon, any given empirical phenomenon can be more or less adequate to its concept.[59]

33. The second way in which Marx departs from Aristotle is in conceiving of moneymaking as grounding a distinct form of society. Aristotle does see exchange as the condition of possibility of society, writing that "a society is maintained by proportionate reciprocity" and that "there would be no community without exchange"; he also views the proper use of wealth as vital to ethical and political virtue and hence to a good society.[60] If moneymaking is a distortion of exchange, as Aristotle suggests it is, and society is maintained by exchange, then moneymaking surely threatens to distort society as a whole. Yet in this connection Aristotle fails to join the dots, perhaps because he tends to think of society as primarily a political realm rather than an economic one; in the political realm those freed from the need to labor (whether by their own wealth or by temporary civic subsidy) discuss what is to be done, thereby fulfilling their nature as political animals, with the economic realm serving solely to provide the ex-

---

58. Marx, *Capital*, vol. 1, 254. The same thought is also expressed at vol. 1, 739: "Except as capital personified, the capitalist has no historical value. . . . It is only to this extent that the necessity of the capitalist's own transitory existence is implied in the transitory necessity of the capitalist mode of production. But, in so far as he is capital personified, his motivating force is not the acquisition and enjoyment of use-values, but the acquisition and augmentation of exchange-values." See also vol. 1, 92: "I do not by any means depict the capitalist and the landowner in rosy colors. But individuals are dealt with here only in so far as they are the personifications of economic categories, the bearers [*Träger*] of particular class-relations and interests," as well as vol. 1, 179, 342.

59. The relation between the conceptual and empirical dimensions of *Capital* is addressed systematically by Robert Albritton in, e.g., *Economics Transformed*; Albritton's approach derives from the work of the Japanese scholar Kozo Uno, especially in *Principles of Political Economy*.

60. See Aristotle, *Nicomachean Ethics* 1132b33–34 and 1133b15–20, as well as IV.1–2.

ternal goods necessary for such activity.[61] Plato, by contrast, conceives of society as a division of labor composed of rulers, soldiers, and poets just as much as carpenters and pilots, and he is therefore alive to the threat that moneymaking poses to the polis as a whole. Something similar is true of Marx. Early in his career he wrote that "religion, family, state, law, morality, science, art, etc. are only *particular* modes of production," and that "*just as* society itself produces *man as man*, so society is *produced* by him."[62] *Capital* continues this way of thinking. As a study of a certain mode of production, it is ipso facto also a study of a certain form of society.[63]

34. To understand how Marx goes beyond Plato in this respect, we need to distinguish two ways in which moneymaking can prevent a society from functioning well. If Marx is right that under capitalism moneymaking is no longer a subjective perversion—the product of individual psychic structure or cognitive error—but rather an objective feature of institutional logic, it looks as though capitalist societies will tend to satisfy social needs only haphazardly. Market incentives will ensure rapid advances in some domains of social production, but other domains will be neglected. If there is little money to be made in adult education, for instance, then we should not expect a capitalist society to provide much of it, no matter how important

---

61. This is not to say that Aristotle would not have had the resources within his theory to join the dots had he wished to. After all, the *Nicomachean Ethics* begins with a snapshot of an integrated economy aimed at the good life, as we saw in Chapter 3.

62. Tucker, *Marx-Engels Reader*, 85.

63. This is implied right at the start of *Capital* when Marx writes that although use values always constitute the material content of wealth, "in the form of society to be considered here they are also the material bearers of . . . exchange-value" (vol. 1, 126). It is also implied when Marx speaks of Asiatic societies, suggesting that if the social division of labor remains the same, so will the social structure more generally (chap. 14, vol. 1, 479). In volume 3, meanwhile, Marx suggests that society is the aggregate of the productive relations in which men stand to each other and to nature: "We have seen how the capitalist process of production is a historically specific form of the social production process in general. This last is both a production process of the material conditions of existence for human life, and a process, proceeding in specific economic and historical relations of production, that produces and reproduces these relations of production themselves, and with them the bearers of this process, their material conditions of existence, and their mutual relationships, i.e. the specific economic form of their society. For the totality of these relationships which the bearers of this production have towards nature and one another, the relationships in which they produce, is precisely society, viewed according to its economic structure" (957).

it is to the good life. As against the ideal of society as a kind of team that works together for the sake of the good life, capitalist societies will therefore tend toward dysfunction.[64] Like the badly managed institutions discussed in Chapter 6, in other words, the social division of labor will be incoherent. From a Platonic point of view, this is an important result in and of itself. But Marx's theory suggests a conclusion still more striking, for on his account capitalist institutions do not render society incoherent so much as repurpose it toward the wrong end. They make it malfunction.

35. For an ideal-typical capitalist society would in fact work as a team. If a capitalist is to earn money from labor—whether her own or someone else's—she must be able to sell her product. Let us assume for the time being that people will buy products that satisfy some need. All other things being equal, the product will therefore have to be socially useful. But this means that the labor has to be socially useful. So market discipline serves as a medium for making sure that all work takes place as part of a division of labor aimed at social needs. The division of labor therefore always sets up what Marx calls a "social labour force"—a team of laborers, in other words.[65] So far this might sound like Smith or Hayek. But Marx emphasizes that capitalism warps the social division of labor in two ways.[66]

36. To begin with, under capitalism it becomes hard for individuals to recognize that they are in fact members of a social labor force. If we imagine a family farm on some isolated prairie, there will be no question about this: individual labor power is obviously deployed only as an instrument of the joint labor power of the family, and only in the service of family needs. Even under feudal exploitation some-

---

64. We might think, for example, of the 2009 report that found that children from the United Kingdom and the United States—countries widely acknowledged be closer to ideal-typical capitalist societies than their rivals—experienced lower levels of well-being than their peers in other OECD countries. See table 2.2 in Organisation for Economic Co-operation and Development, *Doing Better for Children*, chap. 2.

65. Marx, *Capital*, vol. 1, 170–173, 201.

66. Hayek respected Marx as an economist, incidentally, praising volume 2 of *Capital* in his London School of Economics lectures during the early 1930s and calling Marx "almost in the position of Adam Smith in general economics." See Ebenstein, *Friedrich Hayek*, 227–228, and the accompanying notes.

thing similar is true: peasants understand that they are part of a social labor force organized for the benefit of their superiors. A social labor force constituted entirely by moneymakers, by contrast, will not seem to be a social labor force at all. To go back to Smith's example, the butcher, brewer, and baker do not produce for the good of society, or even for anyone in particular, but rather for personal profit. Yet the more entrenched the division of labor becomes—and markets tend to deepen it, as Smith observed—the more dependent each individual becomes on the social division of labor. The irony, then, is that we are becoming at once more and more dependent on society and more and more likely to conceive of ourselves as self-standing, independent agents: "The division of labour is an organization of production which has grown up naturally, a web which has been, and continues to be, woven behind the backs of the producers of commodities."[67] In Platonic terms, the more teamwork becomes important to our livelihoods, the harder it becomes to cognize; we may grasp it theoretically, but we no longer simply see it.

37. By itself, this would seem to be fairly innocuous: after all, if Marx is right then we are working as a team whether we recognize it or not. The problem is that our blindness to teamwork makes us blind to the nature of the team for which we are working. In theory we are becoming ever more capable of constituting a true society in which all our needs are met, "a society in which the full and free development of every individual forms the ruling principle."[68] But under capitalism the social division of labor is brought together and directed by the quasi-animate force that is capital:

> The cooperation of wage-labourers is entirely brought about by the capital that employs them. Their unification into one single productive body, and the establishment of a connection between their individual functions, lies outside their competence. These things are not their own act, but the act of the

---

67. Marx, *Capital*, vol. 1, 201; see also 170–173, 200–203, 471–472.
68. Ibid., 739.

capital that brings them together and maintains them in that situation.[69]

This means that the goal of the team is no longer to benefit its players. "The directing motive and determining purpose of capitalist production," Marx writes, "is the self-valorization of capital to the greatest possible extent."[70] Writ large, this implies that in an ideal-typical capitalist society the goal of the "combined social process"—all the activities that go to make up society—is capital accumulation rather than the good life. This is Aristotelian moneymaking on a grand scale: what should be a means has become an end in itself, and the concept of true wealth has been lost in the process. Coherence has been achieved at the price of perversity.

38. The malfunctioning of social labor under capitalism has a palpable effect on our daily lives. To see why, we must accept Marx's famous invitation to follow him down into the realm (the inferno, we might say) of production.[71] His most obvious goal is to demonstrate the exploitation inherent to capitalist production. If the *telos* of social production is to realize as much surplus value as possible, so that "the worker exists for the process of production, and not the process of production for the worker," this will entail "the greatest possible exploitation of labour-power" and hence immiseration and class conflict.[72] But in my view Marx also wants us to see something else, which has to do with what is actually produced under capitalism. Just as Marx speaks of capitalists in the precise sense, so he also speaks

---

69. Ibid., chap. 13, 449–450. Marx goes on to say that "the interconnection between [the workers'] various labours confronts them, in the realm of ideas, as a plan drawn up by the capitalist, and, in practice, as his authority, as the powerful will of a being outside them, who subjects their activity to his purpose." His point, however, is that this is simply an appearance: although the capitalist seems to be the one directing things, he is just the agent of capital. Obviously this refers to the ideal-typical case rather than real-world cases.

70. Ibid., chap. 13, 449.

71. See Roberts, *Marx's Inferno*.

72. Marx, *Capital*, vol. 1, chap. 13, 449, and chap. 15, 621. See also chap. 12, 436–437: "Capital . . . has an immanent drive, and a constant tendency, towards increasing the productivity of labour, in order to cheapen commodities and, by cheapening commodities, to cheapen the worker himself." For the core of Marx's account of exploitation, see chaps. 7–12.

of their products—commodities—in the precise sense. To a capitalist, the specific purpose that her product serves, its use value, is immaterial. If it were possible go from M to M^1 without passing through C, she would.[73] But this changes the ontology of the product for Marx, since he retains the Platonic-Aristotelian idea that the being of a craft object depends on its form and function.[74] As Aristotle puts it, a shoe comes into existence for the sake of protecting feet. This function determines what the shoe is: to use a shoe as a shoe is to wear it.[75] And the shoemaker will obviously bear this in mind when making his product: the parts—leather, laces, soles, etc.—will be organized toward the end of satisfying the human need for foot protection. Even if on the marketplace it appears as an exchange value, that is, as worth half a pillow or ten dollars, the product is at bottom a good or a use value. It would not be what it is if its form and function were different. In capitalism, on the other hand, commodities come into being for the sake of augmenting a stock of capital, and their form is dependent on that function. Even if it has to appear as a use value to attract a buyer, a commodity is at bottom an exchange value. The standards of success that guide its production are those of profit, not use. Only as such does it become a commodity in the precise sense.[76]

---

73. Marx thinks M-M^1 is the form of finance capital, but he insists that finance capital is logically secondary to productive capital, since for him real value can be added only in the labor process. See *Capital*, vol. 1, chap. 5, 267.

74. See Marx's account of the labor process: "[The worker] sets in motion the natural forces which belong to his own body, his arms, legs, head and hands, in order to appropriate the materials of nature in a form adapted to his own needs. . . . At the end of every labour process, a result emerges which had already been conceived by the worker at the beginning, hence already existed ideally. Man not only effects a change of form in the materials of nature; he also realizes [*verwirklicht*] his own purpose in those materials" (*Capital*, vol. 1, 283–284).

75. Aristotle, *Politics* I.9, 1257a.

76. See especially Marx, *Capital*, vol. 1, 148–154. It is perhaps unfortunate that Marx does not give us a different term for the simple-exchange form of commodity, where the use-value dimension is dominant. In my explication I have simplified by equating "exchange value" and what Marx calls "value": strictly speaking, exchange value is a surface phenomenon that both expresses and veils a deeper dimension, "value," where that amounts to what we might call "labor-time value." So the two dimensions are not in fact use value and exchange value but use value and labor-time value. But although this complication is crucial for understanding many aspects of

39. So a commodity in the precise sense is essentially an exchange value and only accidentally a use value or a good: it comes into being for the sake of augmenting a stock of capital, not for the sake of satisfying a human need. But this ontological shift is not simply a reversal of priority between the two dimensions. When exchange value becomes the dominant dimension of an object, this shapes its use value (or qualitative character) as well.[77] As we saw earlier, a commodity must be marketable if it is to serve the purpose of augmenting capital. This means it must at least appear to be a good, whether by satisfying needs or by creating them.[78] But a commodity is not defective qua commodity if it fails to satisfy any real needs, so long as it finds a buyer. This is not to say that a commodity will never satisfy real needs, nor that a craft product will necessarily do so.[79] The point is simply that a commodity in the precise sense does not, at base, even aim at being a real good. At the same time, it must endeavor to appear as one. A commodity in the precise sense therefore masquerades as a real good. This logic will influence choices concerning both material and form during the production process, and over the course of time those choices will influence the nature of the product. An extreme manifestation of this logic is "planned obsolescence," whereby consumer demand is maintained by deliberately designing products to fail after a certain period. This is just a specific instance of the general phenomenon of products being designed to make a sale rather than to meet social needs.

40. If Plato is right that human flourishing depends on goods that we can access only through cooperation, then the logic of produc-

---

Capital, including the notion of exploitation as the extraction of "surplus value," it only serves to cloud the aspect that I am bringing out here.

77. See the preceding note: technically I should be speaking of the "value" dimension, where that means "labor-time value" rather than the "exchange-value" dimension. But while this is relevant for Marx's economics, the complexity it introduces is likely to obscure the point concerning the teleological ontology of a commodity.

78. On want creation in capitalism, see Marx, *Capital*, vol. 1, 201: "Perhaps the commodity is the product of a new kind of labour, and claims to satisfy a newly arisen need, or is even trying to bring forth a new need on its own account."

79. As we saw earlier in this chapter, Aristotle points out that "the products of a craft determine by their own qualities whether they have been produced well." See *Nicomachean Ethics* II.4.

tion under capitalism ought to be of serious concern to us. As we saw in Chapter 3, the *Republic* offers an extraordinarily rich way of thinking about what social production would ideally entail. Socrates suggests that each of our artefacts builds in and therefore communicates a vision of human life. From statues and temples to couches and chairs, we are surrounded by what Sally Haslanger calls "schematically structured and practice-imbued material things"—items, that is, that both encode a way of looking at the world and provide us with scripts for interacting with one another, making it hard to think or act differently.[80] These objects influence us imperceptibly from childhood onward, molding the beliefs and desires of our plastic psyches. It follows that we are in a cave of our own creation. In producing our material world, we produce ourselves. (As Marx puts it, man "acts upon external nature and changes it, and in this way he simultaneously changes his own nature.")[81] This is why Socrates thinks it so important to ensure that craftsmen do not "represent—whether in pictures, buildings, or any other works—a character that is vicious, unrestrained, slavish, and graceless" (400e–401b). If craftsmen can be brought to produce in the right way, the cultural environment will transmit true beliefs about what counts as just, beautiful, and good. As a result, Socrates says, "our young people will live in a healthy place and be benefited on all sides as the influence exerted by those fine works affects their eyes and ears like a healthy breeze from wholesome regions, and imperceptibly guides them from earliest childhood into being similar to, friendly toward, and concordant with the beauty of reason" (401c–d). The ideal is of an utterly coherent social order that reinforces itself by orienting citizens toward the good and the true at every step—a beautiful city, as Socrates calls it. In Chapter 6 we saw that this ideal need not be illiberal, since citizens can in principle serve as stewards of the social environment without further supervision. This would entail each citizen forming a conception of the good life and how their works could best promote it, given their skills and the needs of the present situation, and then carrying out the tasks in question. No doubt a

---

80. Haslanger, "But Mom, Crop-Tops Are Cute!," 417.
81. Marx, *Capital*, vol. 1, 283.

certain amount of dysfunction would result, given divergent conceptions of the good life and so on. But philosophical citizenship would still bring society closer to the ideal, no matter how incrementally. As a result, I argued, it ought to be part of the ideal of liberal democracy. Under the ideal-typical capitalism described by Marx, however, philosophical citizenship becomes impossible since the goal at which labor aims is settled from the start. All our labors are disciplined via the impersonal medium of market forces toward ongoing capital accumulation. And the product of those labors, as we have just seen, will satisfy social needs only accidentally. If a certain style of advertising is suspected to increase rates of anxiety, for instance, that will not be allowed to affect workplace deliberations unless it would also affect the bottom line. The result is that our cultural environment is beyond anyone's control. It is not anarchic in the manner of Socrates' caricature of democracy, but rather governed by an underlying logic tied to the imperatives of capital accumulation. If ruling is a matter of shaping souls, as Plato thought, then the implication is clear. In a capitalist society we are not ruled by poets or philosophers—we are ruled by capital.[82]

§3 Ideal and Critical Theory

41. The characterization of certain societies as malfunctioning makes sense only against the background of an ideal of a well-functioning society, such as Plato's ideal of a coherent division of labor aimed at fostering the good life.[83] Yet Marx was notoriously reluctant to engage in any kind of ideal theory. It was pointless to

---

82. This is not to deny that from perspective of Plato's psychology the results of rule by capital might be similar to the results of democratic rule: the growth of unnecessary and lawless appetites. Nor is it to assert that capitalist culture will generally tend to serve capitalist interests, as certain explanatory functionalist accounts might have it. Given that there is no agent "controlling for" any particular cultural result, the imperatives of capitalist production might just as well end up contributing to the creation of a culture that actually undermines capital accumulation. For a hypothesis of this kind, see Bell, *Cultural Contradictions of Capitalism*, 33–84. On the extent to which the commodity form shapes every aspect of capitalist society, meanwhile, the classic account is Lukács, *History and Class Consciousness*.

83. Compare the notion of a functional society in Tawney's *Acquisitive Society*.

offer "recipes for the cook-shops of the future," he thought, when a new form of production could come about only through the unfolding of contradictions immanent in the present.[84] "We do not attempt dogmatically to prefigure the future," Marx wrote in an 1844 letter to Arnold Ruge, "but want to find the new world only through criticism of the old. . . . We develop new principles to the world out of its own principles."[85]

42. The approach sketched in the letter to Ruge has come to be known as "critical theory." Like "capitalism" and "neoliberalism," this is a term whose usage can be so loose as to provoke weary skepticism but that nevertheless remains indispensable. Nancy Fraser uses it to refer to any social theory that "frames its research program and conceptual framework with an eye to the aims and activities of those oppositional social movements with which it has a partisan though not uncritical identification."[86] The trouble with this definition is that it must either cover too much to be of any use—should the motivated reasoning of the Klu Klux Klan count as critical theory?—or restrict the category of "oppositional social movements" to groups whose goals are desirable by the standards of an independently derived normative theory. The latter account surely fails to capture Marxian critical theory, since Marx followed Hegel in viewing self-standing normative theory as "one-sided and empty ratiocination." If a theory "builds itself a world *as it ought to be*," Hegel wrote, "then it certainly has an existence, but only within [the theorist's] opinions—a pliant medium in which the imagination can construct anything it pleases."[87] The only way to make respectable normative claims, Hegel thought, was to derive them from the logic of

---

84. For the "cook-shops" remark, see the postface to the 2nd German edition, translated by Ben Fowkes, of volume 1 of *Capital*, 99. For the view more generally, see the whole of vol. 1, chapter 32, as well as vol. 1, chapter 45, 619: "The development of the contradictions of a given historical form of production is the only historical way in which it can be dissolved and then reconstructed on a new basis."

85. Tucker, *Marx-Engels Reader*, 12–14. The text was an open letter, published in the journal that Marx and Ruge coedited.

86. Fraser, "What's Critical about Critical Theory?," 97. Sally Haslanger quotes Fraser in the preface to her *Critical Theory and Practice* and adds, "I think of critical theory as asking questions that are important for bringing about social justice in a particular time and place" (8).

87. Hegel, *Elements of the Philosophy of Right*, 20–22.

contemporary social practices so that the resulting theory could be at once normative and descriptive. So although Marxian critical theory is indeed supposed to be a form of political action, as Fraser suggests, both the theory and the action are somehow supposed to involve nothing more than grasping the nature of existing practices. Whether this is truly possible is another matter, but to understand the idea it helps to view critical theory as a species of immanent critique.

43. What I mean by immanent critique is a mode of argument in which a given standpoint is shown to fail with respect to its own standards—to give an obvious example, a Founding Father who affirms both that racist laws are justified and that "all men were born equal" might be hoist by his own petard. The great advantage of immanent critique is that there is no need to bring in normative standards from the outside, since the reasons given by the critic are always "internal" in the sense made famous by Bernard Williams—there is no question, that is, of how they could get a grip on the person being criticized, since the person in question already subscribes to them in one form or another.[88] As a result, immanent critique is often thought to be politically efficacious.[89]

44. What differentiates critical theory from other forms of immanent critique is that it takes as its object not individual viewpoints but whole forms of life. A form of life can be said to be contradictory if its constitutive elements create pressures in one direction while simultaneously closing them off, as in Hegel's picture of classical Athens as riven by tension between the individualism fostered by its democratic institutions and the collectivist ethos those institutions presumed.[90] Hegel's critical theory takes the past as its object—"The owl of Minerva begins its flight only at the onset of dusk"—but Marx, like other so-called Young Hegelians, believed that the present can and should be the object of critique. As Marx puts it in the letter to Ruge, "If the designing of the future and the

---

88. Williams, "Internal and External Reasons," reprinted in *Moral Luck*, 101–113.

89. See, e.g., Walzer, *Interpretation and Social Criticism*, chap. 2.

90. See Hegel, *Lectures on the Philosophy of History*, pt. 2; and Hegel, *Lectures on the History of Philosophy*, vol. 1, *Greek Philosophy to Plato*.

proclamation of ready-made solutions for all time is not our affair, then we realize all the more clearly what we have to accomplish in the present—I am speaking of a *ruthless criticism of everything existing.*"[91] In revealing the incoherence of a social order that throws up possibilities that it must then suppress in order to survive, critical theory liberates us from ideological illusions concerning the impossibility of meaningful change.[92] But it does so without invoking any kind of external standard. A future that transcends the present is simply one in which the existing society lives up to its own manifest potential. In Marx's formulation, "it will transpire that mankind begins no *new* work, but consciously accomplishes its old work."[93]

45. The obvious weakness of critical theory so sketched is that it gives us no way of judging which of the many possibilities inherent in the present ought to be embraced. Unless we simply assume that whatever is newest is best—an assumption that even those who subscribe to progressive theories of history would have good reason to reject—we seem to need some kind of normative standard with respect to which we can judge certain possibilities better than others.[94] So the question is whether critical theory can really do without normative theory.

46. In the letter to Ruge, Marx assumed a quasi-Hegelian ideal of objective rationality as his normative standard:

---

91. Tucker, *Marx-Engels Reader*, 13.

92. In this vein, Geuss, *Idea of a Critical Theory*, 2, defines a critical theory as "a reflective theory which gives agents a kind of knowledge inherently productive of enlightenment and emancipation." On the emancipatory ambitions of critical theory, see also Horkheimer, "Traditional and Critical Theory," in *Critical Theory*, 188–243.

93. Tucker, *Marx-Engels Reader*, 15. Clearly this account does not do justice to all that goes under the name of "critical theory" even within the Marxist tradition—Habermas's theory has a different shape, for instance, as do those of Adorno and Horkheimer from the *Dialectic of Enlightenment* onward. For an argument about why the Frankfurt school moved away from the model I have described, see Postone, *Time, Labor, and Social Domination*, chap. 3.

94. As Herbert Marcuse writes in the introduction to *One-Dimensional Man*, "Certainly value judgments play a part. The established way of organizing society is measured against other possible ways, ways which are held to offer better chances for alleviating man's struggle for existence; a specific historical practice is measured against its own historical alternatives" (xlii).

Reason has always existed, only not always in reasonable form. The critic can therefore start out by taking any form of theoretical and practical consciousness and develop from the *unique* forms of existing reality the true reality as its norm and final goal. . . . The state everywhere presupposes that reason has been realized. But in just this way it everywhere comes into contradiction between its ideal mission and its real preconditions.[95]

Whether and to what degree Marx continued to endorse this ideal of "realizing reason" is open to debate. What is clear, though, is that he frequently adverted to some kind of ideal, even in his later works. In volume 1 of *Capital*, for instance, he asks us to "imagine, for a change, an association of free men, working with the means of production held in common, and expending their many different forms of labour-power in full self-awareness as one single social labour force."[96] When he turns to the goals of that social labor force in volume 3, he suggests that they consist in achieving two kinds of freedom. First we must achieve freedom from natural necessity, which requires that "the associated producers govern the human metabolism [or exchange] with nature in a rational way, bringing it under their collective control instead of being dominated by it as a blind power; accomplishing it with the least expenditure of energy and in conditions most worthy and appropriate for their human nature."[97] Then, once our natural needs have been met, we can turn to "the true realm of freedom," which consists in "the development of human powers as an end in itself."[98]

---

95. Tucker, *Marx-Engels Reader*, 14.
96. Marx, *Capital*, vol. 1, chap. 1, 171. Marx goes on to say that "the veil is not removed from the countenance of the social life-process, i.e. the process of material production, until it becomes production by freely associated men, and stands under their conscious and planned control" (173), which strongly suggests a Hegelian ideal of realizing reason.
97. Marx, *Capital*, vol. 3, 958–959.
98. Ibid., 959. This chimes with Marx's youthful claim, while commenting on James Mill, that "the ideal relationship to the respective objects of our production is, of course, our mutual need," along with his characterization of that need in terms of the development and actualization of our natural powers in the 1844 manuscripts. See *Comments on James Mill*, 17; and Tucker, *Marx-Engels Reader*, 85–93. In the *Critique of the Gotha Program*, meanwhile, Marx speaks of communism as changing the structure

47. Marx was certainly coy about this ideal. When he speaks of the emerging possibility of "a society in which the full and free development of every individual forms the ruling principle"—its *archē*, Plato might say, the goal that unifies its various activities— he adopts the tone of a natural scientist dispassionately observing the transition of a living being into "a higher form."[99] But that only raises the question of what makes one form of society higher than another. Marx might point to the dialectic posited by historical materialism, according to which the constitutive contradictions of one form of society call forth the creation of a new, and therefore higher, form.[100] But to insist that this exhausts the content of the term "higher" would surely be bad faith, since Marx clearly welcomed the future he predicted. To explain why, we need to refer to his vision of a society that brings about the good life for all.

48. Marx's vision of a well-functioning society has much in common with Plato's. Both conceive of society as produced through our daily actions, so that labor becomes crucial to political theory, and both think that labor should be consciously directed toward the common good by a central authority.[101] As to what that good consists in, meanwhile, both propose a two-stage answer whereby the primary purpose of society is to satisfy our basic need for self-reproduction, but its ultimate purpose is to enable us to realize our natures. There are important differences in how they conceive of self-realization, of course. Marx's picture of human psychology is fundamentally egalitarian and this leads him to reject the "monopoli-

---

of work so that labor becomes "not only a means of life but life's prime want," with the reuniting of mental and physical labor leading to the "all-round development of the individual" and "all the springs of cooperative wealth [flowing] more abundantly" so that individual needs can all be satisfied. Tucker, *Marx-Engels Reader*, 531.

99. Marx, *Capital*, vol. 1, 739.

100. For a stimulating (if ultimately misleading) treatment of this theory, see Cohen, *Karl Marx's Theory of History*.

101. See Marx, *Capital*, vol. 1, chap. 13: "All directly social or communal labour on a large scale requires, to a greater or lesser degree, a directing authority, in order to secure the harmonious co-operation of the activities of individuals, and to perform the general functions that have their origin in the motion of the total productive organism, as distinguished from the motion of its separate organs. A single violin player is his own conductor: an orchestra requires a separate one" (448–449).

zation of social development (including its material and intellectual advantages) by one section of society at the expense of another."[102] Plato, by contrast, sorts people into three kinds, with some having a greater potential for intellectual development than others, if not necessarily a greater claim on material resources. Relatedly, perhaps, Marx seems to conceive of the development of human capacities as potentially infinite, such that it can constitute "the true realm of freedom," whereas Plato seems to think of human capacities as finite in the way that animal capacities are finite; for Plato our labors should therefore aim to create an environment that fosters human health, whereas for Marx they should aim to create a *"humanized* nature" through which we can recognize ourselves as free.[103] Another important difference concerns the division of labor: Plato suggests that citizens should stick to the job in which they can best serve social needs, whereas Marx (following Smith) suggests that human flourishing requires individuals to pursue a variety of occupations.[104] But although Marx certainly deplores the kind of division of labor that leads to the "development in a man of one single faculty at the expense of all others," he never denies that different people should occupy different roles for the sake of carrying out a particular task. Indeed, the element of the capitalist mode of production that he thinks will be preserved in the transition to communism is precisely its achievement

---

102. Marx, *Capital*, vol. 3, 958.

103. Marx, *Economic and Philosophical Manuscripts of 1844*, 89. Marx's emphasis on our freedom and our (supposedly) never-ending capacity for development clearly reflects his inheritance from Rousseau and the German Romantics, not to mention Hegel, but that is too large a theme to explore here.

104. Marx and Engels state this point in a particularly exaggerated way in *The German Ideology*, lamenting that "as soon as the distribution of labour comes into being, each man has a particular, exclusive sphere of activity, which is forced upon him and from which he cannot escape" and advocating a society in which "nobody has one exclusive sphere of activity but each can become accomplished in any branch he wishes," so that it is possible for me "to hunt in the morning, fish in the afternoon, rear cattle in the evening, criticise after dinner, just as I have a mind, without ever becoming hunter, fisherman, shepherd or critic" (160). In *Capital* Marx writes, more soberly, that "some crippling of body and mind is inseparable even from the division of labour in society as a whole" (vol. 1, chap. 14, 484). From the interpretation of the *Republic* that I developed in Chapter 2, the tasks required of citizens in Kallipolis may in fact change during the course of their lives, since philosopher-rulers have to adapt the division of labor in light of changing circumstances. The point is just that Plato does not see such change as representing any kind of good in itself.

of society-wide cooperation or "the socialization of labour."[105] Hence there is a level of description at which the Marxian ideal and the Platonic ideal have a common structure.

49. The ideals also illuminate and bolster each other. To begin with, Marx is surely right that challenging and varied work is part of the good life, so that entrenched specialization impoverishes us. This insight can be incorporated into the Platonic conception relatively easily, as can the egalitarian proposition that each member of society has an interest in developing their intellectual capacities. For as we saw in Chapter 6, the Platonic ideal can survive a certain amount of surgery while retaining its core claim regarding the need for philosophical governance. If freedom of occupation is sacrosanct, for instance, then individuals can be asked to orient their own labors. Likewise, if the good life involves exercising our intellectual capacities in the course of our daily labors then that fact should affect citizens' deliberations concerning the common good: each of us should try to bring about a social world in which work is stimulating and enriching for everybody.[106] So the Marxian ideal can enrich political Platonism in fairly obvious ways.

50. But the Platonic ideal can also breathe life into Marxian theory. For although Marx clearly had an ideal in mind, he failed to argue for it as such. This might have been because he thought the situation obvious from an evaluative point of view, or because he viewed normative argument as unscientific, or because he was trapped by his claims regarding the nature of ideology.[107] Whatever his reasoning,

---

105. See Marx, *Capital*, vol. 1, chap. 14, 474, and chap. 32, 929. I take Marx's considered view on the division of labor to be expressed in chapter 15, 618: "That monstrosity, the disposable working population held in reserve, in misery, for the changing requirements of capitalist exploitation, must be replaced by the individual man who is absolutely available for the different kinds of labour required of him; the partially developed individual, who is merely the bearer of one specialized social function, must be replaced by the totally developed individual, for whom the different social functions are different modes of activity he takes up in turn."

106. For powerful arguments to this effect, see Ruskin, "The Nature of Gothic," in *Unto This Last and Other Writings*, 84–88, and Morris, "Useful Work *versus* Useless Toil," in *News from Nowhere and Other Writings*, 296–305.

107. For a helpful overview of the long and involved debate regarding whether Marx thought capitalism unjust, for instance, see Geras, "Controversy about Marx and Justice." On ideology, see Michael Rosen, *On Voluntary Servitude.*

Marx's reticence on normative matters encouraged the impression that there are no standards with respect to which capitalist societies can be better or worse, which is surely false. Worse still, it allowed him to duck vital questions regarding the relative importance of freedom of occupation and social cohesion—questions that proved to be extremely important for twentieth-century attempts to realize his ideal. But it also prevented him from developing anything as sophisticated as Plato's vision of a harmonious social order permeated by models that convey true beliefs about the good life. And this in turn made him blind to the possibility of using an ideal to shift the social imaginary and thereby alter the political landscape.[108]

---

108. In particular, Marx never saw fit to publish his most philosophically sophisticated ideal, namely that found in the *Economic and Philosophical Manuscripts of 1844*, where he invites the reader to imagine a society in which production is no longer alienated, so that "*society* is the consummated oneness in substance of man and nature—the true resurrection of nature—the naturalism of man and the humanism of nature both brought to fulfilment" (85). His point is that production has the capacity to transform the world so that we can see our collective will expressed in it and therefore overcome the subject-object split that haunted Hegel: "man is not lost in his object only when the object becomes for him a *human* object or objective man. This is possible only when the object becomes for him a *social* object, he himself for himself a social being, just as society becomes a being for him in this object" (88). The result of such self-conscious (and hence free) transformation of nature, Marx claims, would be a steady transformation (and liberation) of the human senses into organs for appreciating the beauty and wealth of the world: "Only through the objectively unfolded richness of man's essential being is the richness of subjective *human* sensibility (a musical ear, an eye for beauty of form—in short, *sense* capable of human gratifications, senses confirming themselves as essential powers of *man*) either cultivated or brought into being. For not only the five senses but also the so-called mental senses—the practical senses (will, love, etc.)—in a word, *human* sense—the humanness of the senses—comes to be by virtue of its object, by virtue of *humanized* nature. The *forming* of the five senses is the labour of the entire history of the world down to the present. . . . The care-burdened man in need has no sense for the finest play; the dealer in minerals sees only the mercantile value but not the beauty and unique nature of the mineral: he has no mineralogical sense. Thus, the objectification of the human essence both in its theoretical and practical aspects is required to make man's *sense human*, as well as to create the *human sense* corresponding to the entire wealth of human and natural substance" (88–89). This passage gives the lie to Hannah Arendt's claim that "the question of a separate existence of worldly things, whose durability will survive and withstand the devouring processes of life, does not occur to [Marx] at all" (*Human Condition*, 108), since it leaves us in no doubt that Marx was intrigued by the way in which human activity can produce a world of durable objects that manifest our wills and reflect them back to us. Indeed, we might fruitfully compare

51. As we saw in Chapter 4, Plato's ideal theory has a political purpose: in inviting Athenians to admire Kallipolis, he was also inviting them to see their city as alien and perverse, and hence to undergo a kind of internal emigration. Such emphasis on the political imagination need not be alien to critical theory. In fact, it ought to be the natural corollary of Marxian ideology critique, as Antonio Gramsci seems to have understood. If capitalist societies maintain themselves in part via institutions such as schools, churches, and newspapers that shape commonsense beliefs concerning what is natural, possible, and desirable, Gramsci thought, then what is needed is a "war of position" in which militants gradually advance a new form of common sense.[109] It seems plausible to suppose that visions of the best possible society can play an important role in such a war. Nor is this their only function. For aside from influencing our tacit presuppositions concerning what is natural, possible, and desirable, ideals can also serve to make salient certain possibilities or potentialities that might otherwise have gone unnoticed, as Herbert Marcuse saw:

> In a situation where such a future [one in which genuine needs and wants are fulfilled] is a real possibility, fantasy is an important instrument in the task of continually holding the goal up to view. . . . Without fantasy, all philosophical knowledge remains in the grip of the present or the past and severed from

---

Marx's vision of social production as training the human senses in beauty with Plato's vision of social production as creating a beautiful city that trains prospective guardians. (Thanks to Noah Chafets for this suggetsion.) Yet Marx does not seem to reflect on the implications of this theory for his own political practice in the way that Plato does (according to the interpretation I gave in Chapter 4): although the Manifesto's glorious evocation of capitalist achievements (475–477) does seem designed to produce a feeling of wonder at mankind's collective capacities, for the most part Marx does not seem to recognize the power of ideals to change the social imaginary and hence to affect political life—otherwise he might have seen the value in publishing and propagating the vision of a beautiful city that we find in the manuscripts. For more on self-realization in the early Marx, see Brudney, *Marx's Attempt to Leave Philosophy*, 143–168, and Leopold, *The Young Karl Marx*, 223–245.

109. See Gramsci, "The Intellectuals," "On Education," and "State and Civil Society," in *Selections from the Prison Notebooks*, 5–23, 26–43, 210–276.

the future, which is the only link between philosophy and the real history of mankind.[110]

Not all ideals can play such a role, of course. As Marcuse emphasizes, for an ideal to have the right kind of traction it must be in some way real or actual: "Like philosophy, [critical theory] opposes making reality into a criterion in the manner of complacent positivism. But unlike philosophy, it always derives its goals only from the present tendencies of the social process."[111] What it means for possibilities to be inherent in the present, on Marcuse's view, is for them to be "within the reach of the respective society" and hence "definable goals of practice." They must be "historical alternatives which haunt the established society as subversive tendencies and forces."[112]

52. No one could plausibly claim that the ideal of Kallipolis haunts contemporary society as a subversive tendency or force. But in my view the ideal according to which citizens should be idealists, reasoning about how their work and their institutions might fit into a coherent whole that aims at promoting the good life, is in fact fairly widespread in contemporary culture. To see this, we can turn to an example that is about as commonplace as they come: the way we talk about the media.

53. More than a quarter of a century after Noam Chomsky and Edward Herman published *Manufacturing Consent*, it is now fairly banal, and even rather tiresome, to bemoan the corruption of American media organizations—those organizations even make the complaint themselves, as in Fox News's endless laments about "the mainstream media."[113] It is nevertheless worth thinking through what the modern media look like from the perspective of the ideal of philosopher-citizens. On the Platonic picture of a functional society, a television news producer would have to think about how her show could best contribute to the good of society, and how its dif-

---

110. Marcuse, "Philosophy and Critical Theory," 71. I take it that Marcuse is using "fantasy" in the Germanic sense "imagination," and that the term is therefore neutral rather than pejorative.

111. Ibid., 64.

112. Marcuse, *One-Dimensional Man*, xliii–xliv.

113. See Herman and Chomsky, *Manufacturing Consent*.

ferent parts could help it make that contribution.[114] Assume the producer is committed to democracy. In the course of her reflections, she might hit on the theory that her show should foster democratic discussion by providing accurate information and invigorating debate. As Thomas Jefferson once wrote, "Whenever the people are well-informed, they can be trusted with their own government."[115] If the antecedent does not hold, Jefferson implies, democracy is dangerous. So the producer's activity would be guided by an ideal of her institution's place in society. This ideal would generate standards of success and failure for her activity: if research showed that regular viewers remained ill informed, for example, she would take herself as having failed and review her decisions accordingly.

54. Obviously this is not the way news organs typically work in America: the principal goal of most large news organizations is to secure greater market share and hence to reward investors (whether shareholders or banks). A vivid example comes from Michael Mann's 1999 film *The Insider*.[116] Based on a true story, *The Insider* ostensibly concerns Jeffrey Wigand (Russell Crowe), a tobacco-industry research scientist who is encouraged to blow the whistle on his company by Lowell Bergman (Al Pacino), a producer for CBS's *60 Minutes*. By itself, this story line is not particularly enthralling: it doesn't come as much of a surprise that tobacco companies try to get customers addicted, or even that they try to silence dissenting voices.[117] What makes the film of enduring interest—beyond the acting and cinematography—is what seems at first to be the subplot, namely the story of how Lowell Bergman becomes a whistle-blower against CBS when it refuses to air his story on dubious grounds. (CBS executives

---

114. Rachel Barney also points to contemporary journalism as a place where Socrates' conception of craftsmanship still does battle with a Thrasymachean one (as she calls it). See Barney, "Socrates' Refutation of Thrasymachus," 50–51.

115. Thomas Jefferson, letter to Richard Price, January 8, 1789, in the Library of Congress online collection, http://www.loc.gov/exhibits/jefferson/60.html.

116. I focus on the film rather than the (true) story on which it is based because Mann is able to bring out a structure that I wish to highlight.

117. Having said that, Wigand does provide some interesting remarks on the gap between the true ontology of a cigarette and the way its users think of it. In reality, he thinks, the essence of a cigarette is specified by its function as a "delivery device for nicotine" and hence, we might say, as a means for augmenting a stock of capital.

claim to fear a "tortious interference" lawsuit, but it seems that what they really fear is the disruption of a takeover bid that would enrich them personally; another factor is that the largest shareholder also owns a tobacco company.) So there are in fact two "insiders" in the film, Wigand and Bergman, their respective resignations made parallel.[118] By titling his film *The Insider* rather than *The Insiders*, Mann sets up a surprise for his viewer. But he also suggests that the film deals with a type, namely the professional who insists on being professional in the face of institutional malfunction.

55. This focus on professionalism or craftsmanship allows Mann to explore some of his characteristic themes, such as the tension between male friendship, whose primal site he tends to picture as a team of risk takers, and the almost purposeless domesticity of family life. But it also allows him to explore what happens when the obverse of professionalism or craftsmanship becomes institutionalized. Early in the film, when Wigand asks Bergman, "Am I just a commodity to you?" Bergman takes the position I have been ascribing to Smith and his followers: "We're all commodities to CBS, but people listen."[119] In other words, it might be true that a given product, such as a news program, is produced for the sake of exchange value or capital and is therefore a commodity in the precise sense—but this does not matter, since the marketplace ensures that the production of exchange value will necessarily be tethered to the production of a use value or good such as information and debate. The intellectual drama of *The Insider* consists of Bergman changing his mind on this question. Toward the end, Bergman and Mike Wallace, the *60 Minutes* anchor played by Christopher Plummer, trade gibes with each other and their bosses concerning the distinction between moneymaking and genuine craft: "C'mon, what are you? Are you a businessman? Or are you a newsman?"; "These people [CBS execs] are putting our whole reason

---

118. Visually speaking, Mann suggests this parallel through the lighting, framing, and mise-en-scène as Wigand and Bergman leave their respective corporate buildings at the beginning and end of the film; these shots bookend the film, after the prologue at least.

119. There is no denying that Mann's dialogue can be clichéd and trite, as if the lines were placeholders awaiting transformation in a later draft of the script. But for my purposes the crudity can be useful.

for doing what we do on the line!"; "We work in the same corporation. Doesn't mean we work in the same profession." If these out-
bursts are clunky from an aesthetic perspective, it is because they
seem to have been scripted expressly to illustrate a Platonic point
about craftsmen and moneymakers. The plot as a whole, meanwhile,
seems to have been designed to illustrate the way in which the logic
of capital—$M\text{-}C\text{-}M^1$ rather than $C\text{-}M\text{-}C^1$—can lead institutions to
malfunction.

56. The idea that corporations can be criticized for preventing professionals from doing their jobs will be new to no one, yet it clearly
implies that the norm should be a situation in which citizens and institutions work for the common good. The ideal of philosophical
citizenship, according to which citizens should reflect on how their
work fits together with that of other citizens to bring about the
common good, is simply a natural outgrowth of this commonplace
thought, as is the ideal of philosophical governance more broadly.
One might even call these ideals obvious. What gives them their
critical force is simply the regularity with which the world flouts them.
Where malfunction has come to be expected, Platonic demands will
seem radical.[120]

57. By the same token, however, it must also be said that a society
in which this kind of critique is commonplace cannot be malfunctioning uniformly or completely. For as Marx suggests in the third
of his theses on Feuerbach, critique always has its roots in actual
social forces: "The materialist doctrine concerning the changing of
circumstances and upbringing forgets that circumstances are
changed by men and that it is essential to educate the educator himself. This doctrine must, therefore, divide society into two parts, one
of which is superior to society."[121] In this passage Marx is objecting
to those who assert that humans are shaped by social circumstances

---

120. Compare one of Wittgenstein's most enduring insights, that one can stray
into confusion by removing a particular concept from the context (or "language
game") within which it finds its natural home. At some level this ought to be obvious.
What gives this observation its critical force is simply our perpetual tendency to
commit the error of which Wittgenstein speaks. See, e.g., *Philosophical Investigations*,
§116.

121. Marx, *Theses on Feurbach*, 144.

without stopping to ask about the ways in which they themselves have been shaped by society. The implication is that any social critique worth its salt ought to be able to explain its own provenance. If a theorist claims that her society shapes people into one-dimensional conformism, for example, how can she explain her own views? Is she "superior to society," as Marx puts it? More likely, surely, is that her society is not unitary or one-dimensional but rather contradictory. The critique is thrown up, as it were, by the society itself. Where there is widespread critique of social malfunction, in other words, there must also be some space, however small, that is still governed by the ideal of a functional society.[122]

58. Consider *The Insider* again. The crucial moments occur when first Bergman and then Wallace recognize that their duties as craftsmen conflict with their bosses' duties as moneymakers, and that it is their bosses who truly represent the essence of the company.[123]

---

122. Where the critical standpoint comes from under capitalism has been the subject of much debate in the Marxist tradition. At the abstract level, there are two types of answers. The first suggests that capitalism produces new potentialities that it simultaneously closes off, and that critical theorists speak from the perspective of those potentialities. We saw earlier, for example, that in Marx's account, capitalism increases the productive forces of society by deepening the division of labor and hence constituting an ever more global "social labor force." We are now an incredibly powerful team, with a wealth of accumulated technical knowledge and a multitude of talents. We therefore have the potential to turn our labors to the common good and hence constitute "a higher form of society, a society in which the full and free development of every individual forms the ruling principle," as Marx puts it in *Capital*, vol. 1, 739, and we can criticize present arrangements from the perspective of this potential. (In Moishe Postone's version of this argument, the potential is specifically related to the possibility of reducing labor time as the productive forces develop. See *Time, Labor, and Social Domination*, 307–384.) A critical standpoint might also be found in something less historically specific, however, such as the potentialities perennially thrown up by human nature. It might be, for instance, that because humans need society in order to realize the good life, functional organization along Platonic lines will always be a natural ideal for us, no matter how hard it is to realize. (It seems to me that those who emphasize Marx's Aristotelian inheritance above his Hegelian one will be more inclined to accept this latter kind of explanation, although it is possible, of course, to read Hegel along Aristotelian lines as well.) Whichever of these theories is correct, the crucial point on a more concrete level is that the critical standpoint must have some roots in present practice.

123. One might object that the corporate executives depicted in *The Insider* were out for their own gain in a one-off trade rather than exemplifying anything about capitalism in general. But the quotations above signal that Mann means to raise that more general question. The executives might just as well have been acting on behalf of

But the fact that this comes as a shock to Bergman and Wallace—or at least that they can convince themselves that it does—shows that CBS News had done a pretty good job of masquerading as a genuine news organization until that point. And the fact that the two of them were part of the corporation in the first place shows that this masquerade involved hiring some genuine craftsmen. As long as masquerade is still necessary, the logic of capitalism cannot be completely hegemonic. To put it another way, we must be in a mixed society rather than an ideal-typical one.

59. If this is right, then the ideal of philosophical citizenship satisfies Marcuse's criteria for a normative contribution to critical theory. Rather than being an empty ideal applied to actuality from the outside, it is grounded in possibilities that are inherent in the present—"historical alternatives which haunt the established society as subversive tendencies and forces." Its real bases are existing practices whereby individuals already exercise the virtues of justice and wisdom in their workplace deliberations. These might represent holdovers from some earlier form of economic organization, but they might also represent new possibilities thrown up by capitalism itself—it might be that service economies are particularly conducive to the notion of work as service, for instance, or that the march of automation naturally provokes people to ask what their work is for.[124] Whatever the case, the ideal of philosophical citizenship makes these practices of craftsmanship salient as objects of political struggle. To use Marcuse's terms, the "definable goals of practice" that are

---

their shareholders, in which case on some level they would simply have been doing their jobs. That points to the possibility of understanding the human tragedy involved in malfunctioning institutions in terms of the clash of duties between doing one's job as a craftsman and doing one's job as a moneymaker. We might think of the recognition this clash produces along Heideggerian lines: moments of breakdown—when things stop working—disclose the articulated but formerly inexplicit purposive structure that constitutes our "lifeworld." See Heidegger, *Being and Time*, division 1, chap. 3.

124. See Engels and Marx, *Manifesto of the Communist Party:* "When people speak of ideas that revolutionise society, they do but express the fact, that within the old society, the elements of a new one have been created, and that the dissolution of the old ideas keeps even pace with the dissolution of the old conditions of existence" (489). On the possibilities thrown up by post-industrial societies, see André Gorz, *Critique of Economic Reason*, 191–212.

"within reach" of present society are clear: they consist in defending zones of craftsmanship where they already exist and creating them where they do not.

60. This will involve action on the part of both individuals and collectives. As individual citizens, each of us ought to reflect on how our particular talents might best be deployed given present social needs. One of those needs will be for a cultural environment conducive to the good life. This might be an environment that fosters the liberal virtues of civility, tolerance, and respect, but (as we saw in Chapter 6) it will also be an environment that fosters the Platonic virtues of justice and wisdom. Where possible, then, citizens ought to ask themselves how they might contribute to creating and sustaining a culture of true craftsmanship. Given that all our works—both products and actions—can be taken up as models, one way is simply to live up to the ideal in one's own career. We all know of people who devote themselves to producing things they genuinely consider to be good and useful, and who therefore insist on certain standards beyond the point of financial rationality. Take the copy editors of the world, for example: making prose intelligible is a service to the reader, yet no one ever responded to a misplaced comma by asking for a refund. Craftsmen like this find fulfillment in doing a job well and are correspondingly pained by the thought of allowing something shoddy into the world. They therefore stand as living refutations of the dogma—or ideology—that it is always rational to pursue our own financial interest in economic affairs. They are not saints of self-sacrifice, but they are nevertheless models. In finding fulfillment through service, they subtly influence our sense of what is natural, possible, and desirable.[125]

61. That said, individual action will obviously not suffice. After all, the whole point of §2 was to show that moneymaking is not simply an individual affliction. Insofar as our economic institutions approach those of ideal-typical capitalism, individuals will be constrained to act as moneymakers whether they like it or not. In the face of competition, for example, the managing editor of a newspaper

---

125. On the importance of meaningful work and craftsmanship to the good life, see Muirhead, *Just Work*; and Sennett, *Craftsman*.

may be forced to reduce the resources devoted to copyediting; workers lower down the hierarchy, meanwhile, may lack the power to make any important decisions regarding the orientation of their labors. If we are to embed a culture of craftsmanship, then, we need to shape our economic institutions.

62. The question of which particular actions are called for can be answered only by a combination of social science and practical wisdom, but at a general level we might say that structures of ownership and accountability are likely to be crucial. Take a case where a culture of craftsmanship has already sprung up around a given institution: one gets the impression, for example, that those who work for the *New York Times* feel a kind of pride in living up the standards set by their predecessors, and that this sense of honor (and so shame) serves as a bulwark against moneymaking pressures.[126] In cases like this the goal must be to conserve rather than to create. But if Marx is right then maintaining a culture of craftsmanship will require insulating institutions against the logic of capital accumulation and therefore considering alternative structures of ownership and accountability.[127] Plato would agree: the point of restricting private property in Kallipolis was (at least in part) to ensure that certain classes of workers deliberated as craftsmen rather than as moneymakers.[128] To speak a little more concretely, it might be that public ownership of certain institutions would make them accountable to

---

126. Just to be clear: I am in no way endorsing everything the *New York Times* does or stands for. The point is simply that it seems to have developed an institutional culture whereby journalists take themselves to have a certain kind of social role and hence to be subject to standards that cannot be entirely explained in narrowly economic terms. A similar example would be the tradition of fact-checking at the *New Yorker*. I should also reiterate something I said earlier in this chapter, that from a Platonic perspective the critique of moneymaking might just as well be the critique of honor seeking. If all our labors are oriented by a desire for honor, where our sense of what is honorable is not governed by investigation into the good life, then we will produce a dysfunctional society in much the same way as moneymakers would. If our institutions are consciously organized around prestige—as Ivy League universities sometimes appear to be—then this will represent a kind of malfunction analogous to that produced by capitalist imperatives.

127. On the need for conservatives to take Marx seriously, see Thakkar, "Why Conservatives Should Read Marx."

128. For a fuller development of this thought, see section 4 of Thakkar, "Moneymakers and Craftsmen."

the state and hence to the standard democratic process. Or it might be that cooperative ownership would make them accountable to workers and consumers and hence to a different kind of democratic process.[129] In industries where workers typically experience high degrees of alienation, exploitation, and insecurity, arrangements that give them some control over the workplace might be particularly useful for spreading an ethos of craftsmanship (even if those designing institutions would also have to take into account other values, such as efficiency and coherence).[130] None of this would amount to anything so grand as the final overcoming of capitalism, of course—but any expansion of true craftsmanship will bring us closer to the ideal of constituting a genuine society. And insofar as we produce ourselves through our work, both by settling into habits of thought and action and by creating a cultural environment that shapes us imperceptibly, that could not be more important.

IN CHAPTER 6 I ARGUED that the ideal of philosopher-citizens is both legitimate by liberal standards and genuinely Platonic. In this chapter I have tried to show that this ideal has both explanatory and normative power, helping us think, albeit at a very general level, about economic life today. Plato's critique of moneymaking might seem outlandish at first, but it turns out to be extremely powerful. Taken on its own, it does not exactly undermine the Smithian logic that has brought so much prosperity to the global economy in the past two centuries, but it does provide a useful corrective to a noxious understanding of how markets and the division of labor are supposed to work. Even in a competitive marketplace, one can and should still play for the team on pain of contributing to society's becoming dysfunctional. When married to Marx's theory of capitalism, the critique of moneymaking becomes more powerful still. For now we have a vision of a whole society whose labors are aimed at capital accumulation rather than the good life—a society that systematically

---

129. See section 5 of Thakkar, "Moneymakers and Craftsmen"; and Thakkar, "Neo-socialism."

130. See Wright, *Envisioning Real Utopias*; and Hahnel and Wright, *Alternatives to Capitalism*.

malfunctions. This new critical category, of malfunction as opposed to dysfunction, allows us to analyze the present in ways that are at once realistic and idealistic and thereby to satisfy the demands of Marxian critical theory while at the same time suggesting the outlines of a positive political program. Whether or not it is true that some forms of ideal theory have nothing to say about the specifics of the world around us, then, the ideal of philosophical citizenship most certainly does.

Conclusion

1. THIS BOOK HAS been an extended essay rather than any kind of treatise. A treatise seeks closure and completion; the dream would be to produce the argument to end all arguments. An essay is more humble and more open-ended. The goal is simply to enrich a conversation, and at some point that requires yielding the floor instead of trying to chart every twist and turn or block every avenue of attack. Whereas treatises pretend to timelessness, essays are self-consciously occasional; they always respond to some circumstance in the life of the author, be it personal or cultural. Plato's *Republic* might be understood as an essay in this sense: however far-flung the interlocutors' proposals become, however powerful their aspiration to transcend time and place, the conversation remains rooted in the courtyard of Polemarchus, where twelve people have gathered during a festival in the Piraeus, so that the work as a whole remains, as Hegel saw, Plato's attempt to grasp his time in thought.[1] My ambitions have been more

---

1. See Hegel, *Lectures on the History of Philosophy*, vol. 2, *Plato and the Platonists*, 96: "the eternal world . . . is reality, not a world above us or beyond, but the present world looked at in its truth, and not as it meets the senses of those who hear, see, &c. When we thus study the content of the Platonic Idea, it will become clear that Plato has, in fact, represented Greek morality according to its substantial mode, for it is the Greek state-life which constitutes the true content of the Platonic Republic. Plato is not the man to dabble in abstract theories and principles; his truth-loving mind has

circumspect, naturally: the goal has simply been to recover Plato's way of thinking about the polis in the hope of freeing us from a knot that currently cramps both political life and political philosophy.

2. Visions of transcendent futures have been noticeably absent from mainstream politics in the last few decades, I claimed in the Introduction, at least in the so-called West and relative to periods such as the 1920s and 1960s. Granted, there has been no shortage of Cassandras prophesying crises over aging populations, mass unemployment, resistance to antibiotics, water shortages, climate change, or nuclear weapons; and nor for that matter of Panglossians who cannot wait for automated production, self-driving cars, domestic robots, space travel, genetic engineering, and extended lifespans. But few of these exercises in futurology are tethered to reflection on the nature of the good life or the possibility of a social order more conducive to human flourishing than our own. And yet as Keynes pointed out back in 1930, the great promise of new technology is precisely that it frees man to face "his real, his permanent problem— how to use his freedom from pressing economic cares, how to occupy the leisure, which science and compound interest will have won for him, to live wisely and agreeably and well."[2] This failure to work out and orient ourselves towards visions of the collective good by no means bespeaks complacency with regard to current arrangements—to the contrary, dissatisfaction with our present way of life is frequently palpable on both Right and Left. If we do not live in relationship with ideals, it is because idealism has somehow come to seem forlorn.

3. The hunch that animated this project was that dissatisfaction with our present way of life and despair at the prospects for orienting

---

recognized and represented the truth, and this could not be anything else than the truth of the world he lived in, the truth of the one spirit which lived in him as well as in Greece. No man can overleap his time, the spirit of his time is his spirit also; but the point at issue is, to recognize that spirit by its content."

2. Keynes, *Economic Possibilities for our Grandchildren*, 6–7; Keynes goes on to predict that in response to this problem, "We shall once more value ends above means and prefer the good to the useful. We shall honour those who can teach us how to pluck the hour and the day virtuously and well, the delightful people who are capable of taking direct enjoyment in things, the lilies of the field who toil not, neither do they spin" (9).

ourselves toward some alternative might be two sides of the same coin—that what ails us might be precisely our inability to live as idealists. To make this case required me to confront those who reject ideal theory as an evasion of real politics and hence as a mode of inquiry that at best lacks practical import and at worst engulfs us in ideological mystification. My attack on this way of thinking was oblique: the idea was to dislodge it by inviting the reader to look at today's world through the eyes of Plato.

4. The *Republic* is one of the most widely read texts in philosophy, yet it remains ill understood. In the first half of the book I argued that Plato intended to influence Athenian life by disseminating ideals and images that might provoke his fellow citizens to perceive their institutions critically, and that this blend of ideal and critical theory was the result of combining the proposition that ruling is largely a matter of shaping the cultural environment with the proposition that ruling well requires constructing and disseminating philosophically models (or ideals) that manifest good and bad form. To build this case I had to argue against the common preconception that for Plato true philosophy is a matter of contemplating a mysterious world of forms that is set apart from our own. On my interpretation, Platonic philosophy is the activity of working out how the world around us might best cohere into a harmonious structure of parts and wholes. Every genuine entity has a function as part of a wider whole, according to this way of thinking, and an entity's true form is the mode of organization that will best enable it to carry out its function. Ruling, meanwhile, is the craft of benefiting subjects by shaping their souls, and since our souls are shaped by our social environment, shaping souls requires shaping whole societies. Ruling therefore requires knowing how citizens can best fit together in a coherent division of labor organized toward creating and sustaining a cultural environment maximally conducive to human flourishing. This in turn requires knowing what human flourishing consists in and hence how the parts of the human psyche might best cohere into a harmonious whole. The kind of knowledge that rulers need is therefore the kind of knowledge that philosophy seeks, namely knowledge of how parts and wholes might best fit together at different levels of the cosmos. This is why rulers should be

philosophers. But for Plato, I argued, it is also the case that philosophers should be ideal theorists, since philosophers use ideals in the sense of models or paradigms in order to test accounts of form and function (even if those accounts must eventually be independent of such heuristics). We can therefore say that in the ideal society rulers would be ideal theorists. So the *Republic* turns out to be surprisingly recursive: in working out ideals of city and soul, Socrates and his interlocutors model the kind of inquiry that the rulers in their ideal city would engage in. Once we notice this recursive structure, something else opens up to view: Plato's ambitions vis-à-vis Athenian society. Philosophical rulers are to shape their fellow citizens' highest values by ensuring that stories and artefacts embody, and therefore transmit, true beliefs concerning the good life. Although this is best done by those who hold political office and can therefore shape the division of labor from above, it is also possible for ordinary citizens to achieve something similar simply by tailoring their labors in line with philosophical inquiry into the good life. This suggests that philosophers can exercise at least some degree of rule even in nonideal societies such as democratic Athens. Indeed the *Republic*, with its "statues" of the just man and the just city, can be seen as an attempt to do just that—to exercise, but also to model, what we might call philosophical citizenship.

5. Plato's view was dependent on a picture of the cosmos as a harmonious order with a comprehensible teleological structure; it was also elitist and illiberal. But in the second half of the book I argued that we can recover Plato's way of thinking for the present if we take inspiration from the model of philosophical citizenship that he gave us through his own activity. In an ideal liberal democracy, I claimed, each citizen would understand themselves as a steward of society, forming an ideal of the good life and the division of labor that might bring it about and then acting in light of that conception. The ideals that such citizens form will be locally grounded visions of the best possible society—visions of the best possible *us*, as I put it, constrained by a sense of practical possibility relative to a particular context in space and time. This notion of philosophical citizenship promises to bolster liberal democracy by making clear that citizens' responsibility for maintaining a liberal-democratic culture goes beyond the obviously

political domain (where it requires complying with the law, paying taxes, voting in elections, and suchlike) and into the realm of day-to-day life (where it guides commonplace interactions, workplace deliberations, career choices, and the governance of nonstate institutions). But it also allows us to transcend the narrow purview of liberal ideals by inviting us to reflect on how our work might best facilitate the good life more generally, whether directly, through satisfying social needs, or indirectly, through shaping institutions or disseminating models.

6. From one perspective the ideal of philosophical citizenship seems obvious; from another it seems far-fetched. The reason, I argued, is that capitalistic economic institutions tend to ensure that workplace deliberations revolve around moneymaking rather than the production of a cultural environment conducive to flourishing. Just as Kallipolis, that most distant of ideals, was able to anchor a critical theory of Athenian democracy, so too, then, can the ideal of philosophical citizenship serve as the basis of a contemporary critical theory. Viewed from the perspective of a revived and revised Platonism, much of our economic life looks warped, from the ideological illusion that the invisible hand justifies any and all self-interested actions to the institutional imperative to maximize shareholder value. Yet this critical perception need not entail despair, since it suggests a relatively straightforward plan of action: to defend and expand those institutional forms that already encourage citizens to act as idealists and thereby model philosophical citizenship for others.

7. Zooming all the way out, we can see that this book has made three main claims, related but distinct: first, that ideals can serve to shift the social imaginary and thereby to generate a vantage point from which to critically perceive the present; second, that in an ideal liberal democracy citizens would comport themselves as idealists; and third, that we should fight for institutions that facilitate our acting in this way. Put together, these three claims allow us to reconcile ideal theory, critical theory, and practical struggle as three moments of political engagement that can inform and reinforce each other. Sometimes ideal theory will come first, disclosing unactualized possibilities for flourishing and thereby setting the agenda both for critical theory, which aims to disclose how present arrangements

simultaneously generate and close off such possibilities, and for practical political struggle, which seeks to alter the balance of forces so that those possibilities can be actualized. But other times the agenda will be set by critical theory or political practice, and in any case each of the three moments can always be conditioned by the other two.

8. Questions remain, of course, both about what has been said and about what has not been said. In the first category we could place a set of concerns regarding the ideal of philosophical citizenship. To begin with, the claim that in an ideal society citizens would be idealists might seem either trivially true or beside the point. Of course it would be better for citizens to have the Platonic virtues as well as the liberal ones, a critic might say—and every other virtue besides, from creativity to courage. But if citizens were angels, we wouldn't need politics in the first place. As James Madison put it in *Federalist* no. 49, "In a nation of philosophers . . . a reverence for the laws would be sufficiently inculcated by the voice of an enlightened reason. But a nation of philosophers is as little to be expected as the philosophical race of kings wished for by Plato."[3] This remark is unfair to Plato, who was well aware that most of us lack the cognitive and psychological capacity to follow reason where it leads; what motivates the transition from the first city to the second, and with it the birth of political philosophy proper, is precisely the waywardness of human desire—or, to put it another way, the fact that citizens are generally not angels. But the criticism would certainly seem to apply to the liberal-democratic Platonism that I have put forward. Following Rawls, I adopted a "political conception of the person" according to

---

3. Wootton, *The Essential Federalist and Anti-Federalist Papers*, 121. Madison's argument is particularly worth considering in this connection because it was directed against a line of thought similar to that expressed in Chapter 2's notion of ruling as refounding, namely Thomas Jefferson's suggestion in *Notes on the State of Virginia* that the best way to prevent the branches of government from exceeding their respective mandates would be to organize constitutional conventions whereby the people could essentially refound the polity anew, a proposal that Jefferson later radicalized into the proposal that each generation should be granted "a solemn opportunity" to "choose for itself the form of government it believes most promotive of its own happiness" by means of a constitutional convention held "every nineteen or twenty years." For the former suggestion, see Jefferson, *Political Writings*, 348; for the latter, see page 216 of the same edition.

which each citizen is assumed, for the purposes of theory-construction, to meet a threshold with respect to the capacities necessary for reasonable and rational self-government. This assumption flattens the human landscape, obscuring the difficulty and sheer painfulness of the philosophical inquiry necessary to achieve reflective equilibrium, and it thereby forestalls the kind of questions that both Plato and Madison wanted to ask about the role of myths and traditions in maintaining a stable social order.[4] The challenge is therefore clear: Isn't the ideal of philosophical citizenship merely wishful thinking, and if so mustn't it distort our perception of real politics?

9. My response is relatively simple: we need to distinguish between different stages of theory construction. If we accept that one of the functions of institutions is to foster—or institutionalize—certain norms of behavior, it follows that there will be a role for reflection on how people would ideally behave. Both the resulting institutional designs and the plans for bringing them about must then be guided by clear-eyed realism about human psychology.[5] But the debate

---

4. For Madison's views on the importance of tradition, see the whole paragraph from which the quotation about Plato is taken: "If it be true that all governments rest on opinion, it is no less true that the strength of opinion in each individual, and its practical influence on his conduct, depend much on the number which he supposes to have entertained the same opinion. The reason of man, like man himself, is timid and cautious when left alone, and acquires firmness and confidence in proportion to the number with which it is associated. When the examples which fortify opinion are ANCIENT as well as NUMEROUS, they are known to have a double effect. In a nation of philosophers, this consideration ought to be disregarded. A reverence for the laws would be sufficiently inculcated by the voice of an enlightened reason. But a nation of philosophers is as little to be expected as the philosophical race of kings wished for by Plato. And in every other nation, the most rational government will not find it a superfluous advantage to have the prejudices of the community on its side. The danger of disturbing the public tranquility by interesting too strongly the public passions, is a still more serious objection against a frequent reference of constitutional questions to the decision of the whole society. Notwithstanding the success which has attended the revisions of our established forms of government, and which does so much honor to the virtue and intelligence of the people of America, it must be confessed that the experiments are of too ticklish a nature to be unnecessarily multiplied." Wootton, *The Essential Federalist and Anti-Federalist Papers*, 120–121.

5. This psychological realism will most likely involve creating institutions compatible with the behavior of self-interested individuals out to maximize their own welfare as they perceive it. But it may also go beyond that, depending on the results of psychological research into individual motivation. It might turn out, for example, that the most psychologically realistic way of designing an institution is to insist upon a given ethos or to maintain certain traditions. In this connection we might return to a

concerning the ideal itself is simply whether it is possible and desirable. I have argued that it would be desirable for each citizen to conceive of herself as a co-steward of the cultural environment regardless of the likelihood of her being joined in that endeavor by other citizens and regardless of the likelihood of them sharing her view of the good life, and that this would require a willingness to reflect on the nature of the good life and the work that would be required to bring it about. The underlying thought is that where achieving a healthy cultural environment is concerned, every little helps, first, so that inching forward is never pointless, and, second, coherence has to be part of the ideal, so that an excellent citizen will take into account the visions of others. This thought is then combined with a contingent empirical proposition to the effect that a society whose citizens act in this way will inch forward towards a healthy cultural environment. The resulting vision is certainly ambitious, but there is nothing utopian about it; attempts to live up to it would never be quixotic.

10. The picture just sketched implies that institutions are only of secondary importance. They can enable or encourage certain kinds of action and proscribe or discourage others, but by themselves they are neither necessary nor sufficient for bringing about a genuine society. They are not sufficient because their influence is never absolute; they are not necessary because in principle we could act as we should even in their absence.[6] But some might say that a theory that pictures demands on individuals as prior to demands on institutions is ethical rather than political. After all, few ethicists would disagree with the thought that individuals ought to form a conception of the common good and then contribute to its realization as best they can. Aristotle suggests that the finest actions we can perform are those aimed at the common good; Kant suggests that we should conceive of ourselves as legislators for a community of equals; and consequentialists

---

suggestion that I made in §4 of Chapter 6, namely that the political conception of the person, though empirically false, could potentially serve as a myth that stabilizes a liberal-democratic social order.

6. Coordinating institutions, such as the highway code, clearly are necessary for a good society even with the assumption of ideal agents, but these are not the kind of institutions to which I am referring.

suggest that we should bring about as much good as possible. These thoughts are by no means equivalent, but they do all seem to bear on the choices we make between and within different careers. In and of itself this does not represent a problem for the ideal of philosophical citizenship, which is supposed to be compatible with a variety of ethical systems. But it does raise the question whether anything differentiates it from a claim concerning the need to act ethically in one's career.

11. A useful comparison in this respect might be "effective altruism," a movement that calls for individuals to consider career options in light of their expected contribution to the good of the world, however they conceive it. This is not the place for a thorough treatment of effective altruism.[7] For present purposes the impor-

---

7. For introductions to effective altruism by its proponents, see William McKaskill, *Doing Good Better*; and 80000hours.org. Effective altruism has received two kinds of critiques. The first accuses it of falling into the standard consequentialist traps, such as treating individuals as nothing more than agents of universal well-being or departing too far from ordinary morality. Some have thought that any ethical theory that supplies a criterion for assessing states of affairs can be redescribed as consequentialist, given that in and of itself, consequentialism implies no particular account of what makes states of affairs good; possible answers include the quality of subjective experience, the satisfaction of preferences or desires, the exercise of distinctively human capacities, and the achievement of rational freedom or mutual recognition, and ethical theories might be profitably distinguished simply by this measure. If it is true that all ethical theories can be redescribed as consequentialist, then it is hard to imagine much being gained from criticisms of consequentialism as such. (For an argument against the possibility of such universal redescription, however, see Campbell Brown, "Consequentialize This.") The second type of critiques leveled at effective altruism focuses not on its underlying structure but rather on the crudeness with which that structure has been fleshed out. McKaskill, for instance, assumes a rather simplistic conception of what it would be to benefit the world in an efficient manner: roughly speaking, he seems to think that it consists in improving the welfare of the poorest humans through schemes that have gone through randomized trials with respect to measurable goals (29–42). This permits him to conclude that the most talented altruists should not work in nonprofits, where there is often someone else who could do the job just as well, but rather "earn to give," working wherever they can accrue the most financial and human capital and then using that capital to produce good outcomes. Graduates of elite institutions such as Oxford and Harvard, for instance, will often (although not always) turn out to be morally obliged to work in investment banks or hedge funds so as to be able to donate more mosquito nets or deworming kits to Africans (90–94, 147–178). Many have found this proposal distasteful. It seems naïve to assume that individuals could work in the financial sector without absorbing nonaltruistic values; that poverty can be resolved by means of donations rather than political or institutional reform; and that randomized trials are

tant point is simply to note the kinds of question that the movement encourages us to ask regarding our careers: How much good would a given career path allow us to produce in the best-case scenario? How likely is that scenario relative to others? And would passing up the opportunity lead to the job being done less well by someone else? Questions of this kind would surely be germane to philosophical citizenship as well. The difference, slight though it is, lies in the word "citizenship." Citizens are always citizens of something. Whereas effective altruism directs us to contribute to good states of affairs wherever and whenever the opportunity arises, philosophical citizenship directs us to contribute to the societies of which we are already members (regardless of whether we count as citizens in the juridical sense). Just as a team is an intentional object for its members, especially those with management responsibilities, so philosophical citizens treat their society as an intentional object, asking how it could be better rather than how the world could be better. This is not to say that philosophical citizens cannot also be concerned with the wider world. But insofar as this concern is not a function of their taking themselves to be members of a given social unit, they would be concerned as moral agents rather than as citizens. We are all members of various cooperative units, of course—families, departments, associations, professions, and nations, among others—and in some circumstances it might make sense to think of the community of humans on earth as one such unit. But even that is bounded such that we can identify members and nonmembers. This is what distinguishes the political from the ethical.

12. As to why we might care about the condition of the various societies of which we are members, ethical commitments can certainly play a part: we might think that the best way to promote

---

always the best way of determining the value of a course of action. Worse still, this naïveté seems to reflect an unattractive combination of self-satisfied scientism and complacent Oxbridge culture. It is open to effective altruists to admit the immaturity of their efforts thus far, however, while retaining the core of their view, which is just that individuals should choose their careers on the basis of an assessment of their expected contribution to the good of the world. For further discussion, see Srinivasan, "Stop the Robot Apocalypse"; and McMahan, "Philosophical Critiques of Effective Altruism."

goodness in the universe at large is to promote it in our little corner, or that freedom or respect or dignity can be realized only in social units of a certain form, or that we have obligations toward those who depend on us. But Plato's own position, it should be noted, is less moralistic than that. The claim is that we should care about the condition of society because our own well-being depends on doing so. There are two dimensions to this. The first gives us an extrinsic motivation. Just as it is hard for an individual soccer player to thrive outside a flourishing team, so it is hard for individuals to lead good lives outside flourishing societies. Each of us depends on social cooperation for a whole array of goods, of which the most important may be psychic health and the ability to pass on a way of life to our children. The larger the unit of cooperation, of course, the greater the attractions of free riding, since the well-being of each individual seems to depend less on society and the condition of society seems to depend less on the behavior of each individual. But this brings us to the second thought, which is that playing a part in the flourishing of social units is intrinsically good for us regardless of its further effects. Plato figured this in terms of maintaining our psychic health, but we could also make the case by drawing on Marxian or Aristotelian claims regarding our nature as cooperative beings or contemporary psychological and sociological research regarding what gives people a sense of meaning in life.

13. Practically speaking, it remains likely that we will be more motivated to play our parts in small social units than in large ones. Not only are the causal chains clearer, so that rewards for cooperation and sanctions for noncooperation can be applied more effectively, but there is also a greater likelihood of our subjectively identifying with the social unit and hence conceiving of our own well-being as bound up with its success. This is especially true when the unit can be conceived as a team that must compete against opposing teams. The presence of an opponent is not necessary for individuals to act as a team—think of mountain-rescue teams—but it can certainly provide a useful source of motivation (which explains why mountain rescuers sometimes anthropomorphize the elements). The global social unit is a case in point: it seems likely that we would be

more motivated by the fate of the human community than we currently are if we discovered it was under threat from alien invaders. But it is important to distinguish the psychological question concerning when a given social unit becomes important to us from the philosophical question of what counts as excellent citizenship of a social unit. It is in answer to this latter question that I have emphasized the importance of justice and wisdom. Like teams, societies depend on cooperation and oversight. How the relevant activities and their corresponding virtues ought to be distributed will depend on the social unit in question: the less hierarchical the arrangement, the more each member will have to exercise both justice and wisdom. In liberal democracies, I argued, each citizen ought to think philosophically.

14. The fact that each of us belongs to a multitude of overlapping social units means that each of us is likely to be subject to competing obligations deriving from citizenship. This is just a special case of a problem that affects all agents, namely the need to weigh different demands and values against one another. A given situation might require us to weigh the obligation to keep a promise, for instance, against the obligation to save a human life. Less dramatically, we often have to weigh our obligations against our own interests in choosing how to act. And even when we are assessing our own interests, we still have to weigh different values against each other: as G. A. Cohen points out, this happens in ordinary cases such as choosing a restaurant.[8] It is not possible to provide an algorithm for such choices; all we can do is elucidate what is at stake in them.[9] Individuals must

---

8. Cohen, *Rescuing Justice and Equality*, 6.

9. See Cohen, *Finding Oneself in the Other*, 145–146: "Philosophers often have something novel to say about what, as it were, ingredients should go into the, as it were, cake even when they can say nothing about the proportions in which these ingredients, or values, are to be combined, across different cases: not because that is not important, but because the problem simply does not yield to general recipe making. . . . Although philosophers cannot produce the weighing that is necessary in any practical discussion, their disposition to notice things in ordinary experience that other people miss means that they can nevertheless make a contribution to an immediately practical question. They can contribute by identifying a value that bears on choice and that is being neglected. Consider an analogy. A bunch of us are trying to

decide for themselves how important the duties deriving from their membership of a given social unit are relative to their other obligations and interests. Being a good parent might sometimes require one to be a bad citizen. So might leading a good life.[10]

15. Recognizing that reasons of citizenship may be outweighed within our all-things-considered judgments about what to do allows us to better understand the Platonic critique of moneymaking, which is likely to seem naïve and moralistic if stated by itself. Some of this impression is dispelled once we remember that the point is not that we should produce altruistically with no thought for wages, but only that our workplace deliberations ought to be guided by our understanding of social needs. It is also worth remembering that deliberating with respect to honor is just as much a subject of Platonic critique as deliberating with respect to money, since both can lead to social dysfunction. But the idea that citizens ought ideally to choose a profession out of a sense of social needs (or a fear of someone doing the job worse than they would) might nevertheless strike us as moralistic. After all, not everyone feels capable of treating themselves as a genuine craftsman. Some feel the need to accumulate wealth in order to protect their children from unexpected calamities; others are simply trying to get by. We can now see that in cases of the first kind the obligations deriving from citizenship of one social unit conflict with those deriving from citizenship of another; such conflicts are inevitable in human life,

---

decide which restaurant to choose. Suppose everybody talks a lot about how good the food is in various restaurants, how much it costs, and how long it takes to get there. Someone, hitherto silent, is uneasy. She feels that we have been leaving something out of account. Then she realizes what it is: 'Like, nobody,' she says, 'is considering the decor!' This person has made a significant contribution to our practical discussion. But we should not expect her now also to say exactly how important a restaurant's décor is compared to other things that matter when we are choosing a restaurant."

10. To return to an example given in Chapter 6, we might draw an analogy with university governance. A university belongs to different cooperative units, from the local neighborhood to the global research community, and its trustees will sometimes have to balance the various obligations that result from those memberships. They may also be forced to weigh the institution's obligation to contribute to the creation of a healthy cultural environment against its need to maintain a clear identity and purpose: the pursuit of academic excellence will often dovetail with the pursuit of social justice, for instance, but at times conflicts will emerge and in such cases governors will have to decide how high a value to place on institutional integrity. Compare Williams, "A Critique of Utilitarianism," in Smart and Williams, *Utilitarianism*, 108–117.

and we must each make difficult choices.[11] With respect to those for whom an ethic of craftsmanship will seem a luxury, by contrast, it is worth reiterating that the theory's analytical emphasis on individual behavior does not imply a corresponding political emphasis.

16. Analytically speaking, it is important to recognize that social structures are constituted by individual actions and interactions, and hence that we all have the potential to affect our cultural environment. Politically speaking, however, we ought to focus less on individual responsibility than on institutions.[12] Sometimes the incentives against treating oneself as a craftsman are so great that only exceptionally virtuous individuals are able to resist; this might be true of the so-called revolving door between public and private employment, for example. In cases like this we can justifiably accuse moneymakers of being bad citizens, but we should also design institutions that remove the incentives in the first place. (Plato was surely right to think this especially important in the case of public officials.) But often the situation is worse than that. For economic structures often constrain individuals to act as moneymakers regardless of their personal preferences, and the ability to escape such constraints is often a privilege of those blessed with what are euphemistically termed "independent means."[13] Rather than criticizing particular individuals for deliberating as moneymakers, then, we

---

11. Plato might seem to have a clearer picture in that Book V of the *Republic* clearly privileges the sociopolitical unit over the familial one. But even there matters are not so clear. We could read Plato as merely working out the logic of a fully functional polis, and hence of citizenship, rather than as dictating our all-things-considered judgments about what to do. His point would be that family obligations and civic obligations must necessarily butt up against one another.

12. For a powerful critique of the contemporary Left's emphasis on individual action, see Srnicek and Williams, *Inventing the Future*, chap. 1.

13. Consider a passage in *Wage Labour and Capital* where Marx draws extremely close to Plato's critique of moneymaking: "The product of [the worker's] activity is not the object of his activity. What he produces for himself is not the silk that he weaves, not the gold that he draws from the mine, not the palace that he builds. What he produces for himself is *wages (der Arbeitslohn)*, and silk, gold, palace resolve themselves for him into a definite quantity of the means of subsistence, perhaps into a cotton jacket, some copper coins and a lodging in a cellar" (205). For Marx, it seems, capitalist institutions constrain not only industrialists but also ordinary workers to act as moneymakers, and in both cases this amounts to an alienation of human "life-activity" *(Lebenstätigkeit)* or "life-expression" *(Lebensäußerung)*.

should ask what it would take for every citizen to be free to deliberate as a craftsman. This will entail analyzing how different institutional structures—including different systems of ownership and
accountability—encourage different forms of workplace deliberation,
and how these structures might interact with the technologies that
currently promise to transform the world of work.[14] It will also entail designing educational programs that foster reflection on the good
life while also drawing out the talents of each and every individual;
the first desideratum will require finding ways to give both children
and adults regular opportunities to grapple with different traditions
of humanistic thinking, and the second will require us to recognize
and valorize forms of craftsmanship that have too often gone unnoticed by theorists of labor, especially those in the field of care.[15] And
finally it will entail formulating proposals for the kind of large-scale
redistribution of property and power that would enable each of us
to seriously consider ourselves as "a co-worker in the kingdom of
culture."[16] These are no small obstacles, but they lie beyond the
bounds of this essay, whose goal has simply been to open the des-
tination to view. For in the way of thinking I have derived from
Plato, idealism is part of the ideal. It is also, as a result, the ground
of critique. The task is to make it a reality.

---

14. See, e.g., Srnicek and Williams, *Inventing the Future*.

15. On the need for an educational system that draws out each individual's distinctive
aptitude for craftsmanship, see Morris, "Useful Work *versus* Useless Toil," in *News from
Nowhere and Other Writings*, 300; on the need for an educational system that allows each
citizen to appropriate past humanistic thinking regarding truth, goodness, and beauty,
see Du Bois, *The Souls of Black Folk*, 66–68. On the neglect of care work in political
theory and practice, meanwhile, see, e.g., Schwarzenbach, *On Civic Friendship*, and
Tronto, *Who Cares?* Note that in counting care work as the potential locus of
craftsmanship, I am rejecting the traditional association of craft with the production of
durable artefacts. In my usage, which derives from that of Plato, crafts are simply
structured activities that aim at producing a distinctive social good, so that ruling is just
as much of a craft as carpentry and caring for the elderly is no less a craft than building
houses. I believe this entails rejecting Hannah Arendt's distinction between labor, work,
and action as activities that produce consumer goods, use-objects, and the "fabric of
human relationships and affairs," respectively, and with it (perhaps) her attempt to
distinguish between the social and the political, but this would take further work to
establish. See *Human Condition*, 94–95, 22–78.

16. Du Bois, *The Souls of Black Folk*, 5. Thanks to Danielle Allen for reminding me
of this phrase, which is at once a fitting capstone for the present project and a poignant
reminder of its limitations.

Bibliography
Index

Bibliography

Ackerman, Bruce. *Social Justice in the Liberal State*. New Haven, CT: Yale University Press, 1980.

Albritton, Robert. *Economics Transformed: Discovering the Brilliance of Marx*. London: Pluto Press, 2007.

Allen, Danielle S. *Why Plato Wrote*. Malden, MA: Wiley-Blackwell, 2010.

Anderson, Elizabeth. *The Imperative of Integration*. Princeton, NJ: Princeton University Press, 2010.

———. *Private Government: How Employers Rule Our Lives (and Why We Don't Talk about It)*. Princeton, NJ: Princeton University Press, 2017.

Annas, Julia. *An Introduction to Plato's "Republic."* New York: Oxford University Press, 1981.

Arendt, Hannah. *The Human Condition*. Chicago: University of Chicago Press, 1998.

Aristophanes. *Clouds*. Translated by Peter Meineck. Indianapolis: Hackett, 2000.

Aristotle. *Categories*. Translated by J. L. Ackrill. In *The Complete Works of Aristotle*, vol. 1, edited by Jonathan Barnes, 3–24. Princeton, NJ: Princeton University Press, 1984.

———. *Constitution of Athens*. Translated by F. G. Kenyon. In *The Complete Works of Aristotle*, vol. 2, edited by Jonathan Barnes, 2341–2383. Princeton, NJ: Princeton University Press, 1984.

———. *Eudemian Ethics*. Translated by J. Solomon. In *The Complete Works of Aristotle*, vol. 2, edited by Jonathan Barnes, 1922–1981. Princeton, NJ: Princeton University Press, 1984.

———. *Generation of Animals*. Translated by A. Platt. In *The Complete Works of Aristotle*, vol. 1, edited by Jonathan Barnes, 1111–1218. Princeton, NJ: Princeton University Press, 1984.

————. *Metaphysics*. Translated by W. D. Ross. In *The Complete Works of Aristotle*, vol. 2, edited by Jonathan Barnes, 1552–1728. Princeton, NJ: Princeton University Press, 1984.

————. *Meteorology*. Translated by E. W. Webster. In *The Complete Works of Aristotle*, vol. 1, edited by Jonathan Barnes, 555–625. Princeton, NJ: Princeton University Press, 1984.

————. *Nicomachean Ethics*. Translated by Sarah Broadie and Christopher Rowe. New York: Oxford University Press, 2002.

————. *On the Soul*. Translated by J. A. Smith. In *The Complete Works of Aristotle*, vol. 1, edited by Jonathan Barnes, 641–692. Princeton, NJ: Princeton University Press, 1984.

————. *Parts of Animals*. Translated by W. Ogle. In *The Complete Works of Aristotle*, vol. 1, edited by Jonathan Barnes, 994–1086. Princeton, NJ: Princeton University Press, 1984.

————. *Physics*. Translated by R. P. Hardie and R. K. Gaye. In *The Complete Works of Aristotle*, vol. 1, edited by Jonathan Barnes, 315–446. Princeton, NJ: Princeton University Press, 1984.

————. *Politics*. Translated by E. Barker and R. Stalley. New York: Oxford University Press, 1995.

Arneson, Richard J. "Liberal Neutrality on the Good: An Autopsy." In *Perfectionism and Neutrality: Essays in Liberal Theory*, edited by Steven Wall and George Klosko, 191–218. Lanham, MD: Rowman & Littlefield, 2003.

Augustine. *Confessions*. Translated by Henry Chadwick. New York: Oxford University Press, 1992.

Austin, John Langshaw. *Philosophical Papers*. Edited by J. O. Urmson and G. J. Warnock. New York: Oxford University Press, 1990.

Badiou, Alain. *The Communist Hypothesis*. Translated by David Macey and Steve Corcoran. London: Verso, 2010.

————. *Plato's "Republic": A Dialogue in 16 Chapters*. Translated by Susan Spitzer. Cambridge: Polity Press, 2012.

Barney, Rachel. "Platonic Ring-Composition and *Republic* 10." In *Plato's "Republic": A Critical Guide*, edited by Mark McPherran, 32–51. Cambridge: Cambridge University Press, 2010.

————. "Socrates' Refutation of Thrasymachus." In *The Blackwell Guide to Plato's "Republic*," edited by Gerasimos Santas, 44–62. Oxford: Blackwell, 2006.

Bell, Daniel. *The Cultural Contradictions of Capitalism*. New York: Basic Books, 1996.

Bercuson, Jeffrey. *John Rawls and the History of Political Thought: The Rousseauvian and Hegelian Heritage of Justice as Fairness*. New York: Routledge, 2014.

Berlin, Isaiah. "Two Concepts of Liberty." In *The Proper Study of Mankind: An Anthology of Essays*, edited by H. Hardy and R. Hausheer, 191–242. New York: Farrar, Straus and Giroux, 1998.

Berman, Scott. "A Platonic Theory of Truthmaking." *Metaphysica* 14, no. 1 (2013): 109–125.

————. "Universals: Ways or Things?" *Metaphysica* 9, no. 2 (2008): 219–234.

Blondell, Ruby. *The Play of Character in Plato's Dialogues*. Cambridge: Cambridge University Press, 2006.

Bloom, Allan. "Interpretive Essay." In *The Republic of Plato*, translated by Allan Bloom, 307–436. New York: Basic Books, 1968.

Boethius. *The Consolation of Philosophy*. Translated by P. G. Walsh. Oxford: Oxford University Press, 1999.

Brennan, Geoffrey, and Philip Pettit. *The Economy of Esteem: An Essay on Civil and Political Society*. Oxford: Oxford University Press, 2005.

Brennan, Jason. *Against Democracy*. Princeton, NJ: Princeton University Press, 2016.

Brill, Sara. "Plato's Critical Theory." *Epoché* 17, no. 2 (Spring 2013): 233–248.

Broadie, Sarah. "Virtue and Beyond in Plato and Aristotle." *Southern Journal of Philosophy* 43 (2005): 97–114.

Brooke, Christopher. "Rawls on Rousseau and the General Will." In *The General Will: The Evolution of a Concept*, edited by James Farr and David Lay Williams, 429–446. New York: Cambridge University Press, 2017.

Brown, Campbell. "Consequentialize This." *Ethics* 121, no. 4 (July 2011): 749–771.

Brown, Lesley. "The Verb 'to Be' in Greek Philosophy: Some Remarks." In *Companions to Ancient Thought*, vol. 3, *Language*, edited by S. Everson, 212–236. Cambridge: Cambridge University Press, 1994.

Brown, Wendy. *Undoing the Demos: Neoliberalism's Stealth Revolution*. New York: Zone Books, 2015.

Brudney, Daniel. *Marx's Attempt to Leave Philosophy*. Cambridge: Harvard University Press, 1998.

Burke, Edmund. *Reflections on the Revolution in France*. Edited by L. G. Mitchell. New York: Oxford University Press, 1993.

Burnyeat, Myles. "Culture and Society in Plato's *Republic*." *Tanner Lectures on Human Values* 20 (1997): 215–324.

———. "Plato on Why Mathematics Is Good for the Soul." In *Mathematics and Necessity: Essays in the History of Philosophy*, edited by Timothy Smiley, 1–81. Oxford: Oxford University Press, 2000.

———. "Sphinx without a Secret." Review of *Studies in Platonic Political Philosophy*, by Leo Strauss. *New York Review of Books*, May 30, 1985, 30–36.

———. "Utopia and Fantasy: The Practicability of Plato's Ideally Just City." In *Plato 2: Ethics, Politics, Religion, and the Soul*, edited by Gail Fine, 297–308. New York: Oxford University Press, 1999.

Castoriadis, Cornelius. *The Imaginary Institution of Society*. Cambridge, MA: MIT Press, 1998.

Chesterton, G. K. *Orthodoxy*. Chicago: Moody Bible Institute, 2009.

Cicero. *The Republic and The Laws*. Translated by Niall Rudd. New York: Oxford University Press, 2009.

Ciepley, David. "Beyond Public and Private: Toward a Political Theory of the Corporation." *American Political Science Review* 107, no. 1 (February 2013): 139–158.

Clay, Diskin. *Platonic Questions: Dialogues with the Silent Philosopher*. University Park: Penn State University Press, 2000.

Cohen, G. A. "Facts and Principles." *Philosophy and Public Affairs* 31, no. 3 (2003): 211–245.

———. *Finding Oneself in the Other.* Princeton, NJ: Princeton University Press, 2013.

———. *If You're an Egalitarian, How Come You're So Rich?* Cambridge, MA: Harvard University Press, 2001.

———. *Karl Marx's Theory of History: A Defence.* Oxford: Oxford University Press, 1978.

———. *Lectures on the History of Moral and Political Philosophy.* Edited by J. Wolff. Princeton, NJ: Princeton University Press, 2013.

———. *Rescuing Justice and Equality.* Cambridge, MA: Harvard University Press, 2008.

———. *Why Not Socialism?* Princeton, NJ: Princeton University Press, 2009.

Collingwood, R. G. *An Autobiography.* Oxford: Oxford University Press, 1939.

Cooper, John M. "The Psychology of Justice in Plato." In *Plato's "Republic": Critical Essays,* edited by Richard Kraut, 17–30. Lanham, MD: Rowman & Littlefield, 1997.

Cross, R. C., and A. D. Woozley. *Plato's "Republic": A Philosophical Commentary.* London: Macmillan, 1964.

Devereux, Daniel. "Separation and Immanence in Plato's Theory of the Forms." In *Plato 1: Metaphysics and Epistemology,* edited by Gail Fine, 192–214. New York: Oxford University Press, 1999.

Dewey, John. *Experience and Nature.* New York: Dover Publications, 2000.

———. *Human Nature and Conduct: An Introduction to Social Psychology.* New York: Cosimo, 2007.

Dreher, Rod. *The Benedict Option: A Strategy for Christians in a Post-Christian Nation.* New York: Sentinel, 2017.

Du Bois, W. E. B. *The Souls of Black Folk.* Seattle: Amazon Classics, 2017.

Dworkin, Ronald. *Law's Empire.* Cambridge, MA: Harvard University Press, 1986.

———. "Liberalism." In *Public and Private Morality,* edited by Stuart Hampshire, 113–143. New York: Cambridge University Press, 1978.

Ebenstein, Alan. *Friedrich Hayek: A Biography.* New York: Palgrave, 2001.

Eck, Job van. "Fine's Plato: A Discussion of Gail Fine, *Plato on Knowledge and Forms.*" *Oxford Studies in Ancient Philosophy* 28 (2005): 303–326.

Eich, Stefan. "Between Justice and Accumulation: Aristotle on the Politics of Money." Unpublished manuscript, 2017.

Engels, Friedrich. "Socialism: Utopian and Scientific." In *The Marx-Engels Reader,* edited by Robert C. Tucker, 683–717. New York: Norton, 1978.

Engels, Friedrich, and Karl Marx. *Manifesto of the Communist Party.* In *The Marx-Engels Reader,* edited by Robert C. Tucker, 469–500. New York: Norton, 1978.

———. *The German Ideology: Part One.* Translated by S. Ryazanskaya. In *The Marx-Engels Reader,* edited by Robert C. Tucker, 146–200. New York: Norton, 1978.

Enoch, David. "Agency, Shmagency: Why Normativity Won't Come from What Is Constitutive of Action." *Philosophical Review* 115, no. 2 (2006): 169–198.

———. "Ideal Theory, Utopianism, and What's the Question (in Political Theory)." Unpublished manuscript, 2016.

———. "Shmagency Revisited." In *New Waves in Metaethics*, edited by Michael Brady, 208–233. New York: Palgrave Macmillan, 2011.

Estlund, David M. *Democratic Authority: A Philosophical Framework*. Princeton, NJ: Princeton University Press, 2009.

———. "What Good Is It? Unrealistic Political Theory and the Value of Intellectual Work." *Analyse und Kritik* 33, no. 2 (2011): 395–416.

———. "Why Not Epistocracy?" In *Desire, Identity and Existence: Essays in Honour of T. M. Penner*, edited by Naomi Reshotko, 53–69. Kelowna: Academic Printing & Publishing, 2003.

Farrelly, Colin. "Justice in Ideal Theory: A Refutation." *Political Studies* 55 (2007): 844–864.

Ferrari, G. R. F. *City and Soul in Plato's "Republic."* Chicago: University of Chicago Press, 2005.

———. "Strauss's Plato." *Arion: A Journal of Humanities and the Classics* 5, no. 2 (Fall 1997): 36–65.

Fine, Gail. "Forms as Causes: Plato and Aristotle." In *Mathematics and Metaphysics in Aristotle*, edited by A. Graeser, 69–112. Bern: Haupt, 1987.

———. "Knowledge and Belief in *Republic* V." In *Plato on Knowledge and Forms: Selected Essays*, edited by Gail Fine, 66–84. New York: Oxford University Press, 2003.

———. "Knowledge and Belief in *Republic* V–VII." In *Plato on Knowledge and Forms: Selected Essays*, edited by Gail Fine, 85–116. New York: Oxford University Press, 2003.

———, ed. *Plato on Knowledge and Forms: Selected Essays*. New York: Oxford University Press, 2003.

Finlayson, Lorna. *The Political Is Political: Conformity and the Illusion of Dissent in Contemporary Political Philosophy*. London: Rowman and Littlefield, 2015.

Finley, M. I. *The Ancient Economy*. Berkeley: University of California Press, 1973.

Floyd, Jonathan. "Is Political Philosophy Too Ahistorical?" *Critical Review of International Social and Political Philosophy* 12, no. 4 (2009): 513–533.

Foot, Philippa. *Natural Goodness*. New York: Oxford University Press, 2001.

Foucault, Michel. *Discipline and Punish*. Translated by Alan Sheridan. New York: Vintage Books, 1995.

Frank, Jill. *Poetic Justice*. Chicago: University of Chicago Press, 2018.

Frankfurt, Harry G. *The Importance of What We Care About: Philosophical Essays*. Cambridge: Cambridge University Press, 1988.

Fraser, Nancy. "What's Critical About Critical Theory? The Case of Habermas and Gender." *New German Critique*, no. 35 (1985): 97–131.

Frede, Dorothea. "Plato on What the Body's Eye Tells the Mind's Eye." *Proceedings of the Aristotelian Society*, n.s., 99 (1999): 191–210.

Frede, Michael. "The Original Notion of Cause." In *Essays in Ancient Philosophy*, edited by Michael Frede, 125–150. Minneapolis: University of Minnesota Press, 1987.

Freeden, Michael. *Liberalism: A Very Short Introduction*. Oxford: Oxford University Press, 2015.

Freud, Sigmund. *The Ego and the Id*. Translated by James Strachey. New York: Norton, 1990.

Fukuyama, Francis. "Are We Approaching the End of History?" Lecture at the University of Chicago Olin Center, Chicago, 1989.

————. "The End of History?" *National Interest* 16 (Summer 1989): 3–18.

Gadamer, Hans-Georg. *The Idea of the Good in Platonic-Aristotelian Philosophy*. Translated by P. Christopher Smith. New Haven, CT: Yale University Press, 1986.

————. *Truth and Method*. New York: Continuum, 1989.

Gaiser, Konrad. "Plato's Enigmatic Lecture 'On the Good.'" *Phronesis* 25, no. 1 (1980): 5–37.

Galston, William A. *Liberal Purposes: Goods, Virtues, and Diversity in the Liberal State*. Cambridge: Cambridge University Press, 1991.

Gaus, Gerald. "The Diversity of Comprehensive Liberalisms." In *The Handbook of Political Theory*, edited by Gerald F. Gaus and Chandran Kukathas, 100–114. London: Sage, 2004.

————. *The Order of Public Reason: A Theory of Freedom and Morality in a Diverse and Bounded World*. Cambridge: Cambridge University Press, 2011.

————. *The Tyranny of the Ideal*. Princeton, NJ: Princeton University Press, 2016.

Gaus, Gerald F., and Chandran Kukathas, eds. *The Handbook of Political Theory*. London: Sage, 2004.

Geras, Norman. "The Controversy about Marx and Justice." *New Left Review* no. 150 (March–April 1985): 47–85.

Gerson, Lloyd. *Aristotle and Other Platonists*. Ithaca, NY: Cornell University Press, 2006.

————. *From Plato to Platonism*. Ithaca, NY: Cornell University Press, 2013.

Geuss, Raymond. *The Idea of a Critical Theory*. Cambridge: Cambridge University Press, 1981.

————. *Outside Ethics*. Princeton, NJ: Princeton University Press, 2005.

————. *Philosophy and Real Politics*. Princeton, NJ: Princeton University Press, 2008.

————. *Politics and the Imagination*. Princeton, NJ: Princeton University Press, 2010.

————. *Reality and Its Dreams*. Cambridge, MA: Harvard University Press, 2016.

————. "The Wisdom of Oidipous and the Idea of a Moral Cosmos." *Arion: A Journal of Humanities and the Classics* 20, no. 3 (Winter 2013): 59–89.

————. *A World without Why*. Princeton, NJ: Princeton University Press, 2014.

Giddens, Anthony. *The Constitution of Society*. Berkeley: University of California Press, 1984.

Gifford, Mark. "Dramatic Dialectic in *Republic* Book I." *Oxford Studies in Ancient Philosophy* 20 (Summer 2001): 37–106.

Gillespie, M. A. 2009. "Players and Spectators: Sports and Ethical Training in the American University." In *Debating Moral Education*, edited by E. Kiss and P. Euben, 296–316. Durham, NC: Duke University Press, 2009.

Giorgini, Giovanni. "Radical Plato: John Stuart Mill, George Grote and the Revival of Plato in Nineteenth-Century England." *History of Political Thought* 30, no. 4 (2009): 617–646.

Gonzales, Francisco. "Propositions or Objects? A Critique of Gail Fine on Knowledge and Belief in Republic V." *Phronesis* 41 (1996): 245–275.

Gorz, André. *Critique of Economic Reason.* Translated by Gillian Handyside and Chris Turner. London: Verso, 1989.

Gosling, J. C. B. "*Doxa* and *Dunamis* in Plato's *Republic.*" *Phronesis* 13 (1968): 119–130.

———. *Plato: The Arguments of the Philosophers.* London: Routledge, 2008.

———. "Republic Book V: *Ta Polla Kala* etc." *Phronesis* 5, no. 2 (1960): 116–128.

Gramsci, Antonio. *Selections from the Prison Notebooks.* Edited and translated by Quintin Hoare and Geoffrey Nowell Smith. London: Lawrence and Wishart, 1971.

Grant, Ruth. *Strings Attached: Untangling the Ethics of Incentives.* Princeton, NJ: Princeton University Press, 2011.

Greco, Anna. "On the Economy of Specialization and Division of Labour in Plato's *Republic.*" *Polis* 26, no. 1 (2009): 52–72.

Green, Jeffery. "Political Theory as Both Philosophy and History: A Defense Against Methodological Militancy." *Annual Review of Political Science* 18 (2015): 425–441.

Grice, H. P. "Reply to Richards." In *Philosophical Grounds of Rationality: Intentions, Categories, Ends,* edited by R. Grandy and R. Warner, 45–108. Oxford: Clarendon Press, 1986.

Guerrero, Alex. "Against Elections: The Lottocratic Alternative." *Philosophy and Public Affairs* 42 (2014): 135–178.

Hahnel, Robin, and Erik Olin Wright. *Alternatives to Capitalism.* London: Verso, 2016.

Haksar, Vinit. *Equality, Liberty, and Perfectionism.* New York: Oxford University Press, 1980.

Halliwell, Stephen. "The Life-and-Death Journey of the Soul: Myth of Er." In *The Cambridge Companion to Plato's "Republic,"* edited by G. R. F. Ferrari, 445–473. New York: Cambridge University Press, 2007.

Hanley, Ryan, ed. *Adam Smith: His Life, Thought, and Legacy.* Princeton, NJ: Princeton University Press, 2016.

Harris, Gardiner. "Talk Doesn't Pay, So Psychiatry Turns Instead to Drug Therapy." *New York Times,* March 5, 2011.

Harte, Verity. *Plato on Parts and Wholes: The Metaphysics of Structure.* Oxford: Oxford University Press, 2002.

Harvey, David. *A Brief History of Neoliberalism.* New York: Oxford University Press, 2005.

Haslanger, Sally. *Resisting Reality.* New York: Oxford University Press, 2012.

———. *Critical Theory and Practice.* Assen: Van Gorcum, 2017.

Hayek, Friedrich. "The Use of Knowledge in Society." *The American Economic Review* 35, no.4 (1945): 519–530.

Hegel, G. W. F. *Elements of the Philosophy of Right.* Edited by A. W. Wood. Translated by H. B. Nisbet. Cambridge: Cambridge University Press, 1991.

_____. *Lectures on the History of Philosophy.* Vol. 1, *Greek Philosophy to Plato.* Translated by E. S. Haldane. Lincoln: University of Nebraska Press, 1995.

_____. *Lectures on the History of Philosophy.* Vol. 2, *Plato and the Platonists.* Translated by E. S. Haldane and F. H. Simson. Lincoln: University of Nebraska Press, 1995.

_____. *Lectures on the Philosophy of History.* Translated by J. Sibree. New York: Dover Publications, 2004.

Heidegger, Martin. *Being and Time.* Translated by John Macquarrie and Edward Robinson. New York: HarperCollins, 1962.

_____. *Plato's "Sophist."* Translated by R. Rojcewicz and A. Schuwer. Bloomington: Indiana University Press, 2003.

Herman, Edward, and Noam Chomsky. *Manufacturing Consent: The Political Economy of the Mass Media.* New York: Pantheon Books, 1988.

Herodotus. *The Histories.* Translated by George Rawlinson. London: Everyman's Library, 1997.

Hobbes, Thomas. *On the Citizen.* Cambridge: Cambridge University Press, 1998.

Hodgson, Geoffrey. "What Are Institutions?" *Journal of Economic Issues* 40, no. 1 (March 2006): 1–25.

Horkheimer, Max. *Critical Theory: Selected Essays.* Translated by Matthew J. O'Connell. New York: Continuum, 1975.

Hurka, Thomas. *Perfectionism.* New York: Oxford University Press, 1993.

Hyland, Drew. *Finitude and Transcendence in the Platonic Dialogues.* Albany: State University of New York Press, 1995.

Irwin, Terence. "Homonymy in Aristotle." *Review of Metaphysics* 34, no. 3 (March 1981): 523–544.

_____. *Plato's Ethics.* New York: Oxford University Press, 1995.

Jefferson, Thomas. *Political Writings.* Edited by Joyce Appleby and Terence Ball. Cambridge: Cambridge University Press, 1999.

_____. Thomas Jefferson to Richard Price, January 8, 1789. Library of Congress. Accessed May 9, 2013. http://www.loc.gov/exhibits/jefferson/60.html.

Johnston, Mark. *Saving God.* Princeton, NJ: Princeton University Press, 2009.

Joseph, H. W. B. *Knowledge and the Good in Plato's "Republic."* Oxford: Oxford University Press, 1948.

Kahn, C. H. "The Greek Verb 'to Be' and the Concept of Being." *Foundations of Language* 2 (1966): 245–265.

Kant, Immanuel. *Groundwork of the Metaphysics of Morals.* Translated by Mary Gregor and Jens Timmerman. Cambridge: Cambridge University Press, 2012.

_____. *Perpetual Peace, and Other Essays.* Indianapolis: Hackett, 1983.

Kasimis, Demetra. "Recovering a Theory of Performativity in Plato's Mimesis." Presentation at the American Political Science Association, San Francisco, September 2015.

Kass, Leon. *The Beginning of Wisdom: Reading Genesis.* Chicago: University of Chicago Press, 2003.

Keenan, Douglas. "My Thwarted Attempt to Tell of Libor Shenanigans." *Financial Times*, July 27, 2012.

Kennedy, J. B. "Plato's Forms, Pythagorean Mathematics, and Stichometry." *Apeiron* 43, no. 1 (2010): 1–32.

Kerr, Clark. *The Uses of the University*. Cambridge, MA: Harvard University Press, 1963.

Keynes, John Maynard. *Economic Possibilities for our Grandchildren*. Accessed October 31, 2017. https://www.marxists.org/reference/subject/economics/keynes/1930/our-grandchildren.htm.

———. *The General Theory of Employment, Interest and Money*. New York: Harcourt, 1953.

Knight, Jack. "The Imperative of Non-ideal Theory." *Political Studies* 12, no. 3 (September 2014): 361–368.

Korsgaard, Christine M. *Self-Constitution: Agency, Identity, and Integrity*. New York: Oxford University Press, 2009.

———. *The Sources of Normativity*. Cambridge: Cambridge University Press, 1996.

Kosman, Aryeh. "Justice and Virtue: The *Republic*'s Inquiry into Proper Difference." In *The Cambridge Companion to Plato's "Republic,"* edited by G. R. F. Ferrari, 116–137. New York: Cambridge University Press, 2007.

Kraut, Richard. "Introduction to the Study of Plato." In *The Cambridge Companion to Plato*, edited by Richard Kraut, 1–50. Cambridge: Cambridge Univeristy Press, 1992.

———. "Politics, Neutrality and the Good." *Social Philosophy and Policy* 16, no. 1 (1999): 315–332.

———. "Return to the Cave: Republic 519–521." In *Plato 2: Ethics, Politics, Religion, and the Soul*, edited by Gail Fine, 235–254. New York: Oxford University Press, 1999.

Kripke, Saul. *Naming and Necessity*. Oxford: Wiley-Blackwell, 1991.

Kurosawa, Akira. *High and Low*. Tokyo: Toho, 1963.

Lane, Melissa. "Antianarchia: Interpreting Political Thought in Plato." *Plato Journal* 16 (2016): 59–74.

———. *Eco-Republic: What the Ancients Can Teach Us about Ethics, Virtue, and Sustainable Living*. Princeton, NJ: Princeton University Press, 2012.

———. "Founding as Legislating: The Figure of the Lawgiver in Plato's *Republic*." In *Dialogues on Plato's Politeia (Republic): Selected Papers from the Ninth Symposium Platonicum*, edited by Noboru Notomi and Luc Brisson, 104–114. Sankt Augustin: Academia Verlag, 2013.

———. "From History to Model: Plato's *Republic* 8 on Office and Rule in a Normative Logic of Social Change." In *How to Do Things with History*, edited by Danielle Allen, Paul Christesen, and Paul Millett. Oxford: Oxford University Press, forthcoming.

———. "How to Emancipate History from the Past: Plato's *Republic* VIII on Office and Rule in Outlining Conjectural Futures." Unpublished manuscript, 2016.

———. *Method and Politics in Plato's "Statesman."* Cambridge: Cambridge University Press, 1998.

———. *Plato's Progeny: How Plato and Socrates Still Captivate the Modern Mind.* Bristol: Bristol Classical Press, 2001.

———. "Popular Sovereignty as Control of Officeholders: Aristotle on Greek Democracy." In *Popular Sovereignty in Historical Perspective*, edited by R. Bourke and Q. Skinner, 52–72. Cambridge: Cambridge University Press, 2016.

———. "The Relation between Liberty, Law, and Rule: Platonic Variations on 'Spartan' Themes." Unpublished manuscript.

———. "Self-Knowledge in Plato? Recognizing the Limits and Aspirations of a Self as Knower." In *Self-Knowledge in Ancient Philosophy*, edited by Fiona Leigh. Oxford: Oxford University Press, 2018.

Lange, Margaret Meek. "Reconciliation Arguments in John Rawls's Philosophy." *Critical Horizons* 15, no. 3 (2014): 306–324.

Larmore, Charles E. *Patterns of Moral Complexity.* New York: Cambridge University Press, 1987.

Lawford-Smith, Holly. "Understanding Political Feasibility." *Journal of Political Philosophy* (2012). doi: 10.1111/j.1467-9760.2012.00422.x.

Lear, Gabriel Richardson. "Plato on Learning to Love Beauty." In *The Blackwell Guide to Plato's "Republic,"* edited by Gerasimos Santas, 104–124. Oxford: Blackwell, 2006.

Lear, Jonathan. "Allegory and Myth in Plato's Republic." In *The Blackwell Guide to Plato's "Republic,"* edited by Gerasimos Santas, 25–43. Oxford: Blackwell, 2006.

———. *A Case for Irony.* Cambridge, MA: Harvard University Press, 2011.

———. "The City Prefect." Review of *Plato: Political Philosophy*, by Malcolm Schofield. *Times Literary Supplement*, August 24, 2007.

———. "Inside and Outside the *Republic*." In *Plato's "Republic": Critical Essays*, edited by Richard Kraut, 61–94. Lanham, MD: Rowman & Littlefield, 1997.

———. *Radical Hope: Ethics in the Face of Cultural Devastation.* Cambridge, MA: Harvard University Press, 2006.Lee, David C. "Interpreting Plato's *Republic*: Knowledge and Belief." *Philosophy Compass* 5, no. 10 (2010): 854–864.

Leiter, Brian. "Marxism and the Continuing Irrelevance of Normative Theory." Review of *If You're an Egalitarian, How Come You're So Rich?*, by G. A. Cohen. *Stanford Law Review* 54, no. 5 (May 2002): 1129–1151.

Leopold, David. *The Young Karl Marx: German Philosophy, Modern Politics, and Human Flourishing.* Cambridge: Cambridge University Press, 2007.

Lippert-Rasmussen, Kasper. "Estlund on Epistocracy: A Critique." *Res Publica* 18, no. 3 (2012): 241–258.

List, Christian, and Philip Pettit. *Group Agency: The Possibility, Design, and Status of Corporate Agents.* Oxford: Oxford University Press, 2011.

Locke, John. *Second Treatise on Government.* Edited by C. B. Macpherson. Indianapolis: Hackett, 1980.

Loux, Michael. *Metaphysics: A Contemporary Introduction.* 3rd ed. New York: Routledge, 2006.

Luban, Daniel. "Forward with Fukuyama." *Point* 10 (2015): 157–176.

Lukács, Georg. *History and Class Consciousness: Studies in Marxist Dialectics.* Cambridge, MA: MIT Press, 1972.

Lukes, Steven. *Power: A Radical View.* New York: Palgrave Macmillan, 2005.

Lysias. Translated by S. C. Todd. Austin: University of Texas Press, 2000.

Macedo, Stephen. *Liberal Virtues: Citizenship, Virtue, and Community in Liberal Constitutionalism.* New York: Oxford University Press, 1990.

MacIntyre, Alasdair. *After Virtue.* Notre Dame: University of Notre Dame Press, 1981.

———. *Against The Self-Images of the Age.* Notre Dame: University of Notre Dame Press, 1989.

Makin, Stephen. "Aristotle on Modality." *Proceedings of the Aristotelian Society,* supplementary volume 74 (2000): 143–161.

Mandeville, Bernard. *The Fable of the Bees.* Edited by Phillip Harth. New York: Penguin Books, 2007.

Mann, Michael, dir. *The Insider.* Burbank, CA: Touchstone Pictures, 1999.

Mann, Michael (sociologist). "The Autonomous Power of the State: Its Origins, Mechanisms and Results." *Archives Européenes de Sociologie* 25 (1984): 185–213.

———. *The Sources of Social Power.* Vol, 1, *A History of Power from the Beginning to AD 1760.* New York: Cambridge University Press, 1986.

Marcuse, Herbert. *One-Dimensional Man.* Boston: Beacon Press, 1964.

———. "Philosophy and Critical Theory." In *Critical Theory and Society: A Reader,* edited by S. Bronner and D. Kellner, 58–76. London: Routledge, 1989.

Markell, Patchen. Review of *Philosophy and Real Politics,* by Raymond Geuss. *Political Theory* 38, no. 1 (2010): 172–177.

Marx, Karl. *Capital.* Vol. 1. Translated by Ben Fowkes. London: Penguin Books, 1990.

———. *Capital.* Vol. 3. Translated by David Fernbach. London: Penguin Books, 1991.

———. *Comments on James Mill,* Éléments D'économie Politique. Accessed October 30, 2017. https://www.marxists.org/archive/marx/works/1844/james-mill/index.htm.

———. *Critique of the Gotha Program.* In *The Marx-Engels Reader,* edited by Robert C. Tucker, 525–541. New York: Norton, 1978.

———. *Economic and Philosophical Manuscripts of 1844.* Translated by Martin Milligan. In *The Marx-Engels Reader,* edited by Robert C. Tucker, 66–125. New York: Norton, 1978.

———. *For a Ruthless Criticism of Everything Existing.* Translated by Ronald Rogowski. In *The Marx-Engels Reader,* edited by Robert C. Tucker, 12–15. New York: Norton, 1978.

———. *Theses on Feuerbach.* In *The Marx-Engels Reader,* edited by Robert C. Tucker, 143–145. New York: Norton, 1978.

———. *Wage Labour and Capital.* In *The Marx-Engels Reader,* edited by Robert C. Tucker, 203–217. New York: Norton, 1978.

McCabe, Mary Margaret. "Plato's Ways of Writing." In *The Oxford Handbook of Plato,* edited by Gail Fine, 88–113. Oxford: Oxford University Press, 2008.

McCarthy, George. *Dialectics and Decadence: Echoes of Antiquity in Marx and Nietzsche.* Lanham, MD: Rowman & Littlefield, 1994.

———, ed. *Marx and Aristotle: Nineteenth-Century German Social Theory and Classical Antiquity.* Lanham, MD: Rowman & Littlefield, 1992.

———. *Marx and the Ancients: Classical Ethics, Social Justice, and Nineteenth-Century Political Economy.* Lanham, MD: Rowman & Littlefield, 1990.

McCloskey, Deirdre N. *Bourgeois Dignity: Why Economics Can't Explain the Modern World.* Chicago: University of Chicago Press, 2010.

McKaskill, William. *Doing Good Better: Effective Altruism and a Radical New Way to Make a Difference.* New York: Avery, 2015.

McKirahan, Richard D. "The *Nomos-Phusis* Debate." In *Philosophy before Socrates: An Introduction with Texts and Commentary*, edited by Richard D. McKirahan, 405–426. Indianapolis: Hackett, 2010.

McMahan, Jeff. "Philosophical Critiques of Effective Altruism." *Philosopher's Magazine* 73, no. 2 (2016): 92–99.

Meikle, Scott. "Aristotle and Exchange Value." In *A Companion to Aristotle's Politics*, edited by David Keyt and Fred D. Miller, 156–181. Oxford: Blackwell, 1991.

———. *Essentialism in the Thought of Karl Marx.* London: Open Court, 1985.

Mill, John Stuart. *On Liberty and Other Essays.* Oxford: Oxford University Press, 1998.

Miller, Arthur B. "Aristotle on Habit and Character: Implications for the *Rhetoric.*" *Speech Monographs* 41 (1974): 309–316.

Miller, David. *Justice for Earthlings.* Cambridge: Cambridge University Press, 2013.

———. *Market, State, and Community: Theoretical Foundations of Market Socialism.* New York: Oxford University Press, 1989.

Miller, Mitchell. "Beginning the 'Longer Way.'" In *The Cambridge Companion to Plato's "Republic,"* edited by G. R. F. Ferrari, 310–344. New York: Cambridge University Press, 2007.

Miller, Seumas. *The Moral Foundations of Social Institutions.* New York: Cambridge University Press, 2010.

Mills, Charles W. "'Ideal Theory' as Ideology." *Hypatia* 20, no. 3 (Summer 2005): 165–184.

———. "Rawls on Race/Race in Rawls." *Southern Journal of Philosophy* 47 (2009): 161–184.

Monoson, S. Sara. *Plato's Democratic Entanglements: Athenian Politics and the Practice of Philosophy.* Princeton, NJ: Princeton University Press, 2000.

Morris, William. *News from Nowhere and Other Writings.* London: Penguin, 2004.

Morrison, Donald R. "The Utopian Character of Plato's Ideal City." In *The Cambridge Companion to Plato's "Republic,"* edited by G. R. F. Ferrari, 232–255. New York: Cambridge University Press, 2007.

Muirhead, Russell. *Just Work.* Cambridge, MA: Harvard University Press, 2004.

Naddaff, Ramona. *Exiling the Poets: The Production of Censorship in Plato's "Republic."* Chicago: University of Chicago Press, 2002.

Nagel, Thomas. *Equality and Partiality*. New York: Oxford University Press, 1991.

———. "Getting Personal: Why Don't Egalitarians Give Away Their Own Money?" Review of *If You're an Egalitarian, How Come You're So Rich?*, by G. A. Cohen. *Times Literary Supplement*, June 23, 2000.

Nails, Debra. *The People of Plato: A Prosopography of Plato and Other Socratics*. Indianapolis: Hackett, 2002.

Nehamas, Alexander. "Plato on the Imperfection of the Sensible World." In *Plato 1: Metaphysics and Epistemology*, edited by Gail Fine, 171–191. New York: Oxford University Press, 1999.

Nietzsche, Friedrich. *On the Genealogy of Morality*. Translated by M. Clark and A. Swenson. Indianapolis: Hackett, 1998.

———. "On the Uses and Disadvantages of History for Life." In *Untimely Meditations*, edited by Daniel Breazeale, translated by R. J. Hollingdale. Cambridge: Cambridge University Press, 1997.

Nightingale, Andrea Wilson. *Spectacles of Truth in Classical Greek Philosophy: Theoria in Its Cultural Context*. Cambridge: Cambridge University Press, 2004.

Nozick, Robert. *Anarchy, State, and Utopia*. New York: Basic Books, 1974.

Nussbaum, Martha. "Perfectionist Liberalism and Political Liberalism." *Philosophy and Public Affairs* 39, no. 1 (Winter 2011): 3–45.

Oakeshott, Michael. *On Human Conduct*. Oxford: Oxford University Press, 1991.

Ober, Josiah. "The Original Meaning of 'Democracy': Capacity to Do Things, Not Majority Rule." *Constellations* 15, no.1 (2008): 3–9.

———. *Political Dissent in Democratic Athens: Intellectual Critics of Popular Rule*. Princeton, NJ: Princeton University Press, 1998.

Okin, Susan M. 1989. *Justice, Gender, and the Family*. New York: Basic Books, 1989.

O'Neill, Martin, and Thad Williamson, eds. *Property-Owning Democracy: Rawls and Beyond*. Oxford: Wiley-Blackwell, 2012.

O'Neill, Onora. "Abstraction, Idealization and Ideology in Ethics." In *Moral Philosophy and Contemporary Problems*, edited by J. D. G. Evans, 55–69. Cambridge: Cambridge University Press, 1988.

———. *Towards Justice and Virtue*. Cambridge: Cambridge University Press, 1996.

Organisation for Economic Co-operation and Development. *Doing Better for Children*. OECD, 2009.

Oswald, Martin. *Nomos and the Beginnings of the Athenian Democracy*. Oxford: Oxford University Press, 1969.

Pack, Spencer. *Aristotle, Adam Smith and Karl Marx: On Some Fundamental Issues in 21st Century Political Economy*. Cheltenham: Edward Elgar, 2010.

Parfit, Derek. "Equality and Priority." *Ratio* 10, no. 3 (December 1997): 202–221.

Parsons, Talcott. *The Social System*. London: Routledge, 1991.

Penner, Terry. "The Forms in the Republic." In *The Blackwell Guide to Plato's "Republic,"* edited by Gerasimos Santas, 234–262. Malden, MA: Blackwell, 2006.

Pettit, Philip. "Rawls's Political Ontology." *Philosophy, Politics and Economics* 4 (2005): 157–174.

———. *Republicanism: A Theory of Freedom and Government.* New York: Oxford University Press, 1997.

———. *The Robust Demands of the Good: Ethics with Attachment, Virtue, and Respect.* Oxford: Oxford University Press, 2015.

Pindar. *Olympian Odes. Pythian Odes.* Translated by William H. Race. Loeb Classical Library, vol. 56. Cambridge, MA: Harvard University Press, 1997.

Plato. *Apology.* In *Five Dialogues*, translated by G. M. A. Grube and J. M. Cooper, 21–44. Indianapolis: Hackett, 2002.

———. *Cratylus.* Translated by C. D. C. Reeve. Indianapolis: Hackett, 1998.

———. *Gorgias.* In *Plato in Twelve Volumes*, vol. 3, translated by W. R. M. Lamb. Cambridge, MA: Harvard University Press, 1967.

———. *Laws.* In *Plato in Twelve Volumes*, vols. 10 and 11, translated by R. G. Bury. Cambridge, MA: Harvard University Press, 1967.

———. *Phaedo.* In *Five Dialogues*, translated by G. M. A. Grube and J. M. Cooper, 93–154. Indianapolis: Hackett, 2002.

———. *Phaedrus.* Translated by A. Nehamas and P. Woodruff. Indianapolis: Hackett, 1995.

———. *Philebus.* In *Plato in Twelve Volumes*, vol. 9, translated by Harold N. Fowler. Cambridge, MA: Harvard University Press, 1925.

———. *Platonis Respublica.* Edited by S. R. Slings. Oxford: Oxford University Press, 2003.

———. *Republic.* Translated by G. M. A. Grube and C. D. C. Reeve. Indianapolis: Hackett, 1992.

———. *Republic.* Translated by C. D. C. Reeve. Indianapolis: Hackett, 2004.

———. *Republic.* Translated by Paul Shorey. Cambridge, MA: Harvard University Press, 1937.

———. *The Republic of Plato.* Translated by Allan Bloom. New York: Basic Books, 1968.

———. *Statesman.* In *Plato in Twelve Volumes*, vol. 12, translated by Harold N. Fowler. Cambridge, MA: Harvard University Press, 1921.

———. *Statesman.* Translated by Christopher Rowe. Indianapolis: Hackett, 1999.

———. *Theaetetus.* In *Plato in Twelve Volumes*, vol. 12, translated by Harold N. Fowler. Cambridge, MA: Harvard University Press, 1921.

———. *Timaeus.* In *Plato in Twelve Volumes*, vol. 9, translated by W. R. M. Lamb. Cambridge, MA: Harvard University Press, 1925.

Polybius. *The Histories.* Translated by Robin Waterfield. New York: Oxford University Press, 2010.

Popper, Karl. *The Open Society and Its Enemies.* Vol. 1, *The Spell of Plato.* Princeton, NJ: Princeton University Press, 1966.

Postone, Moishe. *Time, Labor, and Social Domination: A Reinterpretation of Marx's Critical Theory.* New York: Cambridge University Press, 1993.

Rawls, John. *Collected Papers.* Edited by Samuel Freeman. Cambridge, MA: Harvard University Press, 1999.

————. *Justice as Fairness.* Cambridge, MA: Harvard University Press, 2001.

————. *Political Liberalism.* New York: Columbia University Press, 1993.

————. *A Theory of Justice.* Cambridge, MA: Harvard University Press, 1971.

Raz, Joseph. "Comments on the Morality of Freedom." *Jerusalem Review of Legal Studies* (forthcoming).

————. *The Morality of Freedom.* New York: Oxford University Press, 1986.

Reeve, C. D. C. *Blindness and Reorientation: Problems in Plato's "Republic."* Oxford: Oxford University Press, 2012.

————. *Philosopher-Kings: The Argument of Plato's "Republic."* Princeton, NJ: Princeton University Press, 1988.

Ricoeur, Paul. *Interpretation Theory: Discourse and the Surplus of Meaning.* Fort Worth: Texas Christian University Press, 1976.

Roberts, William Clare. *Marx's Inferno: The Political Theory of Capital.* Princeton, NJ: Princeton University Press, 2016.

Robeyns, Ingrid. "Ideal Theory in Theory and Practice." *Social Theory and Practice* 34, no. 3 (2008): 341–362.

Rosen, Michael. *On Voluntary Servitude: False Consciousness and the Theory of Ideology.* Cambridge: Polity Press, 1996.

Rosen, Stanley. *Plato's "Republic": A Study.* New Haven, CT: Yale University Press, 2005.

Rosenblum, Nancy, ed. *Liberalism and the Moral Life.* Cambridge, MA: Harvard University Press, 1989.

Rossi, Enzo, and Matt Sleat. "Realism in Political Theory." *Philosophy Compass* 9, no. 10 (2014): 689–701.

Rothschild, Emma. *Economic Sentiments: Adam Smith, Condorcet, and the Enlightenment.* Cambridge, MA: Harvard University Press, 2002.

Rousseau, Jean-Jacques. *The Basic Political Writings.* Translated and edited by Donald A. Cress. Indianapolis: Hackett, 2011.

————. *On the Social Contract.* In *The Basic Political Writings,* translated and edited by Donald A. Cress, 153–252. Indianapolis: Hackett, 2011.

Runciman, W. G. *Great Books, Bad Arguments: "Republic," "Leviathan," and "The Communist Manifesto."* Princeton, NJ: Princeton University Press, 2010.

Ruskin, John. *Unto This Last and Other Writings.* London: Penguin, 1997.

Russell, Bertrand. *The Problems of Philosophy.* Oxford: Oxford University Press, 2001.

Ryan, Alan. *The Making of Modern Liberalism.* Princeton, NJ: Princeton University Press, 2012.

————. *On Politics: A History of Political Thought.* Vol. 1, *Herodotus to Machiavelli.* New York: Norton, 2012.

Saint-Simon, Henri Comte de. *Selected Writings.* Translated by F. M. H. Markham. New York: Macmillan, 1952.

Sandel, Michael. *Democracy's Discontent: America in Search of a Public Philosophy.* Cambridge, MA: Harvard University Press, 1996.

————. *Liberalism and the Limits of Justice.* New York: Cambridge University Press, 1982.

————. *Public Philosophy: Essays on Morality in Politics.* Cambridge, MA: Harvard University Press, 2006.

———. *What Money Can't Buy: The Moral Limits of Markets*. New York: Farrar, Straus and Giroux, 2012.

Santas, Gerasimos. "The Form of the Good in Plato's *Republic*." In *Plato 1: Metaphysics and Epistemology*, edited by Gail Fine, 247–274. New York: Oxford University Press, 1999.

Satz, Debra. *Why Some Things Should Not Be for Sale: The Moral Limits of Markets*. New York: Oxford University Press, 2010.

Scanlon, T. M. *The Difficulty of Tolerance*. Cambridge: Cambridge University Press, 2003.

———. "Rawls on Justification." In *The Cambridge Companion to Rawls*, edited by Samuel Freeman, 139–167. New York: Cambridge University Press, 2003.

Schofield, Malcolm. "Plato on the Economy." In *Saving the City: Philosopher-Kings and Other Classical Paradigms*, 69–81. Abingdon: Routledge, 1999.

Schumpeter, Joseph A. *History of Economic Analysis*. New York: Oxford University Press, 1954.

Schwab, Whitney. "Understanding *Epistēmē* in Plato's *Republic*." *Oxford Studies in Ancient Philosophy* 51 (2016): 41–85.

Schwarzenbach, Sibyl A. *On Civic Friendship: Including Women in the State*. New York: Columbia University Press, 2009.

———. "Rawls, Hegel, and Communitarianism." *Political Theory* 19, no. 4 (November 1991): 539–571.

Searle, John. *The Construction of Social Reality*. New York: The Free Press, 1995.

———. "Social Ontology: Some Basic Principles." *Anthropological Theory* 6, no. 1 (2006): 12–29.

Sedley, David. "Philosophy, the Forms, and the Art of Ruling." In *The Cambridge Companion to Plato's "Republic*," edited by G. R. F. Ferrari, 256–283. New York: Cambridge University Press, 2007.

Sen, Amartya. *The Idea of Justice*. Cambridge, MA: Belknap Press of Harvard University Press, 2009.

———. "Rational Fools: A Critique of the Behavioral Foundations of Economic Theory." *Philosophy and Public Affairs* 6, no. 4 (Summer 1977): 317–344.

Sennett, Richard. *The Craftsman*. London: Penguin, 2008.

Sewell, William. *Logics of History: Social Theory and Social Transformation*. Chicago: University of Chicago Press, 2005.

Sher, George. *Beyond Neutrality: Perfectionism and Politics*. New York: Cambridge University Press, 1997.

Shields, Christopher. *Aristotle*. Abingdon: Routledge, 2007.

Silverman, Allan. *The Dialectic of Essence: A Study of Plato's Metaphysics*. Princeton, NJ: Princeton University Press, 2002.

Simmons, A. John. "Ideal and Nonideal Theory." *Philosophy and Public Affairs* 38, no. 1 (2010): 5–36.

Skidelsky, Robert, and Edward Skidelsky. *How Much Is Enough? Money and the Good Life*. New York: Other Press, 2012.

Skinner, Quentin. "Meaning and Understanding in the History of Ideas." *History and Theory* 8, no.1 (1969): 3–53.

Smart, J. J. C., and Bernard Williams. *Utilitarianism: For and Against.* Cambridge: Cambridge University Press, 1973.

Smith, Adam. "History of Ancient Logics and Metaphysics." In *Glasgow Edition of the Works and Correspondence of Adam Smith*, vol. 3, *Essays on Philosophical Subjects*, edited by W. P. D. Wightman and J. C. Bryce. Indianapolis: Liberty Fund, 1982.

———. *An Inquiry into the Nature and Causes of the Wealth of Nations.* In *Glasgow Edition of the Works and Correspondence of Adam Smith*, vol. 2, edited by R. H. Campbell and A. S. Skinner. Indianapolis: Liberty Fund, 1981.

———. *The Theory of Moral Sentiments.* In *Glasgow Edition of the Works and Correspondence of Adam Smith*, vol. 1, edited by D.-D. Raphael and A. L. Macfie. Indianapolis: Liberty Fund, 1982.

Srinivasan, Amia. "Stop the Robot Apocalypse." *London Review of Books* 37, no. 18 (September 24, 2015): 3–6.

Srnicek, Nick, and Alex Williams. *Inventing the Future: Postcapitalism and a World without Work.* London: Verso, 2016.

Stanczyk, Lucas. "Productive Justice." *Philosophy and Public Affairs* 40, no. 2 (2012): 144–164.

Stemplowska, Zofia. "What's Ideal about Ideal Theory?" *Social Theory and Practice* 34, no. 3 (2008): 319–340.

Stern, Tom. "Some Third Thing: Nietzsche's Words and the Principle of Charity." *Journal of Nietzsche Studies* 47, no. 2 (Summer 2016): 287–302.

Strabo. *Geography.* Translated by H. L. Jones. Cambridge, MA: Harvard University Press, 1932.

Strauss, Leo. *The City and Man.* Chicago: University of Chicago Press, 1964.

Strawson, P. F. *The Bounds of Sense: An Essay on Kant's "Critique of Pure Reason."* London: Routledge, 2002.

———. *Individuals.* Abingdon: Routledge, 1959.

Swift, Adam. "The Value of Philosophy in Nonideal Circumstances." *Social Theory and Practice* 34, no. 3 (2008): 363–387.

Tawney, R. H. *The Acquisitive Society.* San Diego: Harcourt, Brace and Howe, 1920.

Taylor, C. C. W. "Plato's Totalitarianism." In *Plato's "Republic": Critical Essays*, edited by Richard Kraut, 31–48. Lanham, MD: Rowman & Littlefield, 1997.

———. "Plato's Totalitarianism." In *Plato 2: Ethics, Politics, Religion, and the Soul*, edited by Gail Fine, 280–296. New York: Oxford University Press, 1999.

Taylor, Charles. "Interpretation and the Sciences of Man." In *Philosophy and the Human Sciences: Philosophical Papers 2*, 15–57. Cambridge: Cambridge University Press, 1985.

———. *Modern Social Imaginaries.* Durham, NC: Duke University Press, 2004.

———. *Sources of the Self.* Cambridge, MA: Harvard University Press, 1989.

Thakkar, Jonny. "Hail Mary Time?" *Point* 4 (Spring 2011): 143–156.

———. "Moneymakers and Craftsmen: A Platonic Approach to Privatization." *European Journal of Philosophy* 24, no.4 (2016): 735–759.

———. "Neo-socialism: A Sketch." Unpublished manuscript.

———. Review of *Blindness and Reorientation*, by C. D. C. Reeve. *European Journal of Philosophy* 23, no. S1 (2015): e1–e22.

———. "Socialism We Can Believe In." Pt. 1. *Point* 6 (Winter 2013): 61–79.

———. "Socialism We Can Believe In." Pt. 2. *Point* 7 (Fall 2013): 13–31.

———. "Why Conservatives Should Read Marx." *Point* 3 (Fall 2010): 129–135.

Thomas Aquinas. *Aquinas on Law, Morality, and Politics.* Translated by R. J. Regan. Edited by W. P. Baumgarth and R. J. Regan. Indianapolis: Hackett, 2003.

———. *A Summary of Philosophy.* Edited and translated by R. J. Regan. Indianapolis: Hackett, 2003.

Thoreau, Henry David. *Walden.* New York: Norton, 1992.

Thorsen, Dag Einar, and Amund Lie. "What Is Neoliberalism?" Oslo: Department of Political Science, University of Oslo, 2002. Available at http://folk.uio.no/daget/What%20is%20Neo-Liberalism%20FINAL.pdf.

Thucydides. *History of the Peloponnesian War.* Translated by Rex Warner. New York: Penguin, 1972.

Titelbaum, Michael G. "What Would a Rawlsian Ethos of Justice Look Like?" *Philosophy and Public Affairs* 36, no. 3 (2008): 289–322.

Tocqueville, Alexis de. *Democracy in America.* Translated and edited by Harvey C. Mansfield and Delba Winthrop. Chicago: University of Chicago Press, 2000.

Tronto, J. C. *Who Cares? How to Reshape a Democratic Politics.* Ithaca, NY: Cornell University Press, 1995.

Tucker, Robert C., ed. *The Marx-Engels Reader.* New York: Norton, 1978.

Uno, Kozo. *Principles of Political Economy: Theory of a Purely Capitalist Society.* Sussex: Harvester Press, 1964.

Urbinati, Nadia. *Representative Democracy: Principles and Genealogy.* Chicago: University of Chicago Press, 2006.

Valentini, Laura. "On the Apparent Paradox of Ideal Theory." *Journal of Political Philosophy* 17, no. 3 (September 2009): 332–355.

Vlastos, Gregory. "Degrees of Reality in Plato." In *Platonic Studies,* 58–75. Princeton, NJ: Princeton University Press, 1981.

Volpi, Franco. "*Being and Time*: A Translation of Aristotle's *Nicomachean Ethics*?" Translated by John Protevi. In *Reading Heidegger from the Start: Essays in His Earliest Thought,* edited by Theodore Kisiel and John Van Buren, 195–212. Albany: State University of New York Press, 1994.

Waldron, Jeremy. *Liberal Rights.* New York: Cambridge University Press, 1993.

Wall, Steven. *Liberalism, Perfectionism and Restraint.* Cambridge: Cambridge University Press, 1998.

Wall, Steven, and George Klosko, eds. *Perfectionism and Neutrality: Essays in Liberal Theory.* Lanham, MD: Roman & Littlefield, 2003.

Walzer, Michael. *Interpretation and Social Criticism.* Cambridge, MA: Harvard University Press, 1987.

Weber, Max. "Science as a Vocation." In *The Vocation Lectures,* edited by David Owen, translated by Rodney Livingstone, 1–31. Indianapolis: Hackett, 2004.

Wenar, Leif. "John Rawls." In *The Stanford Encyclopedia of Philosophy*, Spring 2017 ed., edited by Edward N. Zalta. https://plato.stanford.edu/archives /spr2017/entries/rawls/.

———. "Political Liberalism: An Internal Critique." *Ethics* 106, no. 1 (1995): 32–62.

White, N. P. *A Companion to Plato's "Republic."* Indianapolis: Hackett, 1979.

Williams, Bernard. *Descartes: The Project of Pure Enquiry.* Abingdon: Routledge, 2005.

———. *Ethics and the Limits of Philosophy.* Cambridge, MA: Harvard University Press, 1986.

———. *In the Beginning Was the Deed: Realism and Moralism in Political Argument.* Princeton, NJ: Princeton University Press, 2005.

———. *Making Sense of Humanity, and Other Philosophical Papers.* Cambridge: Cambridge University Press, 1995.

———. *Moral Luck.* Cambridge: Cambridge University Press, 1981.

———. *Philosophy as a Humanistic Discipline.* Edited by A. W. Moore. Princeton, NJ: Princeton University Press, 2006.

———. *The Sense of the Past.* Princeton, NJ: Princeton University Press, 2006.

———. *Shame and Necessity.* Berkeley: University of California Press, 1993.

Wittgenstein, Ludwig. *Philosophical Investigations.* Translated by G. E. M. Anscombe. Oxford: Blackwell, 1969.

Woerther, Frédérique. *L'éthos aristotélicie: Genèse d'une notion rhétorique.* Paris: Librairie Philosophique J. Vrin, 2007.

Wootton, David, ed. *The Essential Federalist and Anti-Federalist Papers.* Indianapolis: Hackett, 2003.

Wright, Erik Olin. *Envisioning Real Utopia.* Brooklyn: Verso, 2010.

———. "Toward a Social Socialism." *Point* 5 (Spring 2012): 145–155.

Xenophon. *Hellenika.* Translated by John Marincola. New York: Anchor Books, 2009.

Index